THE ART OF PASCAL CAMPION

3dtotalPublishing

3dtotal Publishing

Correspondence: publishing@3dtotal.com
Website: www.3dtotal.com

First published in the United Kingdom, 2022, by 3dtotal Publishing.

Address: 3dtotal.com Ltd,
29 Foregate Street, Worcester
WR1 1DS, United Kingdom.

Hard cover ISBN: 978-1-912843-66-4

Printing and binding: Gutenberg Press Ltd (Malta)
www.gutenberg.com.mt

Visit www.3dtotalpublishing.com for a complete list of available book titles.

Managing Director: Tom Greenway
Studio Manager: Simon Morse
Lead Editor: Samantha Rigby
Lead Designer: Joseph Cartwright
Editor: Jenny Fox-Proverbs
Designer: Imogen Williams

FSC www.fsc.org
MIX
Paper from responsible sources
FSC® C022612

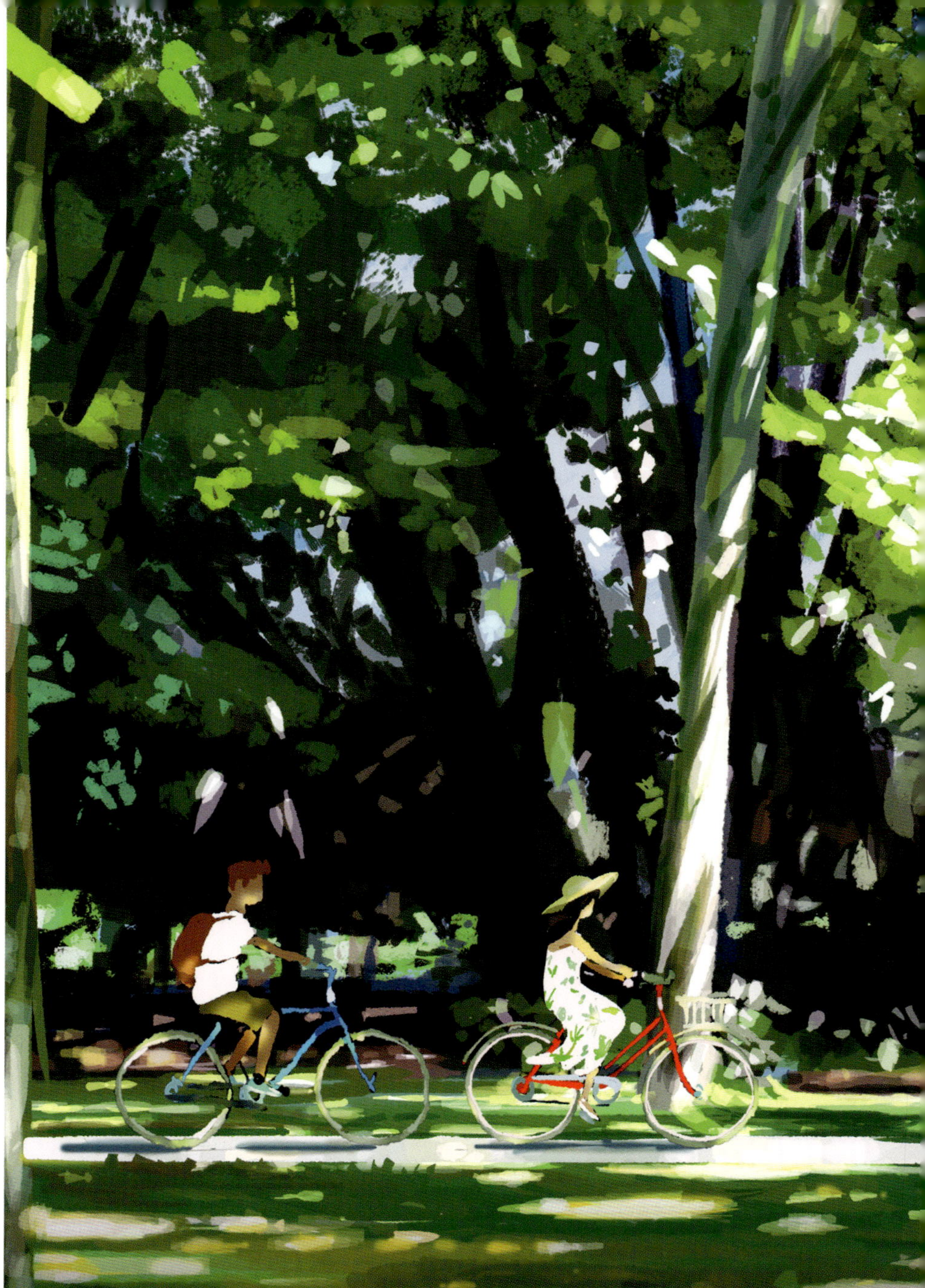

ONE TREE PLANTED FOR EVERY BOOK SOLD

We at 3dtotal Publishing donate 50% of our profits to charity. For every book sold, we give to reforesting charities to plant new trees. This is just one part of our annual donation to a large number of the most effective charities, covering causes such as humanitarian work, animal welfare, and the protection of existing rainforests. We also aim to be a carbon-neutral publisher with carbon-neutral products, which means that by buying from 3dtotal Publishing, you are helping to balance the environmental damage caused by the publishing, shipping, and retail industries, as well as supporting many other causes. See 3dtotal.com/charity for full details.

CONTENTS

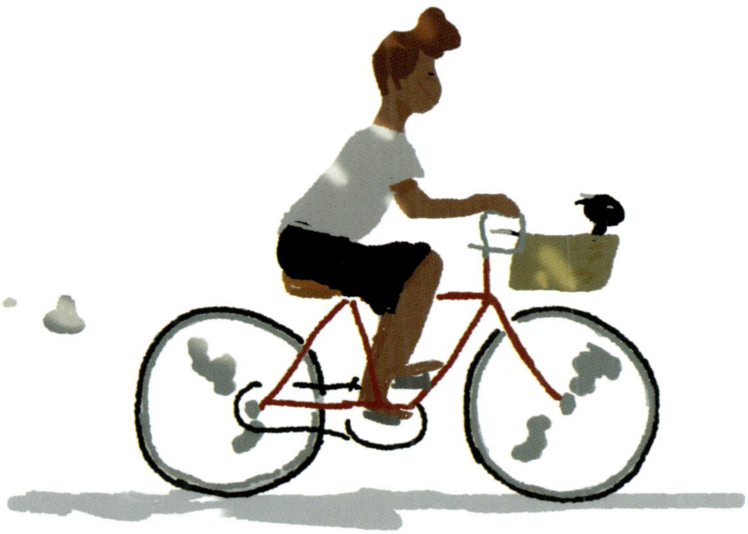

INTRODUCTION

Thank you for opening this book.

It wasn't an easy book to make. Not because I didn't know what should go *in*, but mostly because it was hard to leave things *out*. There is only so much room here, so we needed to make choices, decisions, cuts.

What is left is this. A book that aims to encapsulate the essence of Kitty Cat and Manly Man, and the way they come to life.

Hopefully, you will enjoy reading their stories as much as I enjoyed working alongside them.

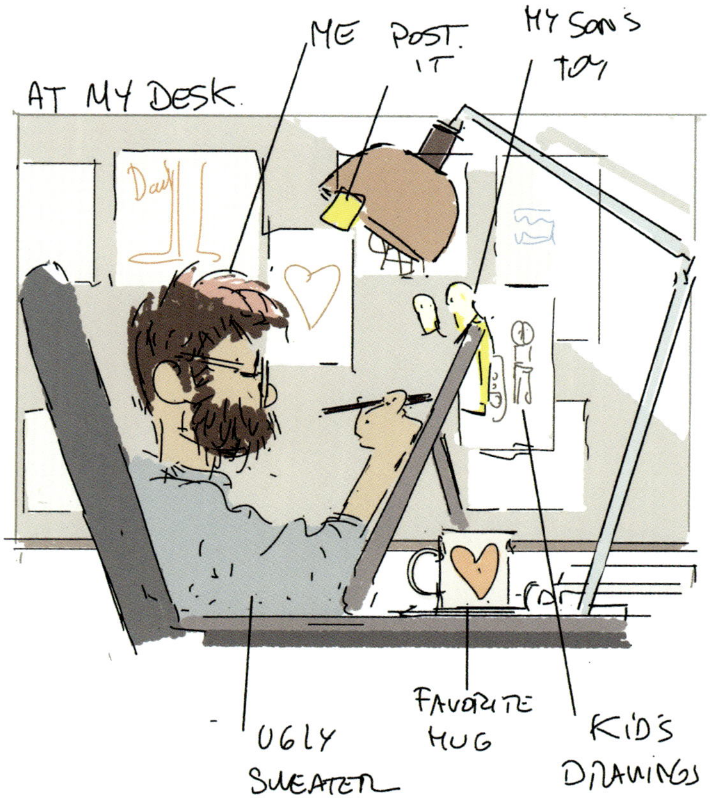

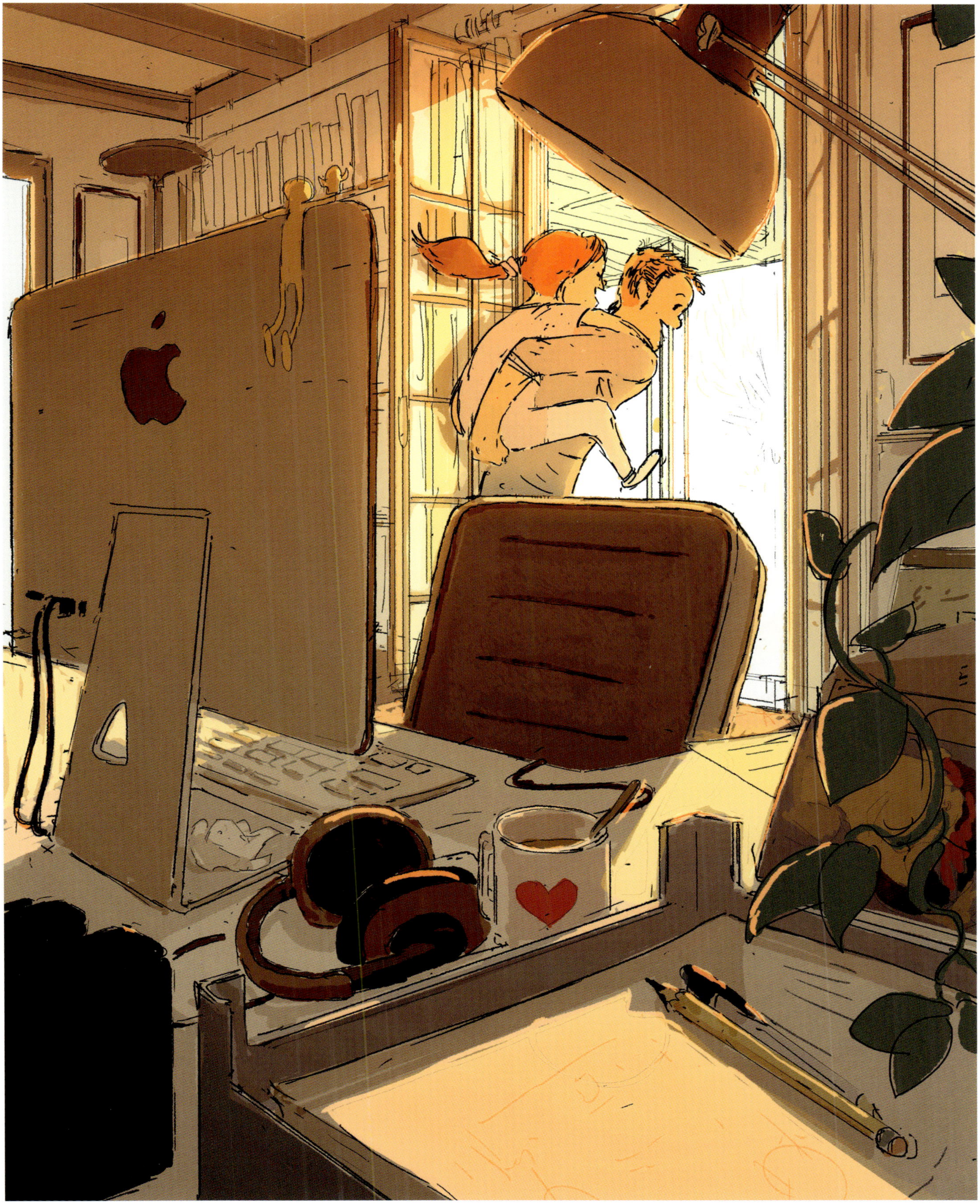

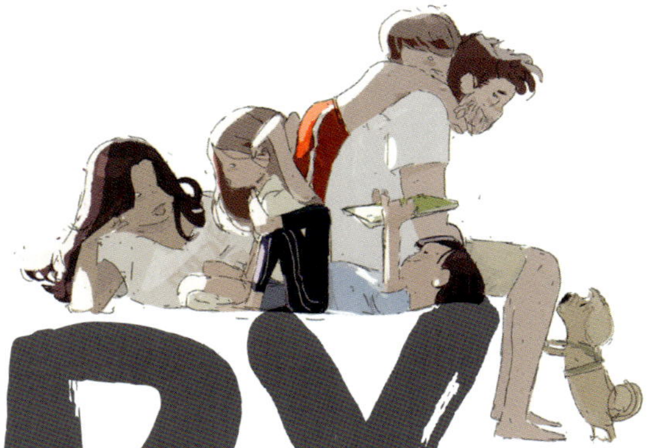

THE STORY SO FAR

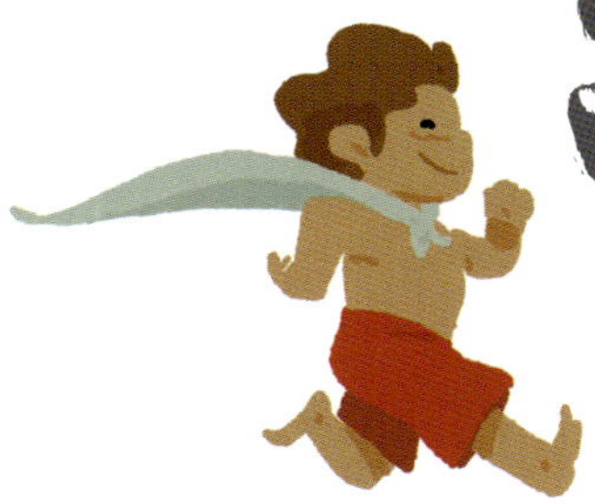

I FEEL LIKE I NEED TO WRITE SOMETHING
WITTY + CLEVER ABOUT MY SELF, BUT CAN'T SEEM TO FIND ANYTHING.

STARTING AT THE START, AS A KID, I WAS QUIET BUT NOT TOO QUIET; RAMBUNCTIOUS BUT NOT BADLY BEHAVED.

I WORKED WELL IN SCHOOL
BUT WASN'T TOP OF MY CLASS...

MORE IMPORTANTLY (TO ME AT LEAST), I DREW A LOT, BUT I WAS NEVER THE BEST IN ART.

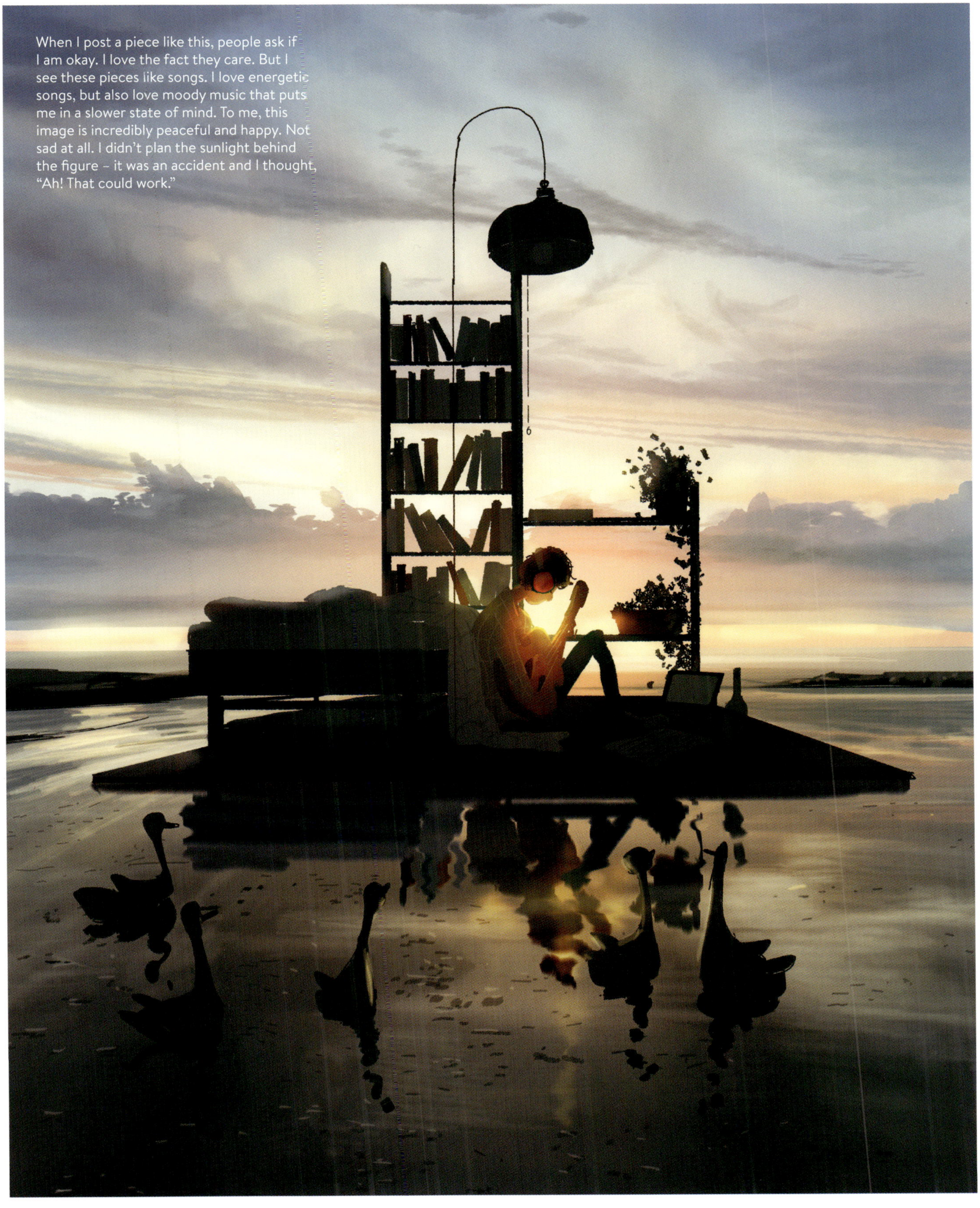

When I post a piece like this, people ask if I am okay. I love the fact they care. But I see these pieces like songs. I love energetic songs, but also love moody music that puts me in a slower state of mind. To me, this image is incredibly peaceful and happy. Not sad at all. I didn't plan the sunlight behind the figure – it was an accident and I thought, "Ah! That could work."

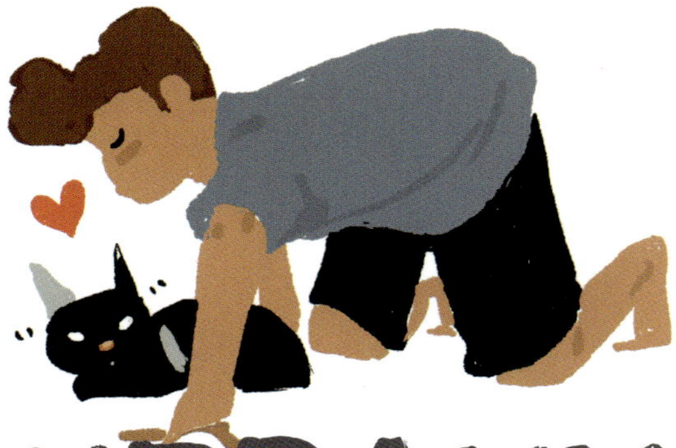

BURBANK VIA HAWAII

As a kid, this was something that always demoralized me: no matter how hard I tried, how long I drew, how much I wanted it, I simply could not be the best artist. It seemed that even my sixth-grade teacher agreed that I could not be the best when it came to drawing. I told him I wanted to be a penciler for Marvel comics when I grew up, and asked for advice on the best way to go about it. The teacher looked me squarely in the eyes, and gently (but also sternly) did what any good teacher who sees no potential in a student would do. He told me to not even think about it, because I simply didn't have "it." And thus began my journey to prove him wrong. To be honest, I could see his point. I can still see his point. I just don't stick to it. I figured a while back that I could see a lot of people's points and still go about doing my own points. I kept drawing and drawing and not being that good. I did this until high school when I finally met other kids who were just as much into comics as I was. They were still better than me, but they thought I wasn't that bad. So we drew together and I felt like I was onto something. We started a school newspaper and I had my very first story in print! It was a proud moment for me. At least six people read it. I was famous.

Even my older sister was proud of me, and if you are a teenager with an older sister, you know how much of an accomplishment this is.

ART SCHOOL

Fast forward to after high school, and a few detours, and I finally enter a proper art school at the late age of 21! I was so ancient. I felt it in my bones. I was at least two to three years older than most kids there. This has been a feeling that I've been lovingly hating for the past few decades. But it's a part of my work at this point, I suppose. That's the thing though – I am still trying to figure out my work – it's still in progress. There was something funny about that art school. They asked me what I liked to do when I entered. And I said I liked to draw. And they said, "Great. Put him in the wood and metal section." And I was... WHAT?

And they were right.

Their goal was to ensure no student entered the school with too narrow an idea of what art could and should be. Someone too passionate about only one thing could miss the possibilities offered by another avenue of art. I vehemently protested. I was older and wiser, and knew exactly what I wanted. By the second trimester, I had forgotten all about that incredible decisiveness. I enjoyed metal and wood, but not nearly as much as making my own paper, playing with architecture, or throwing wet clay around in what I assume was a sculpting class. In fact, I enjoyed it so much that by the time I had to choose a major, I hesitated for almost a full ten seconds before choosing illustration.

I know, it doesn't sound like much, but it was a major shift in my inner tectonic plates. In fact, when I was finally in illustration, I now wasn't sure which type I wanted to do. That was a true gift. Even if it took me several years after leaving school to realize it. Not knowing what I wanted to specialize in allowed me the freedom to appreciate other forms of graphic expression that I would not acknowledge before. A big focus was on children's book illustration, mostly because it was wide enough an area that we could explore everything, from how to tell stories sequentially to how to create images for print. (Note that I didn't say, "...how to *draw* images for print.")

The process of creating stories was the core fundamental of the next few years, and that is something that is still with me to this day. Telling stories. If it's one image, ten images, or a hundred images, it's always about telling a story. It's such a huge part of my art that it has become incredibly difficult, not to say impossible, for me to simply draw a beautiful image (which, ironically, is a huge part of my professional career, but more on that later... Maybe).

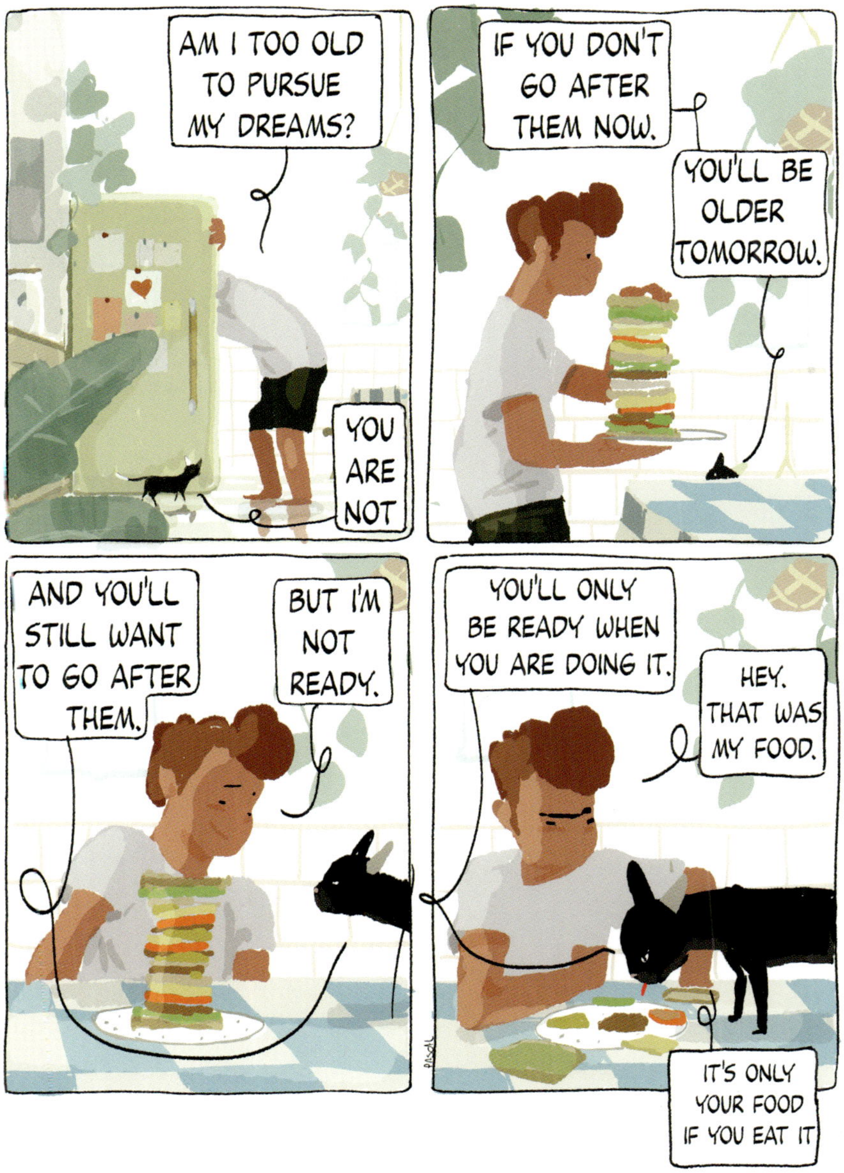

STARTING OUT

There was a bunch of stuff that happened between getting into and out of school, but for the sake of storytelling, I am creating an artistic ellipsis to get to the next point.

Ellipsis!

Remember that particular bit of punctuation when you tell a story – such a powerful tool...

I journey out west. Across the ocean and into the wild land of Kansas City! Actually, not wild at all, but incredibly beautiful and serene. The place left a major impact on me that I can still see in my art when I do nature landscapes. Every experience helps in building you and, in turn, building your art. Even if you can't understand it in the moment. It's funny how that works.

Soon, I get a job at an animation studio. (I say "soon," but for the few months before I was dying with anxiety, hating my awful life decision of going into art, pitying my lack of talent, and overall being in a bit of a mood. Sigh. Oh, such good times in retrospect, right?)

At the time, a lot of commercial animation was done with cut-out puppets. Digitally. And so began the computers-will-never-replace-hand-drawn-animation era, when so much of what we did was a translation of analog techniques to digital techniques (geezes! I'm talking as if I was a dinosaur. This was only five, seven, twenty years ago! Pffff).

I learned nothing about analog because I did everything digitally; I didn't understand why things worked as they did. I didn't even like animation in cut-outs. So I stopped doing that, moved into storyboarding, and got my first inkling of why my school pushed me to understand what that little space between the panels does.

I *loved* storyboarding and I was, I think, pretty good at it. Too bad the company folded. Moved to Hawaii. What can I say? It's Hawaii. It's everything I didn't know could exist and more. I loved it. Met a girl there too. But more on that later.

COMMERCIAL ART

I moved back to the mainland and started working in commercials. I hit the big time (in my mind!). My first project was a series of twenty-four interstitial shows for Cartoon Network. Move over, Glen Keane; make room, Eric Goldberg, here I come. That was... an experience. A good one. Again, in hindsight, it was a good one.

That was when I was really born as a commercial artist, I believe. I mean, the pain and joy of it alone would justify that statement. I learned to breathe slowly so I could work longer, to drink less so I didn't have to... well, you know. But I also learned how to draw faster, more efficiently. I learned how to listen to people and hear what they *meant*, not necessarily what they *said*. It felt like clients spoke a special language that only they knew about. The rest of us had to translate by trial and error.

I LOVED STORYBOARDING
AND I WAS, I THINK, PRETTY GOOD AT IT.
TOO BAD THE COMPANY FOLDED.

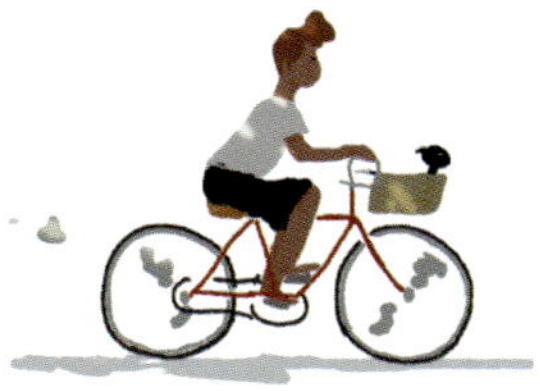

MOVED TO HAWAII. WHAT CAN I SAY?
IT'S HAWAII. IT'S EVERYTHING I DIDN'T KNOW COULD EXIST AND MORE.
I LOVED IT.
MET A GIRL THERE TOO.
BUT MORE ON THAT LATER.

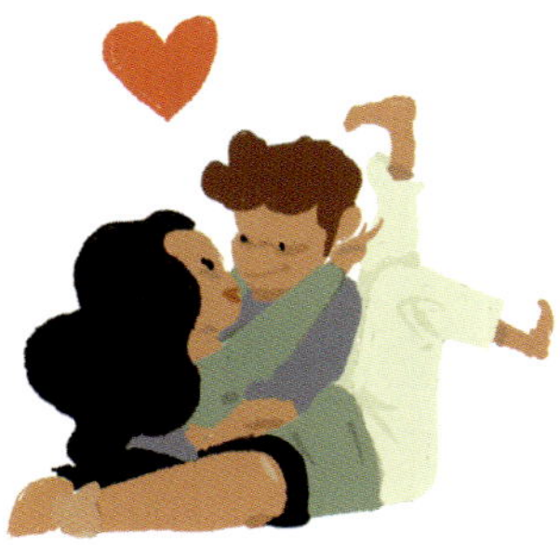

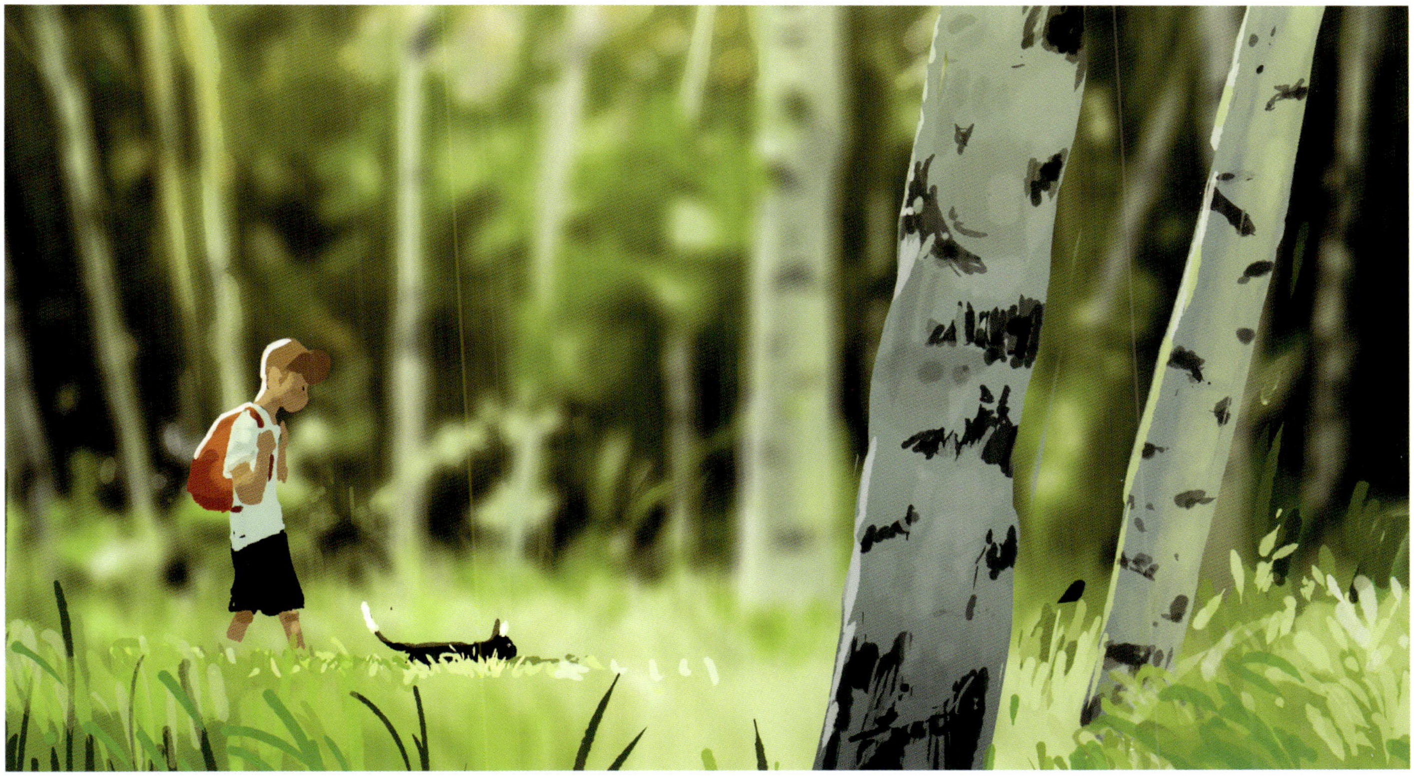

Commercials could be fun and exciting to work in, but also incredibly soulless. But still fun. A weird combo. One night, I got a call from that girl from Hawaii who was not in Hawaii anymore, but in San Francisco. I want to say that I was there the next day but it might have taken a little longer. But, hey! It would be a good story if I had moved the very next day. I didn't though.

FUN? NOT GAMES

I did eventually make it to San Francisco and started working in games (for kids!). Going from the seedy underbelly of Portland to the corporate cleanliness of the Bay Area, after the sun-soaked beaches of Hawaii, was quite a contrast. I enjoyed it... for a while.

Oddly enough, I have *nothing* bad to say about my time in games. I was treated with respect, paid well, got benefits, and lived in a beautiful area. I met amazing people who have been and still are a huge influence on me. But, the funny thing is, unless I am writing something about my professional journey, I rarely if ever think back to that time. I remember exactly one project I worked on there, but I know there must've been others. I was there for almost two years after all. I guess games are not my cup of tea. At least, not working in them. I can't quite say what it was about it, but I know that this is where I started doing a sketch every day. What I *do* remember is not being able to draw very much while I was working in games because most of my day was spent managing teams or writing notes.

A lot of the rest of the day was making sure sounds were connected to the right cues and that pixels didn't exceed a certain number that seemed to change every day. There was a bit of art in there too. I think. With some friends, we decided to fight the boredom of corporate America (it sounds *so* bad when I say it like that, but, truly, it wasn't...).

DAY ONE OF MANY

That's when we decided as a group to do a quick sketch every day and send it to each other. I started posting it on my blog too. And that's how I started drawing again (because up until that point, I had been doing mostly animation, storyboarding, or writing notes. I hadn't done a colored illustration in a few years!).

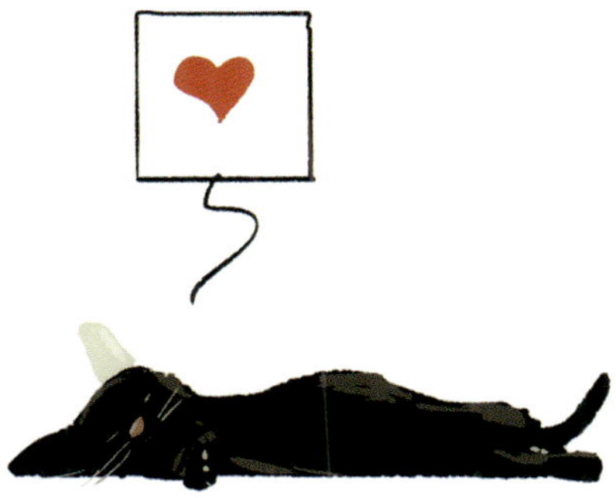

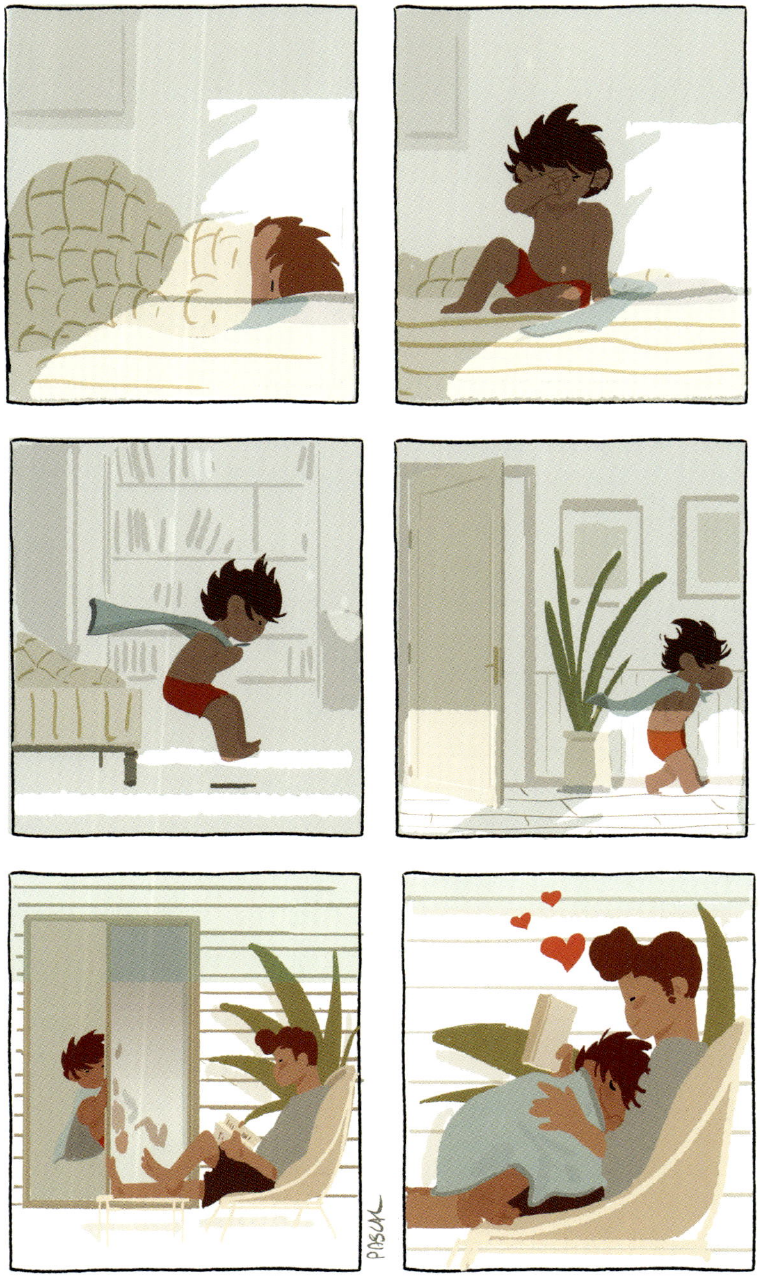

Seventeen years later, I am still doing that daily sketch. Not the same as it started, for sure, but still that *one* big thing I have a need to do every day. When it started, it was just a sketch. I even used pencils and paper at the time. Wow. What a throwback! Prismacolor Col-Erase. I loved the way they glided over the paper. I barely had to press down to get a mark and If I did apply pressure, a thick, greasy, beautiful mark would appear. So organic, so full of life. It was so easy.

It didn't make me a better artist, but it was really fun. That said, most of the sketches I did were in Macromedia Flash simply because it was faster. It started with simple monster characters, and within a few days, evolved to stories. I think after a few designs with just one character, I couldn't figure out what to draw anymore or how to tell a story. So, I started going my own way and making these sketches more and more involved.

MOVING TO BURBANK

Eventually someone noticed because I started working for Disney TV, then DreamWorks, and eventually Disney features. (I am so shortening this bit, but these are all fun stories! Just take my word for it.) All through these projects, I found time to get married and we now have three beautiful kids (teenagers at this point, but I can still see the beauty in them! Just kidding, I love them all, even...).

After some time, we moved to Burbank. The real Hollywood! That's something I didn't know back then. When you are in animation and you say you move to LA, you actually don't really move to LA. You move to Burbank because that's where most of the studios are located. At least, in my experience. As far as I can tell, the only studio that I worked at that was in Los Angeles proper was Paramount. That experience should be a whole book in itself (and yes, they do have golf carts running around the lot and yes, it's quite big and they do shoot movies in those huge hangars, and yes, you run the risk of being run over by a star in her car!). Oh... the good times!

Someone should do a comic on that!

Hmm...

Which is finally the end!

Phew.

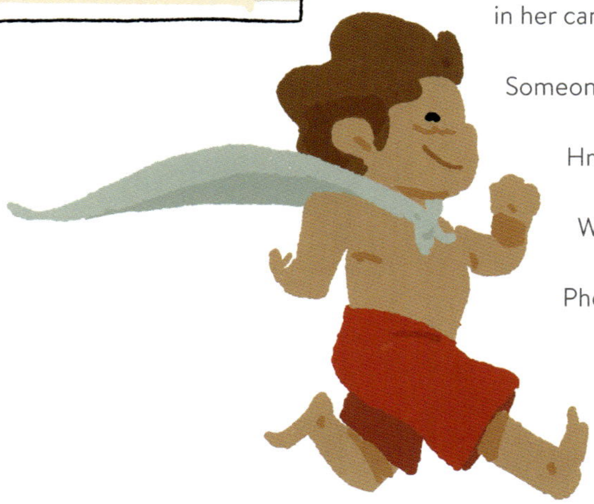

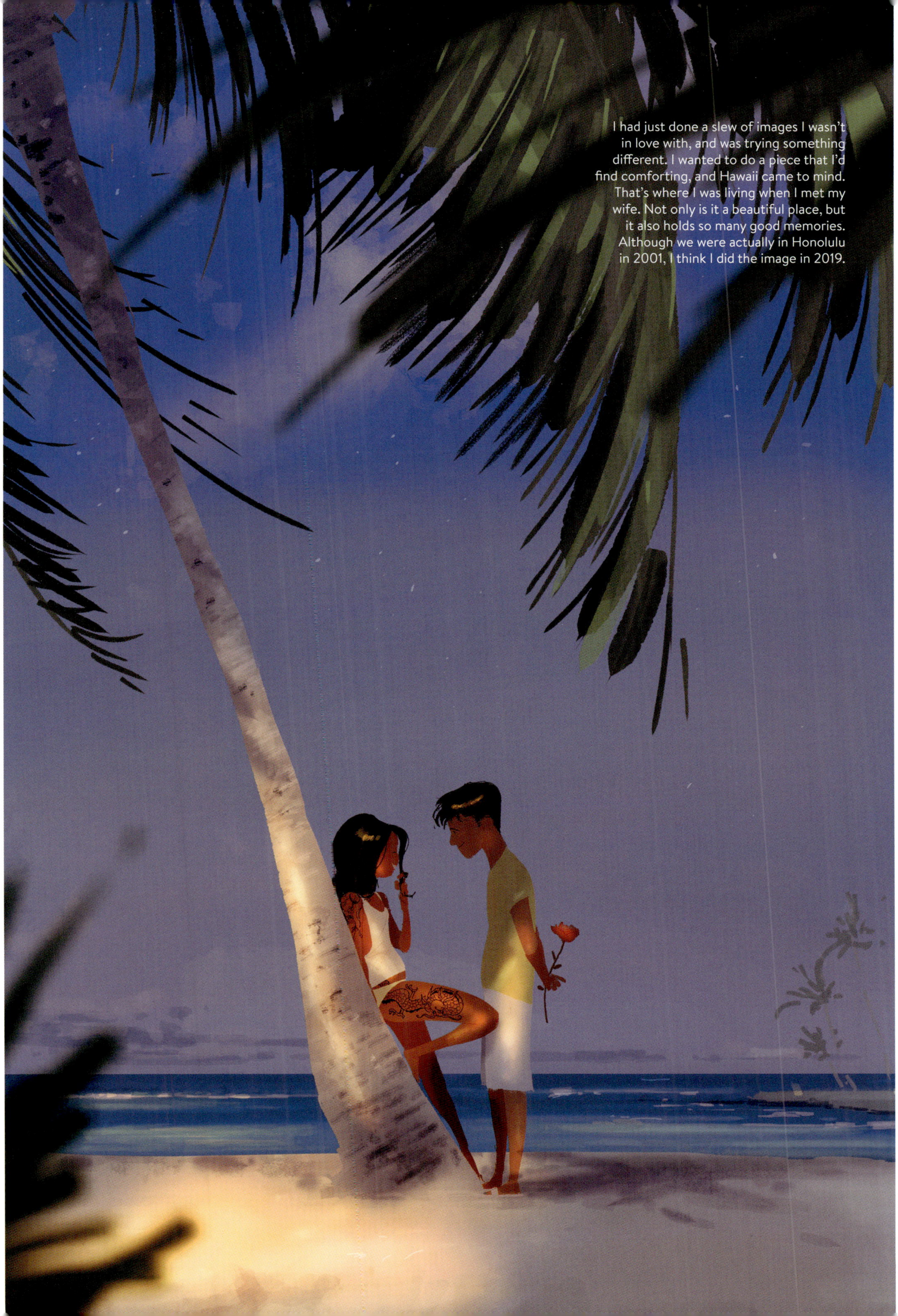

I had just done a slew of images I wasn't in love with, and was trying something different. I wanted to do a piece that I'd find comforting, and Hawaii came to mind. That's where I was living when I met my wife. Not only is it a beautiful place, but it also holds so many good memories. Although we were actually in Honolulu in 2001, I think I did the image in 2019.

EVERYDAY STORYTELLING

When I started doing those daily sketches, I wasn't really worried about anything except getting an image out. That was the plan. I remember a teacher in school being confused why art students didn't draw every day. It doesn't matter what you draw, but draw something every day. How else can you make progress? Somewhere he was right; somewhere he might've been off a bit.

CAREFREE CREATIVITY

Drawing every day does wonders for your skills. This is true. But it can become a burden and freeze your brain a bit. There is a pressure that comes with this sort of habit, tradition, or ritual – whatever you call it. At some point, you have to surrender your conscious mind and let your body take over. Take a back seat. When you become known for a certain type of art, there is a nagging feeling in your stomach that tells you to keep going even if your brain tells you that you should be trying something different.

There was a period of time when I started following what the audience wanted. Or what I *felt* they wanted, anyway. I was happy to oblige, happy to get the likes, and happy to be doing this. Until I wasn't. Nothing had changed, except that I wasn't getting that rush any longer. No more feelings of satisfaction of a job well done, no more excitement at trying and achieving something new. And worse – when I tried something new, it seemed no one cared. As much as I knew it shouldn't matter, it bothered me.

One of the favorite images I have ever done (see page 37) is one that most people would look at and go, "Meh! Not my favorite." But it had everything *I* wanted in it. The simplification, the emotion, the feel.

One of my most famous images from a while back, the one that an executive pulled out in a meeting and suggested we do the project in that style, the one that become a banner, a poster, a calling card, is one I almost did not post. I felt it was so boring and too simple. I had done this type of image a thousand times before and it came easily. Too easily. There was nothing to it in, my opinion.

Anyhow...

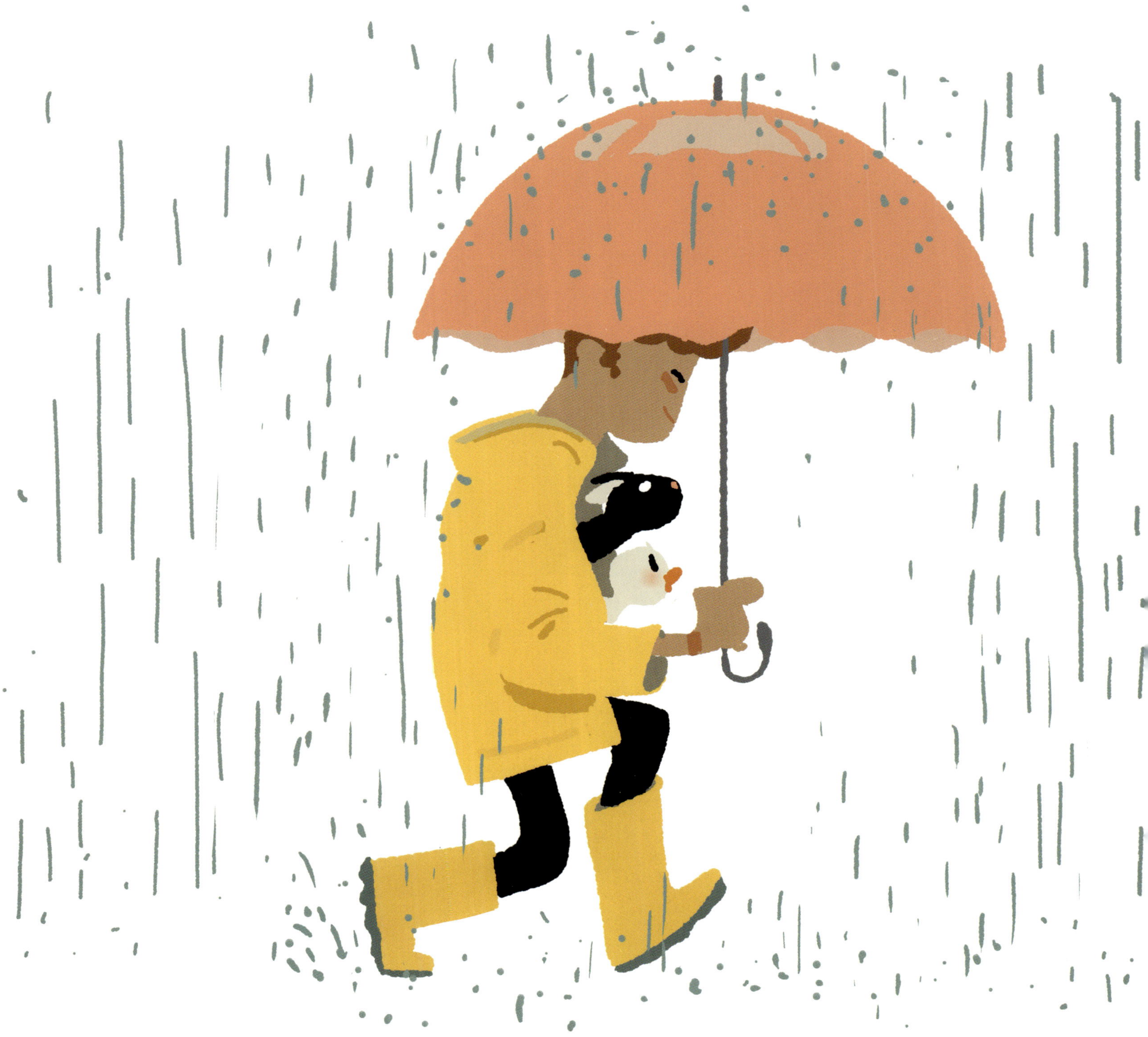

I started working on a big project a while back. It took up a lot of my time and a lot of my brain space. I was still doing daily sketches, but because my attention was diverted, I didn't care about their impact as much. This allowed me to explore different things stylistically because suddenly, it was like nobody was watching. If they were, I didn't know. I started using lines because up till then, my line work was always extremely bad. It's still rough, but I can do a strong enough outline that, when filled in with color, looks intentional. I started playing with themes. Exploring what I always thought I didn't want to explore, what I thought I could not explore. In that sense, I think that period of time was good. I had nothing to lose because I didn't care as much, and it became very creative for me.

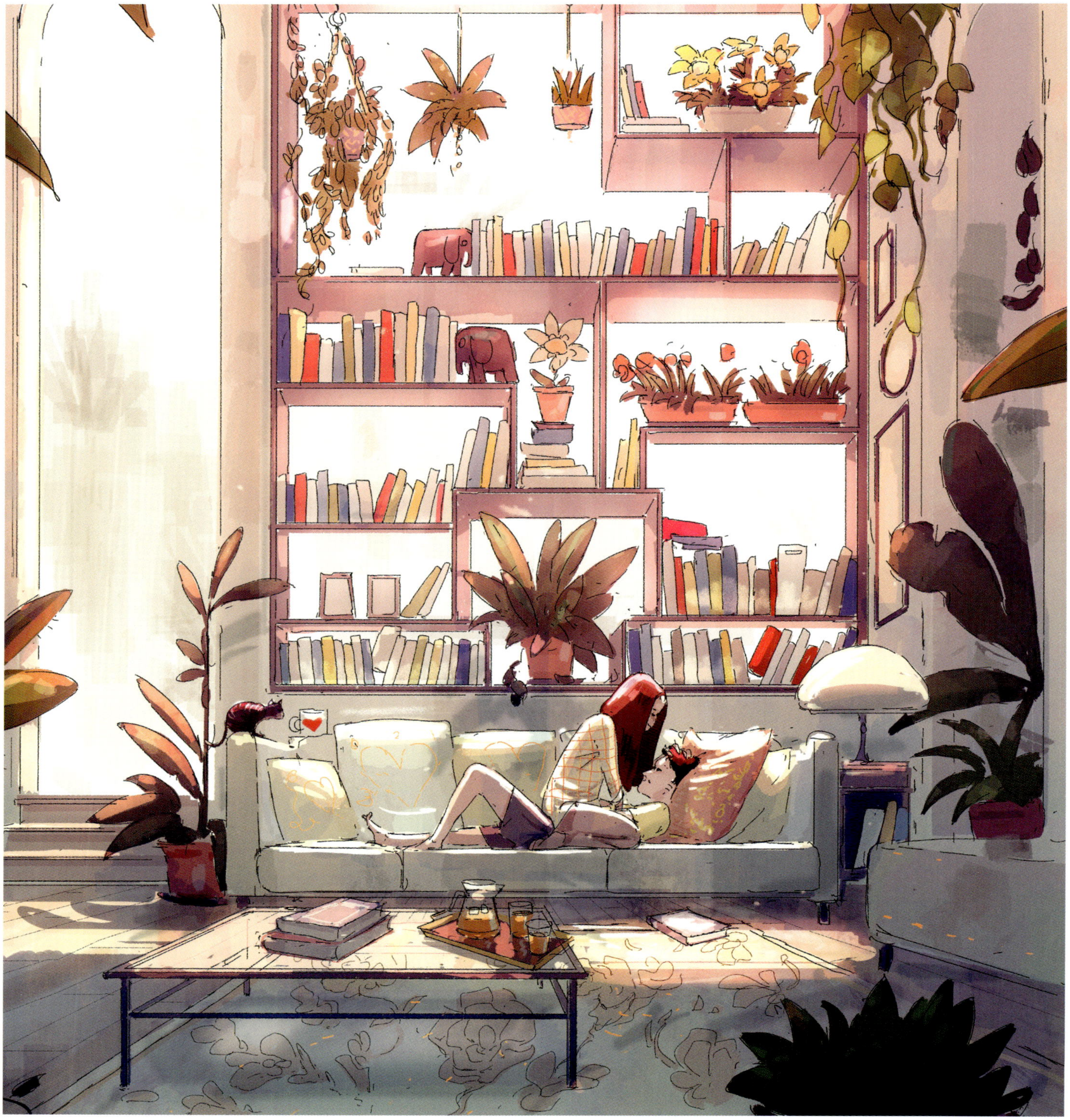

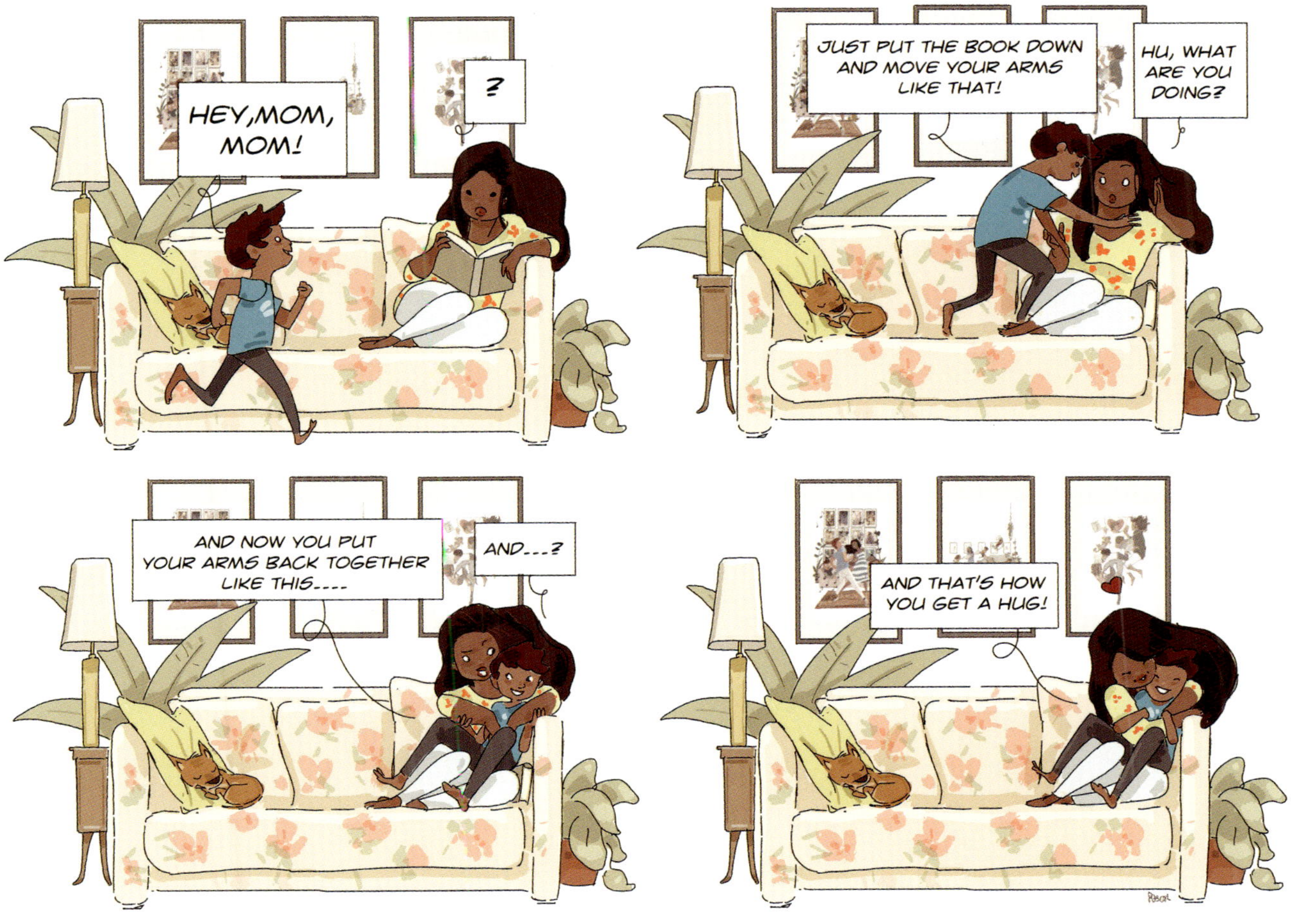

THE DAILY DRAW

Until 2020, I had been doing more realistic work. I had just wrapped up work on a project that called for visual development with more references – it was interesting work, if not fun. It was a different approach, more technical, more picture based. There was room for creativity, but it was far from the gestural, spontaneous approach I was used to. Once the project wrapped, I kept exploring this path for a while. One day, I did an image that took a lot out of me mentally. I thought it was good, but couldn't connect with it. It was all surface and no feelings, and made me question why I had done it. It was time to try something different...

My dream was always to do graphic novels, but I started with small stories I could do in one sitting. It was painful to go from so many years of colored illustration to simple black-and-white sketches – it was hard at first. But eventually, I learned how to simplify my approach and be happy with it (that's what has always been a hard thing for me – being happy about my work. I am happy *doing* the work, but I have a hard time looking back and being happy *about* the work. So, I keep moving forward hoping that I don't have to stop and look at it for too long).

Then the 2020 pandemic began, and the world as everyone knew it stopped moving. Quite literally stopped moving in Los Angeles (yes, yes, Burbank!). The freeways were empty, and we all discovered we were so much closer to the mountains than we thought since the air was clean now. We could see down the street. It was empty. It was scary and eerie and fantastic (in the sense that you could walk on the overpass and literally see no cars on the freeway in either direction). Straight out of a movie.

At this point, I had a short story in the graphic novel series *Flight* (I can't remember which volume). I had also done a couple of short stories for Marvel, and debated mentioning it here for fear somebody might dig them up and embarrass me with the bodies, but, oh well! I had an itch to do more sequential art. I'm not sure if I was getting bored with my sketches, or maybe reading way too many graphic novels, or simply getting old. But it was time to do something a little different.

So I started doing little strips...

I wanted to push my art and explore ideas that had been swirling in my mind for years, but could never really find a way out. I liked the black-and-white strips a lot. I loved the process, even if it took so much longer for me. I was meticulous. I would write down a text then edit it until only the essential message was left. Often, I had no idea what the imagery would be but it felt like starting daily sketches all over again. It was exciting. I did a whole series of sketches on being an artist, then I ran out of ideas with this one.

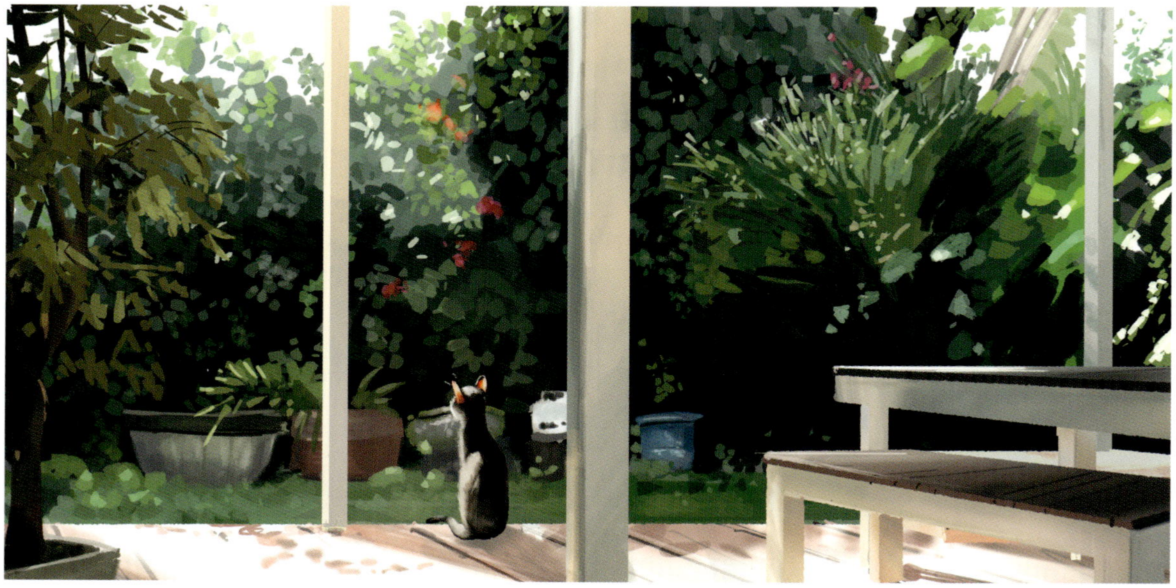

This simple sketch was done to relax while working on a complex movie. Next to the simple colorwork I do on shows now, it seems complex. Funny how we perceive everything in relationship to something else.

ENTER PURSUED BY A CAT

Like many, my head was spinning back in 2020. I mean, it was spinning more than usual, and faster, or maybe it was just in a different rotation. Something like that. One evening, I was with my wife (the girl from Hawaii, who was actually not from Hawaii) on the bed. I was sketching, and a black cat popped into my strip and explained the meaning of life to the main character.

I had *no* idea how that happened. But it did.

I can't remember what the story was about, but I knew it was mostly about articulating some thoughts I had in my head. I wrote them all down and got lazy. I didn't have the energy left to do a bunch of different panels, so I figured I'd be clever – I would draw a single panel, reproduce it a few times, and just change a few details. The panel was a man on a roof, his back to us, looking away. The changing detail was a black cat coming in and sitting next to him. You can see the results on pages 20–21.

So, why a black cat? Honestly, it's because of my mom. Yeah. I know. Growing up, she always had cats at home. She loved cats (still does). She had little statues, paintings, and pictures of cats. It made sense that I would love cats. And I do. I really love cats. But I don't actually have a cat. My wife is allergic to them. Funny, I know.

I've always drawn cats in my images. In college, I would practice drawing my mom's cats. Now, I realize I don't really know how to draw cats. Kitty Cat is always sitting or lying. These are a few of the poses I've learned how to draw and can reproduce fairly well. It's also faster that way. I should've picked a worm.

So much easier to draw.

Sigh.

And then was born Kitty Cat and Manly Man. A few years later, here we are with a few hundred strips and stories and art with Kitty Cat and Manly Man.

BUT WHO *ARE* THEY?

Originally, Manly Man was going to be me, and Kitty Cat… well, I am not sure what Kitty Cat was meant to be. Whatever the idea was, it evolved into something I could not have predicted. Pretty quickly though, I realized that Manly Man couldn't be me. Mostly because I have *zero* opinions about anything and, although I am grumpy, I am just not nearly as grumpy as Manly Man. I needed to push the boundaries of what it is to create what could be, and that is what Manly Man is. What could be. Now, there is some overlap between us, for sure. But a lot of the time, I push or create new qualities for him that I simply don't have. Same with the rest of his family. It's a fun way to talk about anything and, well, it's OK I suppose if people think Manly Man is me.

His wife is based on my wife, but my wife is much better. I just needed to point this out.

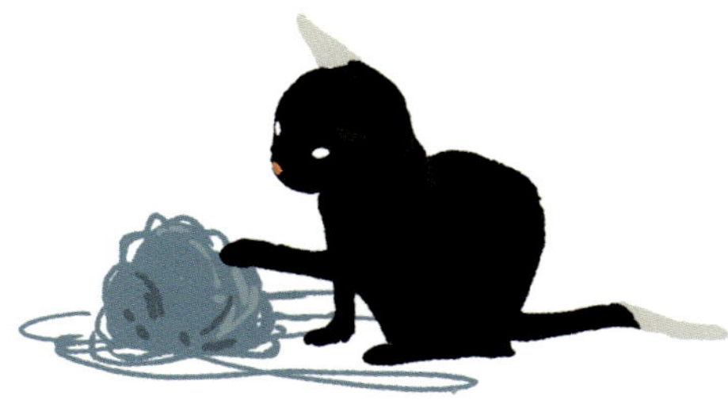

IT MADE SENSE THEN THAT I WOULD
LOVE CATS.
AND i DO.
I REALLY LOVE CATS.
BUT i DON'T ACTUALLY
HAVE A CAT.
MY WIFE IS ALLERGIC TO THEM.
FUNNY, I KNOW.

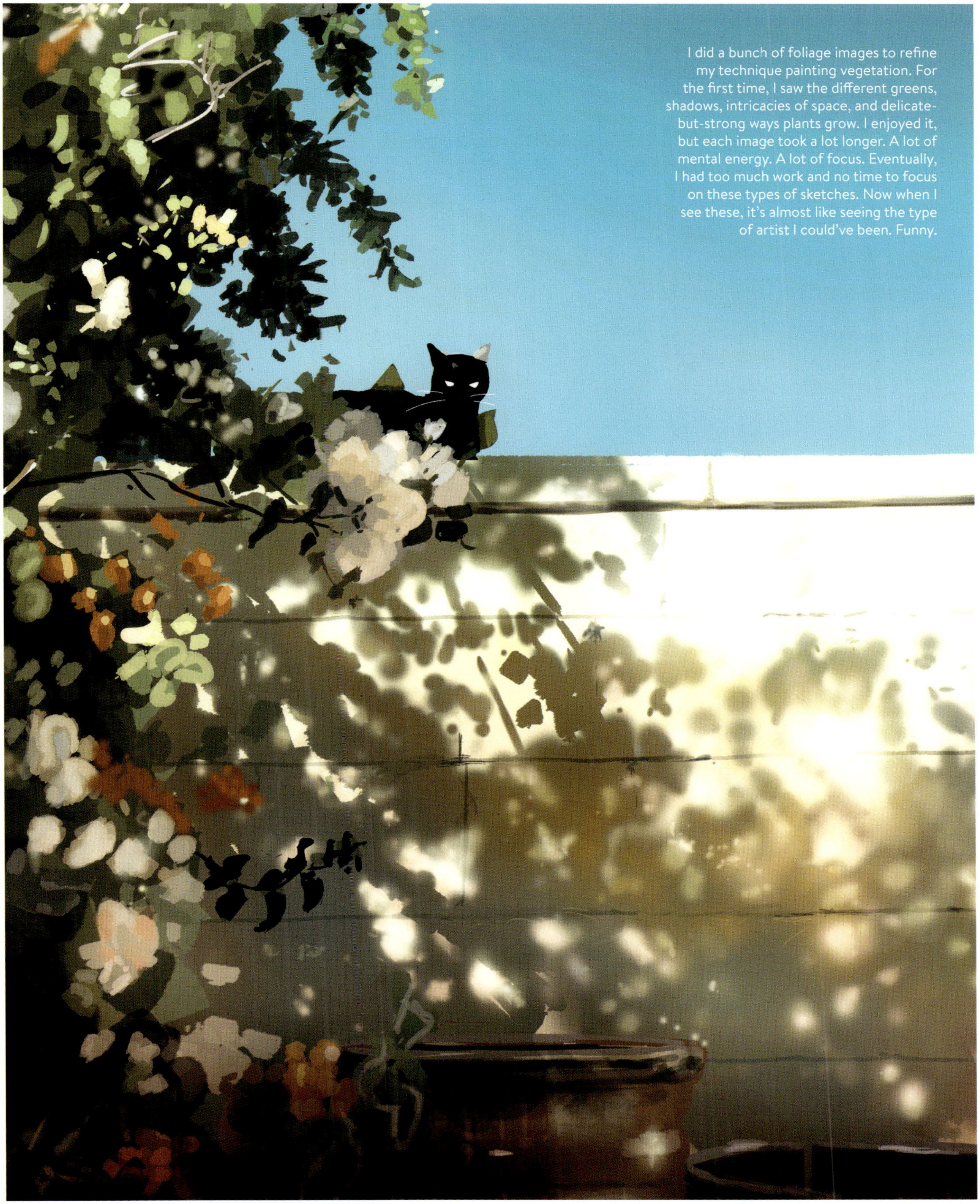

I did a bunch of foliage images to refine my technique painting vegetation. For the first time, I saw the different greens, shadows, intricacies of space, and delicate-but-strong ways plants grow. I enjoyed it, but each image took a lot longer. A lot of mental energy. A lot of focus. Eventually, I had too much work and no time to focus on these types of sketches. Now when I see these, it's almost like seeing the type of artist I could've been. Funny.

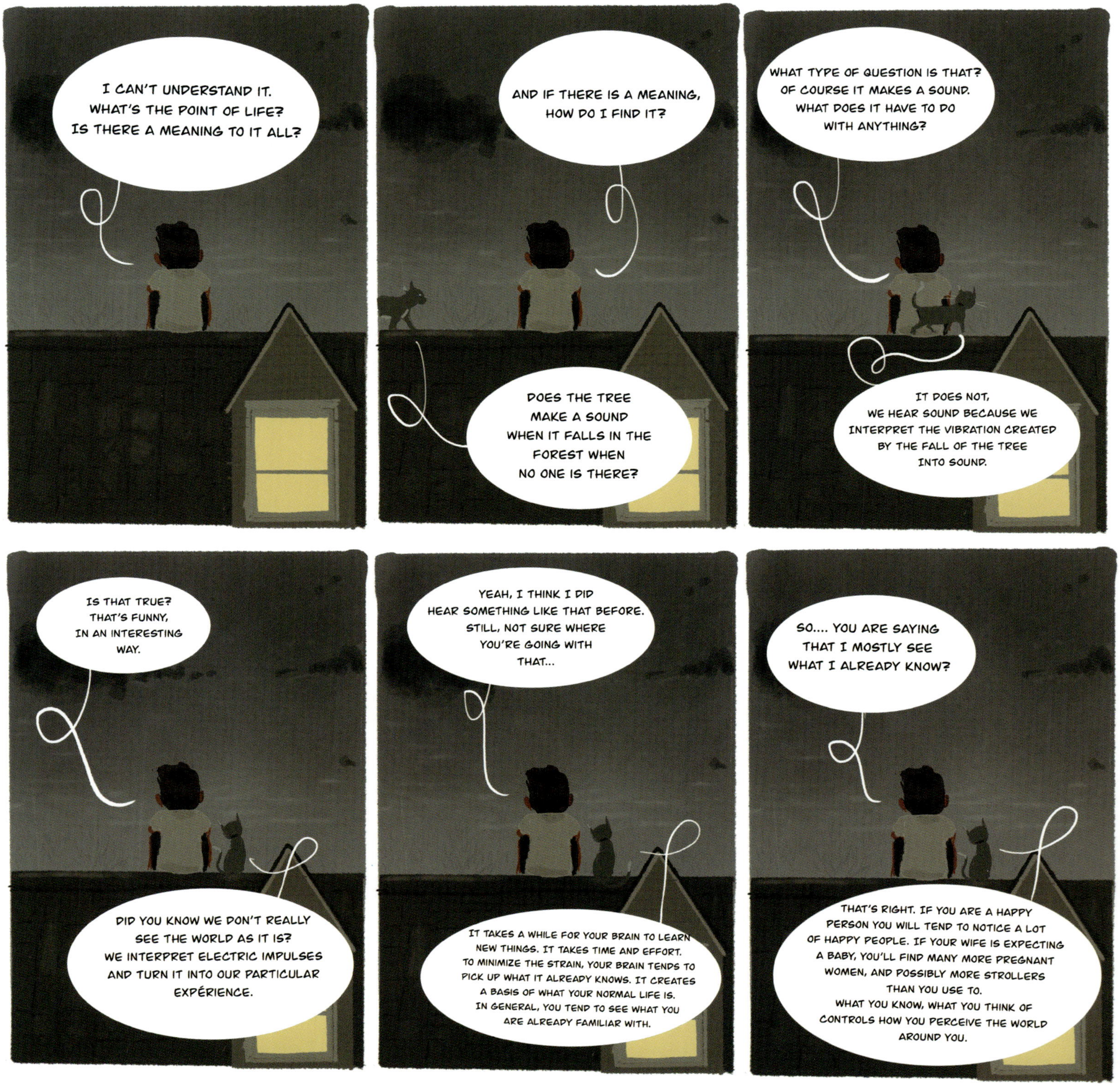
I CAN'T UNDERSTAND IT. WHAT'S THE POINT OF LIFE? IS THERE A MEANING TO IT ALL?
AND IF THERE IS A MEANING, HOW DO I FIND IT?
DOES THE TREE MAKE A SOUND WHEN IT FALLS IN THE FOREST WHEN NO ONE IS THERE?
WHAT TYPE OF QUESTION IS THAT? OF COURSE IT MAKES A SOUND. WHAT DOES IT HAVE TO DO WITH ANYTHING?
IT DOES NOT, WE HEAR SOUND BECAUSE WE INTERPRET THE VIBRATION CREATED BY THE FALL OF THE TREE INTO SOUND.
IS THAT TRUE? THAT'S FUNNY, IN AN INTERESTING WAY.
DID YOU KNOW WE DON'T REALLY SEE THE WORLD AS IT IS? WE INTERPRET ELECTRIC IMPULSES AND TURN IT INTO OUR PARTICULAR EXPÉRIENCE.
YEAH, I THINK I DID HEAR SOMETHING LIKE THAT BEFORE. STILL, NOT SURE WHERE YOU'RE GOING WITH THAT...
IT TAKES A WHILE FOR YOUR BRAIN TO LEARN NEW THINGS. IT TAKES TIME AND EFFORT. TO MINIMIZE THE STRAIN, YOUR BRAIN TENDS TO PICK UP WHAT IT ALREADY KNOWS. IT CREATES A BASIS OF WHAT YOUR NORMAL LIFE IS. IN GENERAL, YOU TEND TO SEE WHAT YOU ARE ALREADY FAMILIAR WITH.
SO.... YOU ARE SAYING THAT I MOSTLY SEE WHAT I ALREADY KNOW?
THAT'S RIGHT. IF YOU ARE A HAPPY PERSON YOU WILL TEND TO NOTICE A LOT OF HAPPY PEOPLE. IF YOUR WIFE IS EXPECTING A BABY, YOU'LL FIND MANY MORE PREGNANT WOMEN, AND POSSIBLY MORE STROLLERS THAN YOU USE TO. WHAT YOU KNOW, WHAT YOU THINK OF CONTROLS HOW YOU PERCEIVE THE WORLD AROUND YOU.

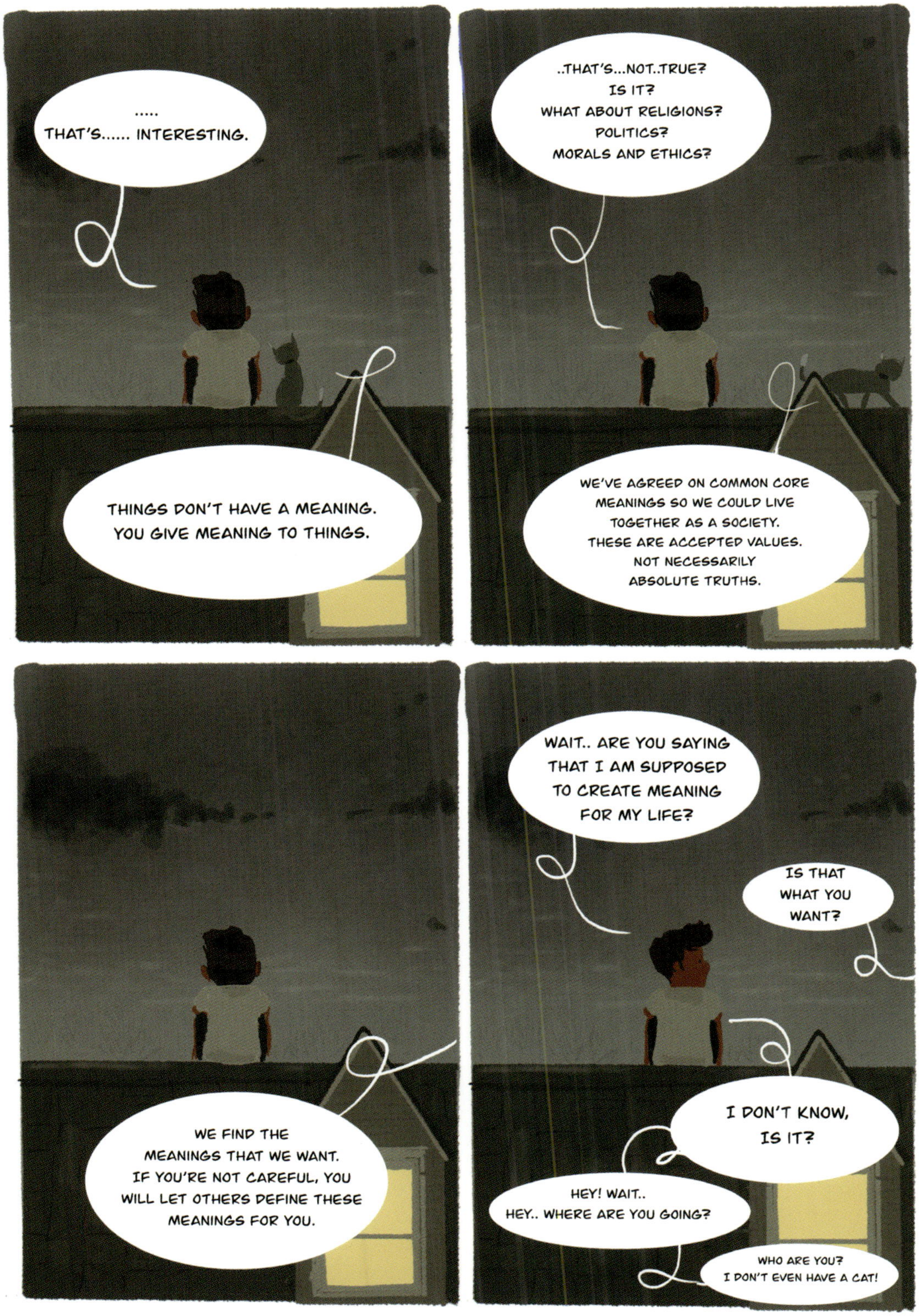

Kitty Cat's debut appearance in 2020, when he first sauntered into (then out of) frame with thought-provoking words of wisdom for a slightly baffled Manly Man.

"WHO ARE YOU? I DON'T EVEN HAVE A CAT"

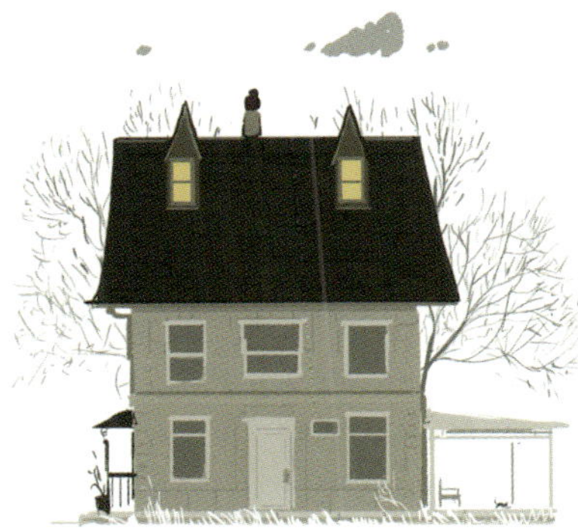

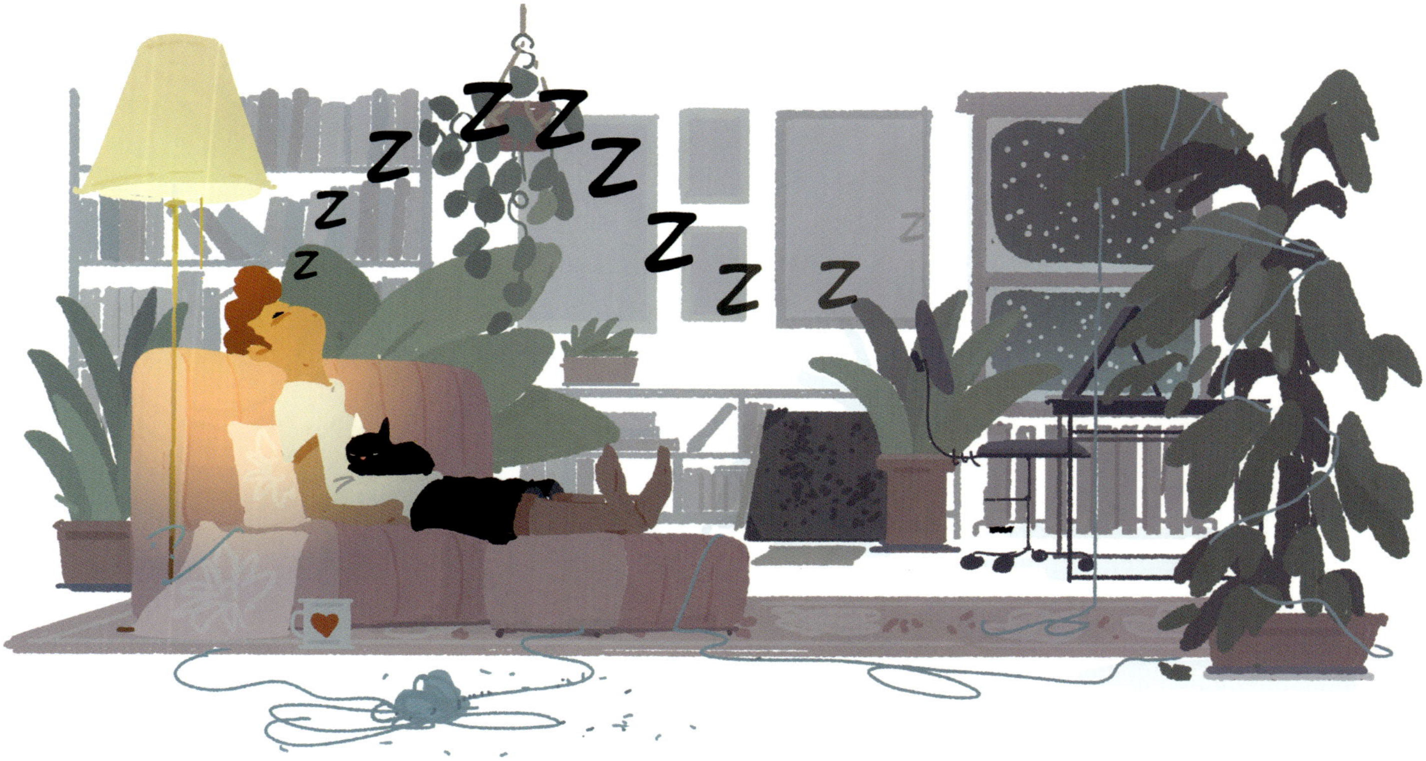

MEET KITTY CAT + MANLY MAN

This seems like a good time to explore more deeply who Kitty Cat and Manly Man are, and how they relate to me as both an artist and a man.

I've already done a lot of talking, so I'm going to pass the keyboard to my muse, biggest fan, and wife – **Katrina**...

“

You know, it's pretty hard to give yourself your own nickname. Nicknames are usually something bestowed on you by your family, close friends or hopefully someone who at least likes you. Nicknames can be legendary, funny, or just a riff on your own name. But not for Manly Man. Manly Man initially irritated me when Pascal used that in his comics. I immediately went cynical. What is a "Manly Man"? Some superhero version of a man? Some super patriarchal figure with big muscles, big thoughts, and big britches? To be honest, I remember recoiling at that term. Maybe it feels like I'm belaboring the point a bit, however I really wondered to myself even at the time why I disliked this moniker so much.

I think today, the definition of a man can bring up so many things, and more than ever has become a bit divisive and a hot topic. The definitions of a man center on many traditional models of being a leader, being a husband and father, being strong both mentally and physically, and being up to a certain standard often defined by our own fathers. It's a generational and cultural definition that I really don't have the expertise to define here, but is for sure fascinating to me.

Where I'm going with this is that I just didn't get it. Pascal was on a journey. To explore and define those terms and assign the meanings of those terms to himself. How can you begin a journey to create your story when the main character is swept up in the current cultural wave of the 2020s, where terms and definitions can bring a great amount of confusion and distress? So, Pascal uses his whimsical illustration style and formats these boxes to dig, to process, and to explore. He shares his vulnerabilities, lessons learned, and his emotional rollercoasters with us.

Through his stories, his illustrations, we can laugh (hopefully), we can heal (maybe), and as fans we can share our love for the wise black cat and the introspective Manly Man.

For me, the journey takes a personal route because not only is Manly Man's journey one that shows our current state of the definition of father, son, and man... but it's defining the meaning of a man in my very household. And healing some deep wounds about the meaning of "man." And giving me so much hope and pride that my sons will feel the freedom and security to explore and define their own manhood with some wise older men, kitty cats, women, and Milo to help guide them along the way.

Katrina

"PASCAL USES HIS WHIMSICAL ILLUSTRATION STYLE... TO DIG, TO PROCESS, AND TO EXPLORE"

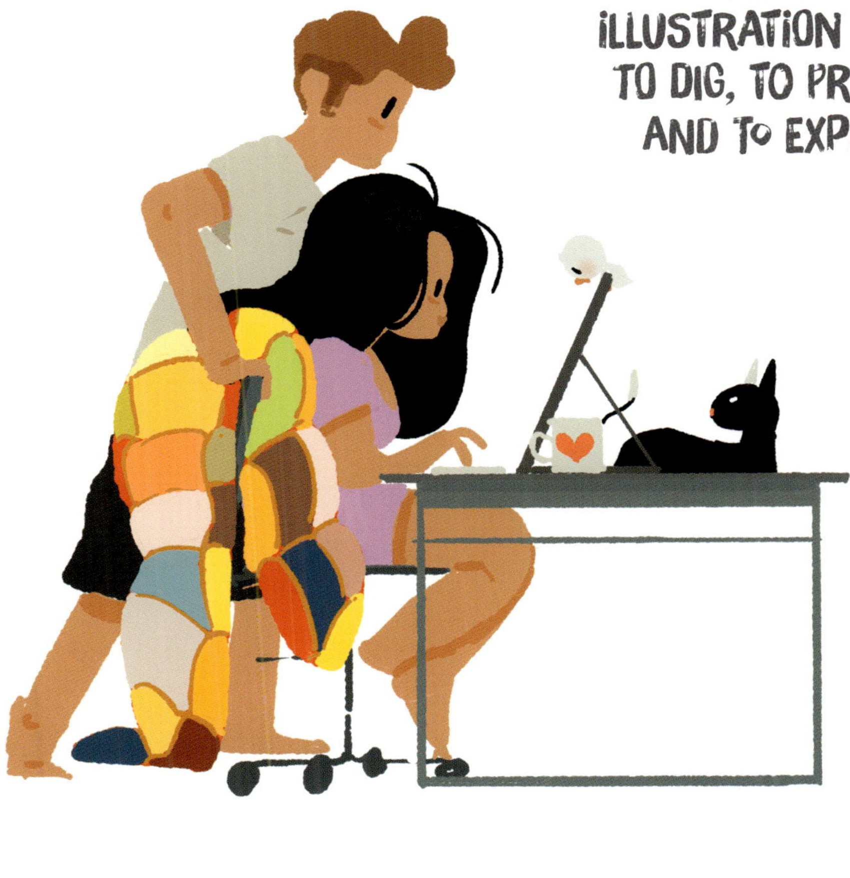

BEING AN ARTIST

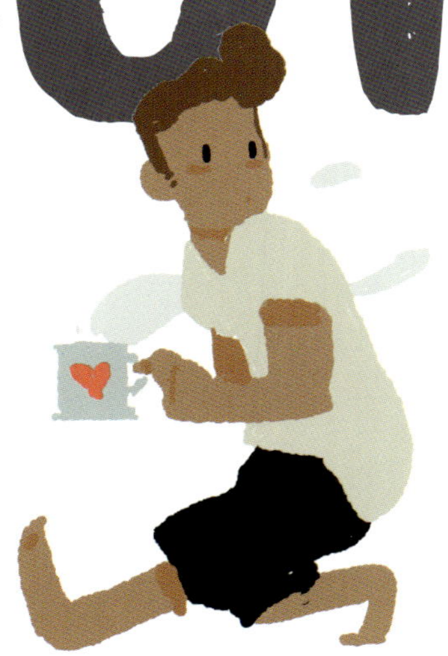

I HAVE A FEW TUTORIALS.
NOT MANY.

I FIND IT HARD TO TALK ABOUT WHAT I DO + HOW I DO IT,
MOSTLY BECAUSE
I FEEL EVERY TIME I DO A PIECE,
IT'S LIKE A PERFORMANCE.

I'M NEVER QUITE SURE I WILL END UP WITH
SOMETHING THAT WORKS.

I KNOW I WILL GET SOMEWHERE,
BUT I DON'T USUALLY KNOW WHERE...

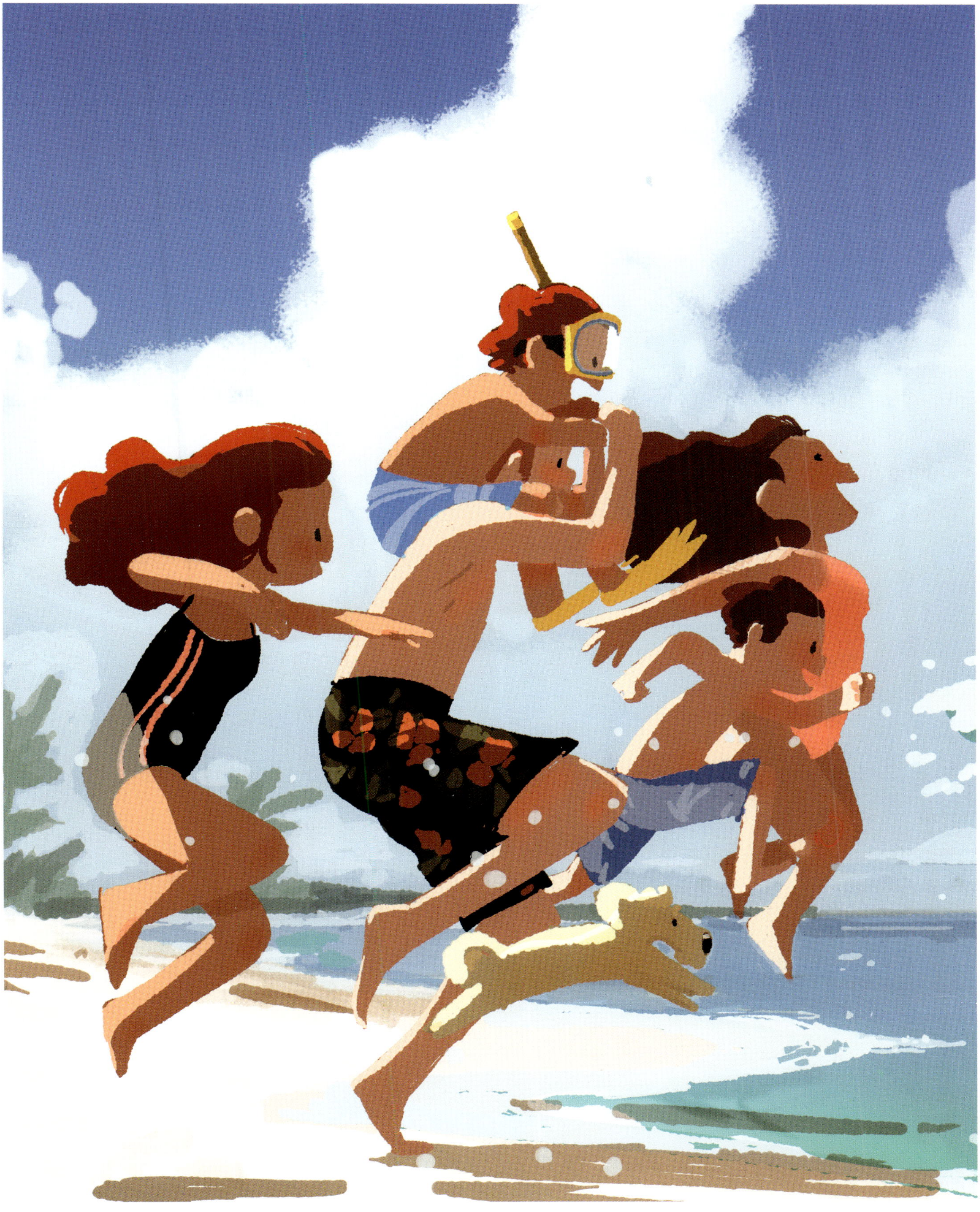

BUT FIRST, WHY STORIES?

One of the questions always on my mind is "Why the heck do I tell stories? Why can't I simply draw a beautiful image and be done with it?" It's something that's always bothered me. Mostly because I think, somewhere, I still want to "learn how to draw." And yes, I know, I know. I "draw" well. I know. *But*. But...

The idea I have in my head of drawing is very different to what comes out on paper. I feel I am always settling for something in between what I can do and what I have in my head. Either by lack of talent or simple laziness. I have a hard time spending too much time on one image because I get bored. This last fact used to worry me because I didn't understand how I could make a living as an artist if I was getting bored doing the art.

The trick I found, or at least one that works for me, is to see the art not as art, but as words. I tell stories through my art because I am not a good enough artist to just draw something and make it "enough" on its own. At least, that's what I tell myself. I think it's pretty common for artists to have a continuous inner dialog with themselves (and I say this with the utmost authority that comes with having asked at least two people about this). My inner dialog is varied. A lot has to do with lunch, but often I ask myself, "What the heck am I doing?" To which I tend to reply, "I have no idea." Since I can't get away from myself, I then ask, "Why don't you try to explain it?" And so on...

I couldn't tell you specifically how I draw a tree, a cloud, or a person, but I can tell you why I thought about putting this car or this light in this place, and what I was hoping the effect would be on the audience. But, in terms of doing it, it's like reinventing the wheel every time. That's what I mean by "I am not a great artist." I can't easily redo what I did. And when I am asked to "Just do what you like," I freeze and give up. What I *can* do is explain what I tend to think about when I tell stories. I can't explain where the stories come from though. I wish I could so that I wouldn't have to work so hard at finding them.

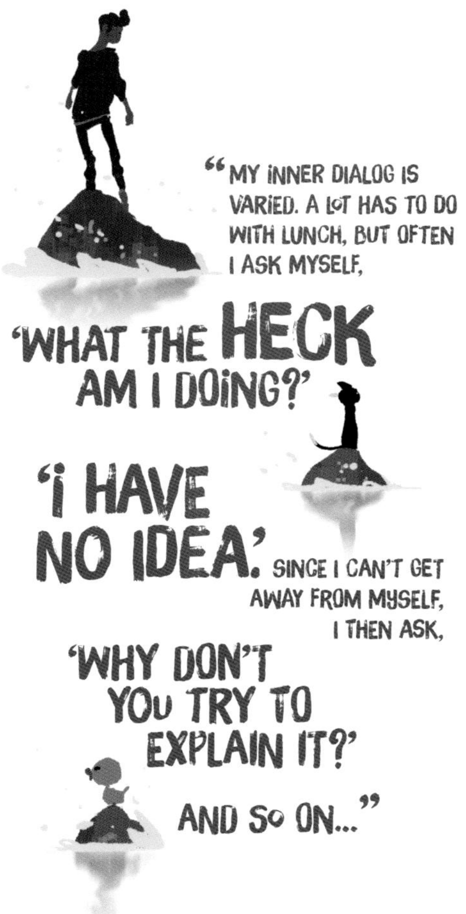

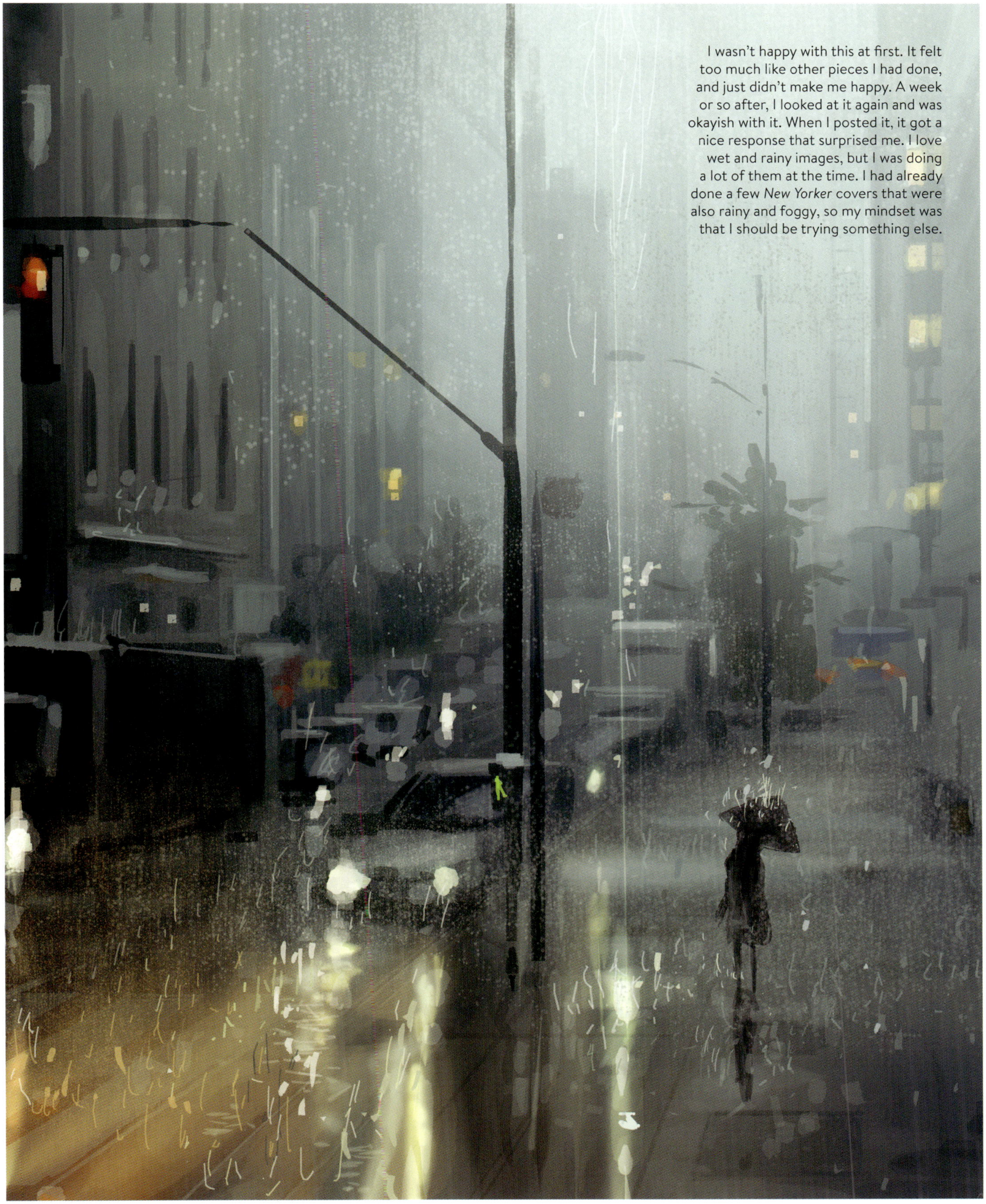

I wasn't happy with this at first. It felt too much like other pieces I had done, and just didn't make me happy. A week or so after, I looked at it again and was okayish with it. When I posted it, it got a nice response that surprised me. I love wet and rainy images, but I was doing a lot of them at the time. I had already done a few *New Yorker* covers that were also rainy and foggy, so my mindset was that I should be trying something else.

THE ART OF STORYTELLING

It's always difficult for me to talk about storytelling. Mostly because I feel that *I* am still trying to understand it. For the longest of time, I kept mixing the craft of storytelling with the story I wanted, or needed, to tell. I also had this need to get stories out, so a lot of them were determined by my energy level. They could be one page, or two, or ten, depending on how much focus I could muster for the session. It's still difficult for me today to pick up a project after having put it down for a bit, so I try to do stories I can finish in one sitting.

Over the years, I've developed tricks to help me sustain my focus over a period of hours, then days.

But it's not natural. In fact, I thought I would never be able to work in comics because I could only focus for short bursts of time.

Didn't realize until much later – I could turn this to my advantage.

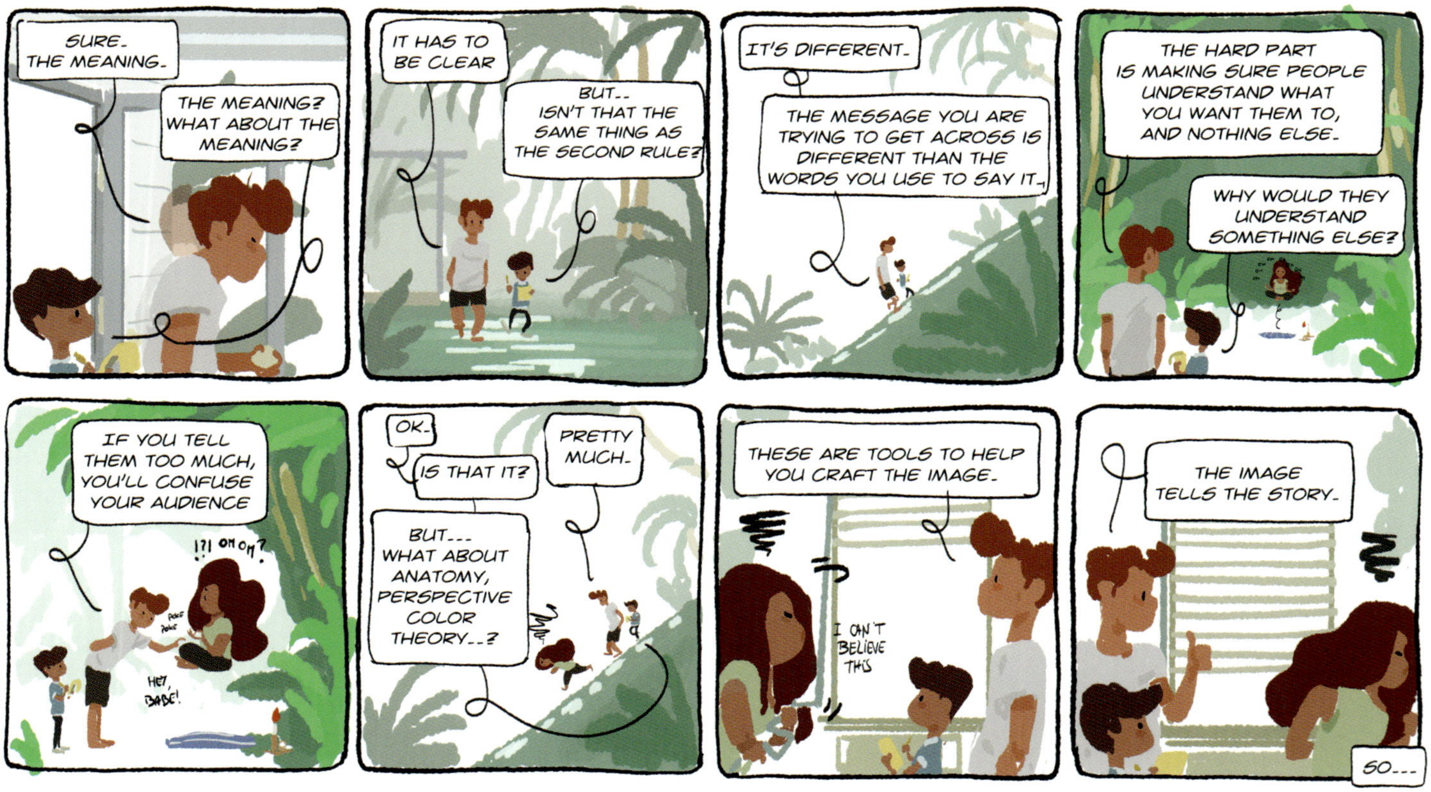

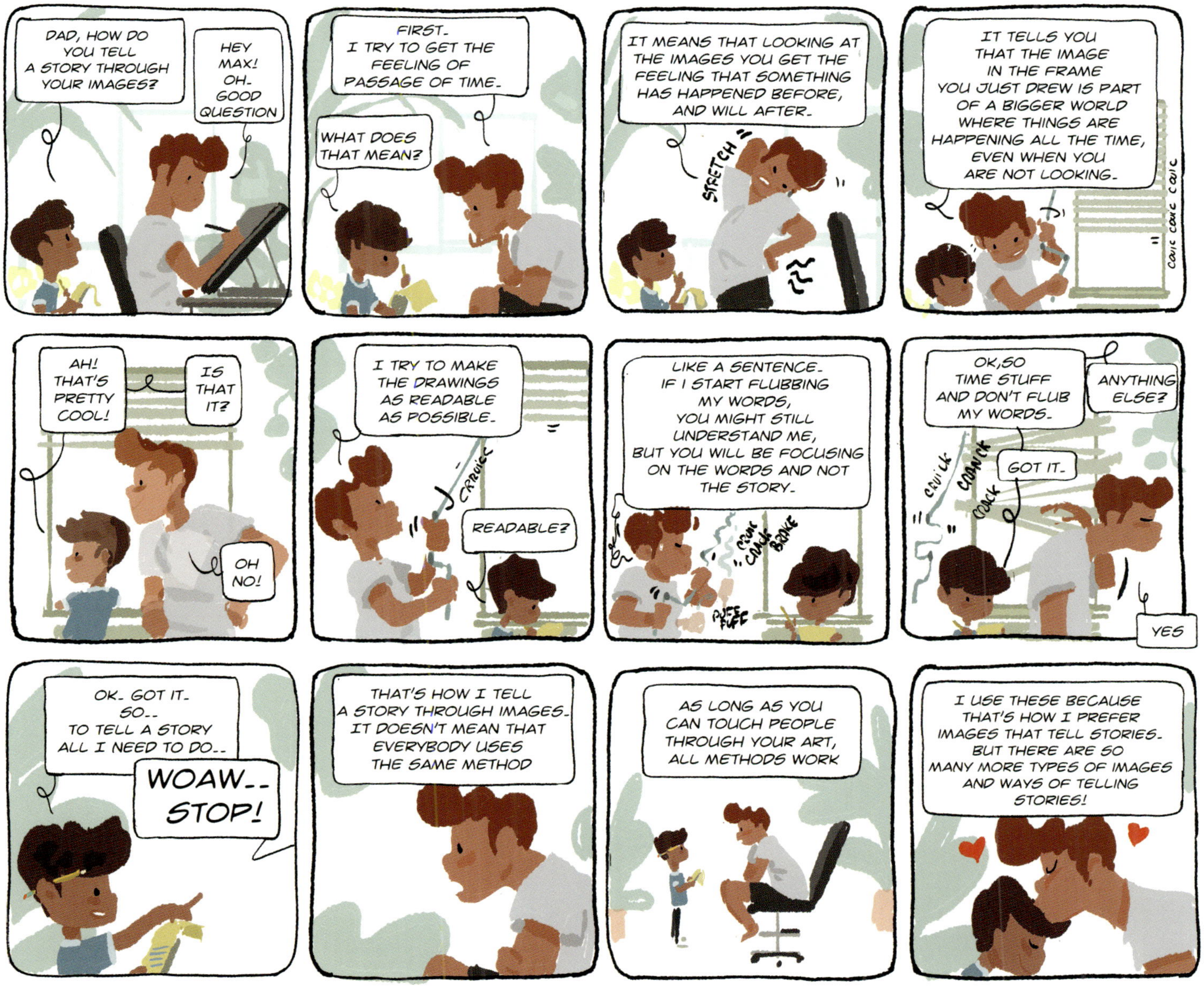

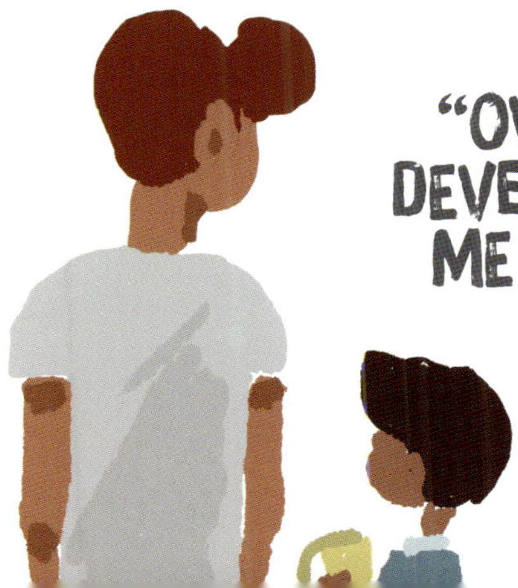

"OVER THE YEARS, I'VE DEVELOPED TRICKS TO HELP ME SUSTAIN MY FOCUS"

THE PASSAGE OF TIME

The number one thing I look for is for the idea of time passing. I feel that if I can capture the idea that something has happened before, or will happen after, what is depicted, you can sense that a larger world exists beyond the limits of the frame. If the image can make you feel like that, it means your brain is filling in the rest and interacting with the story on paper.

Time passing is, for me, easily done with light or weathered elements, or things out of their normal place.

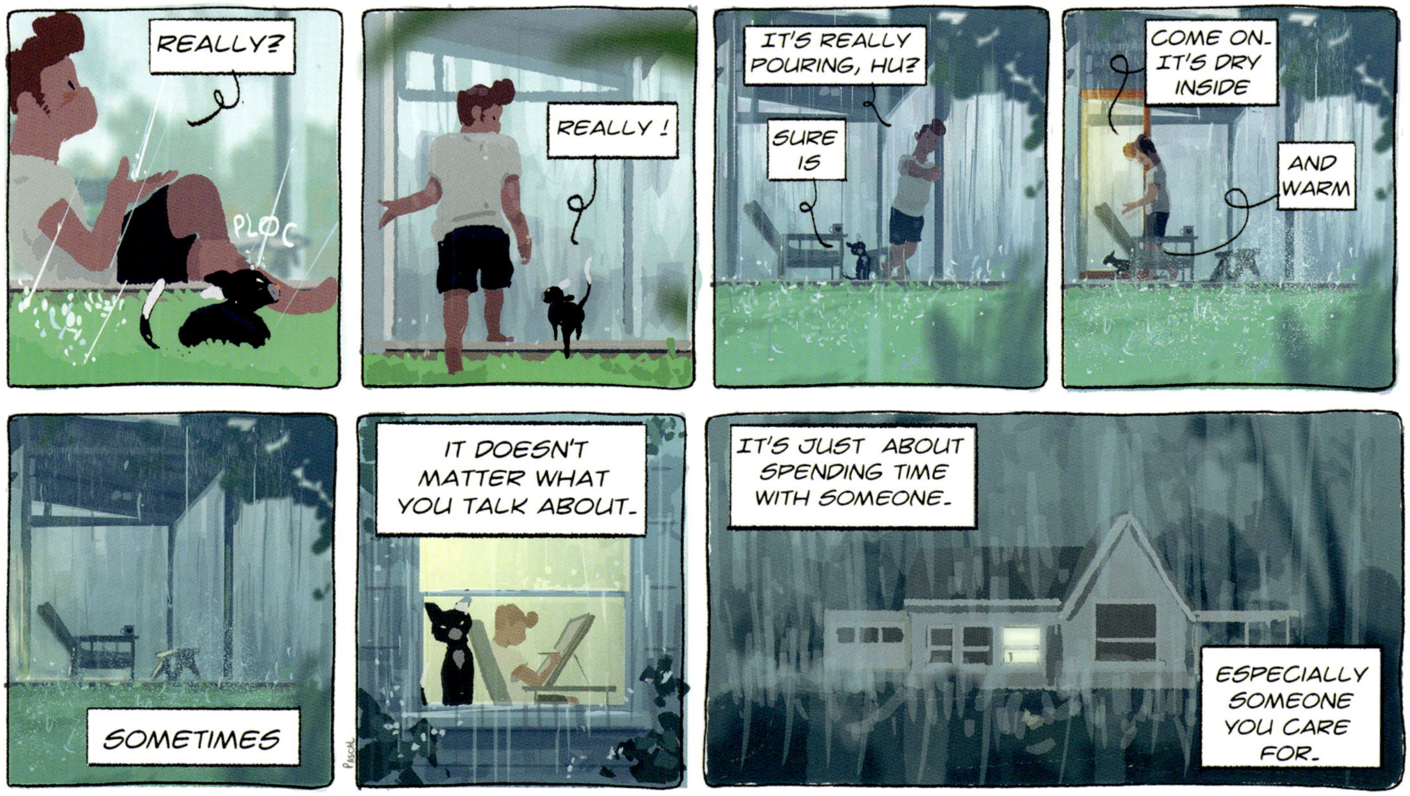

"IF THE IMAGE CAN MAKE YOU FEEL LIKE THAT, IT MEANS YOUR BRAIN IS FILLING IN THE REST..."

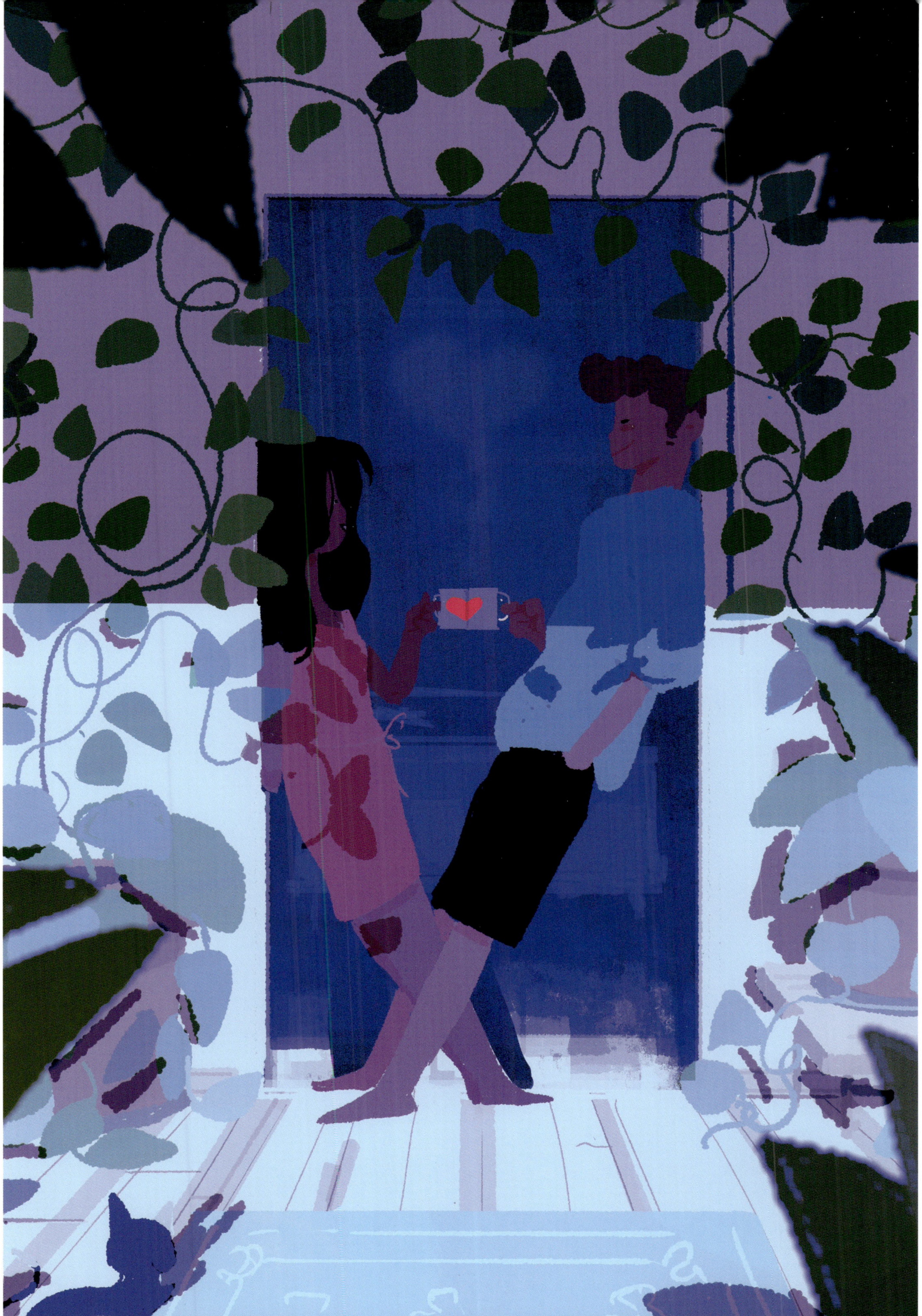

This is part of a series showing people in their own cabin, on water. I had just drawn two cabins crossing paths. This continued the story, one metaphor being about creating a bigger cabin for a growing family. There is a nice balance of hot and cold, and despite some technical clumsiness, it emotes quite a bit. This is a case of the story being stronger than the art (for me, at least).

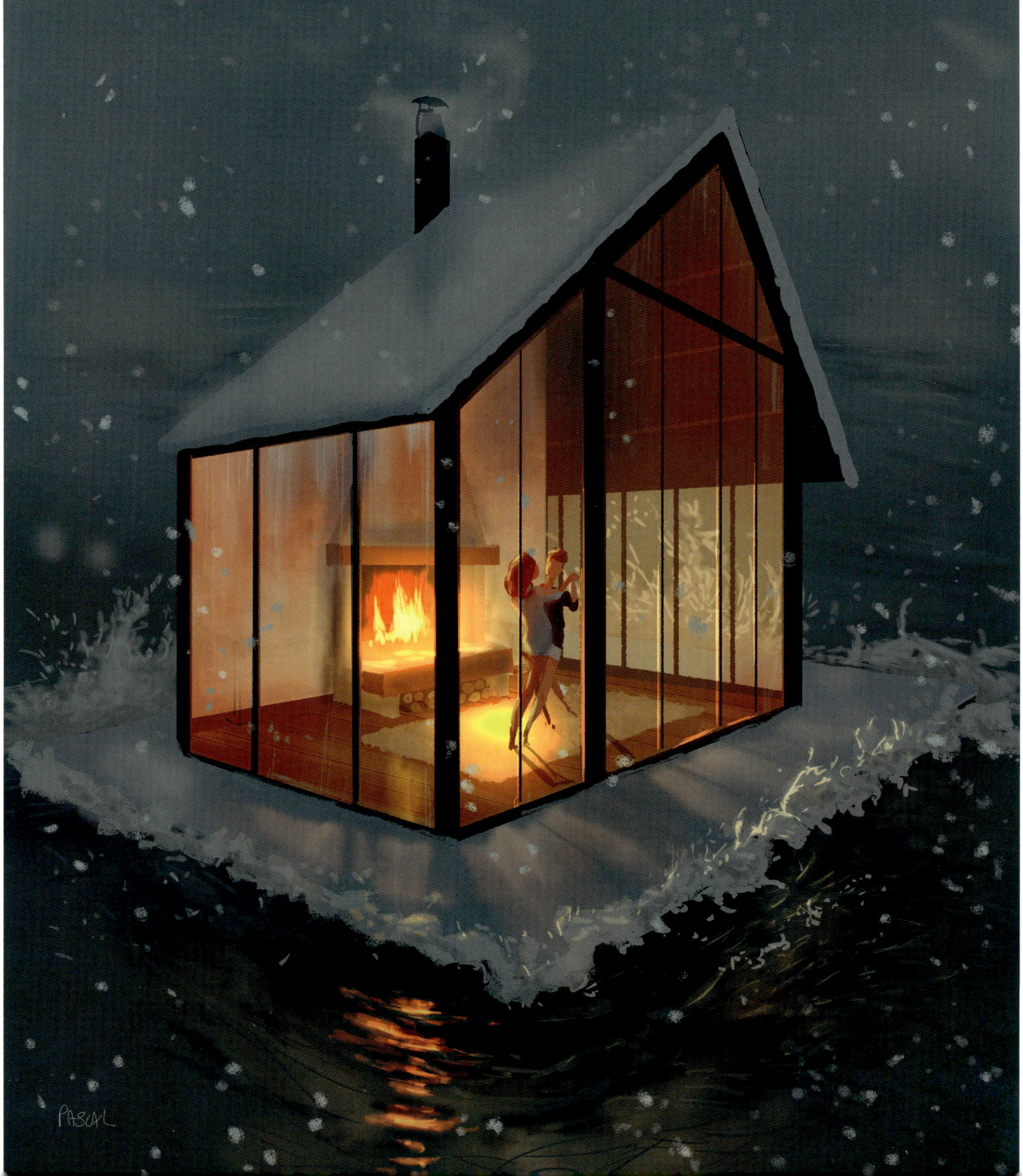

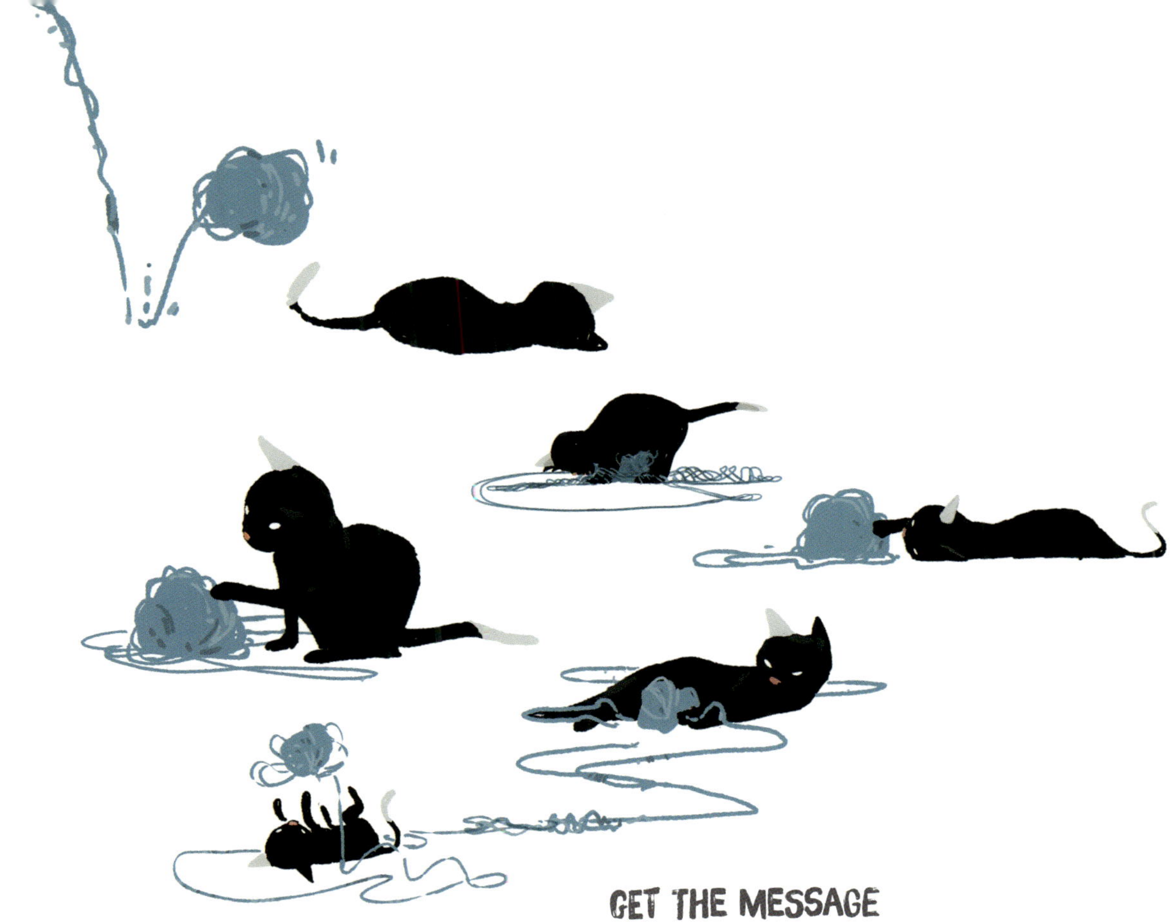

GET THE MESSAGE

Another thing I do when storytelling is to try to be as clear as possible. Both in the art and in the message. I feel this one is both good and bad for me. I still struggle with creating appealing art or deeper stories because I have a need for simplification. But all in all, I try to make my art as readable as possible. If you can't understand what you are looking at in less than a second, then I think I might have lost your attention. Especially today, with the incredibly high demand on everybody's attention. It's the same with words. I am not a writer, so sometimes my words come off as a big, messy jumble, but the goal is usually to be as clear as possible. To that effect, I found that simplifying things works best. Both in what I say and how I say it. Again, this is a double-edged sword. Oversimplification can sometimes alter the meaning of what you are trying to say, especially if you are talking about something subtle. But if you add too many details, you run the risk of losing your way and your audience.

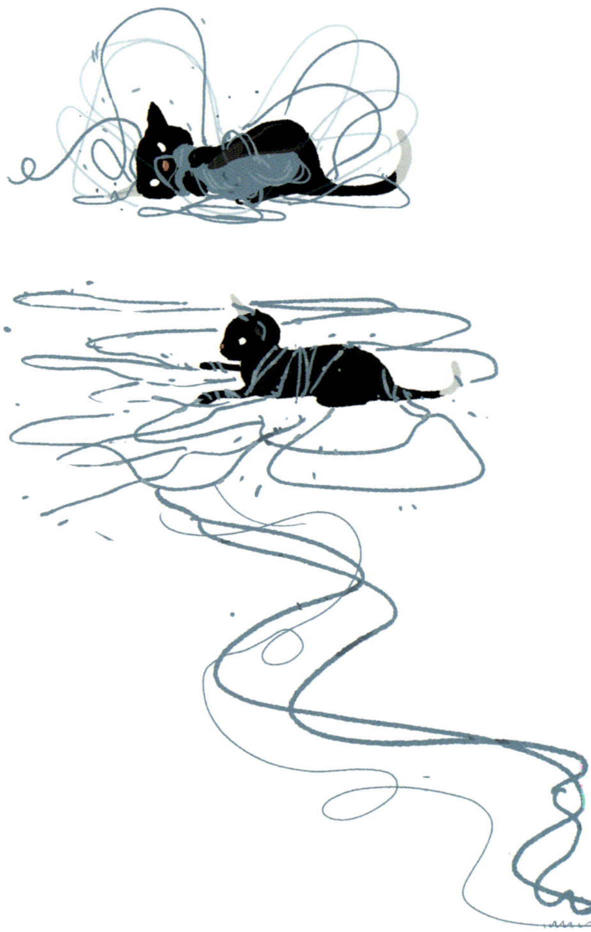

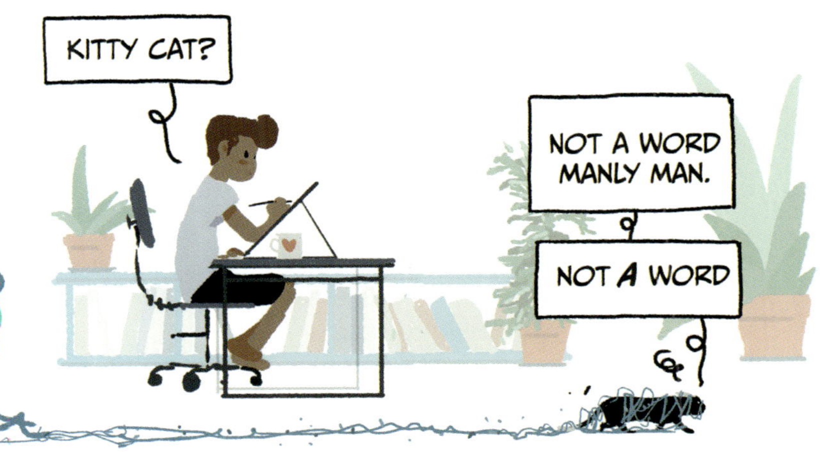

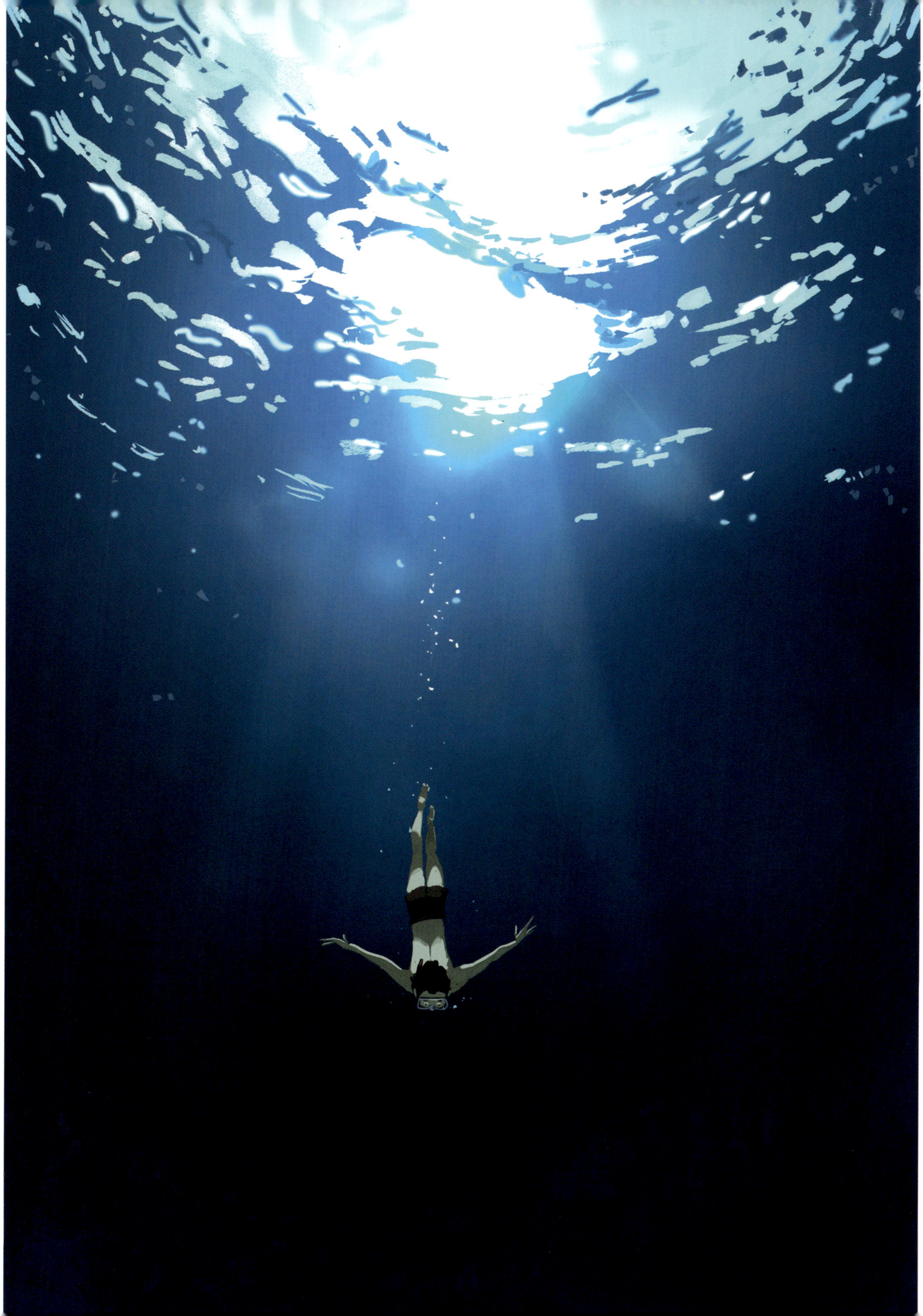

This piece (opposite) was quick and easy, coming to me almost fully formed. The idea of disappearing into my own thoughts is a frequently recurring theme for me, as is the boldly lit character. The water was almost secondary, which is why I think I painted it so quickly. This is one of my favorite pieces because of how easily and precisely it came out – I wanted to do "this," and "this" came out. It's rare that it happens this way for me.

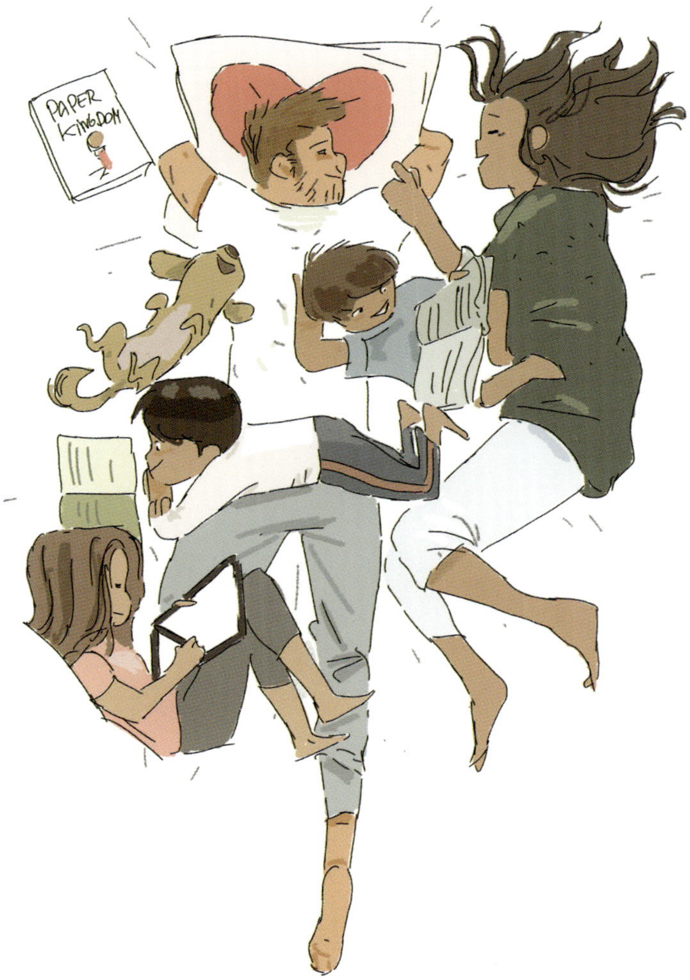

LESS IS MORE

When you look at an image, I want you to understand what is going on in half a second or less. And *feel* the emotion in roughly the same amount of time. Because of that, I often reduce the number of details in the image so that your eye reads the whole piece as quickly as possible. It's not a hard law. More of a rule of thumb. I like the idea that very few details can make you feel a lot of things. It's a balance between what is said and what is suggested.

I like adding details such as books, and pictures on the wall, because to me, I feel that if there are paintings on a wall, *somebody* must've put them there at some point. And that implies a story that has been happening off-screen. I love those little things. At the same time, too many details make me feel like I don't know where to look. At least, the way I draw them. I've seen and loved works of other artists that are incredibly intricate. It's just not something that works for my brain.

It's the same with the characters. I like to get their emotions across with as few details as possible. A line on a face that suggests a smile – that is everything to me. At the same time, I marvel at artists who are able to draw and paint beautifully rendered faces. I look at the works of Thomas Fluharty or Peter de Sève and just cannot understand how they do this. It's an interesting thing to realize that what I like to *see* is not the same as what I like to *do*. This is something that took me years to figure out and accept.

"A LINE ON A FACE THAT SUGGESTS A SMILE – THAT IS EVERYTHING TO ME"

SETTING THE MOOD

I tend to do a lot of moody images, mostly because I am better at drawing nighttime images than daytime ones. I have a harder time with brighter colors and love the dark. I'm not sure if it has to do with me being an introvert and generally preferring silence and solitude to big, busy places, but I have a strong affinity with half-tones and shadows in my images. The way I approach them is fairly simple actually. I draw everything with flat colors, I darken the whole image, and I paint the light over it.

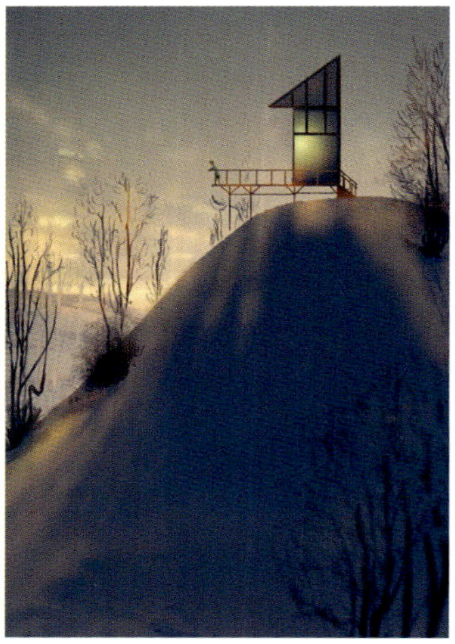
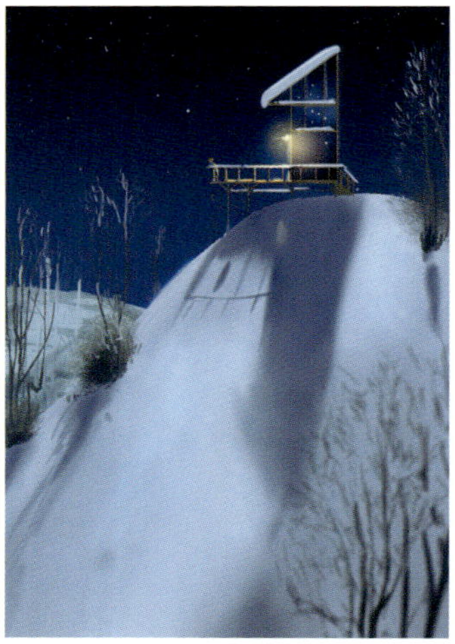
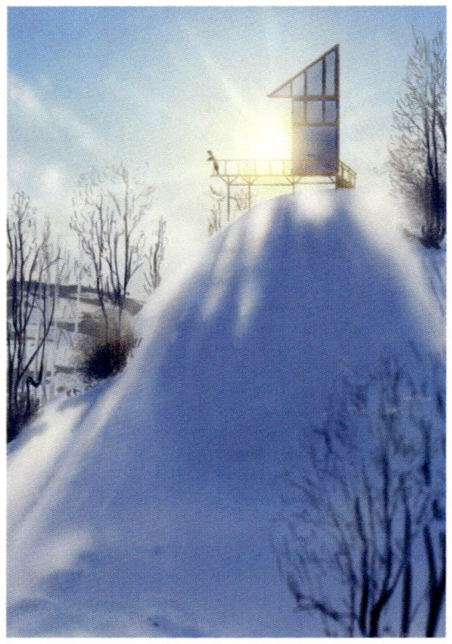
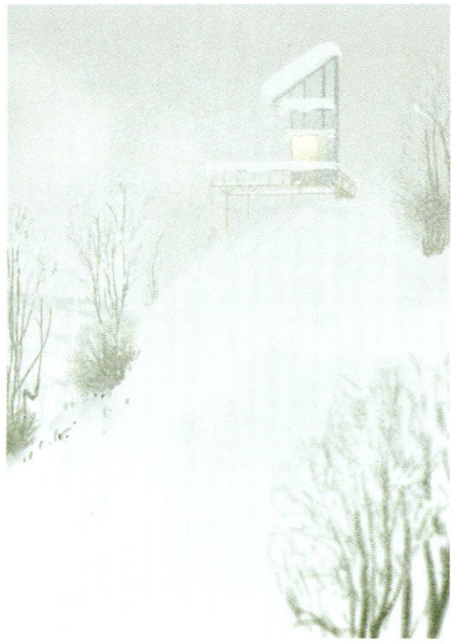

"I HAVE A STRONG AFFINITY WITH HALF-TONES AND SHADOWS"

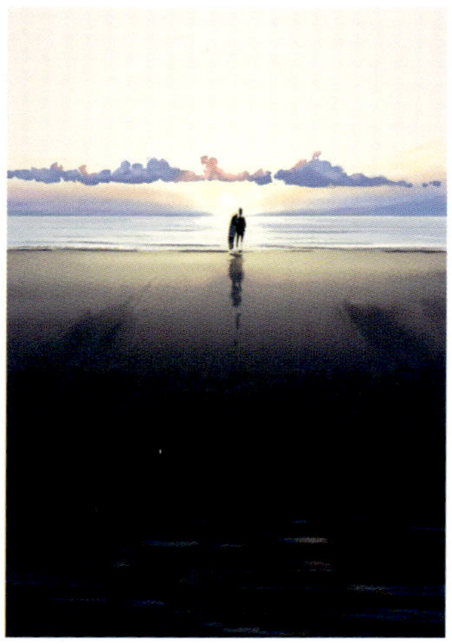
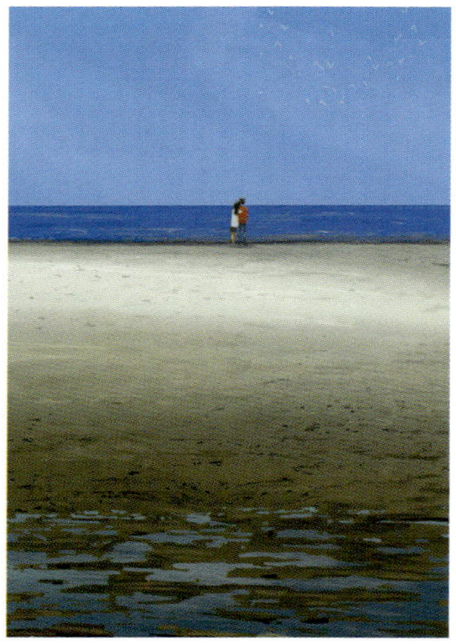

People don't see why this piece (opposite) is one of my favorites – I understand. In the past, the result of using dark colors was something being totally black or unreadable. When I drew this, it was a hot night and I was tired. Instead of trying to *make* it happen, I tried to *let* it happen. And it did, almost by itself. Adding the white shirt against the stark background triggered a vibration – *I did it!* I'd captured the feeling of walking in the woods at the end of a long, hot day. No-one else relates to this. I still love it.

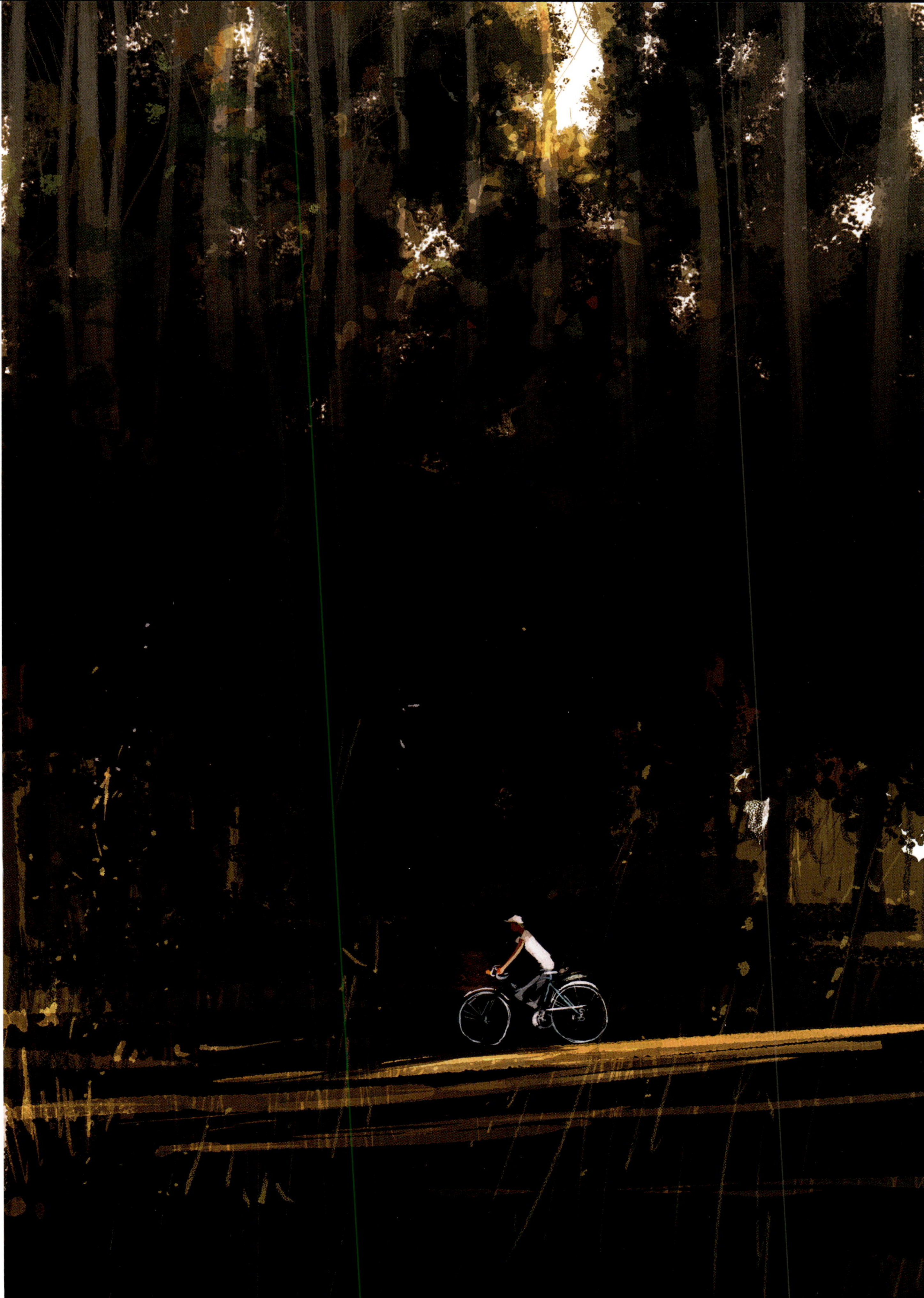

TRICKS WITH ASYMMETRY

Your brain tends to want everything to be organized. When you draw a room in which the chair is off to the side of the desk rather than under it, your brain picks that up as, "Hey, this should be put under the table cleanly and in order." Your brain thinks about why the chair is not under the table. Who did not return it there? How rude! It's a small detail, but it forces you to think about why it's out of place.

Our brains are funny that way. So powerful and so easily tricked! You can use this device with composition too (I mean, every film, comic, illustration, or picture does this to some degree.) If you put something dead center it is, well, like the name says... dead. Again, your brain wants to organize everything. When you look at something, you tend to make it the center of your attention. When you draw a character off to the side of an image, your brain automatically wonders about why this is not in the center. And boom, you've engaged the mind in the image!

That's why a lot of images are usually off-centered. It makes them more visually interesting for your brain. (Again, this is my own explanation. Yours can be different, but this works for me!)

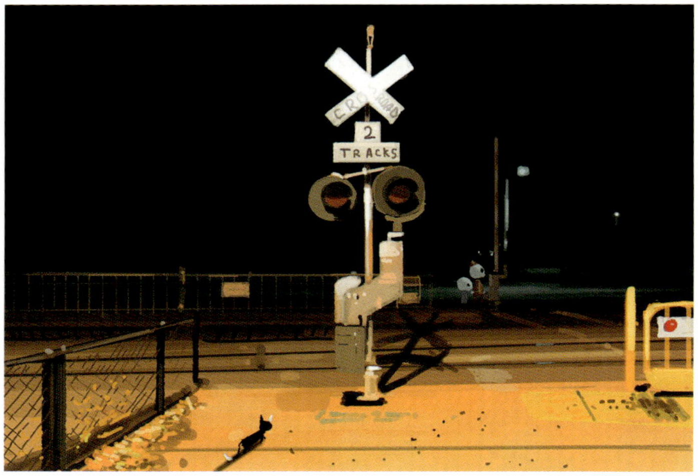

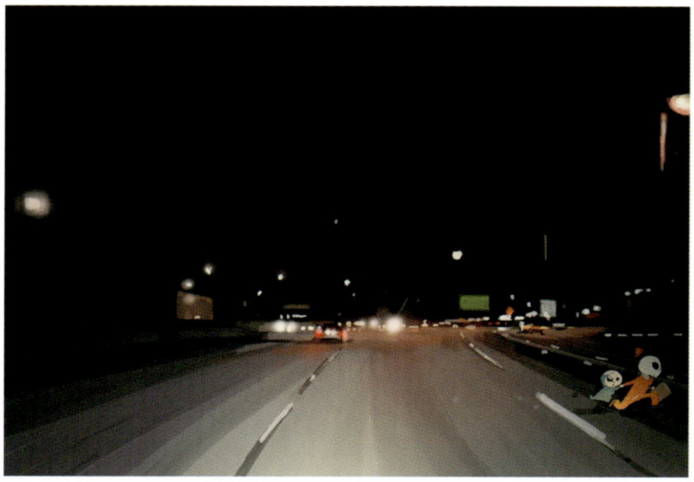

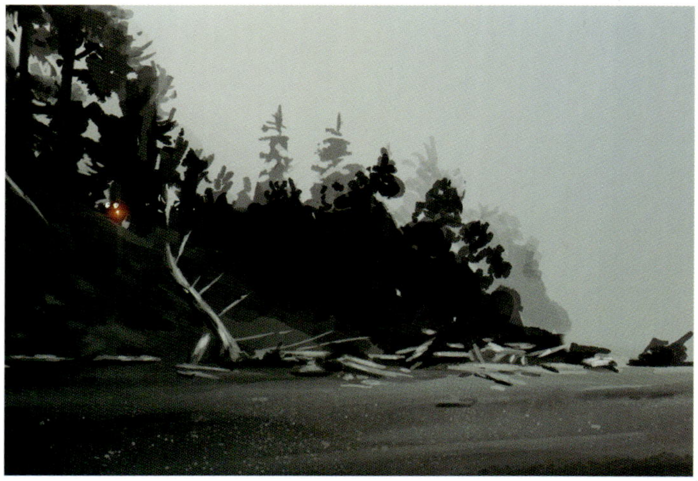

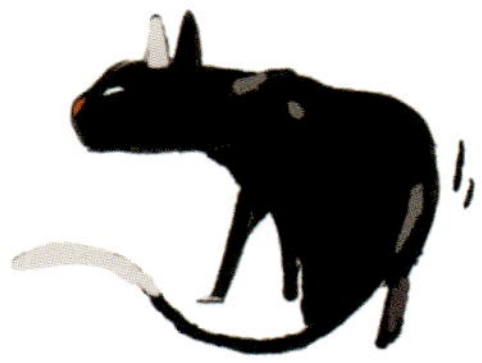

> "IF YOU LOOK AT THE STRIPS OF KITTY CAT, YOU CAN SEE **WOBBLY** LINES."

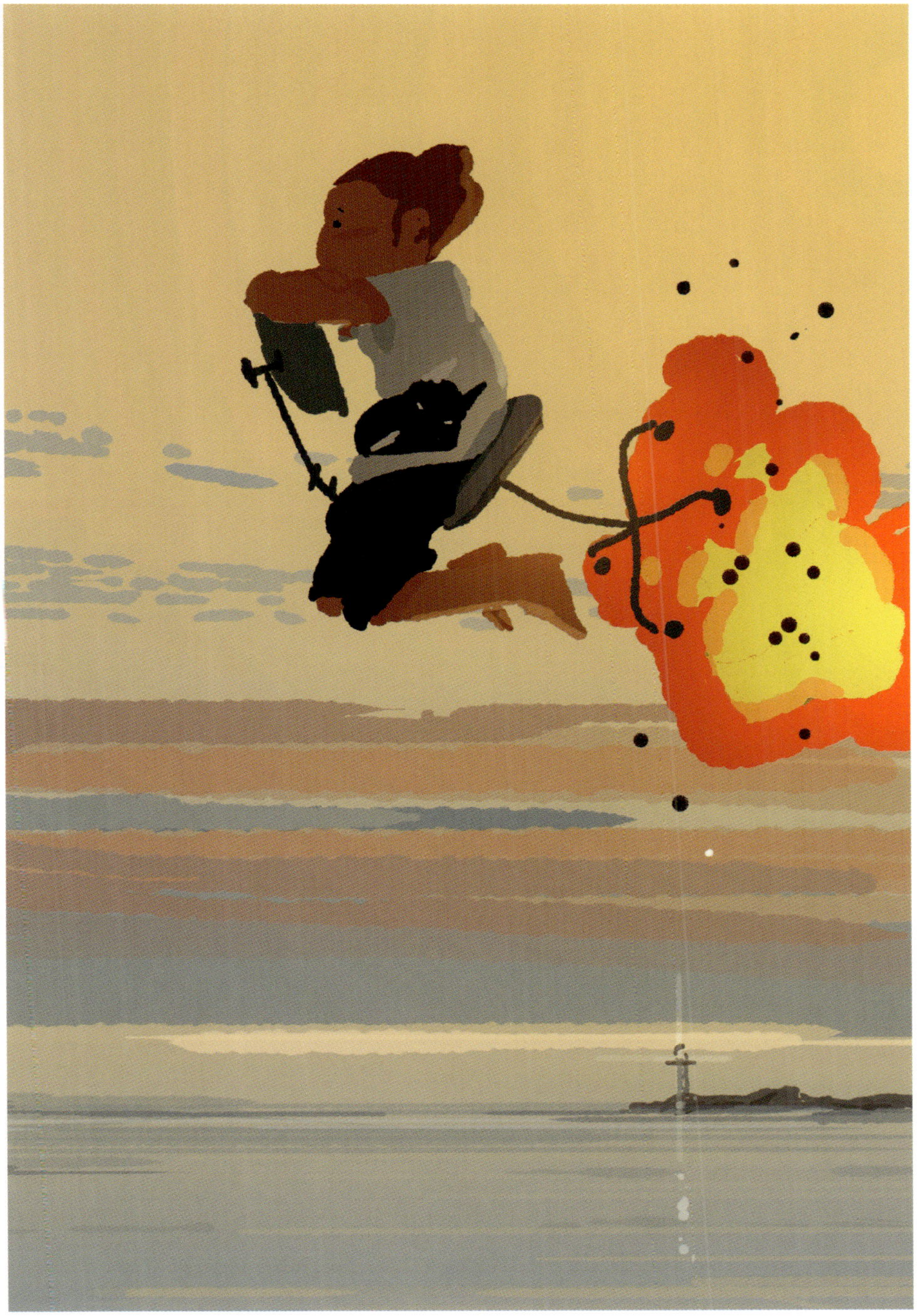

BRUSH TACTICS

Technically, for my art, I use a thick brush when I do strips. I also use a thick brush when I do my art so that I don't add the details at the beginning and get lost in them. If you look at the strips of Kitty Cat, you can see wobbly lines. The brush is simply too thick for me to do details. It goes faster too.

When I started drawing digitally, I used Adobe Flash. It had only one brush at the time, so I got used to using a single brush for everything. When I switched to Adobe Photoshop, I kept hearing about people using all kinds of brushes... So I bought a ton of brushes. And used a ton of brushes of all kinds. And did all kinds of messes.

I then found Kyle Webster's brush packs, liking them because they were pretty simple. Eventually, I stripped *everything* back to the round default brush in Photoshop, adding a bit of "scattering" to stop the line looking *too* perfect, and *voilà*! I use a square brush for cityscapes, and a stipple brush for texture if I really want to go there. But ninety percent of my work is done using that round brush with the scattering.

I *do* think brushes can bring a lot to an artist's work. I really do. It's a tool with a purpose. I don't have much use for different brushes, but they definitely bring a lot to the table when used with a goal in mind.

HOW I DRAW OUR STRIPS

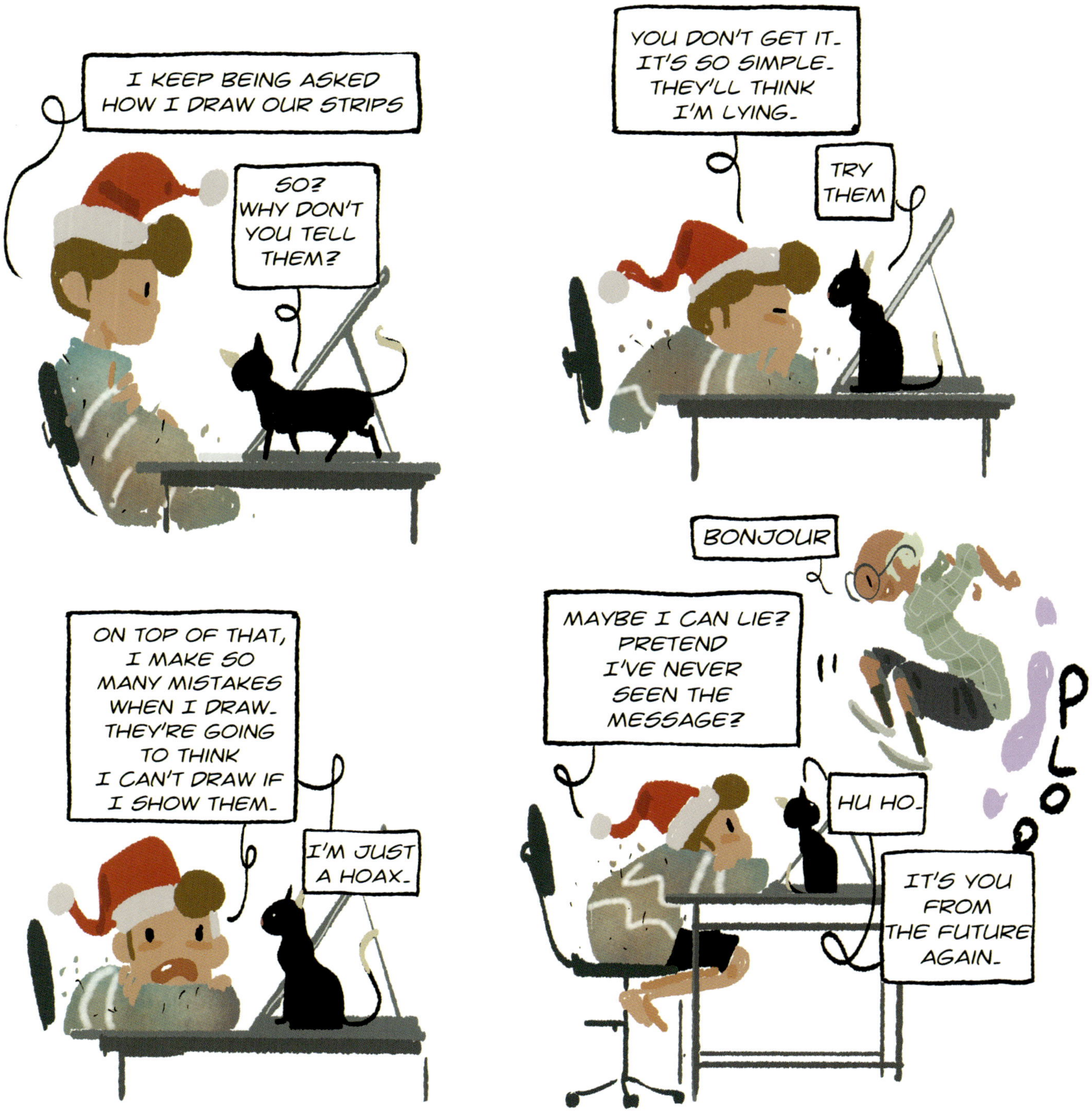

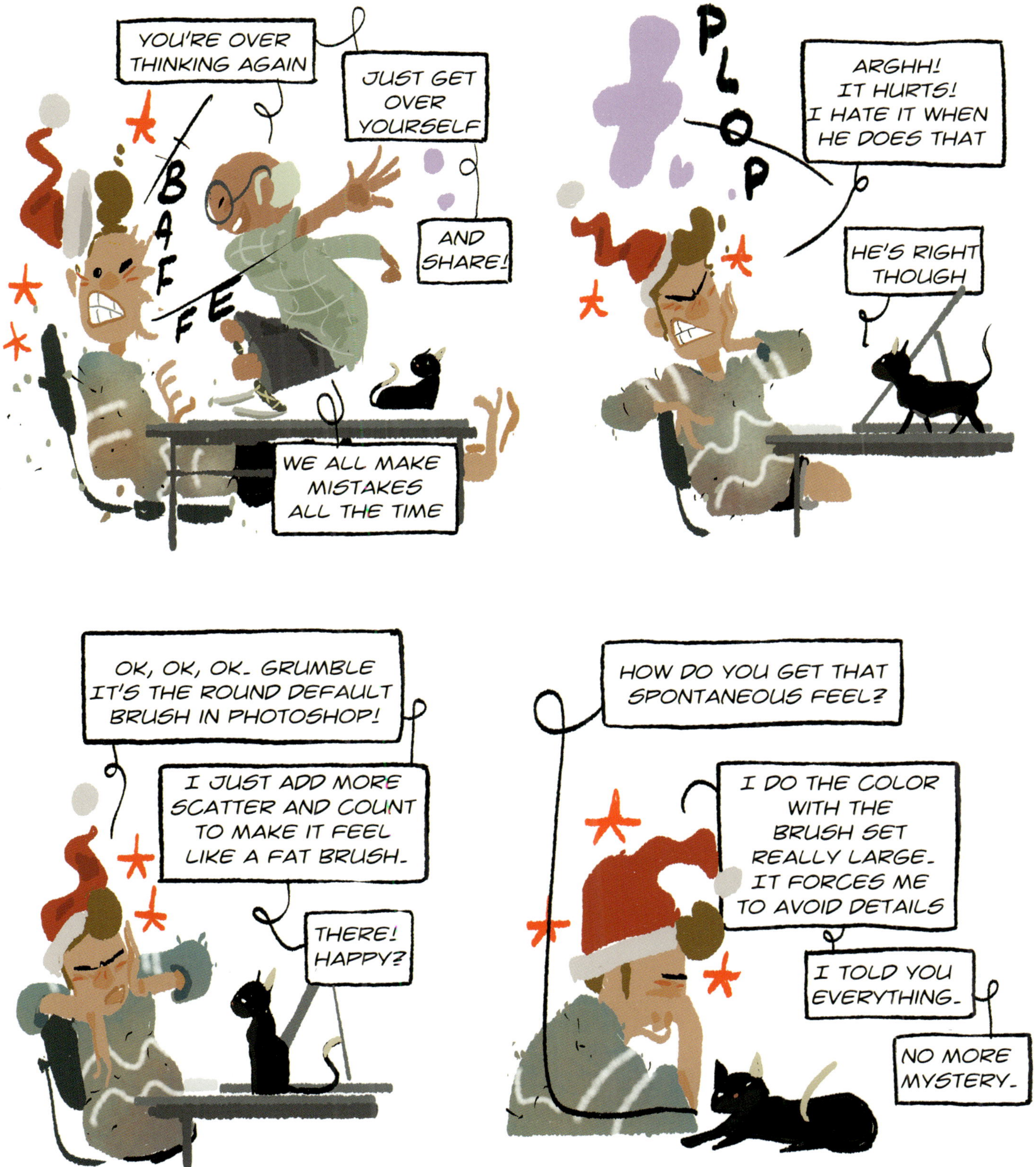
YOU'RE OVER THINKING AGAIN
JUST GET OVER YOURSELF
AND SHARE!
BAFF
FE
WE ALL MAKE MISTAKES ALL THE TIME
PLOP
ARGHH! IT HURTS! I HATE IT WHEN HE DOES THAT
HE'S RIGHT THOUGH
OK, OK, OK. GRUMBLE IT'S THE ROUND DEFAULT BRUSH IN PHOTOSHOP!
I JUST ADD MORE SCATTER AND COUNT TO MAKE IT FEEL LIKE A FAT BRUSH.
THERE! HAPPY?
HOW DO YOU GET THAT SPONTANEOUS FEEL?
I DO THE COLOR WITH THE BRUSH SET REALLY LARGE. IT FORCES ME TO AVOID DETAILS
I TOLD YOU EVERYTHING.
NO MORE MYSTERY.

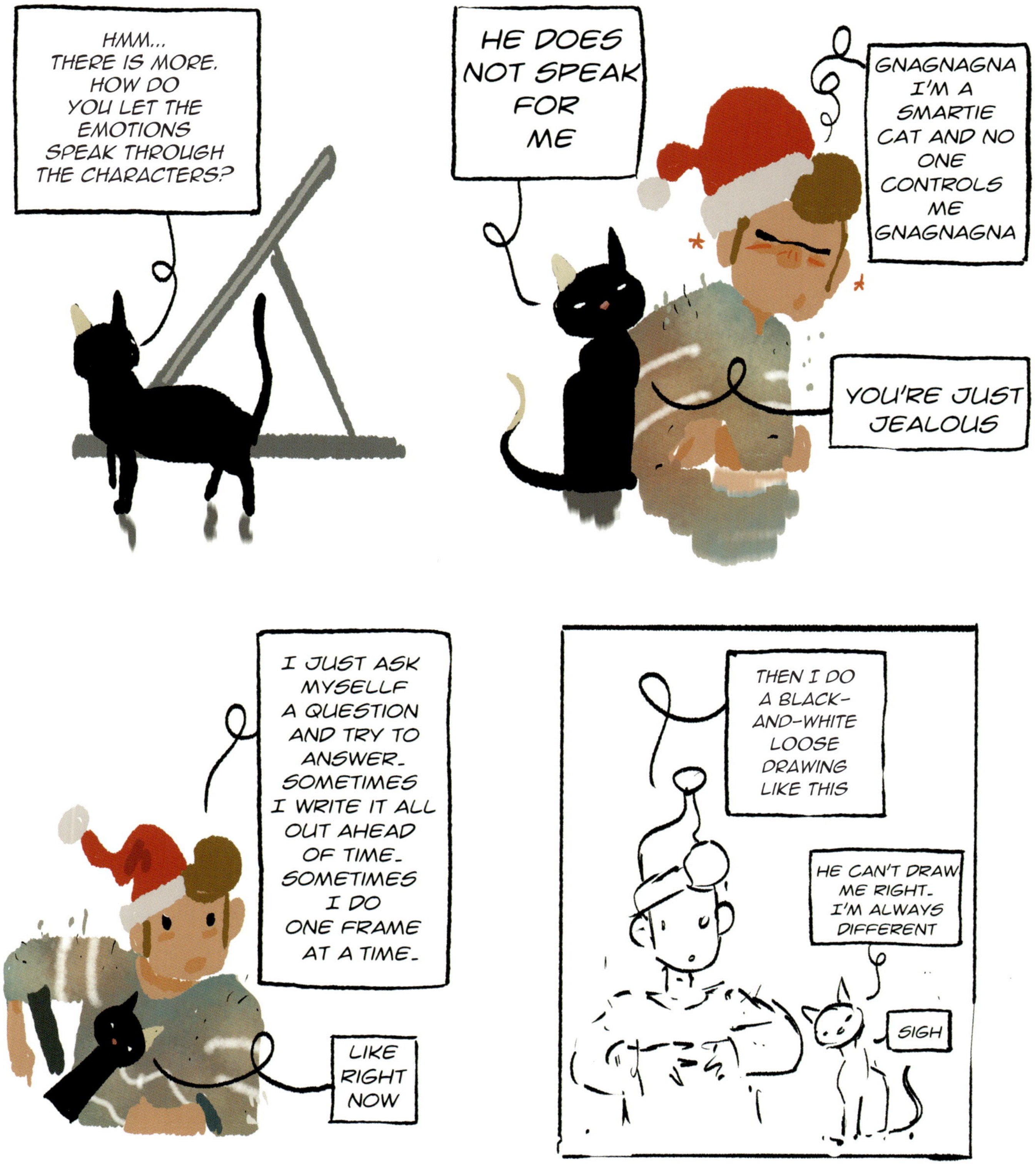
HMM...
THERE IS MORE.
HOW DO
YOU LET THE
EMOTIONS
SPEAK THROUGH
THE CHARACTERS?
HE DOES
NOT SPEAK
FOR
ME
GNAGNAGNA
I'M A
SMARTIE
CAT AND NO
ONE
CONTROLS
ME
GNAGNAGNA
YOU'RE JUST
JEALOUS
I JUST ASK
MYSELLF
A QUESTION
AND TRY TO
ANSWER.
SOMETIMES
I WRITE IT ALL
OUT AHEAD
OF TIME.
SOMETIMES
I DO
ONE FRAME
AT A TIME.
LIKE
RIGHT
NOW
THEN I DO
A BLACK-
AND-WHITE
LOOSE
DRAWING
LIKE THIS
HE CAN'T DRAW
ME RIGHT.
I'M ALWAYS
DIFFERENT
SIGH

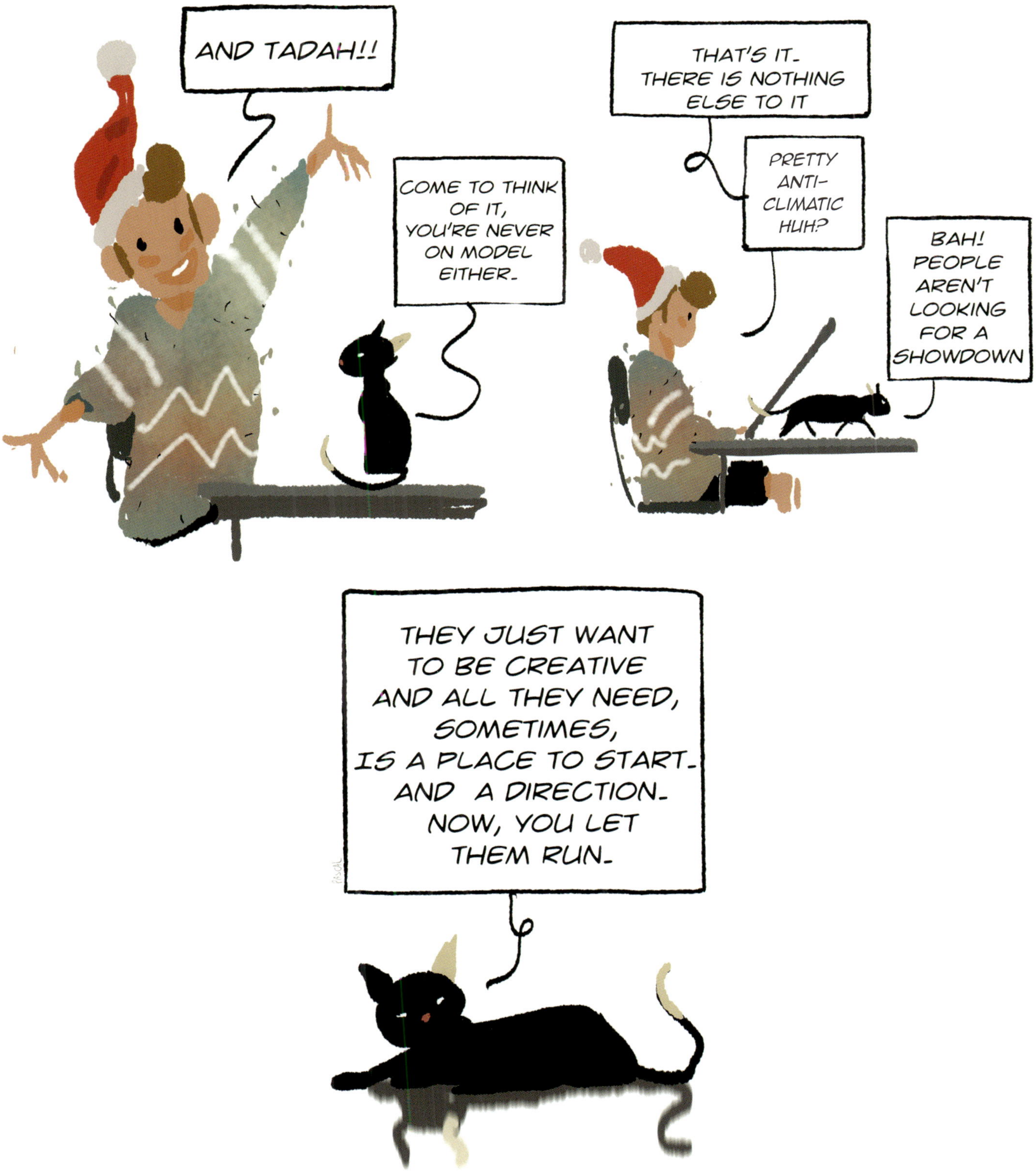
AND TADAH!!
COME TO THINK OF IT, YOU'RE NEVER ON MODEL EITHER.
THAT'S IT. THERE IS NOTHING ELSE TO IT
PRETTY ANTI-CLIMATIC HUH?
BAH! PEOPLE AREN'T LOOKING FOR A SHOWDOWN
THEY JUST WANT TO BE CREATIVE AND ALL THEY NEED, SOMETIMES, IS A PLACE TO START. AND A DIRECTION. NOW, YOU LET THEM RUN.

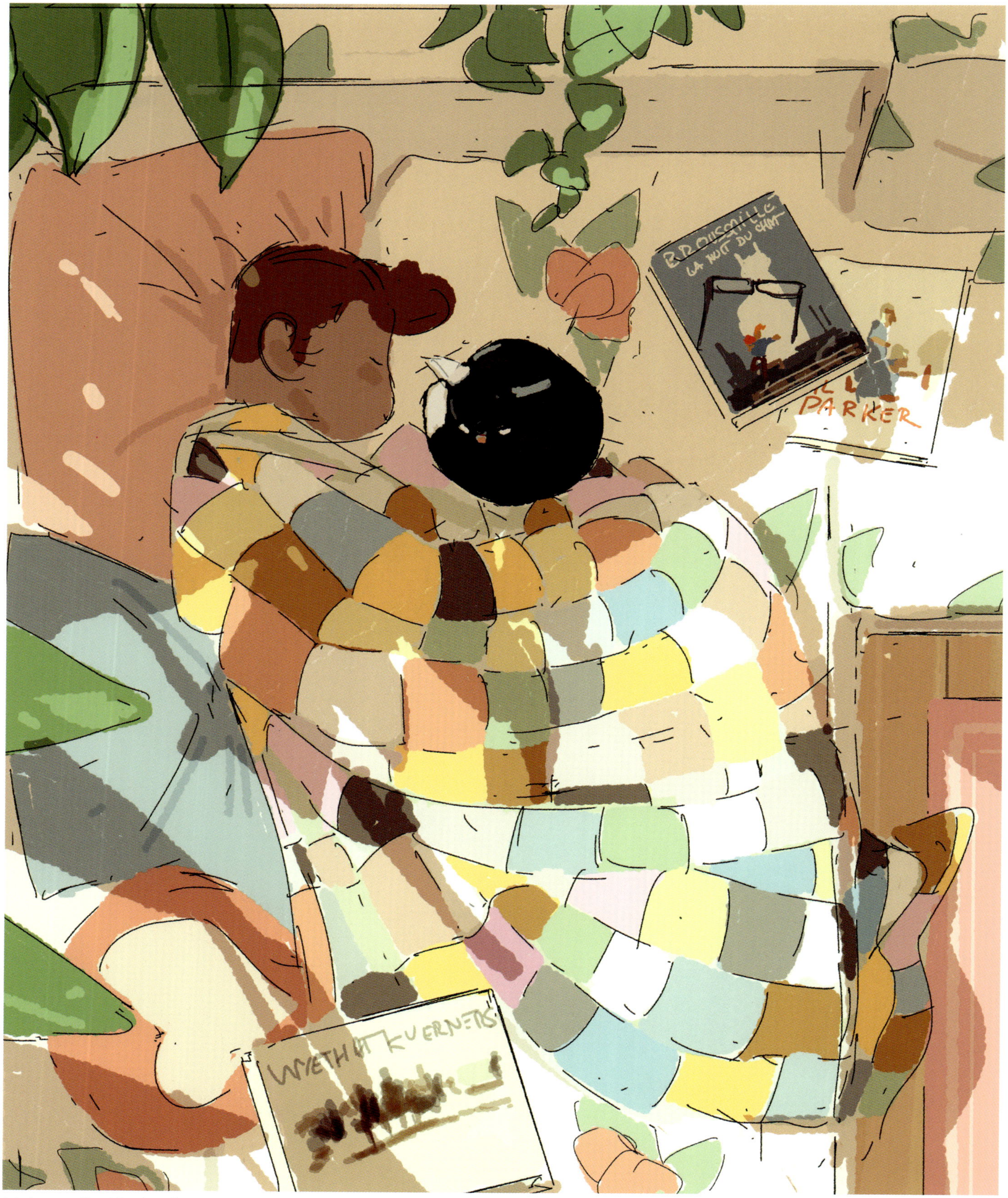

I do images like this when I'm sick, using scratchy linework as I can't focus on color (you can tell by the absence of interesting lighting or color harmonies). But it's not a bad piece of art – just driven by lines rather than my usual color blocking. To be honest, I quite like this style – it's very enjoyable.

WAYS WITH LINEWORK

When I started getting interested in comics, I was fascinated by what they represented. It wasn't that the art was beautiful (to me), it was that they communicate something. Especially when I would compare American comics, comic strips, and French graphic novels. I was aware that the images were not realistic. They were just lines arranged on a flat piece of paper that made me think I was seeing characters move, run, jump, love, live. It was fascinating to me.

I discovered the work of Munoz and Sampayo, Hugo Pratt, and Pellejero. One work that would affect my perception of graphic storytelling forever was the graphic novel *La Nuit du Chat* (*The Night of the Cat*) by Belgian comic artist Frank. What fascinated me was how a simple black line created so much with so little.

Originally, I had no intentions of becoming an artist. I simply wanted to to tell stories through images. I realized that to do that, I needed to know how to draw, so I figured I'd learn how to draw *just* enough to tell the stories. Also, my big brother played a big role in getting me into drawing! It's only now that I see how many little events caused big directional changes in my life. Funny how realizations work.

So, I set out to learn how to draw the *right* way.

Aahahah!

For the longest time, I believed in this *right* way to draw. First, I would learn anatomy (which I did by picking out details from superhero comics) and second, I would practice drawing in tiny little squares (which I couldn't do for the life of me. I didn't know back then that the art was drawn bigger then reduced in size). So, I started drawing with big pens and markers because I didn't like drawing with crayons that I had to stop to sharpen every few minutes. The thing was, I was really bad at drawing. I would see these beautiful lines in the strips but no matter how hard I tried, my work was always so, so messy. I struggled to focus on my cleanliness: it just wasn't working.

"IT'S ONLY NOW THAT I SEE HOW MANY LITTLE EVENTS CAUSED BIG DIRECTIONAL CHANGES IN MY LIFE"

At some point I was going to give up on art – I simply didn't have it. (It didn't help that an art teacher told me the same thing!) I eventually met a teacher in art school who was all about sketching as quickly as possible. Monsieur Carpentier. He was not the most beloved teacher because, as soon as we entered his classroom, he made us move all the tables and chairs to one corner, and we would stand. In his classroom, drawing was an activity, not a passivity. We would hold our pencils by the side, not by the stem, and would not look at our paper when we drew – we needed to focus on what we were seeing.

Basically, it was unlearning everything we had learned originally.

Monsieur Carpentier's classes weren't specifically about drawing – they were about *seeing*. More exactly, about seeing *space* and translating it onto paper through lines. This new way of thinking revolutionized my approach. Eventually, I stopped trying to do clean lines or drawings, instead focusing on getting "space" onto the paper.

It turned out that my sketchy lines weren't so bad after all because the more I approached drawing that way, the better I got. I never got to a clean line, but I got good at blocking out spaces, and people in spaces. So, now, I tend to use my linework in the same way. It's just a blocking method for me, because relying on *just* the linework to do the art is very difficult. This is why so much of my body of work is color blocking.

FINDING MY WAY

A few years back, I got tired of feeling that linework was my weakest spot. When asked to doodle with a pen, I became self-conscious because my illustrative approach was so different. (It took me a long, long, *long* time to realize that my way of doing art was just as valid as anybody else's!) To improve, I decided to do ten images that were line-driven rather than color-block-driven. The first few tries were horrible. I am not even sure I kept them. I was trying to do a clean line and simply couldn't. Even worse, it felt like my ability to see space was gone.

Eventually, I relaxed and started loosening up. Rather than draw, I told myself I'd "sketch" and keep it loose – suggestive rather than representative. I wouldn't draw the people; I would draw the space around them. I was tricking my mind. The first image I did in this style was a couple lying on their bedroom floor. I colored in the lines and to my surprise, I could "see" an image and a story. I was in shock. I did another, and another, until I'd done the ten pieces. I was happy with this process so kept going. Now I have about a hundred pieces.

I don't draw with lines nearly as much, because it is time consuming. I understand that for most, lines are quicker, but since I only consider my sketches done when color and lighting are applied, the extra step of creating lines that worked on their own was a lot harder. Applying the color and staying more or less within the lines was also extremely difficult – I have little patience for precision work.

But, once in a while, I find it fun to approach the art differently and draw with lines. That said, even when I do color blocking, which is when you see the art with no lines visible around the shapes, I often start with a rough sketch. This is mostly for placement, sizes, and an idea of space. Then I go off-road and improvise as I go along.

CASE STUDY: LINE-DRIVEN PROCESS

Linework is key to the foundation of the picture. I will add details and that all-important depth later.

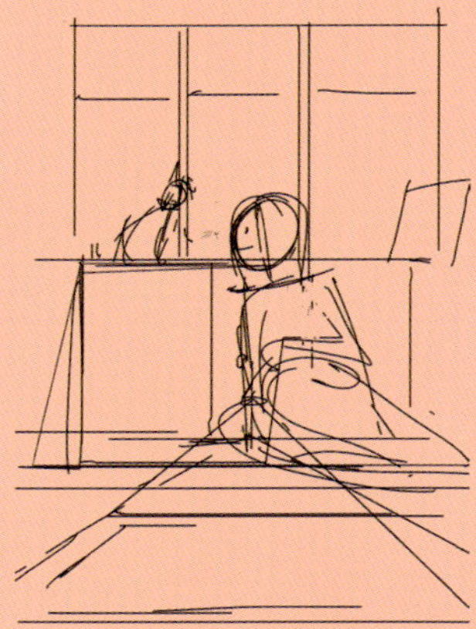

1. PLANNING

Lines help me figure out the space and general position of elements. I like to break up negative space with lines at this stage.

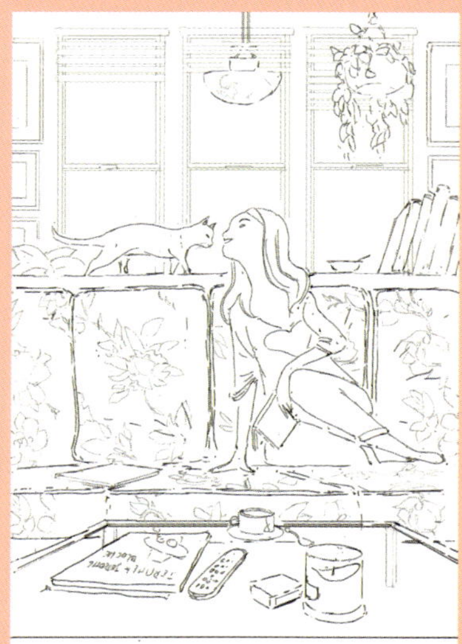

2. DRAWING

Most time is spent defining details; posing characters in their definitive state. This is also my final line. The style is rough, so I try to retain a manufactured look to the outlines. It's all about the storytelling.

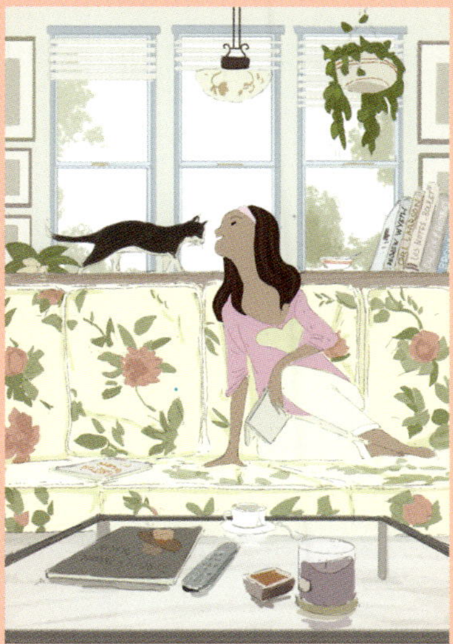

3. COLORING

In this phase, I add flat colors with no lighting. Some texture – not much. The goal here is to harmonise the values so the characters read, and the environment works without overwhelming the main subject.

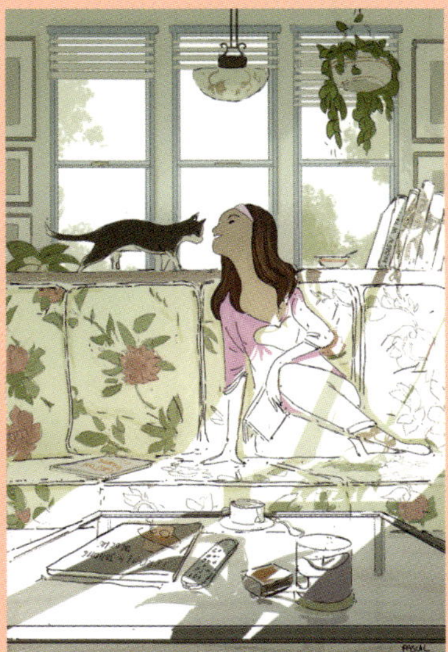

4. LIGHTING

In this phase, I set up mood lighting. I balance the darks with the brights to convey emotions, temperature, and overall feeling.

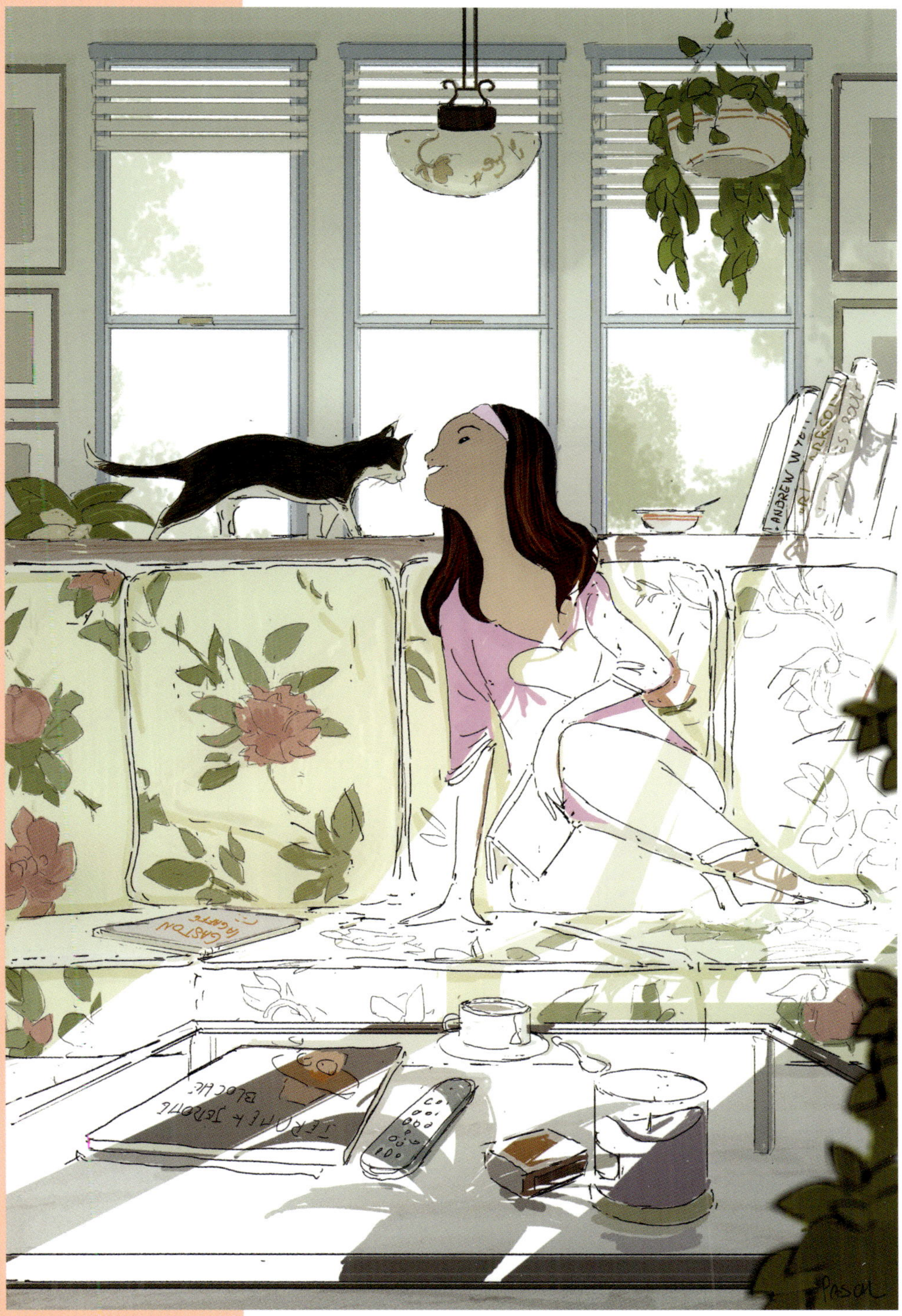

5. FINAL DETAILS

The finishing touches are all about making sure there is warmth and modulation of the lights and shadows. This also gives the scene depth, turning a flat image into something you can look into – imagine looking across the room and out of the window. Nothing much changes from the previous stage, but it's the last ten percent that pushes the image.

CASE STUDY: COLORBLOCK-DRIVEN PROCESS

This is a good example of how I use lines to set up a stage, but not as a final piece of the image. I love the idea that depth can be suggested on a flat piece of paper. A few lines that converge and *voilà* – you have a path that leads away from you.

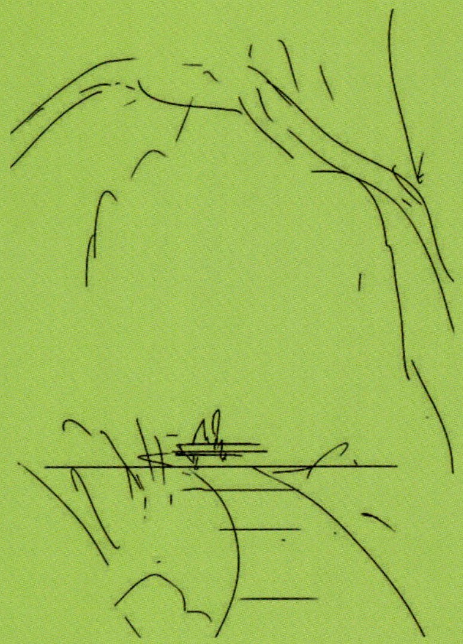

1. BACKGROUND BLOCKING

I block out a tree on the right because I'm afraid the composition will be too empty (even if my goal is to paint a lot of dark vegetation). There is something refreshing and appealing for me about walls of leaves getting lost in the shadows. For this painting, I use a square brush all the way – the same brush I use for my cityscapes – to deter me from drawing details of leaves and branches too soon.

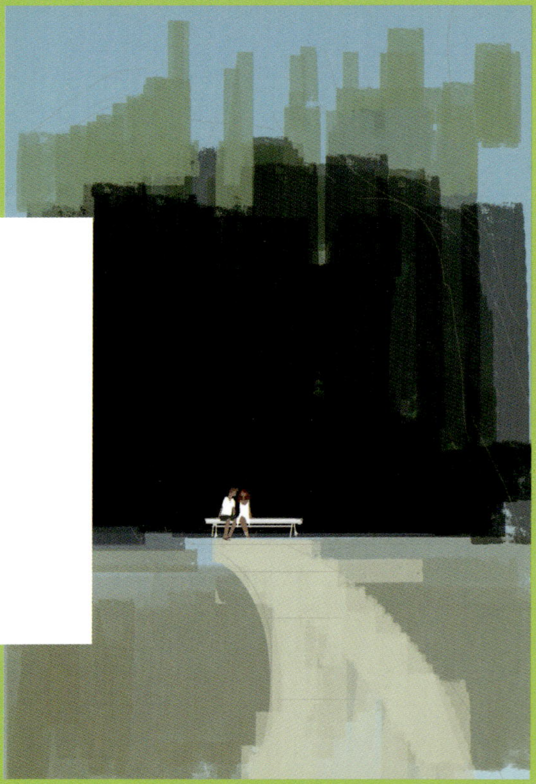

2. ANCHORING

Once I've blocked in some shapes and colors, I place my two characters to create an anchor and sense of story. The main goal for this piece is to capture the feeling of a sunny day contrasting with the coolness of the shadows from the trees. However, I also need a human connection to materialize the feeling.

3. FOREGROUND BLOCKING

After I've blocked out a good portion of the background, I start blocking out the foreground. I try to find colors and value contrasts that stand out from the background without feeling out of place. It's an exercise in finding out how many variations of green I can play with. Green has always been a color I wanted to avoid because I couldn't figure out how to use it properly. In the past few years, I've pushed myself to work more with green because I didn't want to feel stuck in that regard.

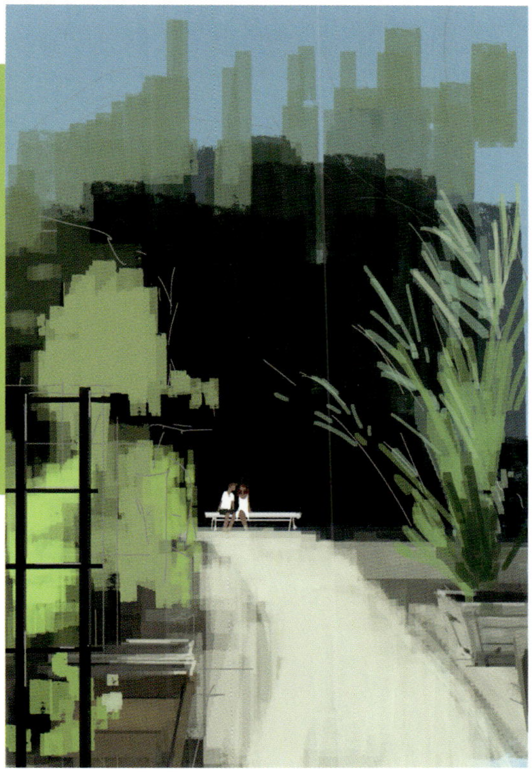

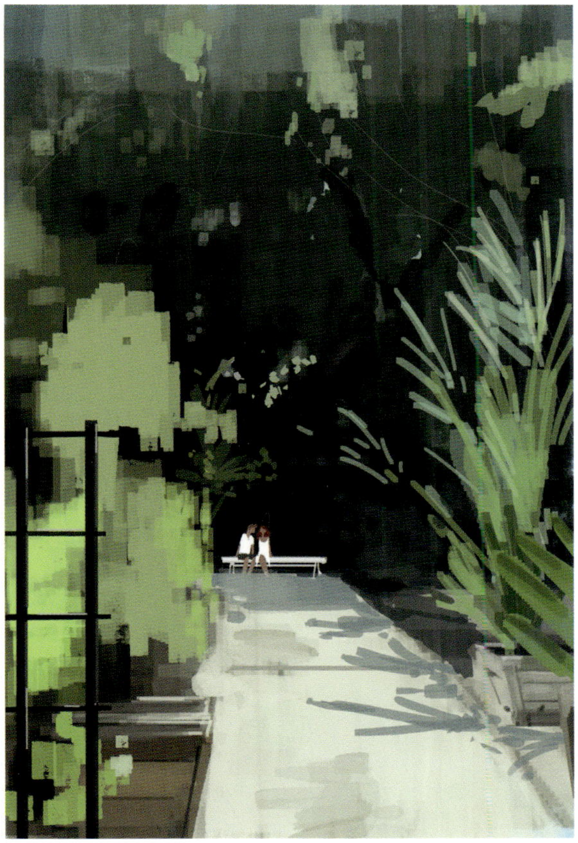

4. PLACING SHADOWS

Once I have good blocking, I start placing shadows. Here, I see shadows as a way to break up the space, and create space within space. Meaning that, if you look at the path, it's just *one* path, but with shadows across it, it feels broken up into different parts, tricking the eye into seeing more space than there actually is. When I do visual development, I use shadow a lot to create a sense of scope; to make an environment feel richer and deeper than it really is.

Lighting is magical this way.

AN ABSTRACT APPROACH TO LIGHT

One of my goals is to draw the light without drawing the objects. An almost abstract approach. I think I have been so conditioned by comics and animation that it is sometimes hard for me to reframe my state of mind to see things differently. Doing these types of paintings helps me get into this new world. The cool thing is that usually, when I do one of these, I'll go for a walk after, and I see the *world* in a very different way. It's funny how art can do that.

5. FINAL DETAILS

Eventually, everything is blocked in, and I start working on details. This is the stage that I love the most – the little dots of lights that pierce through the dark foliage. It's like dappled light to me, a sensorial experience that I really enjoy. At this point, I am still using my square brush. I just made it smaller, and keep tapping my screen with it.

A few years ago, I was adding details to an image like this. My wife heard the taptaptap of my stylus on the screen and said, "Ah! You sound like Bob Ross." "Who's Bob Ross?" I asked. And that is how I discovered happy little trees and a new idol!

I didn't do any major color variations on this piece like I do for cityscapes. I began with an image in mind and wanted to stick to it. I might have pushed the contrast a bit more at the end, but that's it.

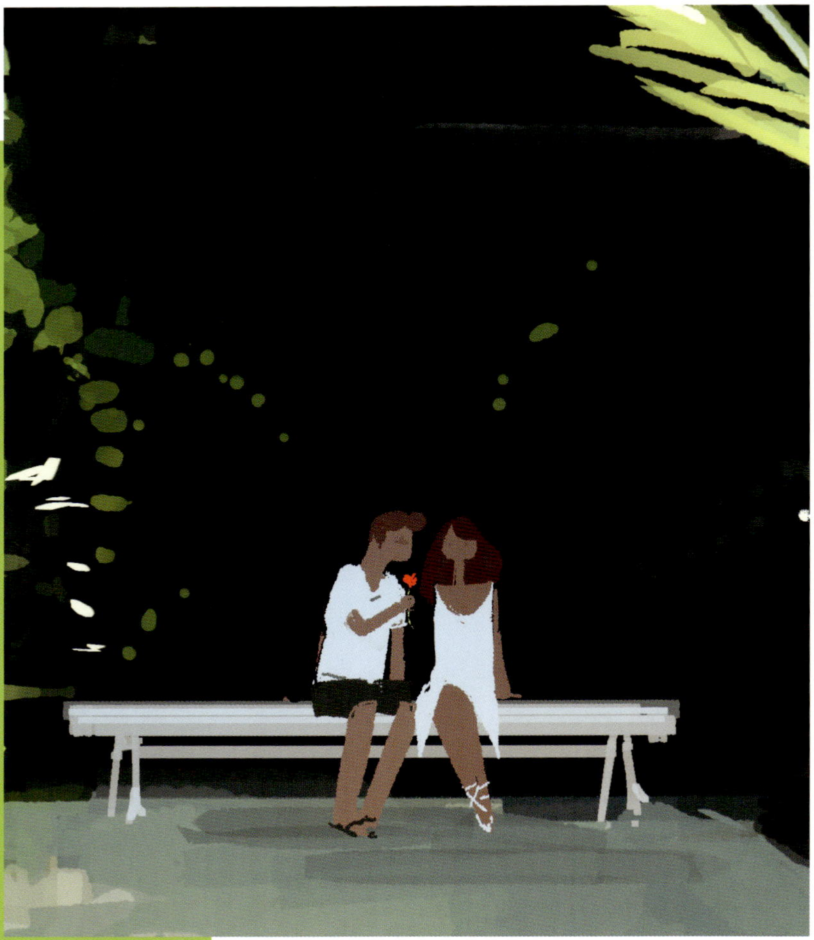

Because I am not yet at the stage where I can go fully abstract with this kind of image and be happy with it, I added the figures to anchor the scene. Maybe someday, though...

"A FEW YEARS AGO, I WAS ADDING DETAILS TO AN IMAGE LIKE THIS.

MY WIFE HEARD THE TAPTAPTAP OF MY STYLUS ON THE SCREEN

AND SAID, 'AH! YOU SOUND LIKE BOB ROSS...'

'WHO'S BOB ROSS?' I ASKED.

AND THAT IS HOW I DISCOVERED HAPPY LITTLE TREES + A NEW IDOL!"

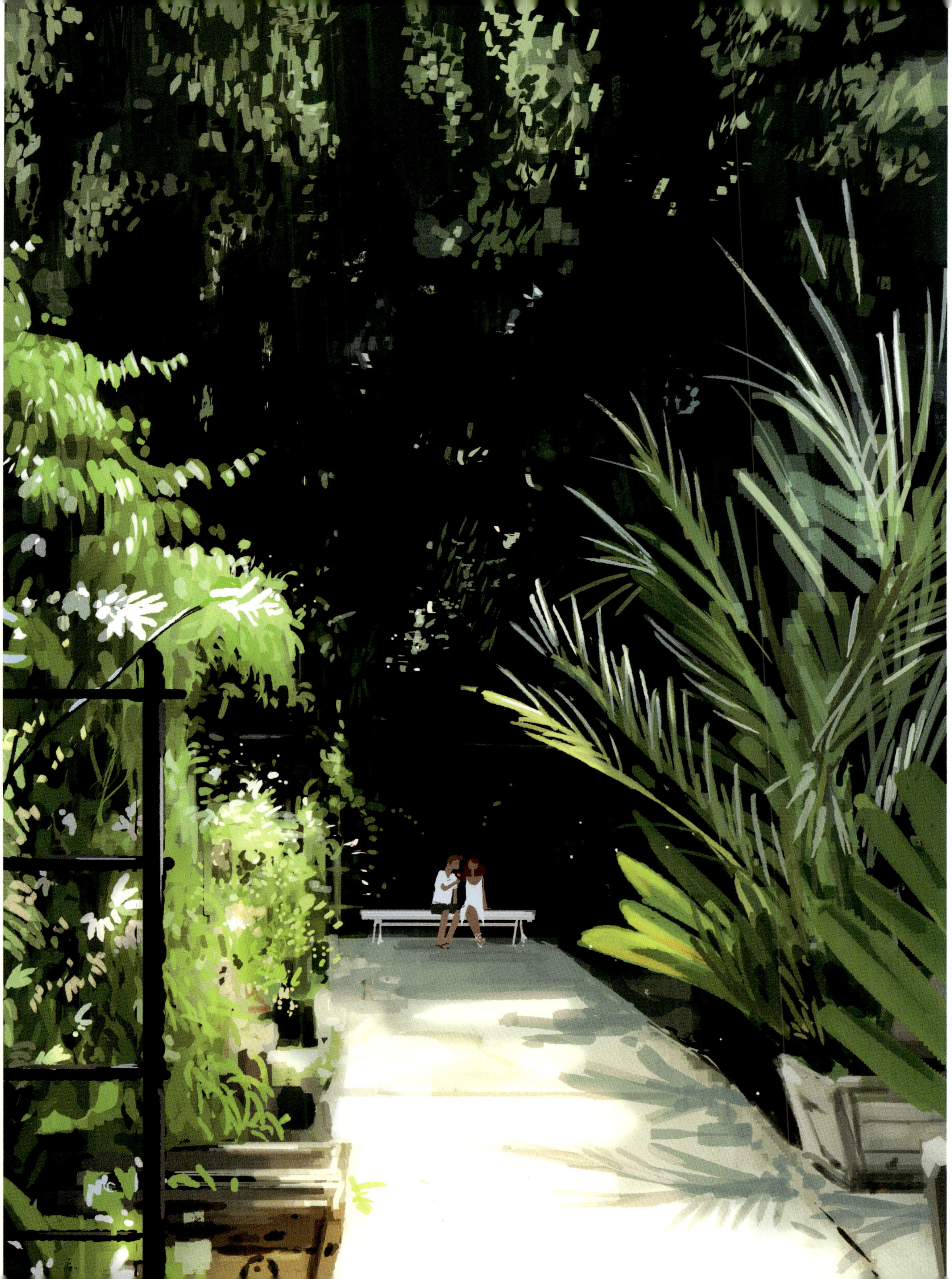

CREATING CITYSCAPES

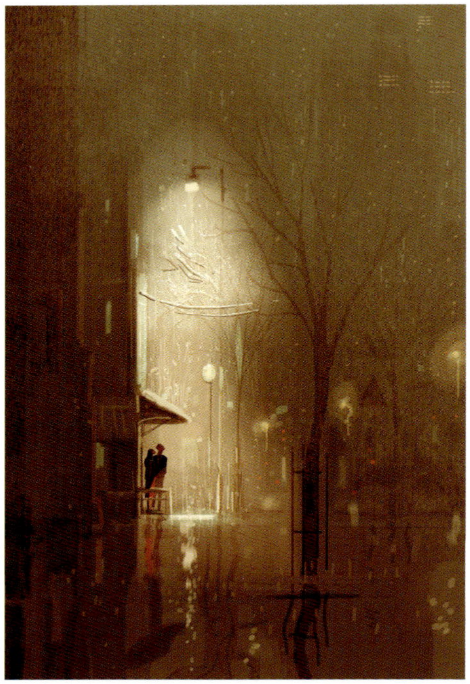

I get asked this a lot. How I do the cityscapes. At this point, I have done a few hundred, so the process has been refined over time. It's a lot easier for me, now, to get closer to the last five percent. But the last five percent – no matter how much more experience I have – is always a struggle, as I'll explain later.

I'll try walking you through the process. I can talk about the tools and the different steps, but some of the choices made come out of in-the-moment emotional reactions, rather than planned ones. It makes it harder to write a recipe for how to make them.

Hopefully this makes a little bit of sense to you. It *still* doesn't make a whole lot of it to me!

1. INITIAL MARK-MAKING

I start with a blank canvas and square brush. I have exactly two digital square brushes that I use. They are both the same, so I am not even sure why I have two. I think at some point I was afraid of losing that brush, so duplicated it and never got around to cleaning my brush palette.

As a side note. I probably have a hundred brushes or so in my Photoshop brush palette and use maybe four of them regularly. Half of which are simply the round brush that I customize by adding scattering.

Anyhow...

I start with a blank canvas and start making marks with the square brush. I typically start with a big brush, I think because I am a bit lazy – drawing something and *then* coloring it, when it's as big as a city, scares me. I think it's also because when I see big cities, it's incomprehensible to me how so much cement and bricks and steel and people are packed into the space, so I approach it as a big mess and try to make sense of it as I go along.

So I just do a few big brush marks on the page, with the opacity set to around thirty percent, sometimes up to sixty. But I tend to stay on the low range – I like how the grays build up, one atop another. It's very abstract at first and seeing shapes emerge little by little fascinates me.

2. Building + Improvising

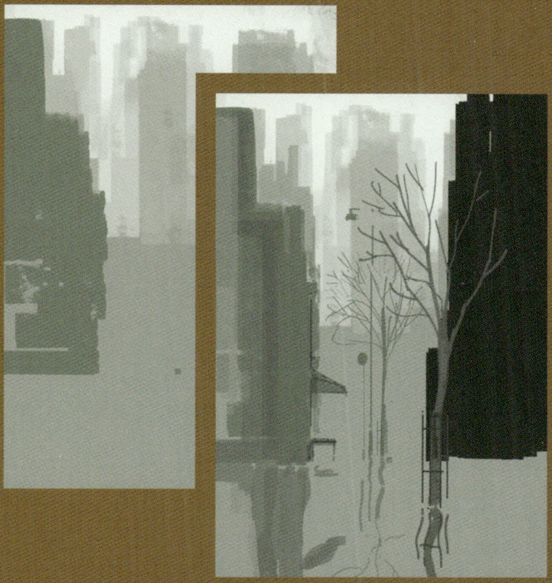

Eventually, after playing around with shapes, I start seeing edges, angles, planes, and begin adding stronger values. I have a very loose approach and try not to fall in love with any mark or shape I put down. If I do, it will stop me improvising as I build up the image, and the improvising – the creating-on-the-go bit – is the reason why I started doing these types of images in the first place.

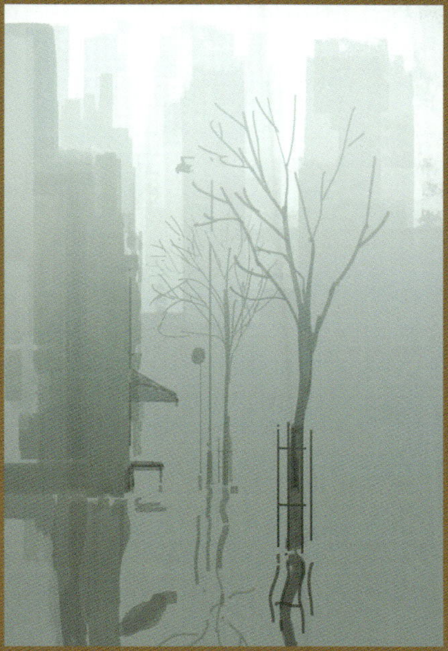

3. Adding Atmosphere

At some point, I add atmospheric perspective. It's like seeing a mountain disappear into the clouds – there is something magical about it to me. I know it's a bit of a "trick" and not an actual skill or decision rooted in some strong foundation of drawing. It's simply because I like the feeling of it.

The more atmosphere I add, the darker it gets, because I use a lot of multiply layers. It helps me attain the "grittiness." I use soft light layers with white or light-grays to create ghost-like effects of windows and architecture. All this is still with the square brush.

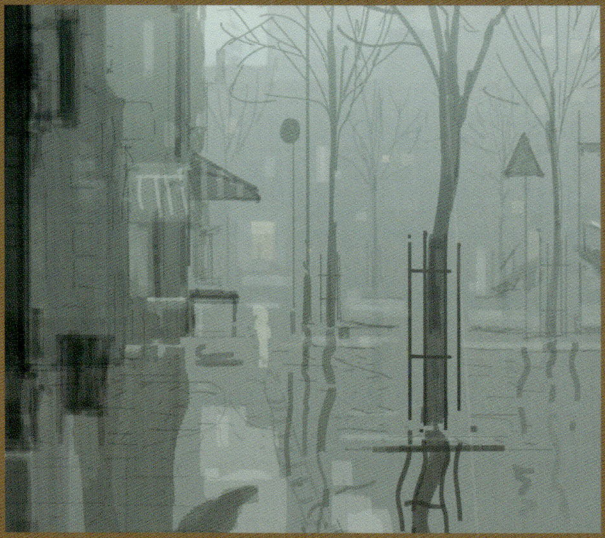

4. Staging the Anchor Point

Finally, when I feel the "architecture" of the scene works, or at least could mean something, I start staging the anchor point.

For me, an anchor point is where your eye is going to look first. It's the detail that will give weight to the whole scene. I usually use people – couples – for this because once your eye reads a classically represented human form, it tends to make sense of the abstract shapes around it. As if the eye recognizes a pattern and accepts it.

5. CREATING HIERARCHY

I make the staging brighter – the characters will have strong values to them, such as a red dress or black coat. The contrast of light and dark draws your eye and creates a hierarchy of values and shapes. Basically, it helps direct how you look at the image.

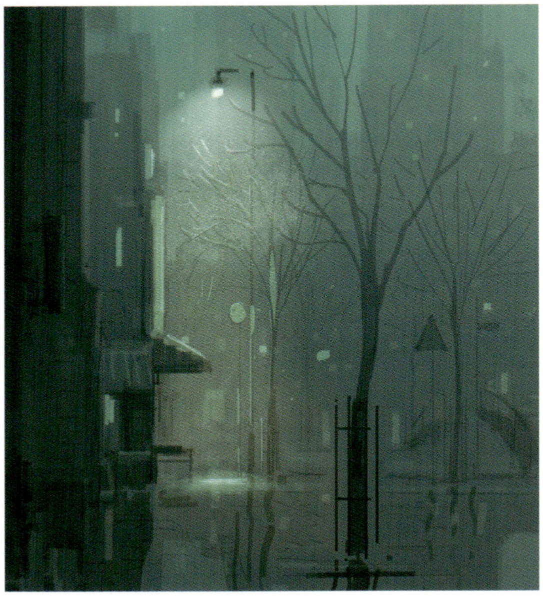

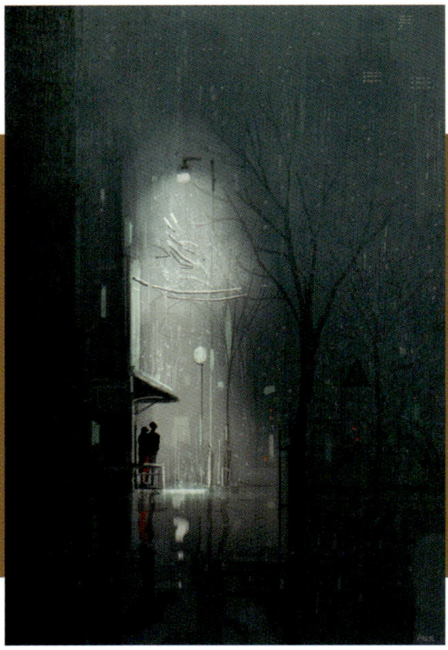

6. PLAYING WITH SHADOWS

Next, I draw the couple, putting them in the shade both because they are under the awning and away from the light, and also because I love playing with darkness and hiding things. I enjoy trying to find the limit of where a simple shape can read as a human, or a hand, or a flower, depending on its value and context. I know it's not the best storytelling process, but I like to try stuff when I do cityscapes.

7. DRAWING RAIN

I add rain to this scene for two reasons. The first is that it's actually fun to draw! There is something cathartic about doing a gazillion little lines on the canvas with no other directive other than "go fast and down."

Secondly, the rain helps create a vibration, graphically. All those little lines make your eye read the colors and values in the back in a more dynamic way, which I like. It's not better or worse if I don't do it, but instead just a choice that I seem to be making over and over. I guess if I have bad habits, this would be one of them.

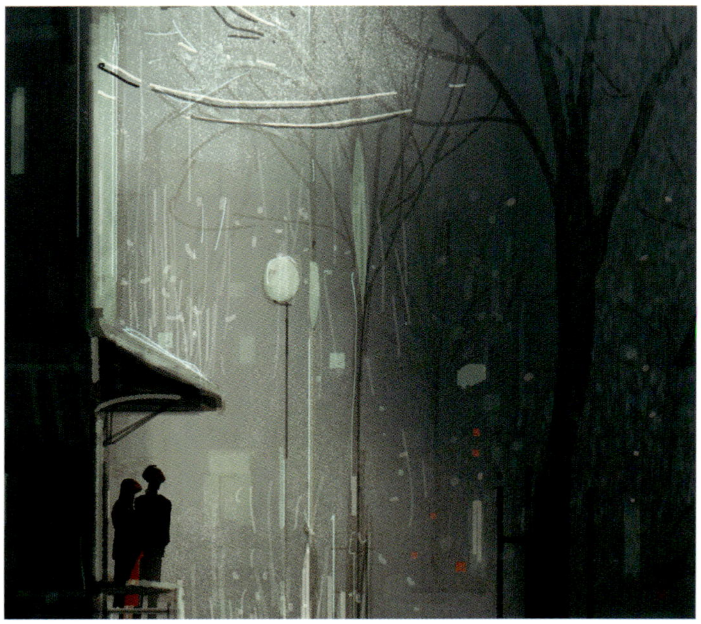

8. AUDITIONING COLORS + VALUES

At this point, I could be done with this. But I can't clearly explain the thought process, other than I am not "feeling" it. When I look at my final image, I like to feel a balance of colors and values. Something that makes me vibrate on the inside. A sort of dopamine hit. It's rare to get this from the first color approach. That's the funny thing about colors and me. I don't understand them. I work a lot with muted colors because I am afraid of using actual colors.

So in this last five percent I use Photoshop to explore the chromatic world. I simply put different values over the image. Either with a soft light layer, or I play with the color balance. I paint over, I subtract, I try anything and everything, and this is the part of the process that drains me the most because there is no real reason in my mind. No theory or knowledge I can leverage my explorations with. It's just a gut feeling.

I'll come up with a value and color combination that works – makes me smile – but I keep trying to find something that will give me a bigger hit. And I go on and on and on. It's very common for me to do ten, twelve, twenty versions of the same image because I am not satisfied with the color and value combination.

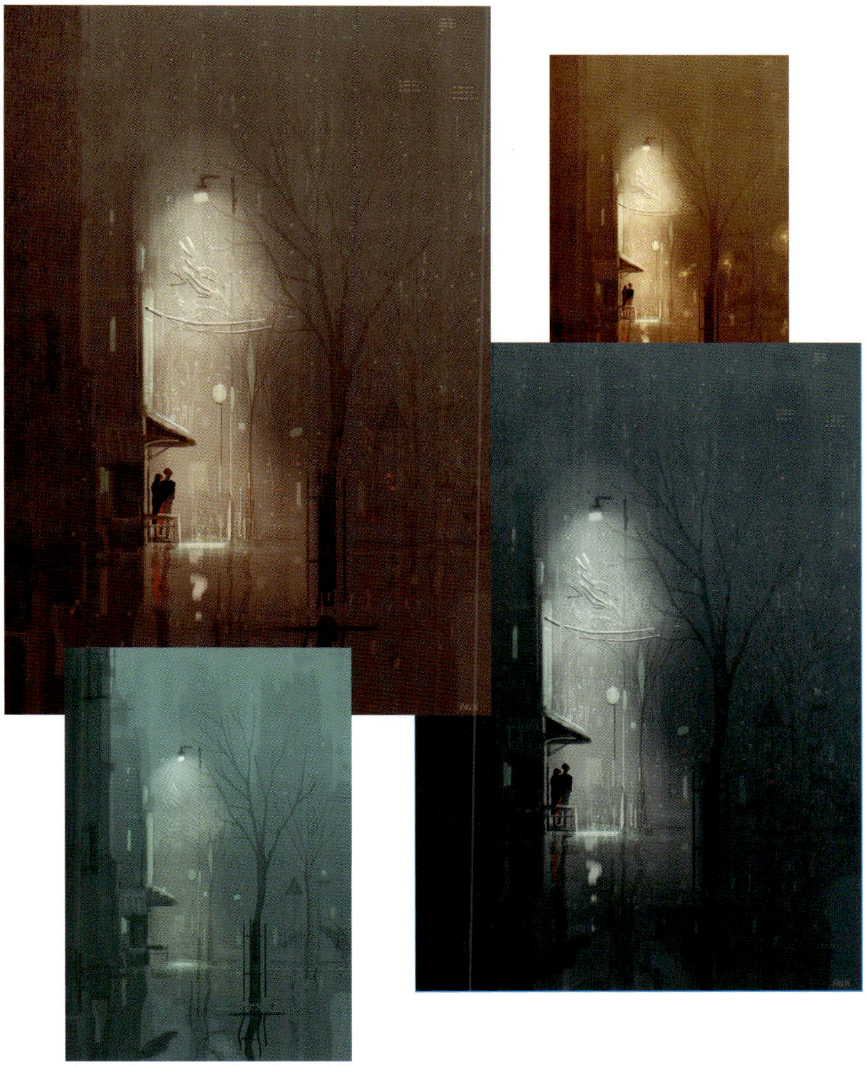

"WHEN I LOOK AT MY **FINAL IMAGE**, I LIKE TO FEEL A **BALANCE** OF COLORS + VALUES. SOMETHING THAT MAKES ME **VIBRATE** ON THE INSIDE. A SORT OF **DOPAMINE HIT**"

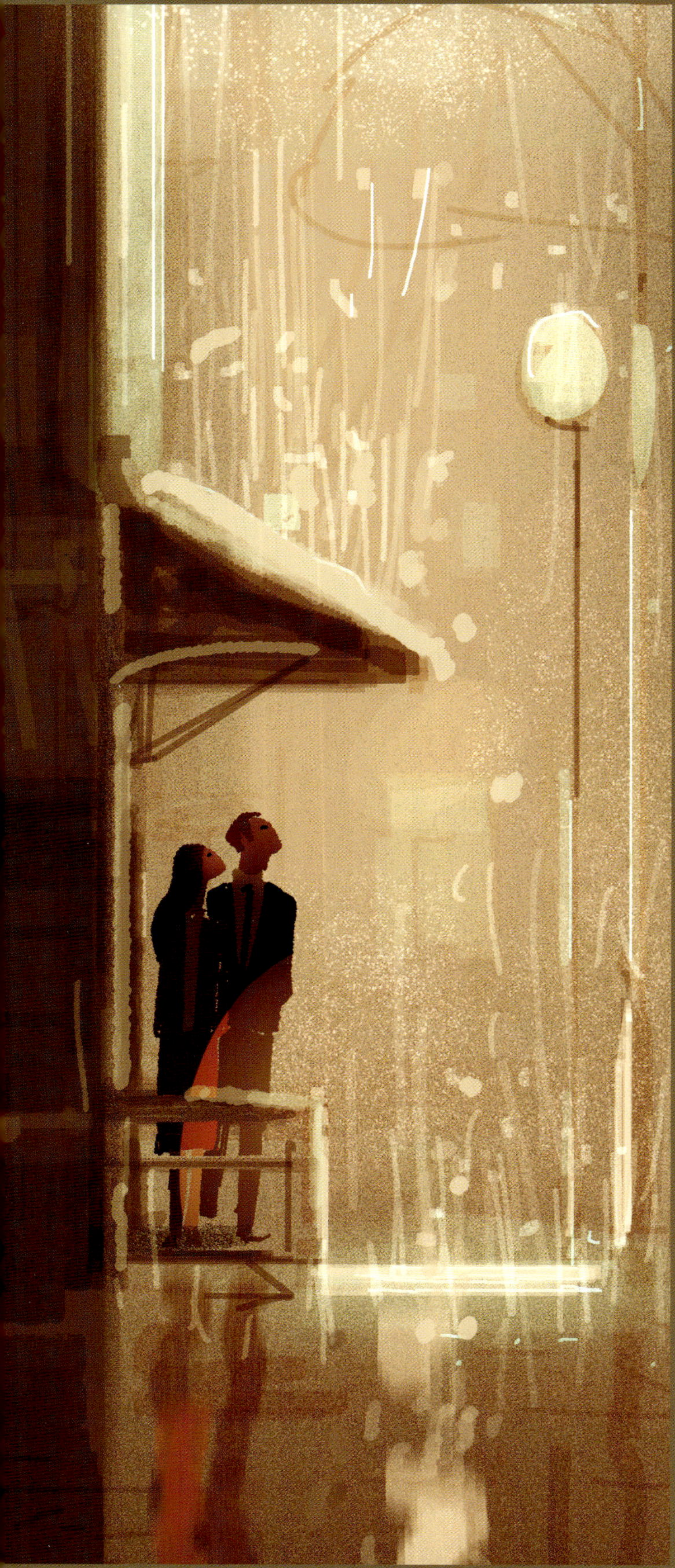

9. THE FINAL IMAGE

At some point, I lose energy and distance, so I need to make a choice. That's usually when I try the complete opposite of what I've been exploring. However, I have to go through the whole process of exploring first. I wish I could simply jump to the end result. It would be so much faster and easier for me to appreciate my own art. Most of the time, I find the final image to be about forty-percent control and sixty-percent accident. It's an interesting feeling.

The final result is a slightly different color combination than I would usually go for. Instead of making it cool, I chose this warm, orange approach. Like liquid gold. To be honest, the idea of gold being liquid scares me since *Game of Thrones*, but I like the expression.

ALTERNATIVE PROCESSES

The process used for the cityscape is very different to the way I create other types of images. The final result for nature images is faster and cleaner to get to because I have a strong idea from the start. In fact, I started doing those little *plein air* images in reaction to these types of cityscapes. I wanted to push myself to understand color so I wouldn't flounder in the last five percent. It hasn't helped for the cityscapes, but it has helped me develop another aspect of art that I am also falling in love with.

The comic-strip process is very direct. It's ninety-percent drawing with a tiny bit of color and I *love* that process. I have so many different types of love in art – it's pretty funny.

Romantic scenes are different again. I would consider them to be a mix between the city/abstract/adventure process, and the comic strips. I know more-or-less where I want to go, but am not entirely sure about the final lighting. However, the characters carry the story so I have room to play with an imperfect balance of light.

I like a space where you can see some of the surroundings, and all the other features disappear into a fog. It feels like a cocoon. A lot of my work evokes this sensation.

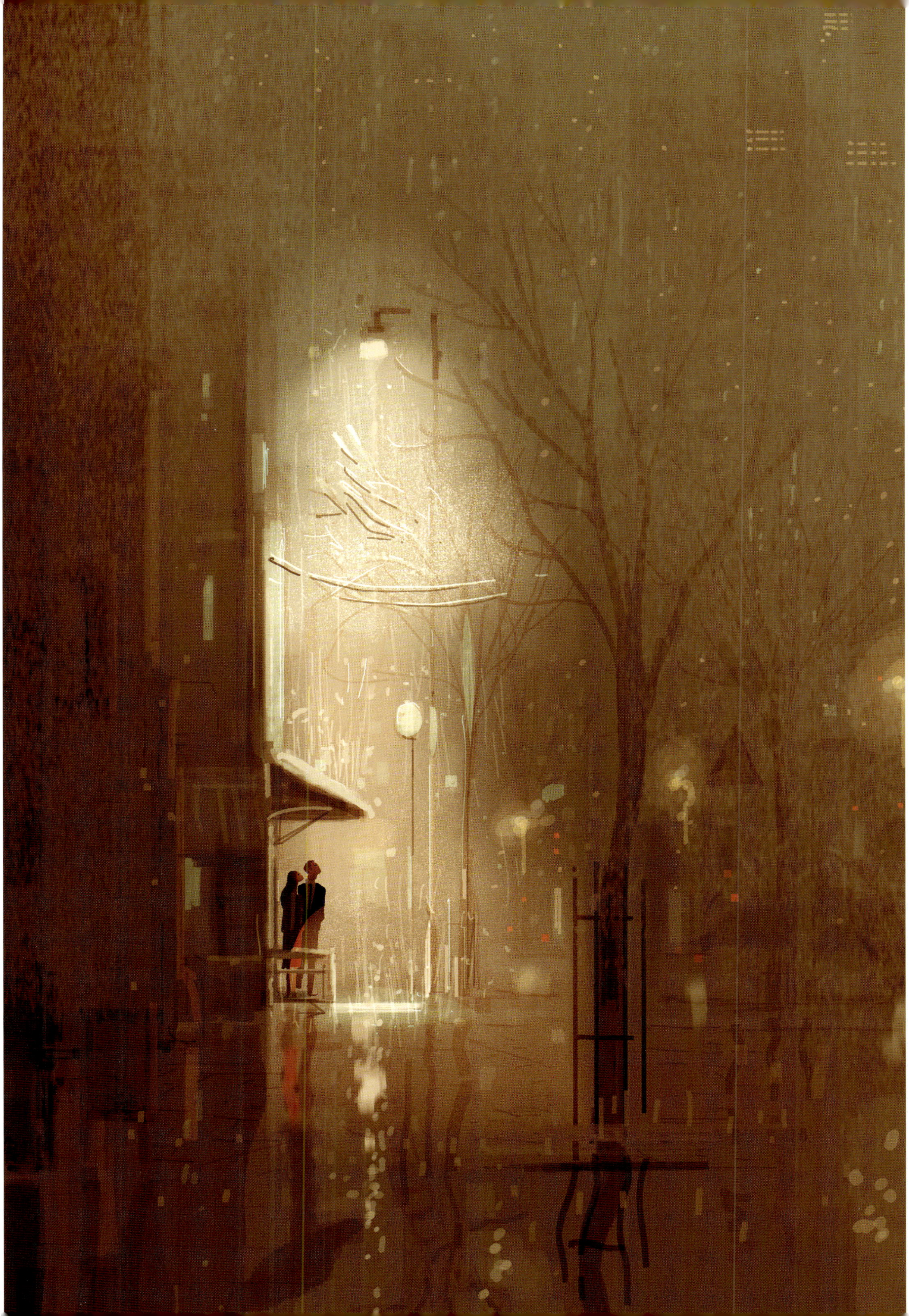

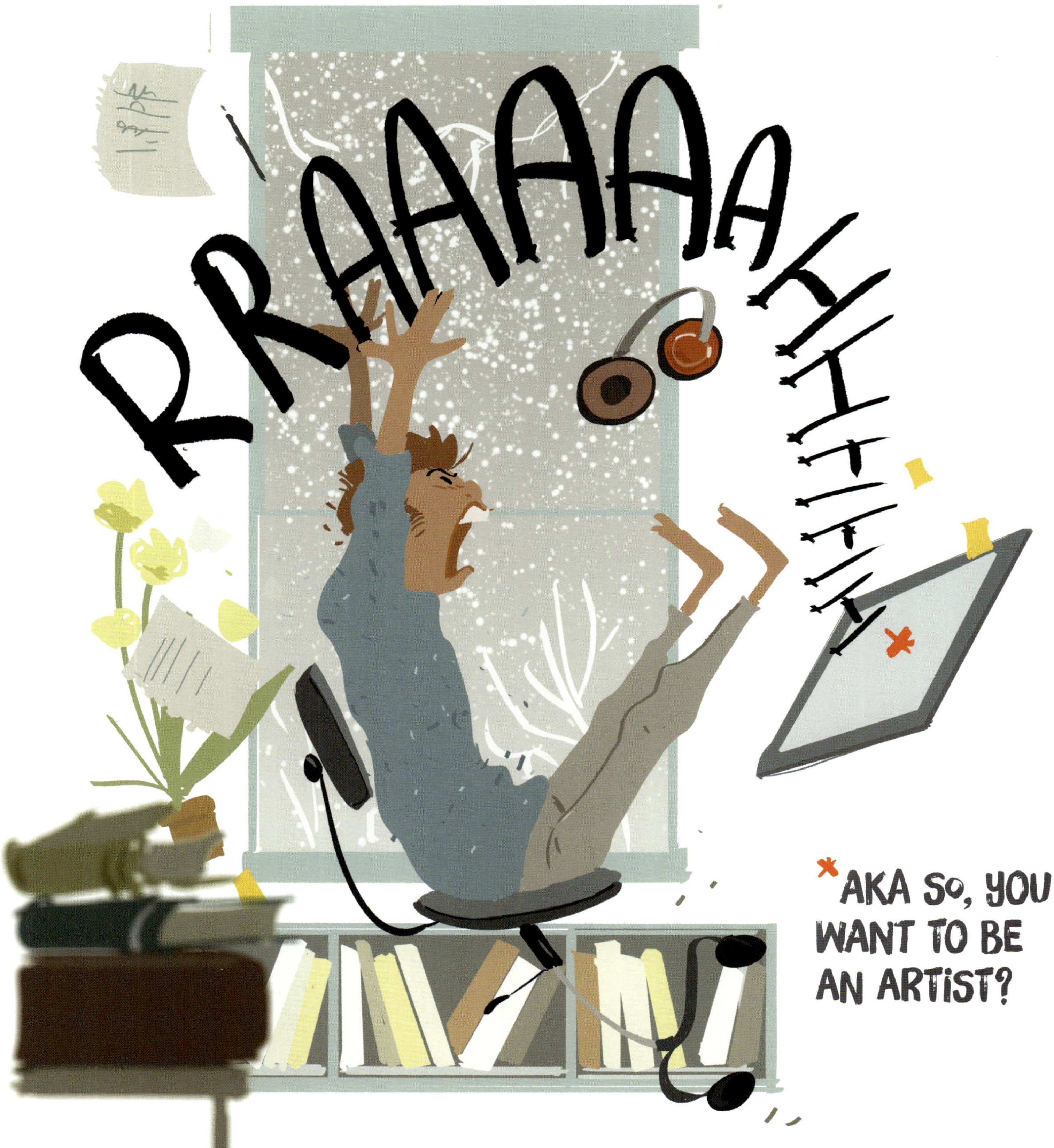
¡RRAAAAAAHHHHH
*AKA SO, YOU WANT TO BE AN ARTIST?

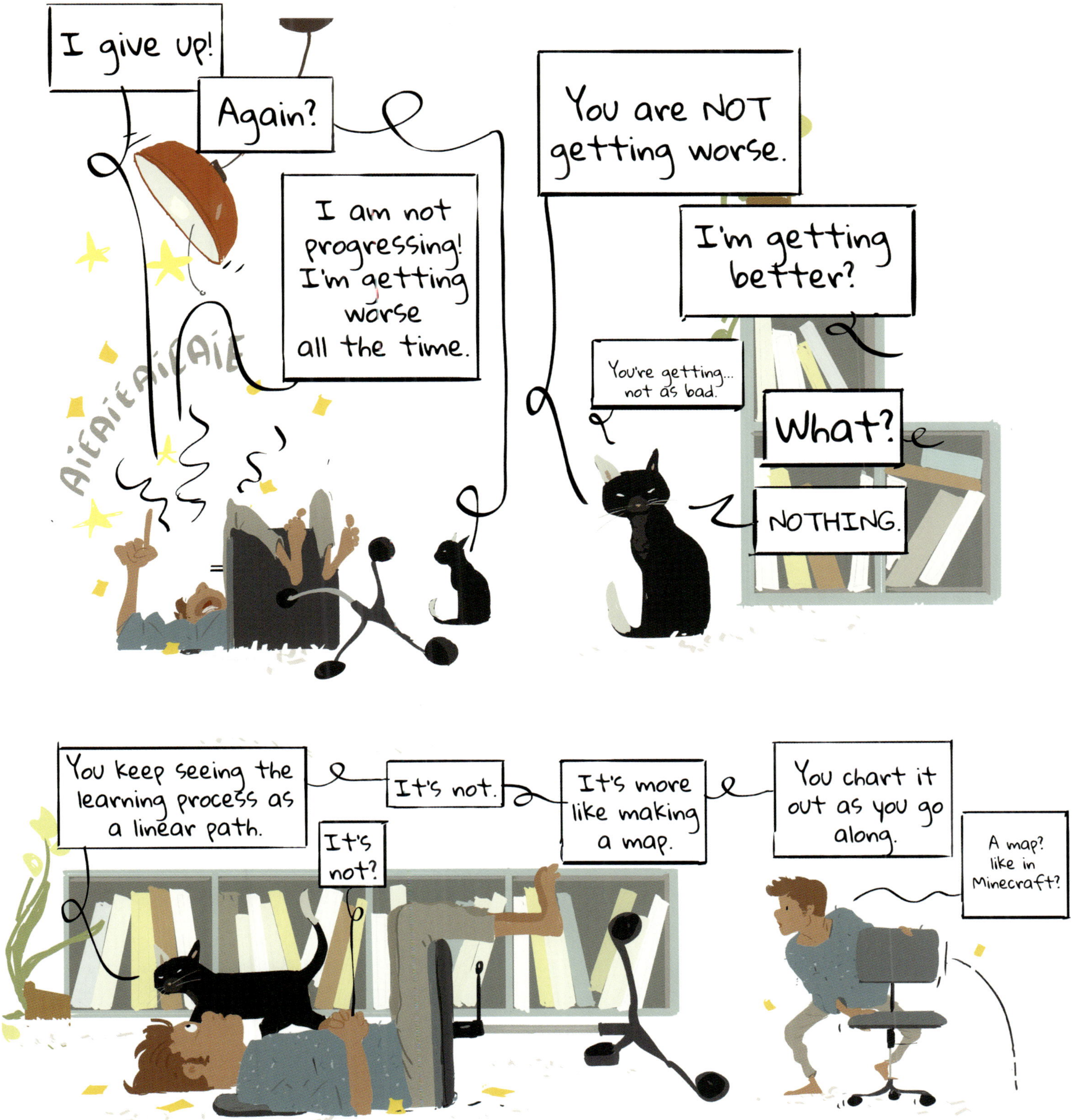

I give up!
Again?
I am not progressing! I'm getting worse all the time.
AIEAIEAIEAIEAIE
You are NOT getting worse.
I'm getting better?
You're getting... not as bad.
What?
NOTHING.
You keep seeing the learning process as a linear path.
It's not.
It's not?
It's more like making a map.
You chart it out as you go along.
A map? like in Minecraft?

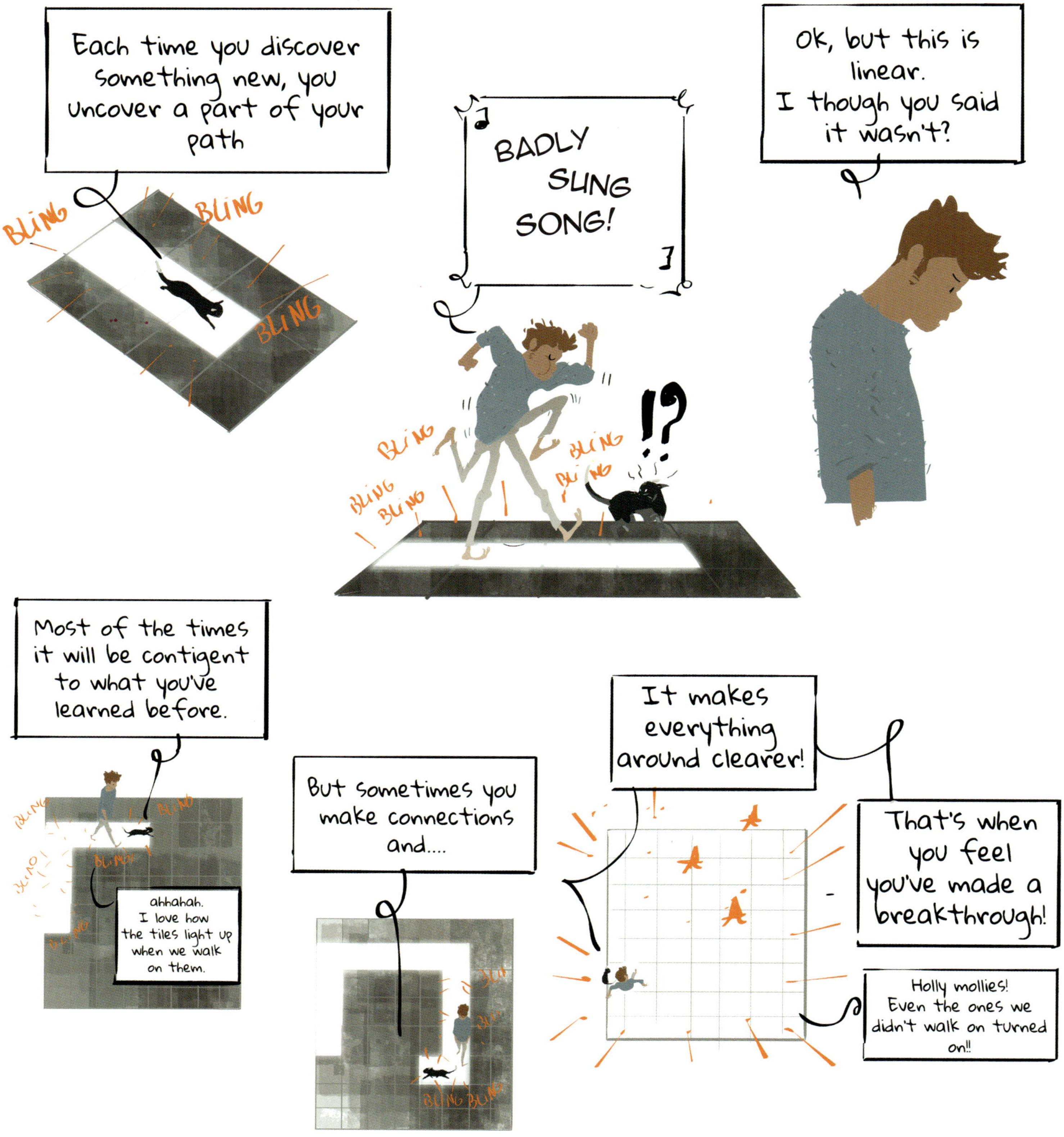
Each time you discover something new, you uncover a part of your path
BLING
BLING
BLING
BADLY SUNG SONG!
BLING
BLING
BLING
BLING
BLING
!?
Ok, but this is linear.
I though you said it wasn't?
Most of the times it will be contigent to what you've learned before.
ahhahah.
I love how the tiles light up when we walk on them.
But sometimes you make connections and....
It makes everything around clearer!
That's when you feel you've made a breakthrough!
Holly mollies!
Even the ones we didn't walk on turned on!!

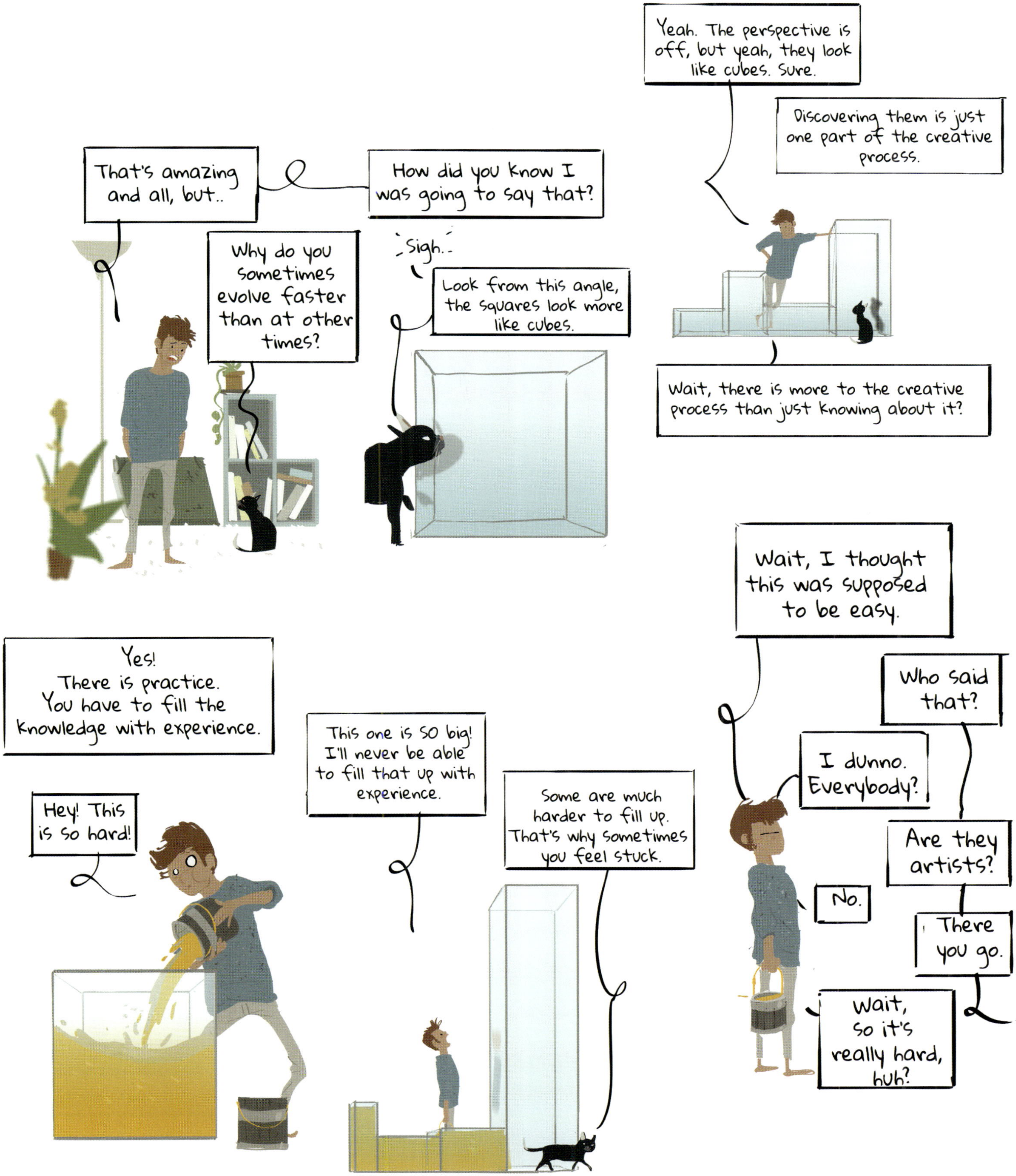

That's amazing and all, but..
How did you know I was going to say that?
Why do you sometimes evolve faster than at other times?
Sigh..
Look from this angle, the squares look more like cubes.
Yeah. The perspective is off, but yeah, they look like cubes. Sure.
Discovering them is just one part of the creative process.
Wait, there is more to the creative process than just knowing about it?
Yes! There is practice. You have to fill the knowledge with experience.
Hey! This is so hard!
This one is so big! I'll never be able to fill that up with experience.
Some are much harder to fill up. That's why sometimes you feel stuck.
Wait, I thought this was supposed to be easy.
Who said that?
I dunno. Everybody?
Are they artists?
No.
There you go.
Wait, so it's really hard, huh?

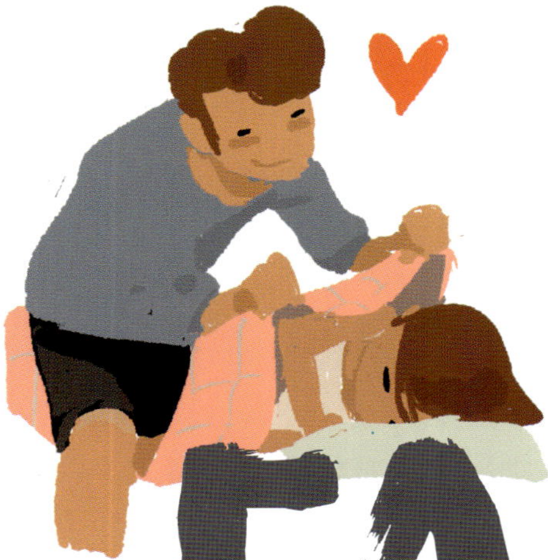

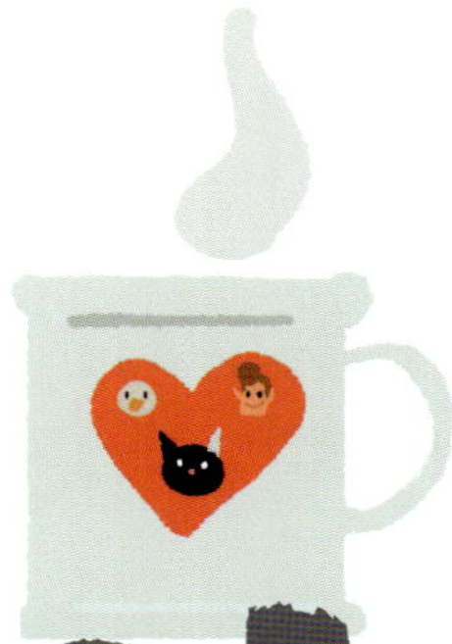

GALLERY: FAMILY, FUN, LOVE!

THERE ARE THE FUN ONES.
THE LIGHT ONES, THE LOVE ONES.

THESE ARE MOST OFTEN FOCUSSED AROUND
MANLY MAN'S FAMILY
AND LOVED ONES
(INCLUDING LITTLE MILO,
WHO WANDERED IN BY MISTAKE).

THEY BRING HIM LIGHT AND LIGHTNESS.
SOMETHING MANLY MAN
CAN USE A LOT MORE OF.

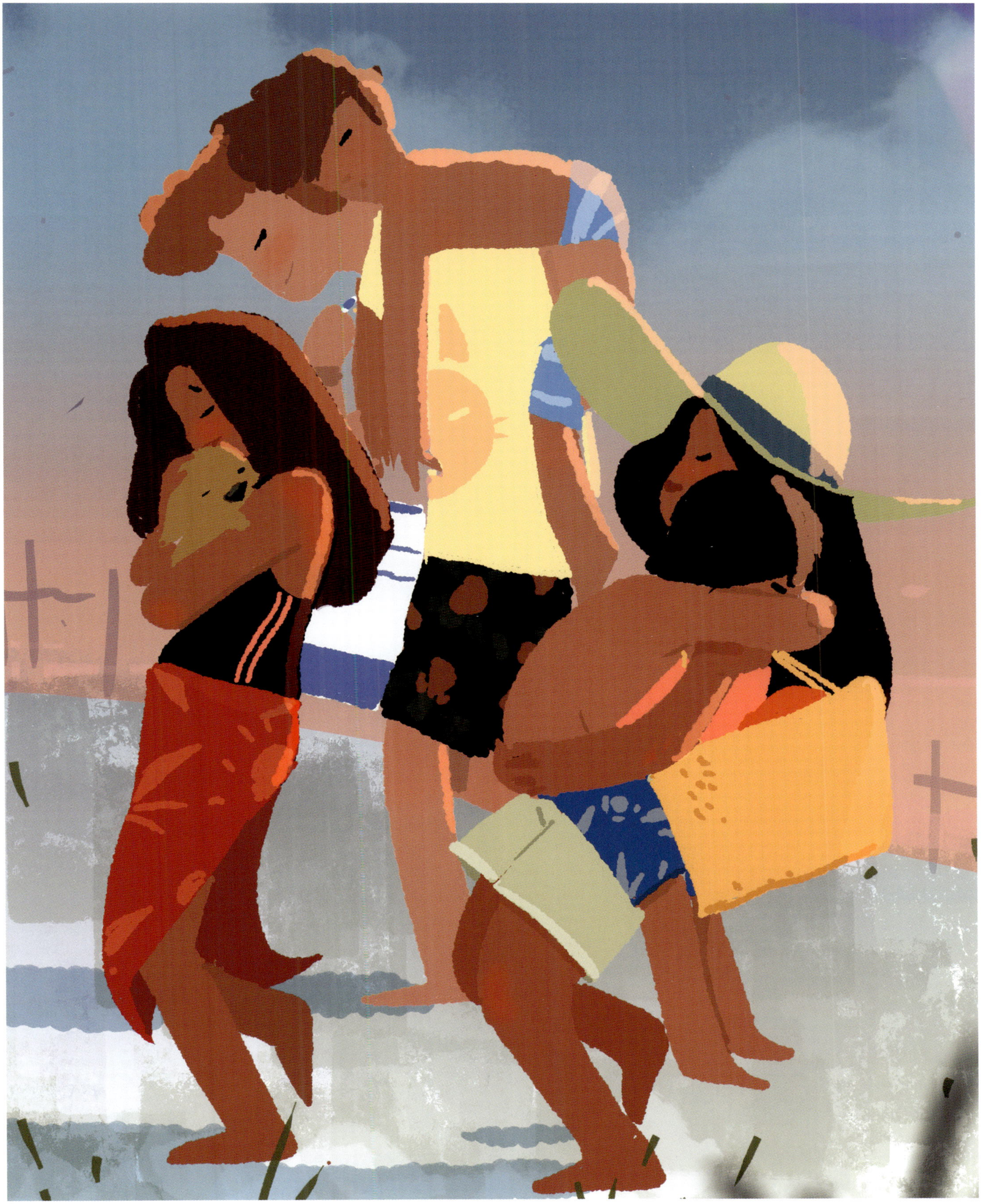

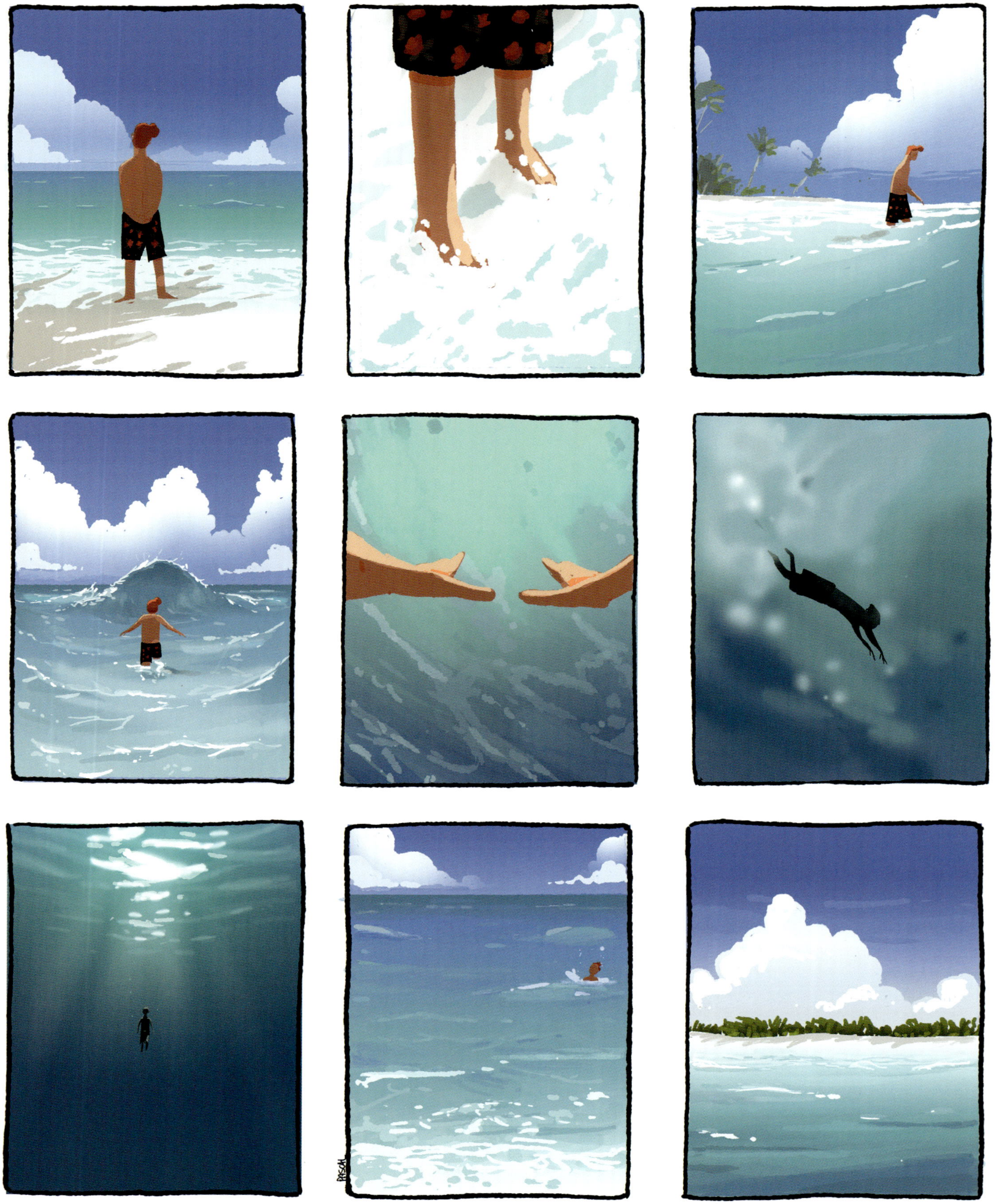

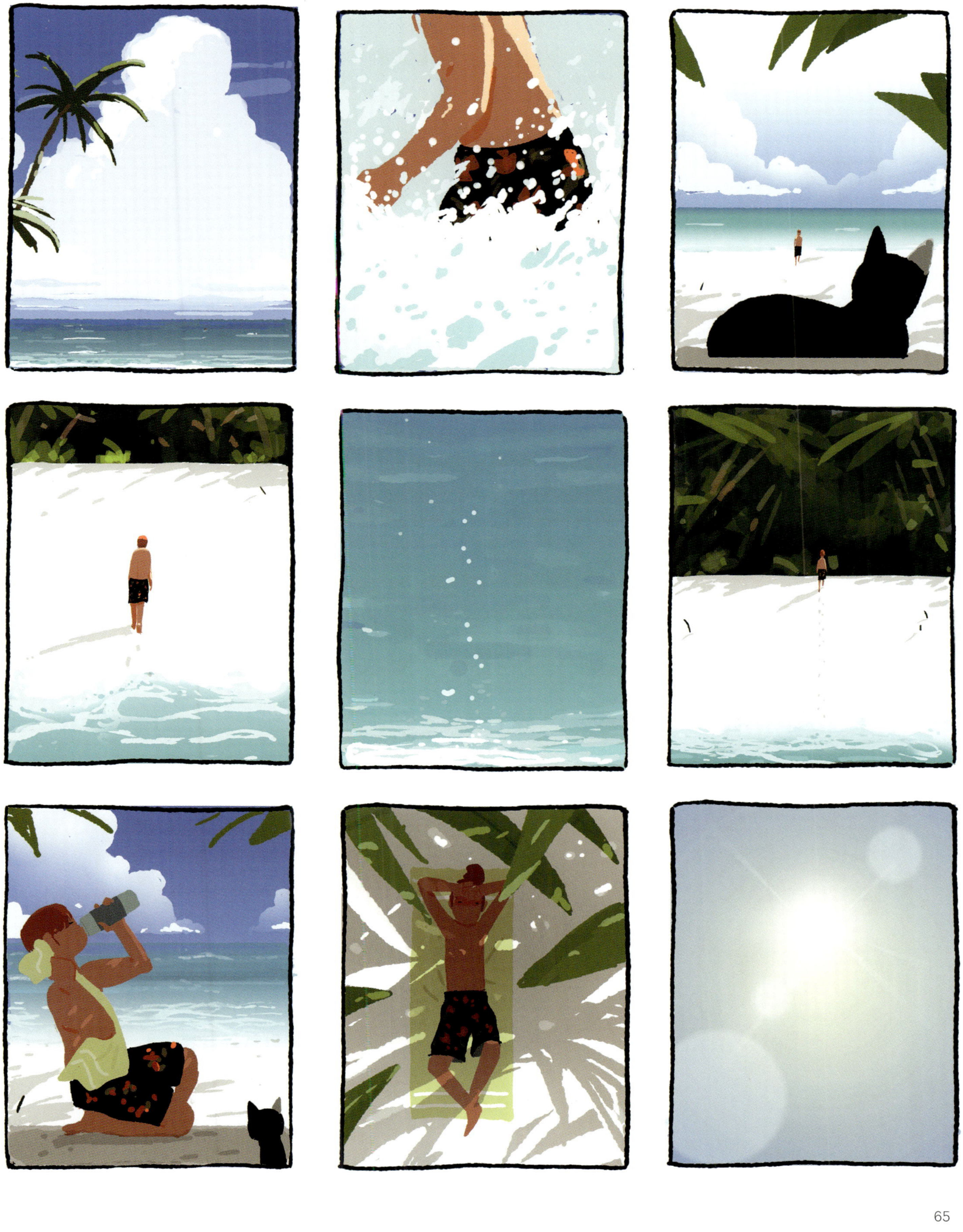

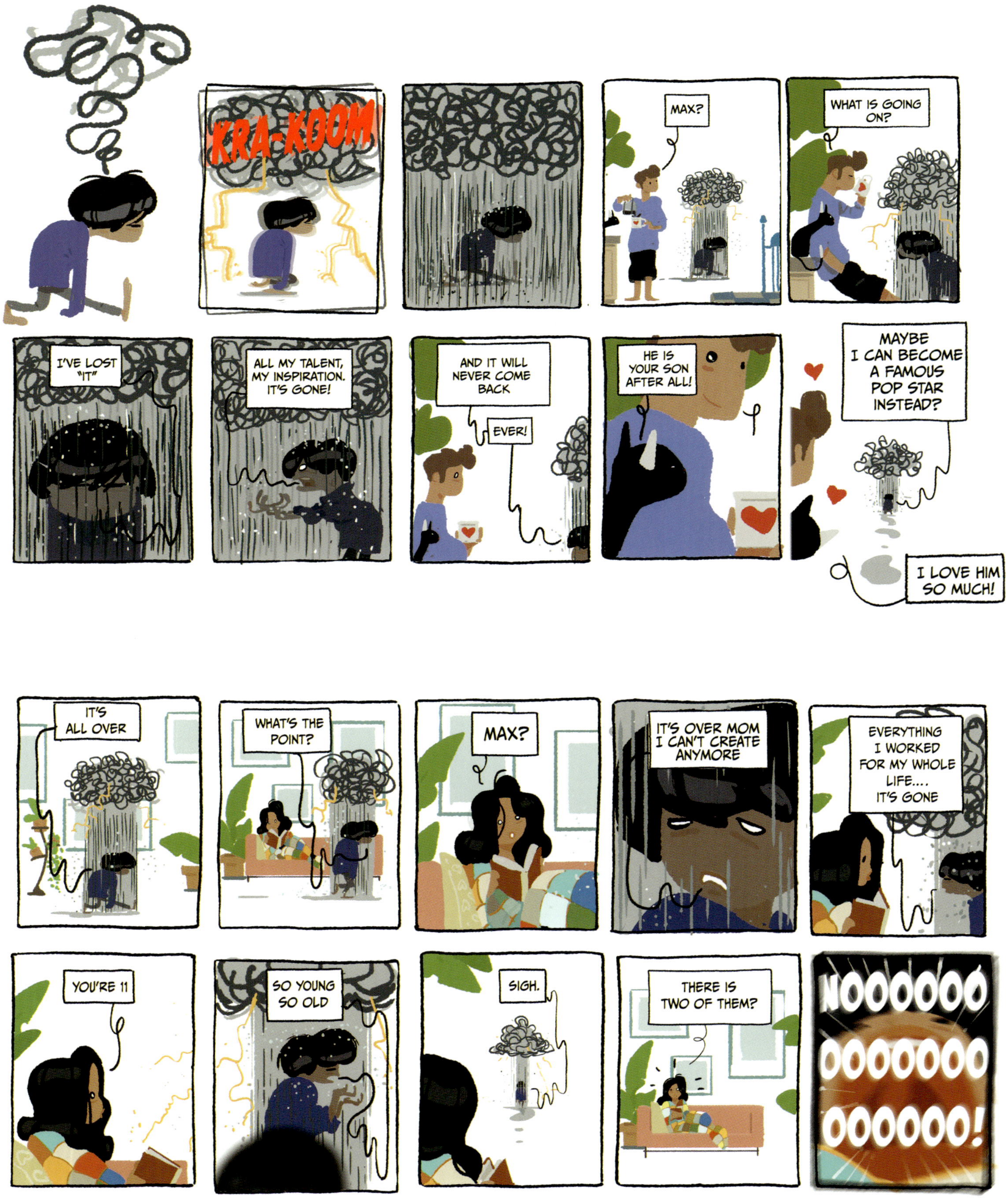
KRA-KOOM
MAX?
WHAT IS GOING ON?
I'VE LOST "IT"
ALL MY TALENT, MY INSPIRATION. IT'S GONE!
AND IT WILL NEVER COME BACK
EVER!
HE IS YOUR SON AFTER ALL!
MAYBE I CAN BECOME A FAMOUS POP STAR INSTEAD?
I LOVE HIM SO MUCH!
IT'S ALL OVER
WHAT'S THE POINT?
MAX?
IT'S OVER MOM I CAN'T CREATE ANYMORE
EVERYTHING I WORKED FOR MY WHOLE LIFE.... IT'S GONE
YOU'RE 11
SO YOUNG SO OLD
SIGH.
THERE IS TWO OF THEM?
NOOOOOOOOOOOOOOOOOOOO!

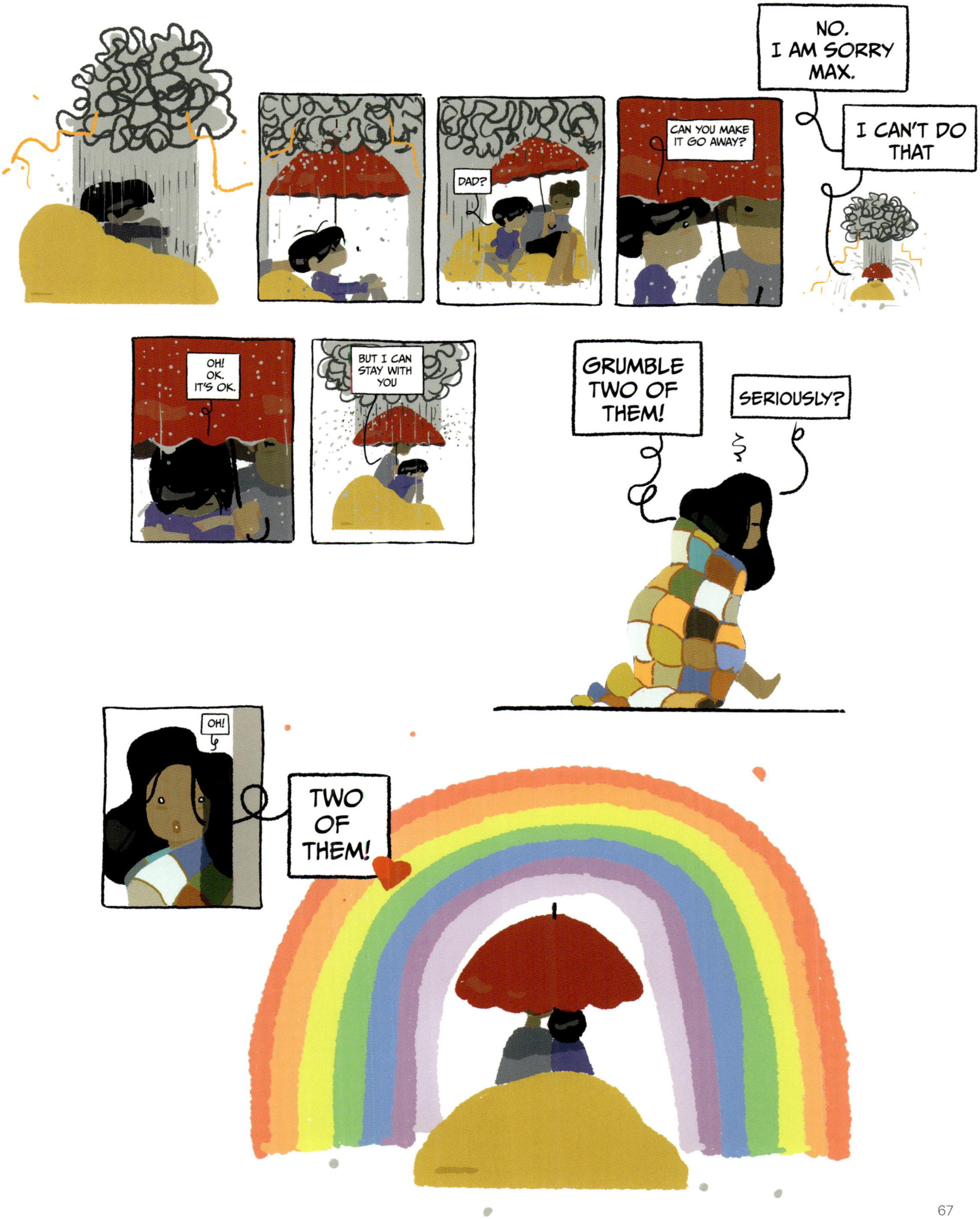
DAD?
CAN YOU MAKE IT GO AWAY?
NO. I AM SORRY MAX.
I CAN'T DO THAT
OH! OK. IT'S OK.
BUT I CAN STAY WITH YOU
GRUMBLE TWO OF THEM!
SERIOUSLY?
OH!
TWO OF THEM!

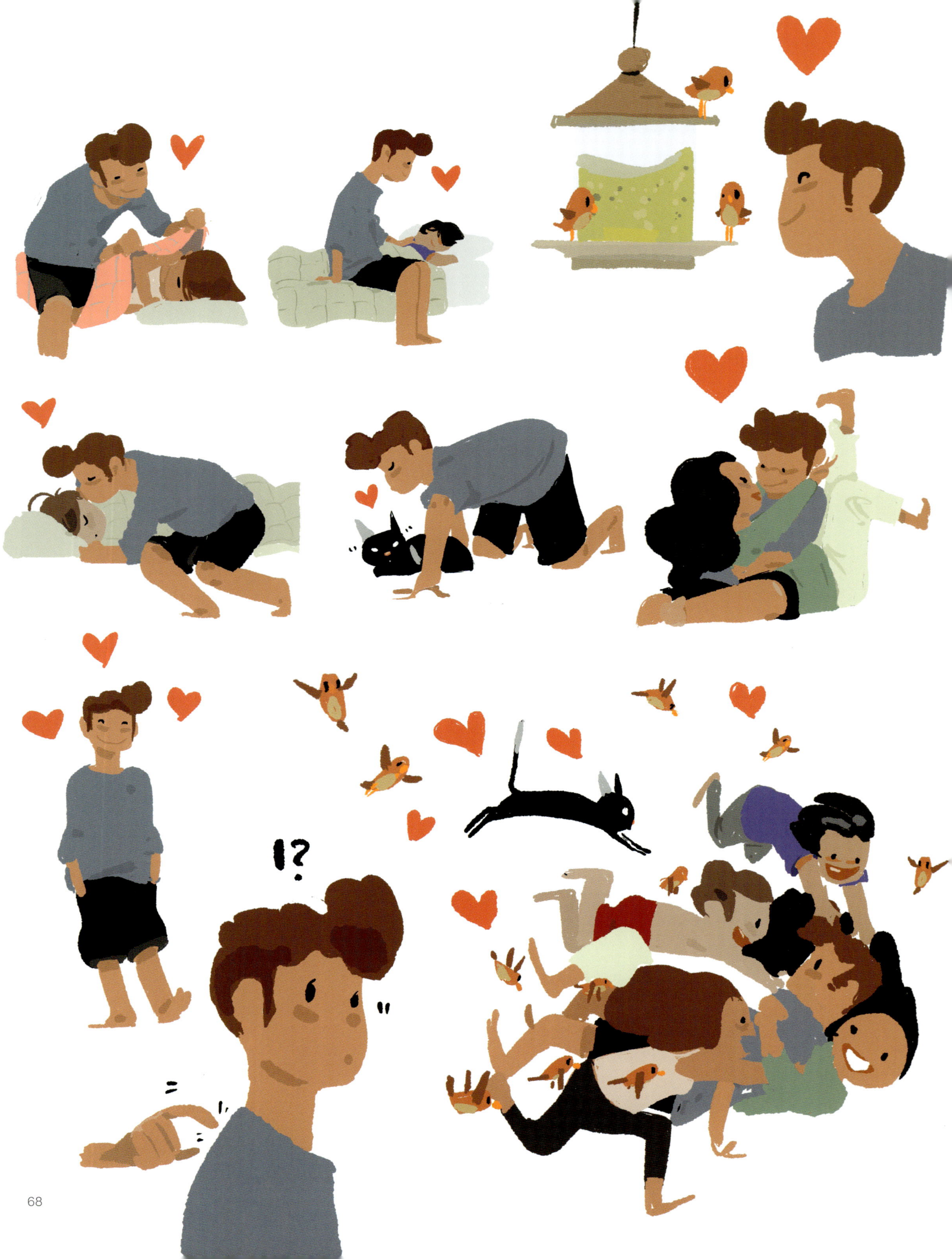

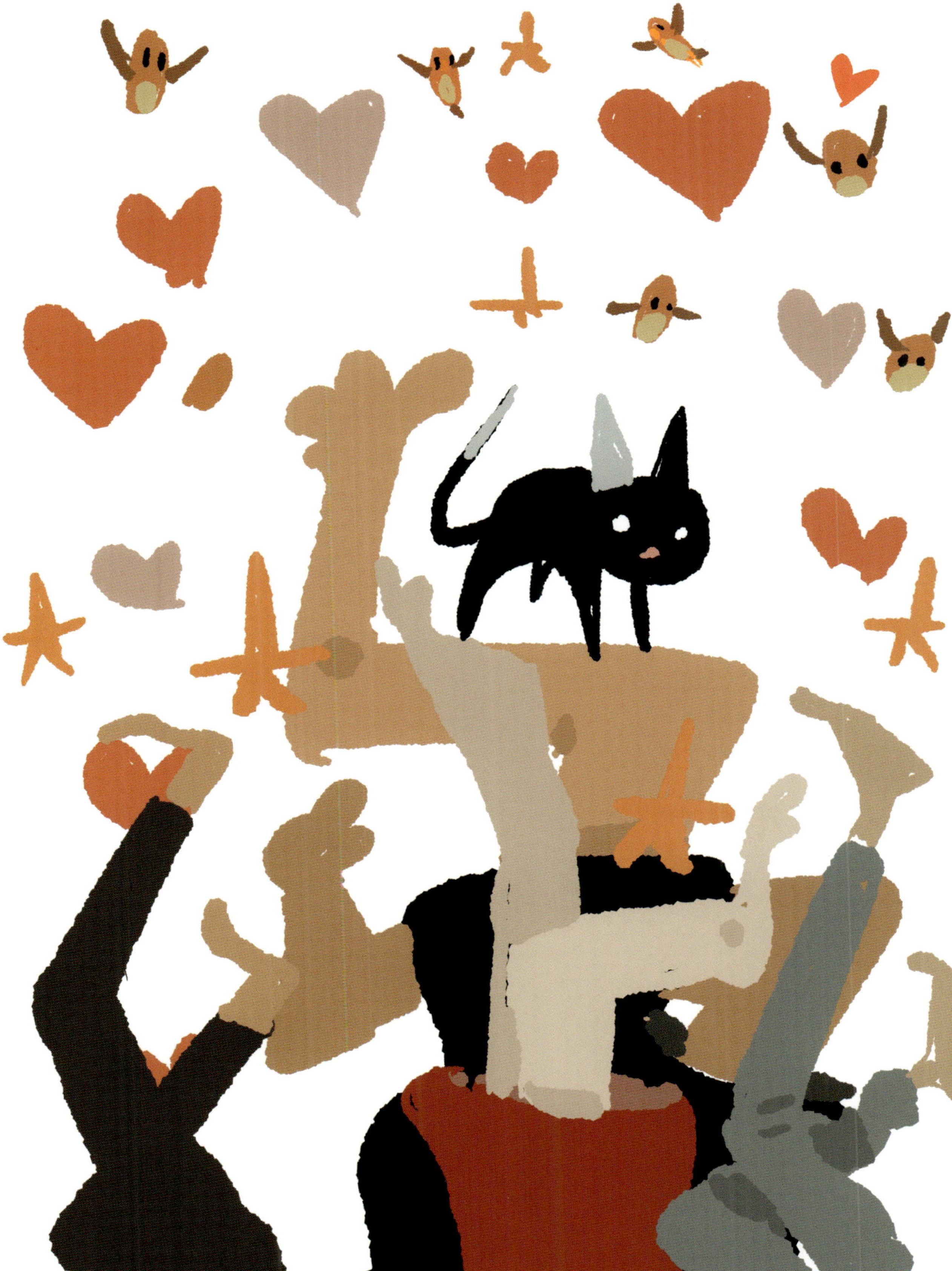

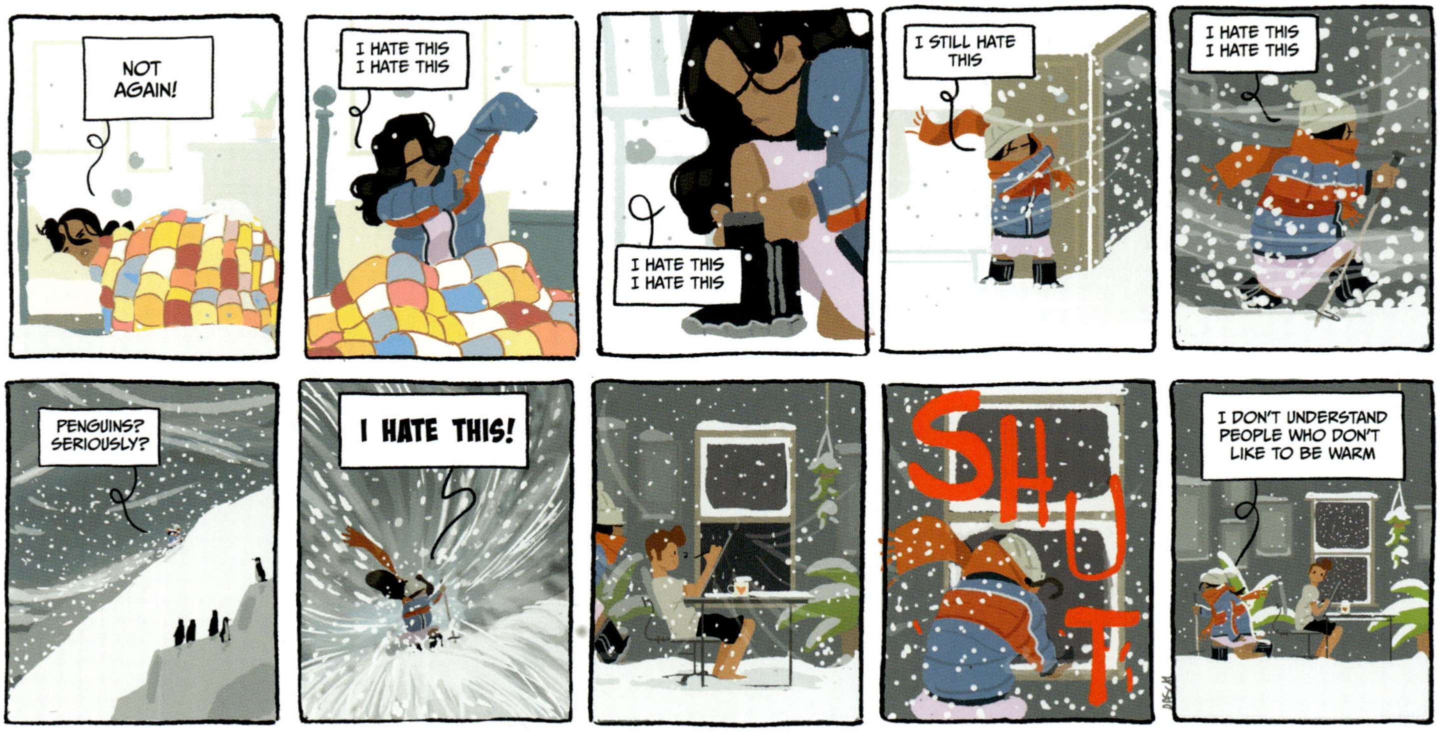
NOT AGAIN!
I HATE THIS I HATE THIS
I HATE THIS I HATE THIS
I STILL HATE THIS
I HATE THIS I HATE THIS
PENGUINS? SERIOUSLY?
I HATE THIS!
SHUT!
I DON'T UNDERSTAND PEOPLE WHO DON'T LIKE TO BE WARM

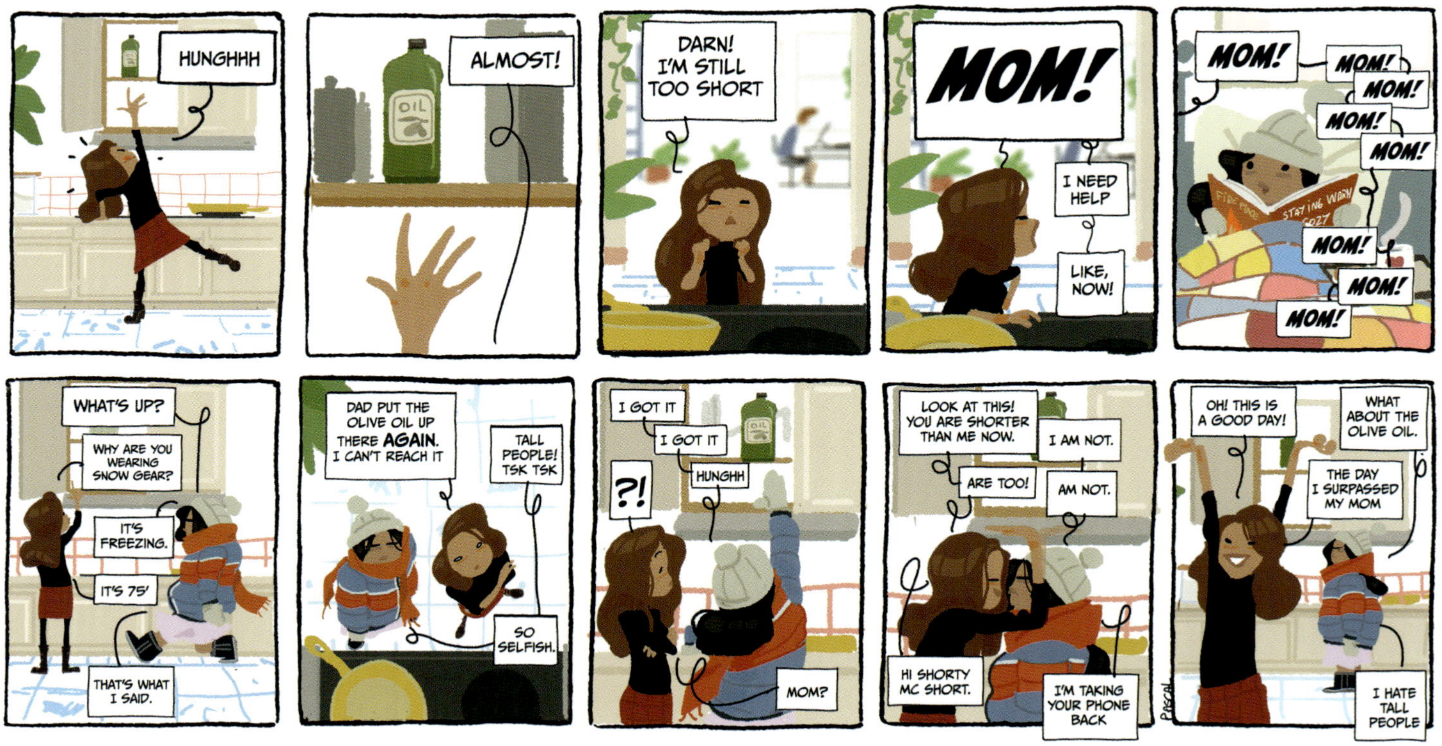
HUNGHHH
ALMOST!
DARN! I'M STILL TOO SHORT
MOM!
I NEED HELP
LIKE, NOW!
MOM!
MOM!
MOM!
MOM!
MOM!
MOM!
MOM!
MOM!
WHAT'S UP?
WHY ARE YOU WEARING SNOW GEAR?
IT'S FREEZING.
IT'S 75°
THAT'S WHAT I SAID.
DAD PUT THE OLIVE OIL UP THERE AGAIN. I CAN'T REACH IT
TALL PEOPLE! TSK TSK
SO SELFISH.
I GOT IT
I GOT IT
HUNGHH
?!
MOM?
LOOK AT THIS! YOU ARE SHORTER THAN ME NOW.
I AM NOT.
ARE TOO!
AM NOT.
HI SHORTY MC SHORT.
I'M TAKING YOUR PHONE BACK
OH! THIS IS A GOOD DAY!
WHAT ABOUT THE OLIVE OIL.
THE DAY I SURPASSED MY MOM
I HATE TALL PEOPLE

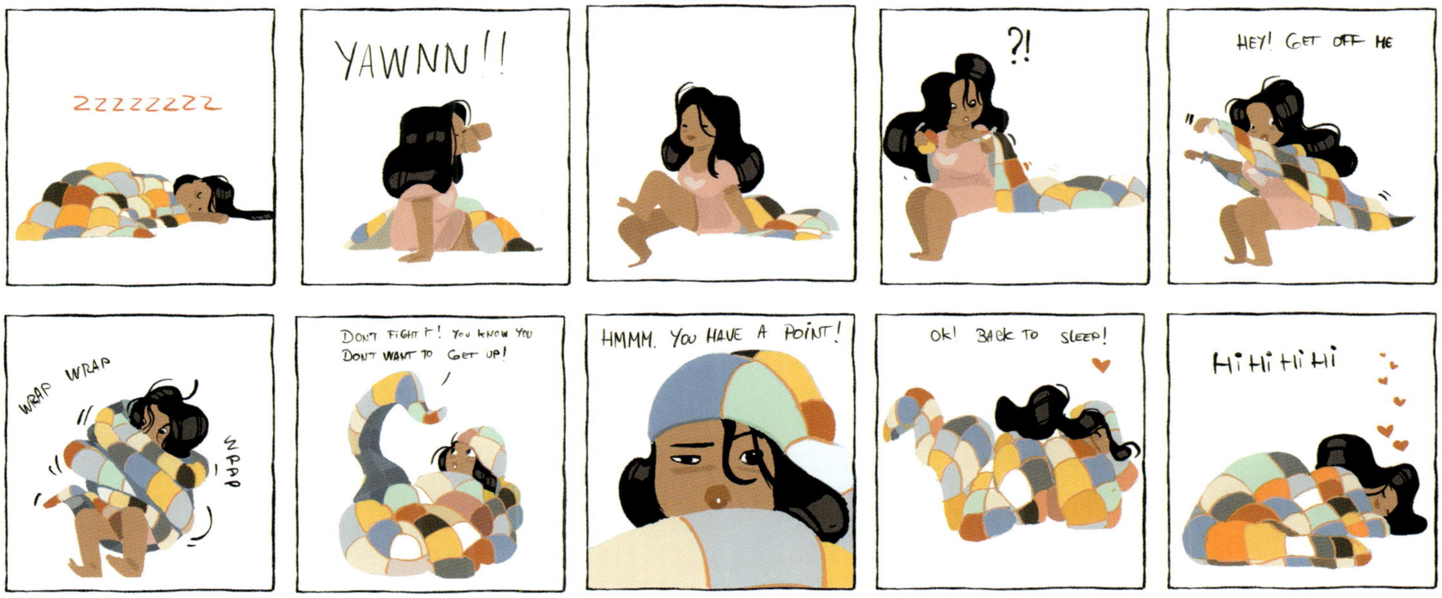
ZZZZZZZZ
YAWNN!!
?!
HEY! GET OFF ME
WRAP WRAP
WRAP
DONT FIGHT IT! YOU KNOW YOU DONT WANT TO GET UP!
HMMM. YOU HAVE A POINT!
OK! BACK TO SLEEP!
HI HI HI HI

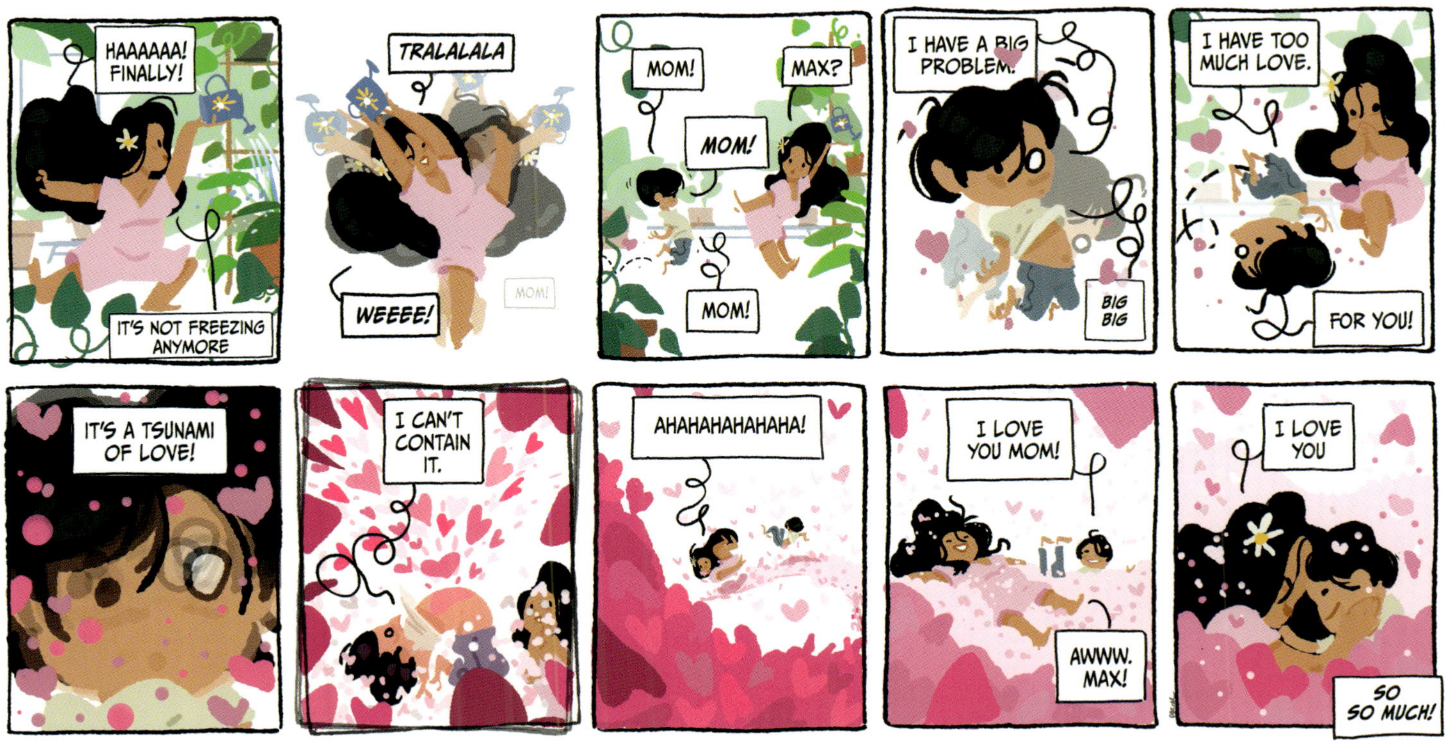
HAAAAAA! FINALLY!
IT'S NOT FREEZING ANYMORE
TRALALALA
WEEEE!
MOM!
MOM!
MAX?
MOM!
MOM!
I HAVE A BIG PROBLEM.
BIG BIG
I HAVE TOO MUCH LOVE.
FOR YOU!
IT'S A TSUNAMI OF LOVE!
I CAN'T CONTAIN IT.
AHAHAHAHAHAHA!
I LOVE YOU MOM!
AWWW. MAX!
I LOVE YOU
SO SO MUCH!

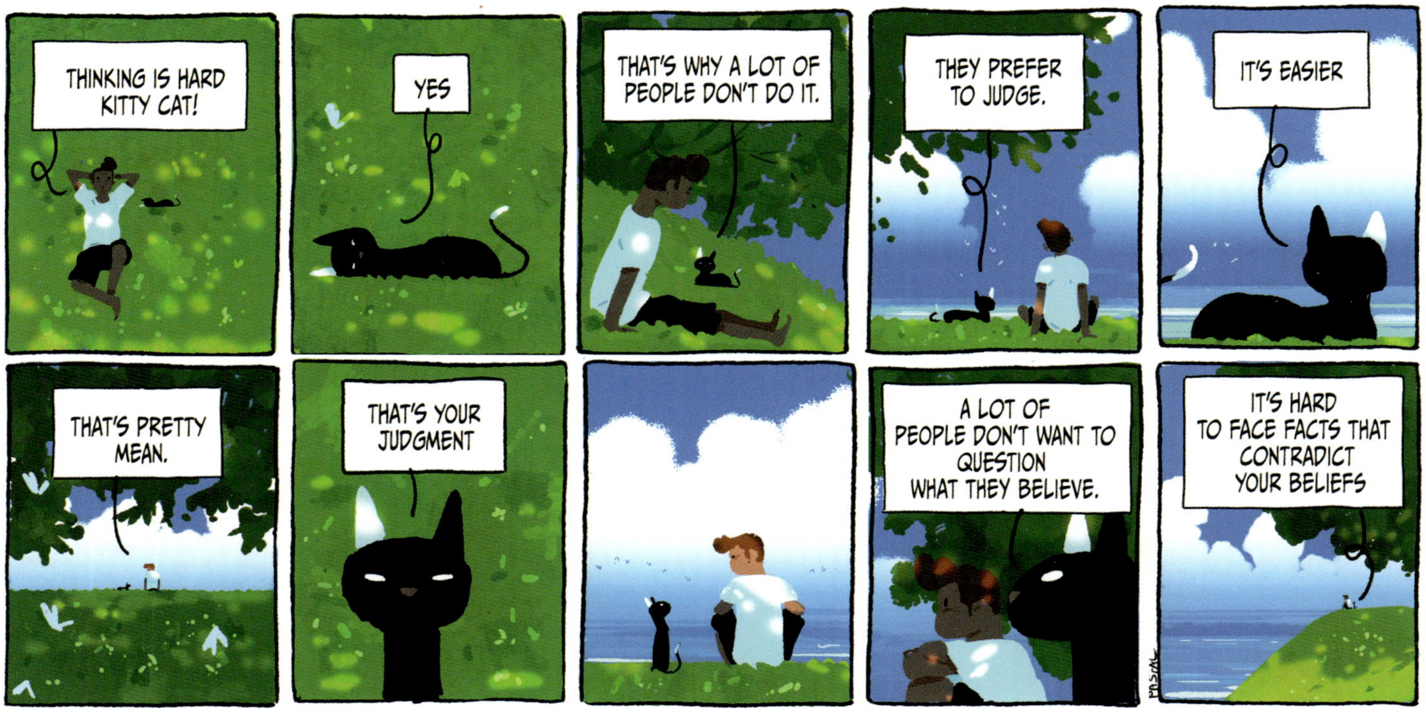
THINKING IS HARD KITTY CAT!
YES
THAT'S WHY A LOT OF PEOPLE DON'T DO IT.
THEY PREFER TO JUDGE.
IT'S EASIER
THAT'S PRETTY MEAN.
THAT'S YOUR JUDGMENT
A LOT OF PEOPLE DON'T WANT TO QUESTION WHAT THEY BELIEVE.
IT'S HARD TO FACE FACTS THAT CONTRADICT YOUR BELIEFS

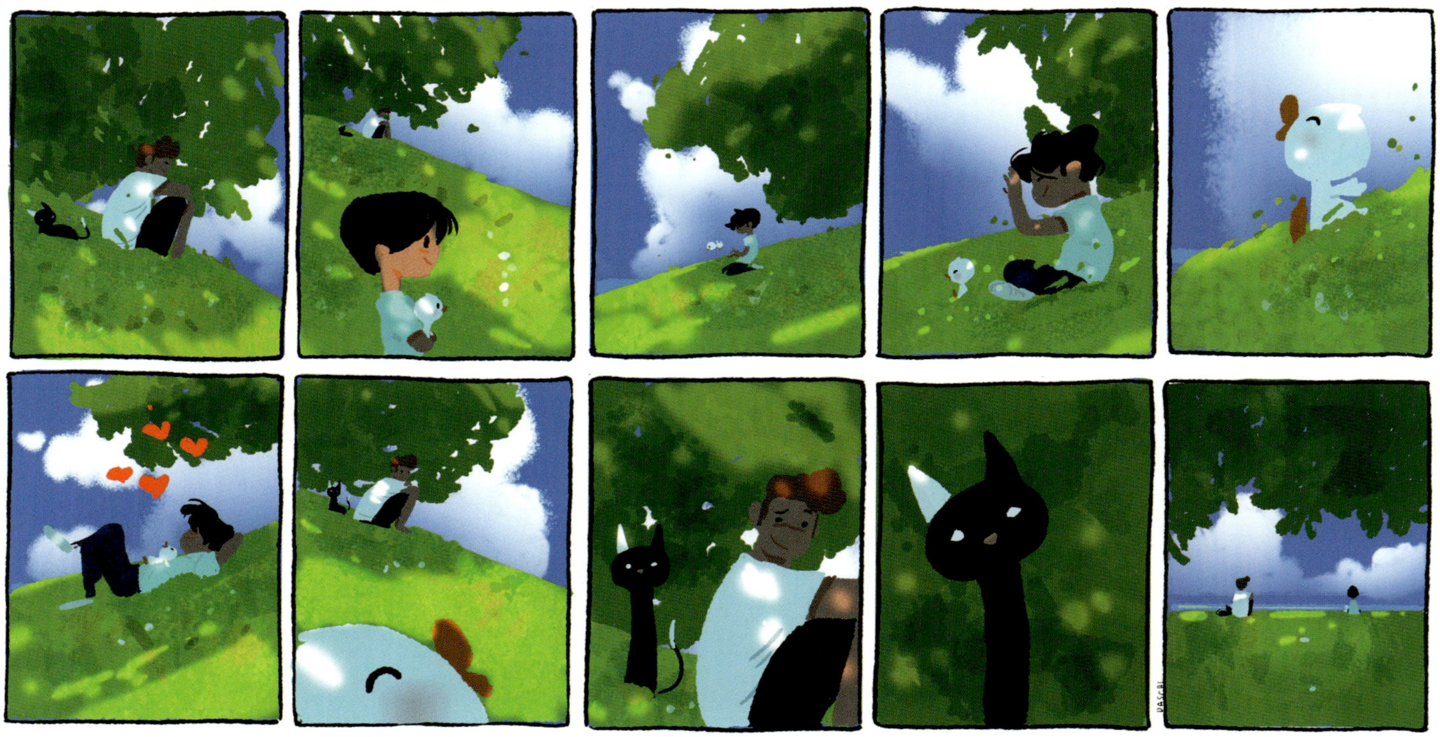

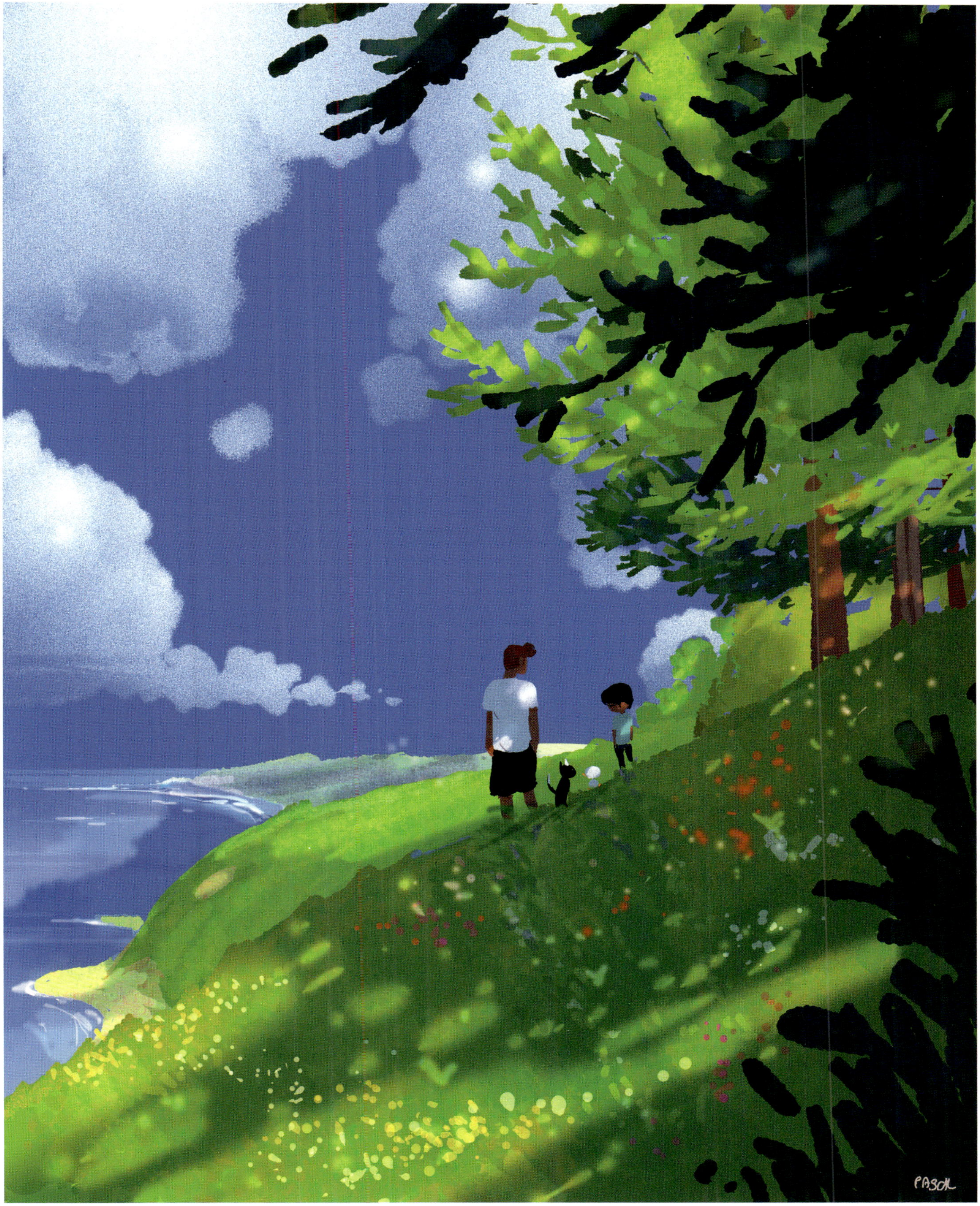

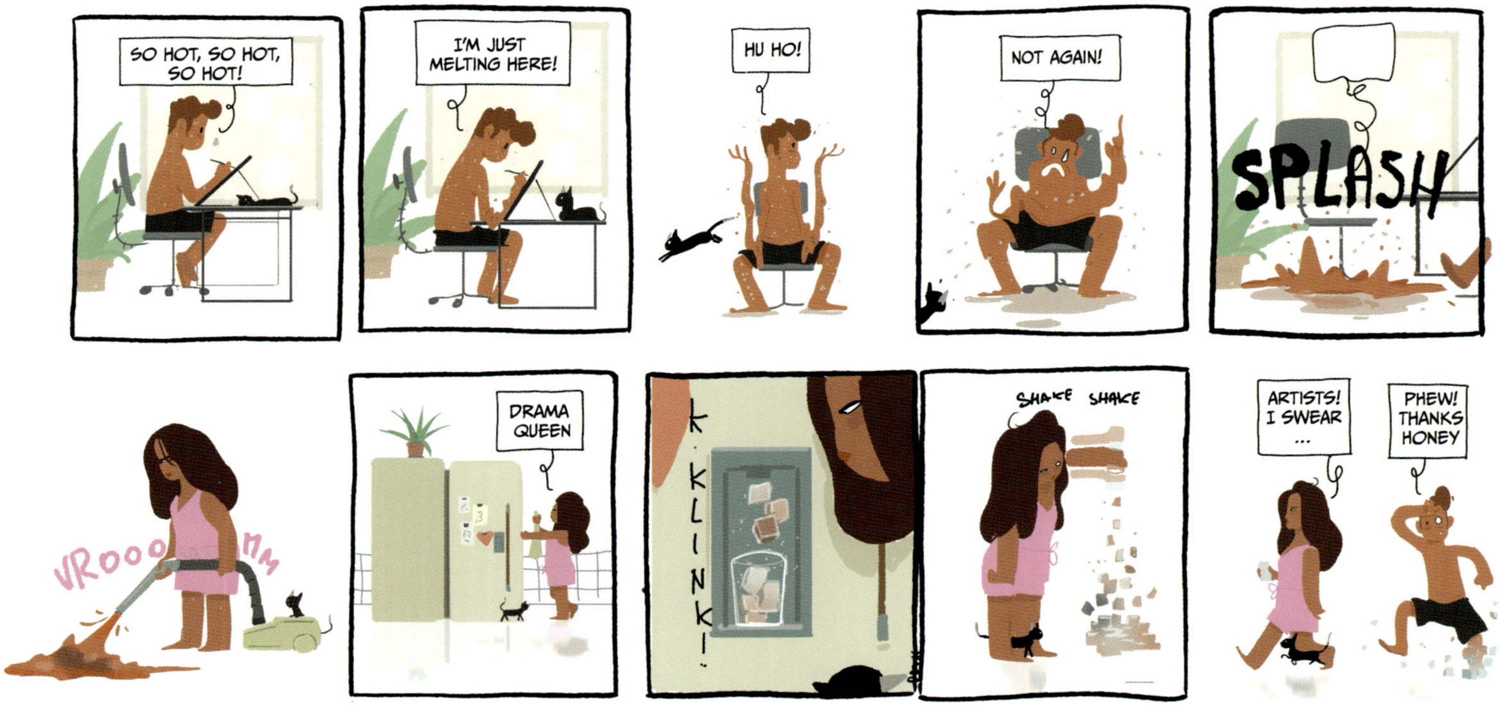
SO HOT, SO HOT, SO HOT!
I'M JUST MELTING HERE!
HU HO!
NOT AGAIN!
SPLASH
VROOOMM
DRAMA QUEEN
K KLINK!
SHAKE SHAKE
ARTISTS! I SWEAR ...
PHEW! THANKS HONEY

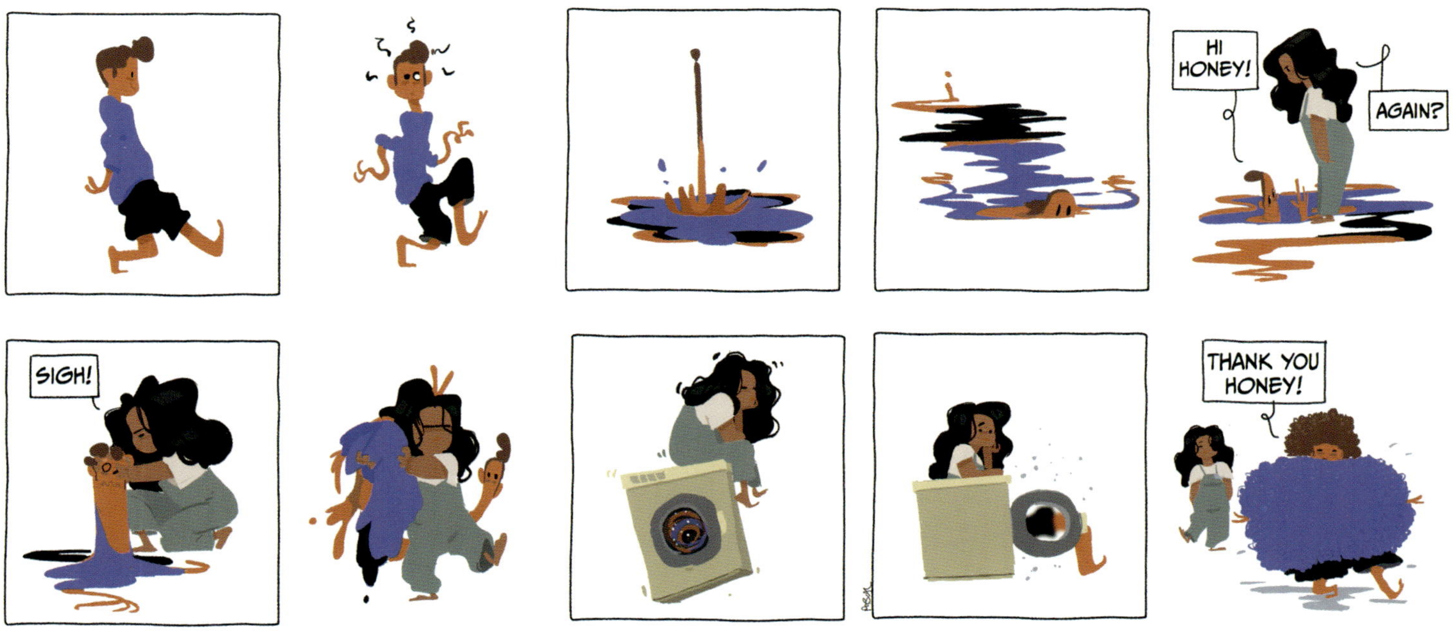
HI HONEY!
AGAIN?
SIGH!
THANK YOU HONEY!

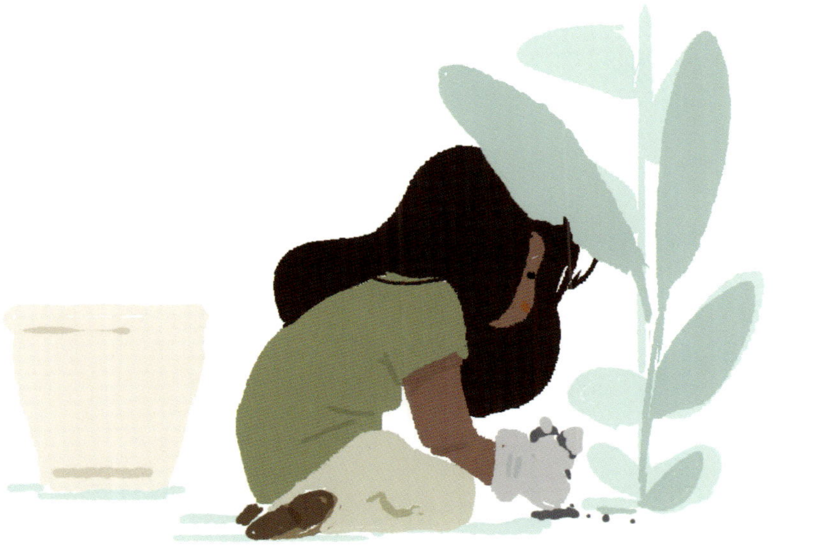

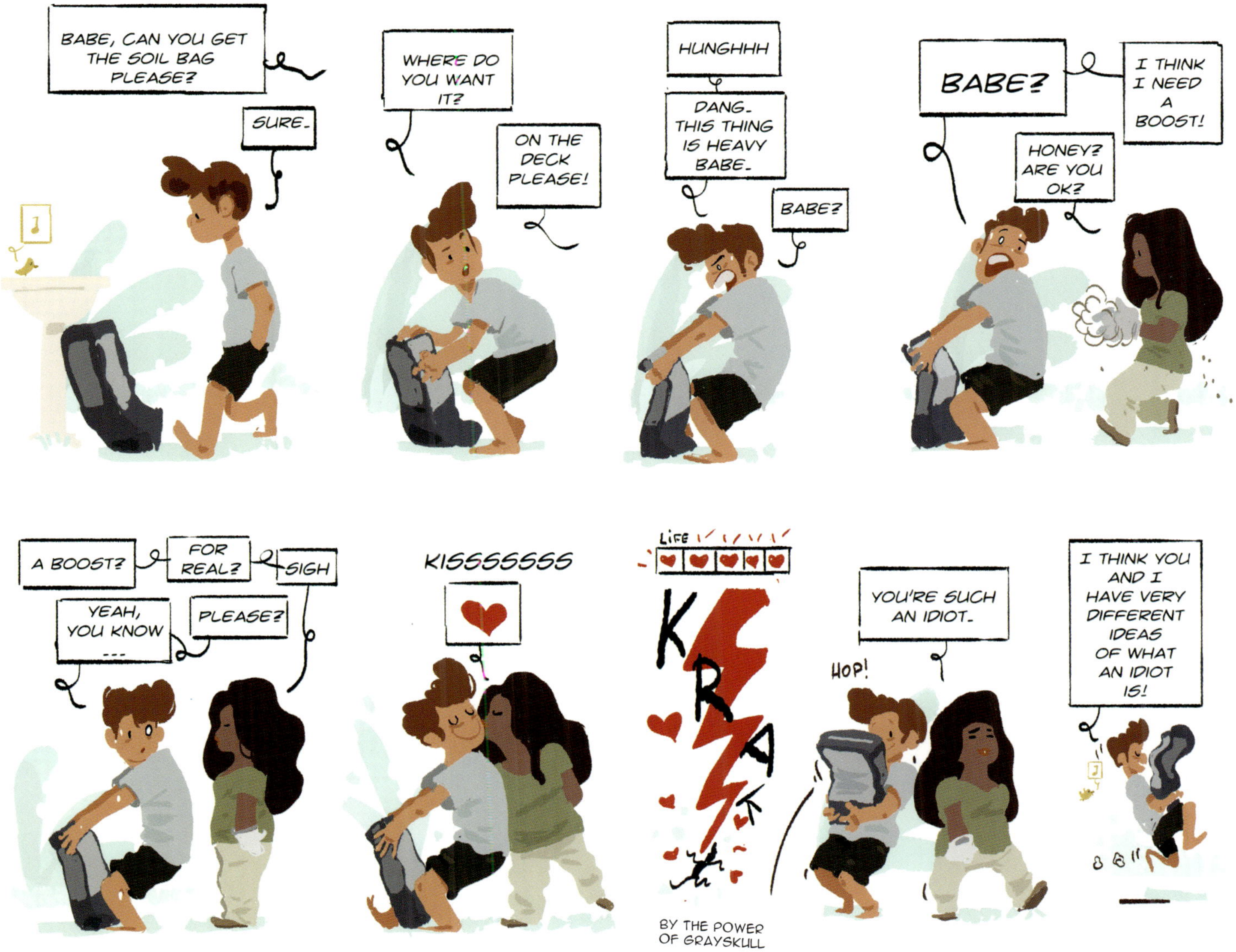
BABE, CAN YOU GET THE SOIL BAG PLEASE?
SURE.
WHERE DO YOU WANT IT?
ON THE DECK PLEASE!
HUNGHHH
DANG. THIS THING IS HEAVY BABE.
BABE?
BABE?
I THINK I NEED A BOOST!
HONEY? ARE YOU OK?
A BOOST?
FOR REAL?
SIGH
YEAH, YOU KNOW ...
PLEASE?
KISSSSSSS
LIFE
KRAAK
BY THE POWER OF GRAYSKULL
HOP!
YOU'RE SUCH AN IDIOT.
I THINK YOU AND I HAVE VERY DIFFERENT IDEAS OF WHAT AN IDIOT IS!

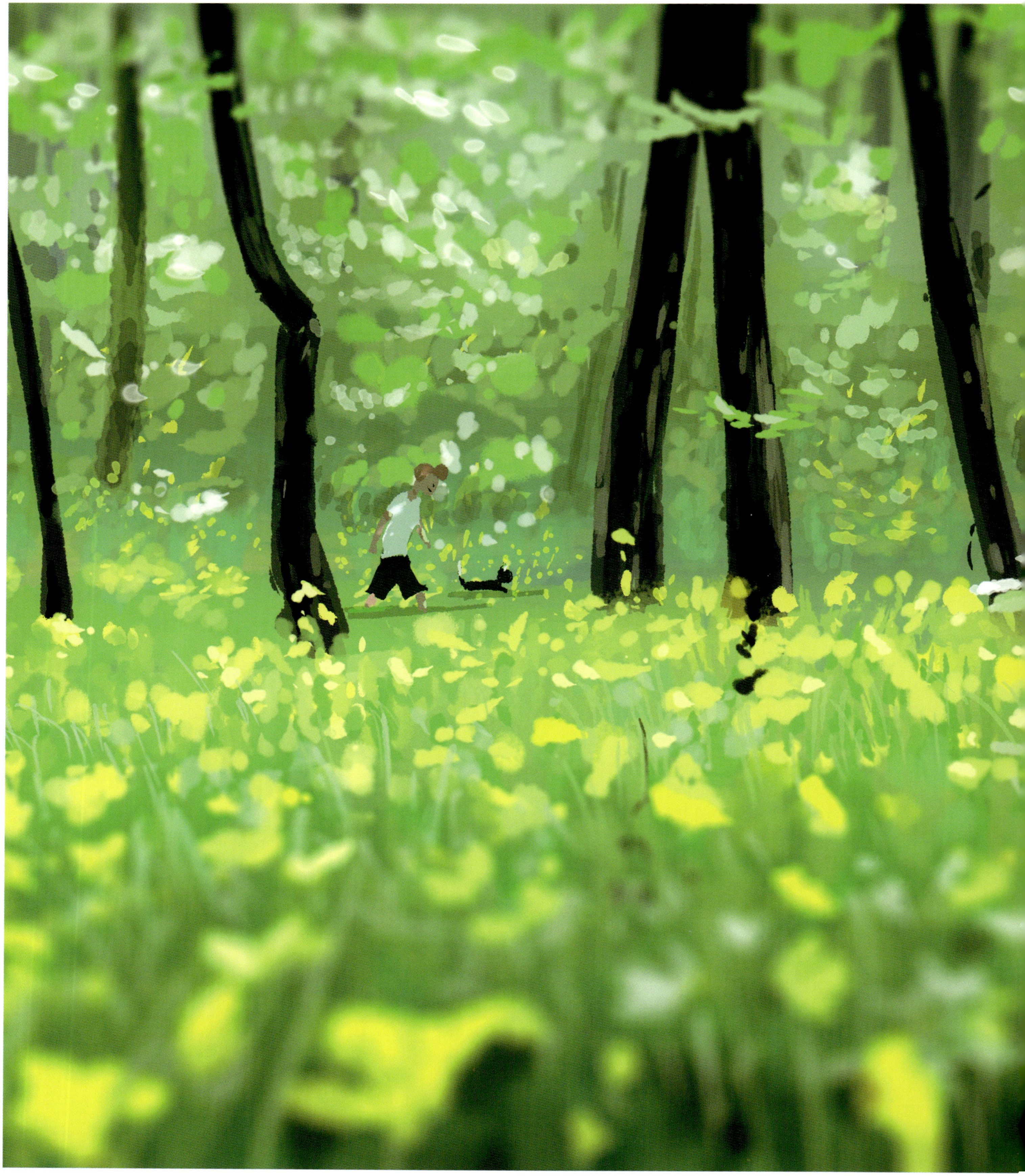

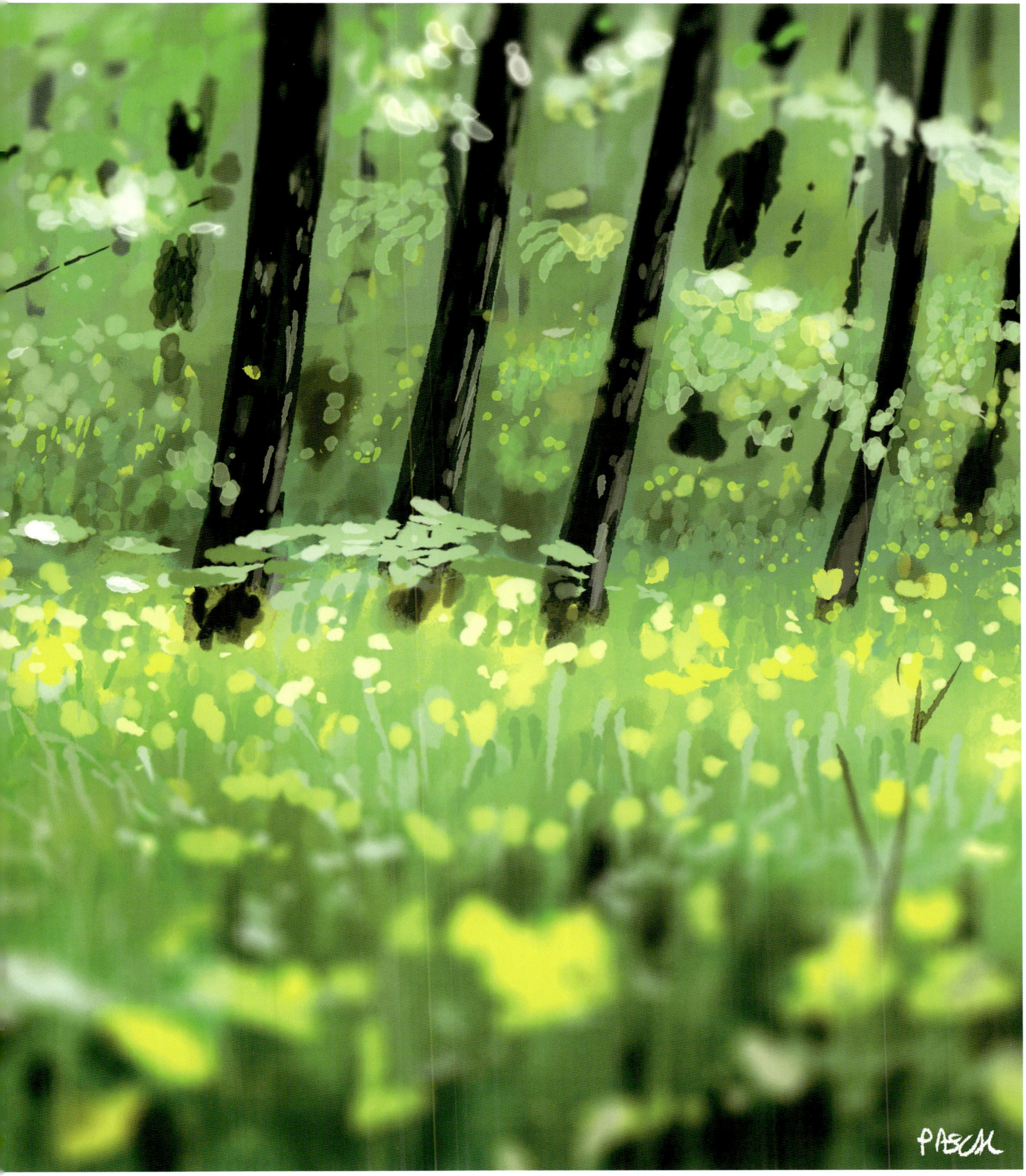
PASCAL

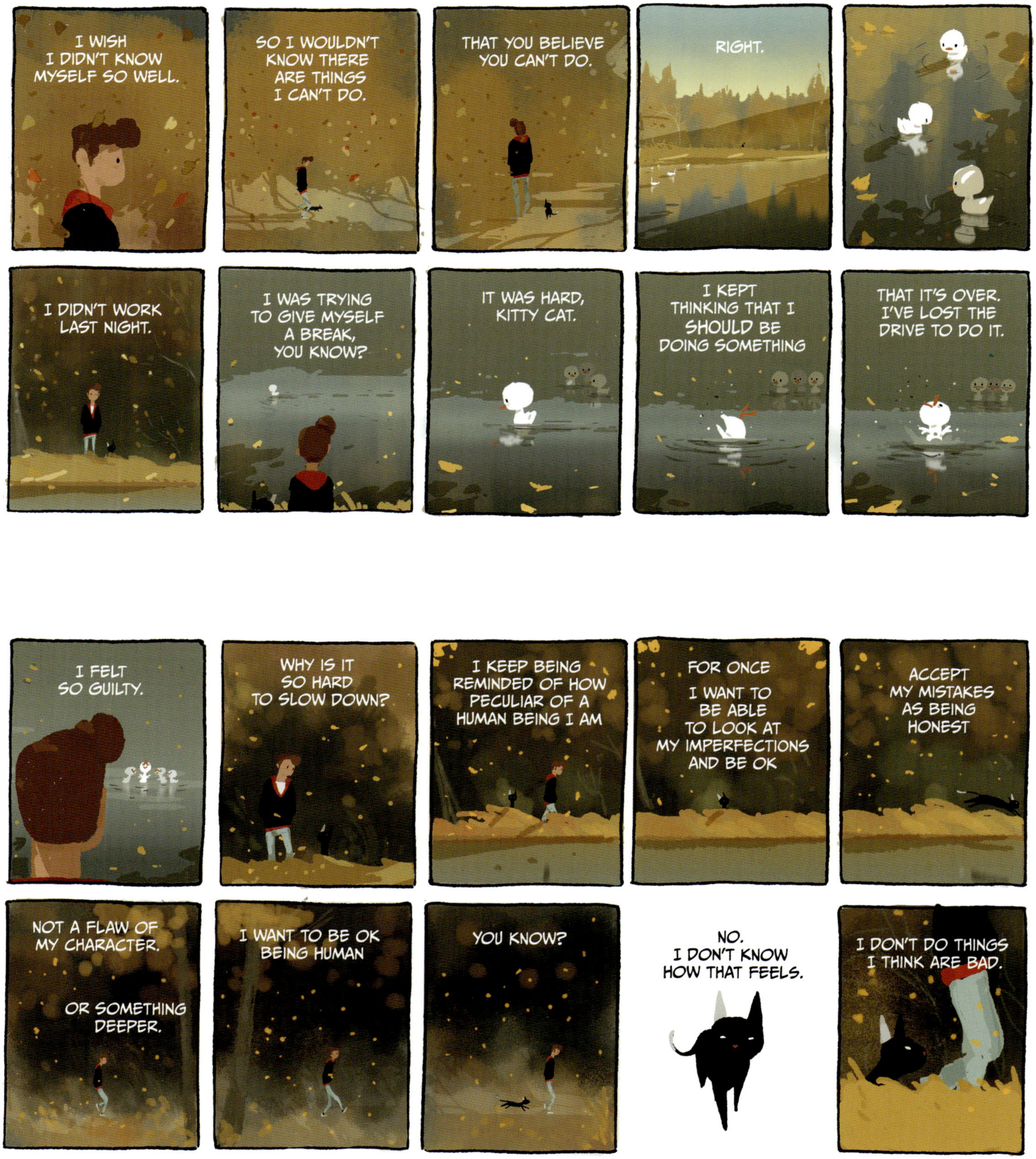

I WISH I DIDN'T KNOW MYSELF SO WELL.
SO I WOULDN'T KNOW THERE ARE THINGS I CAN'T DO.
THAT YOU BELIEVE YOU CAN'T DO.
RIGHT.
I DIDN'T WORK LAST NIGHT.
I WAS TRYING TO GIVE MYSELF A BREAK, YOU KNOW?
IT WAS HARD, KITTY CAT.
I KEPT THINKING THAT I SHOULD BE DOING SOMETHING
THAT IT'S OVER. I'VE LOST THE DRIVE TO DO IT.
I FELT SO GUILTY.
WHY IS IT SO HARD TO SLOW DOWN?
I KEEP BEING REMINDED OF HOW PECULIAR OF A HUMAN BEING I AM
FOR ONCE
I WANT TO BE ABLE TO LOOK AT MY IMPERFECTIONS AND BE OK
ACCEPT MY MISTAKES AS BEING HONEST
NOT A FLAW OF MY CHARACTER.
OR SOMETHING DEEPER.
I WANT TO BE OK BEING HUMAN
YOU KNOW?
NO. I DON'T KNOW HOW THAT FEELS.
I DON'T DO THINGS I THINK ARE BAD.

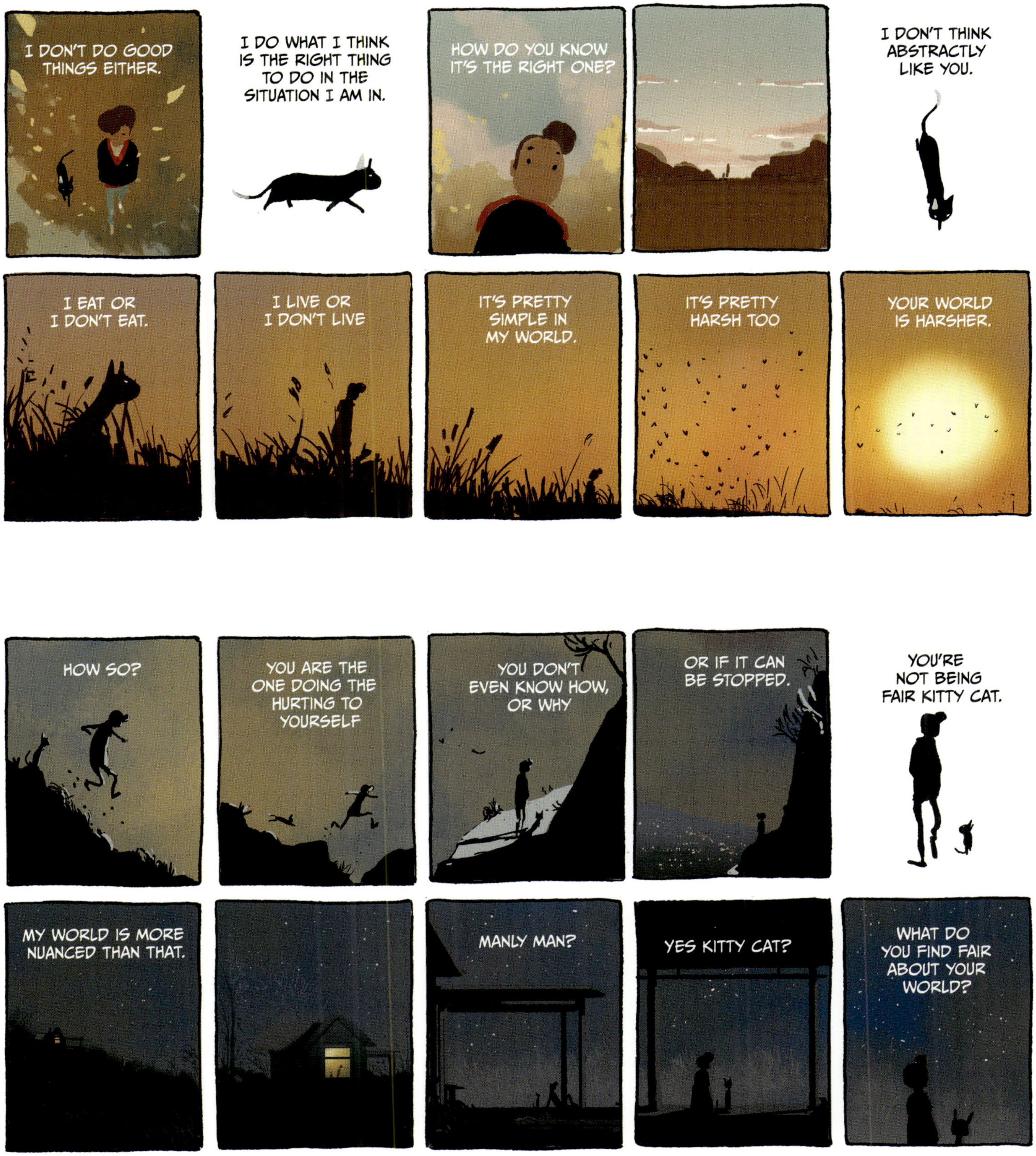
I DON'T DO GOOD THINGS EITHER.
I DO WHAT I THINK IS THE RIGHT THING TO DO IN THE SITUATION I AM IN.
HOW DO YOU KNOW IT'S THE RIGHT ONE?
I DON'T THINK ABSTRACTLY LIKE YOU.
I EAT OR I DON'T EAT.
I LIVE OR I DON'T LIVE
IT'S PRETTY SIMPLE IN MY WORLD.
IT'S PRETTY HARSH TOO
YOUR WORLD IS HARSHER.
HOW SO?
YOU ARE THE ONE DOING THE HURTING TO YOURSELF
YOU DON'T EVEN KNOW HOW, OR WHY
OR IF IT CAN BE STOPPED.
YOU'RE NOT BEING FAIR KITTY CAT.
MY WORLD IS MORE NUANCED THAN THAT.
MANLY MAN?
YES KITTY CAT?
WHAT DO YOU FIND FAIR ABOUT YOUR WORLD?

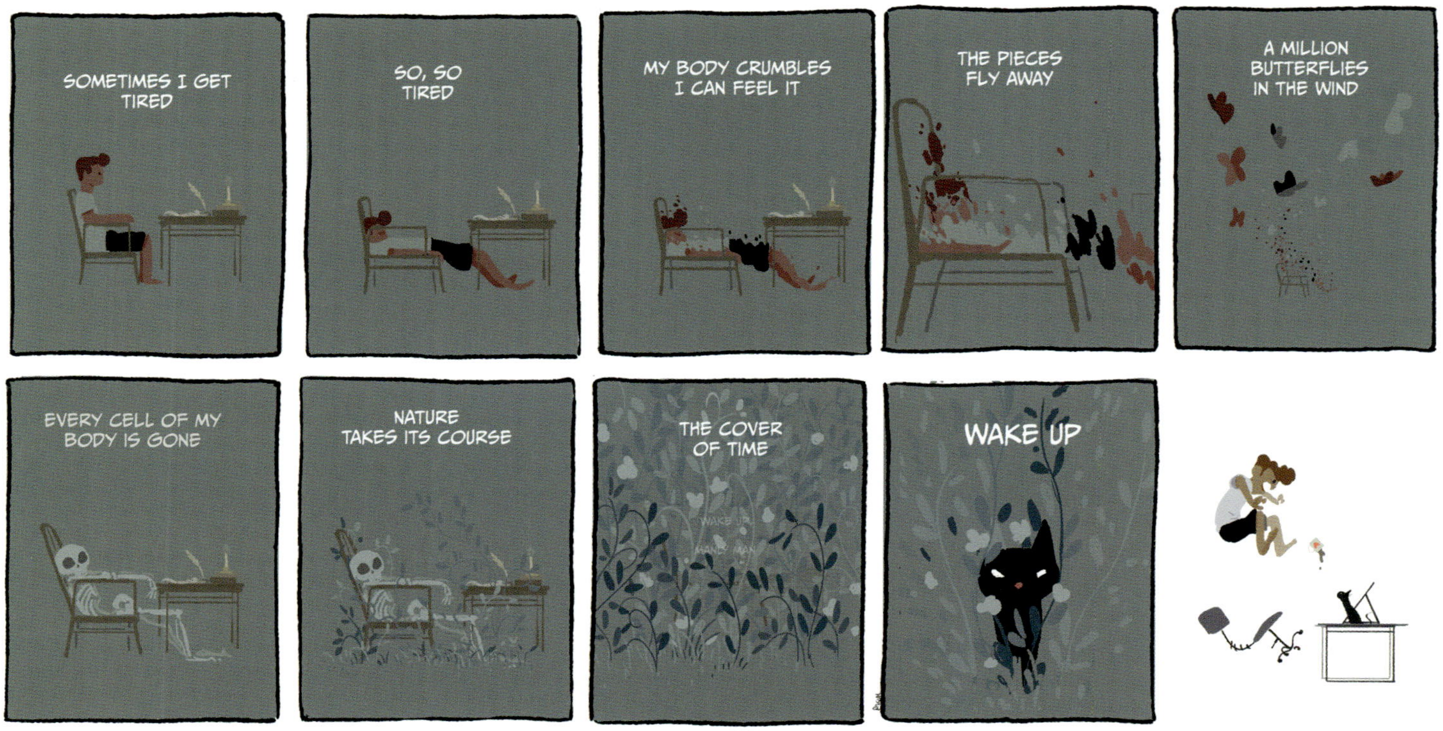

SOMETIMES I GET TIRED
SO, SO TIRED
MY BODY CRUMBLES I CAN FEEL IT
THE PIECES FLY AWAY
A MILLION BUTTERFLIES IN THE WIND
EVERY CELL OF MY BODY IS GONE
NATURE TAKES ITS COURSE
THE COVER OF TIME
WAKE UP

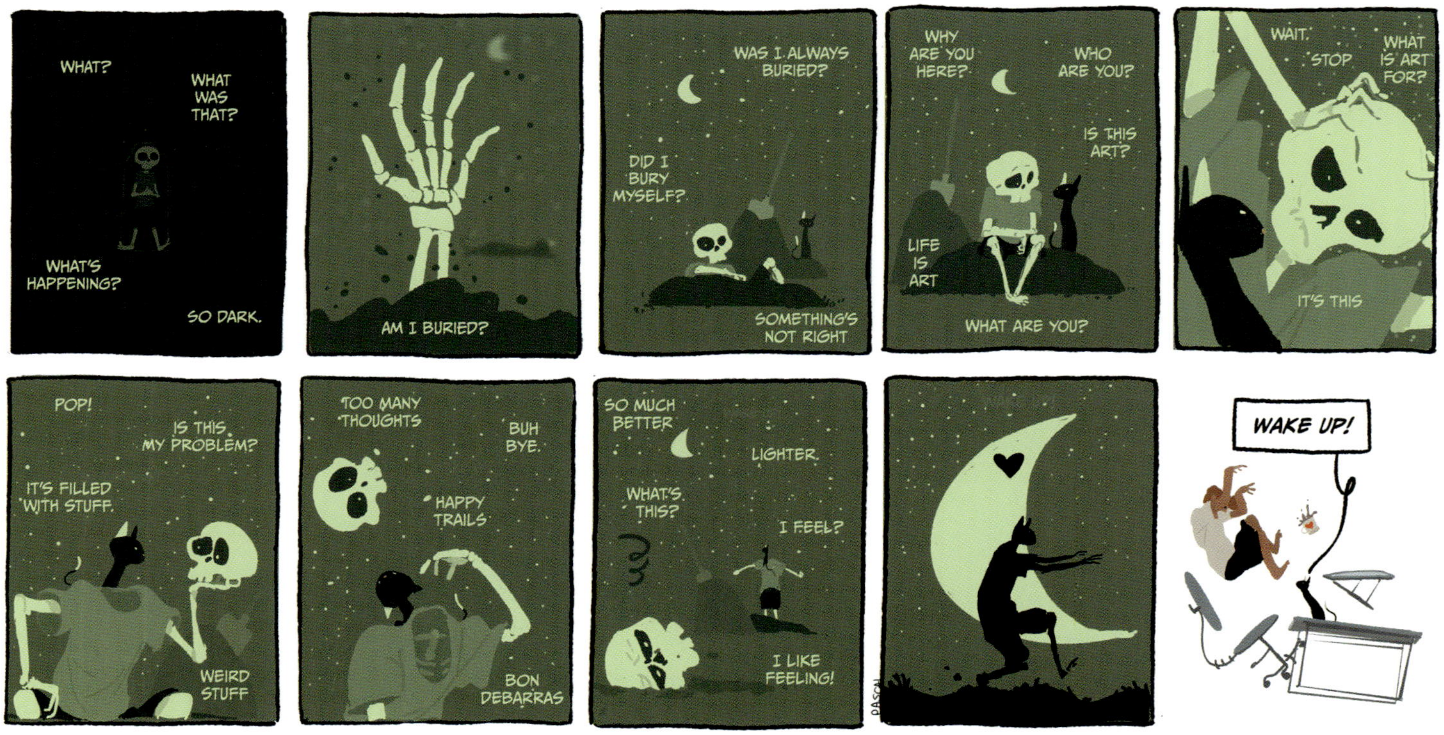

WHAT?
WHAT WAS THAT?
WHAT'S HAPPENING?
SO DARK.
AM I BURIED?
WAS I ALWAYS BURIED?
DID I BURY MYSELF?
SOMETHING'S NOT RIGHT
WHY ARE YOU HERE?
WHO ARE YOU?
IS THIS ART?
LIFE IS ART
WHAT ARE YOU?
WAIT.
STOP
WHAT IS ART FOR?
IT'S THIS
POP!
IS THIS MY PROBLEM?
IT'S FILLED WITH STUFF.
WEIRD STUFF
TOO MANY THOUGHTS
BUH BYE.
HAPPY TRAILS
BON DEBARRAS
SO MUCH BETTER
LIGHTER.
WHAT'S THIS?
I FEEL?
I LIKE FEELING!
WAKE UP!

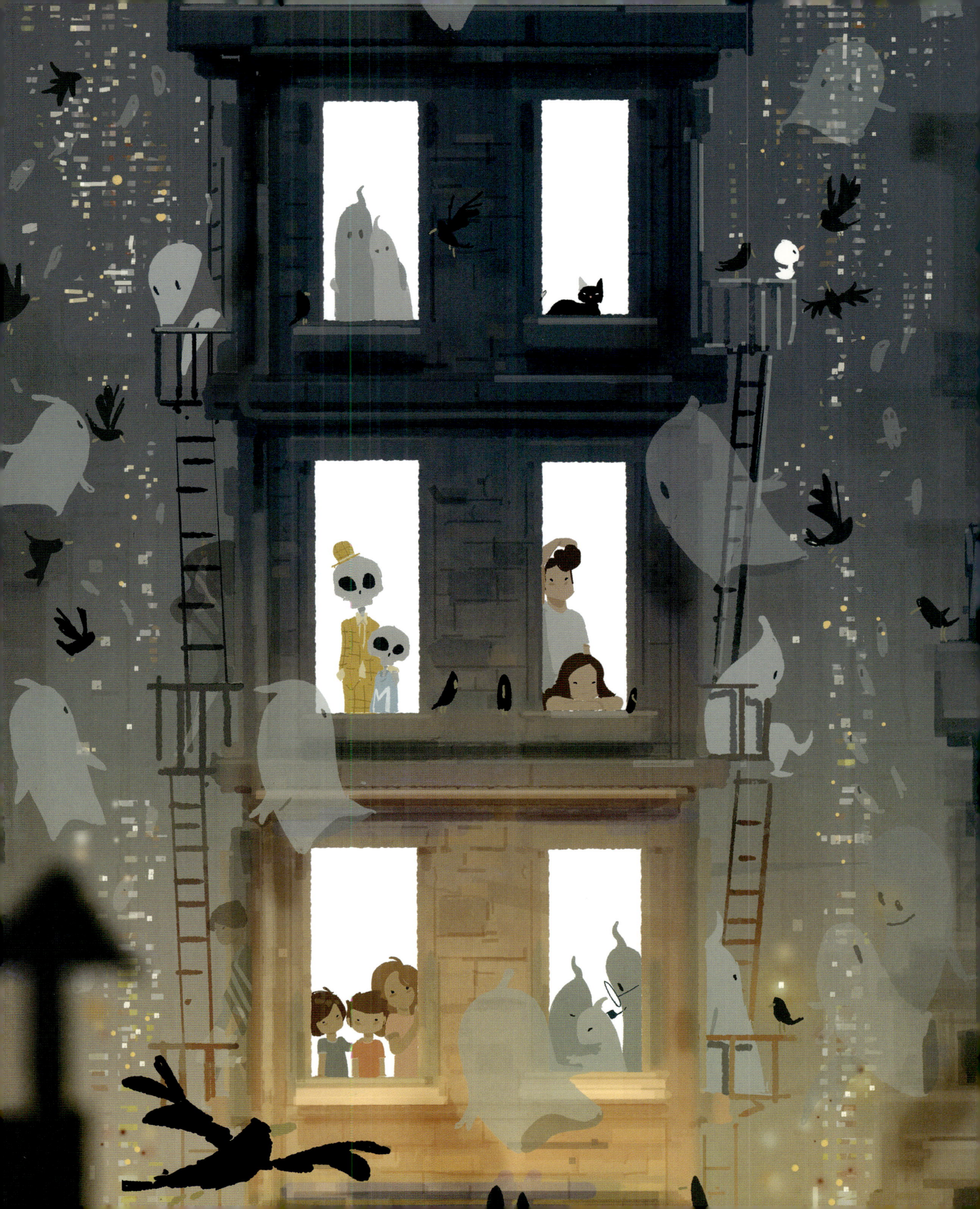

A SERIES OF STRIPS FEATURES 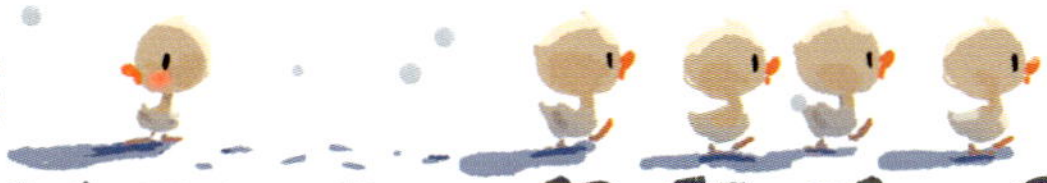
THIS FAMILY OF **DUCKS, SWIMMING** AROUND.

SEEMS BIRDS HAVE BEEN A
THEME SINCE THE BEGINNING.

MILO IS A LOST LITTLE DUCKLING.

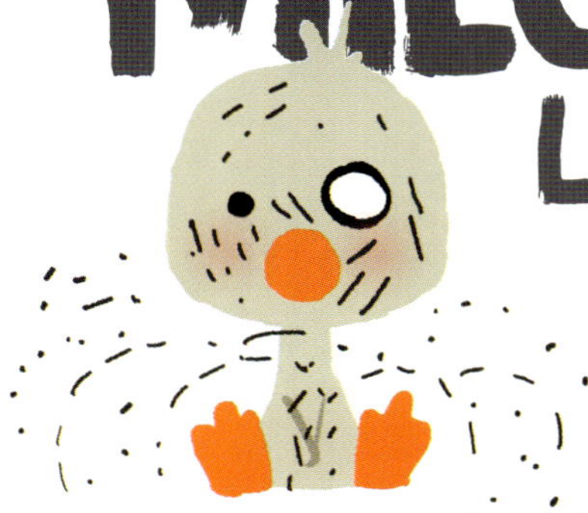

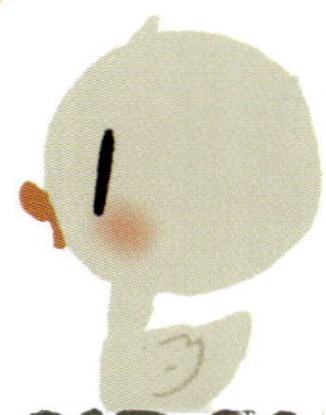

HE TURNED UP IN THE STRIPS BY **ACCIDENT**.
I WASN'T PLANNING A NEW CHARACTER.

HE'D JUST... GOT LOST.

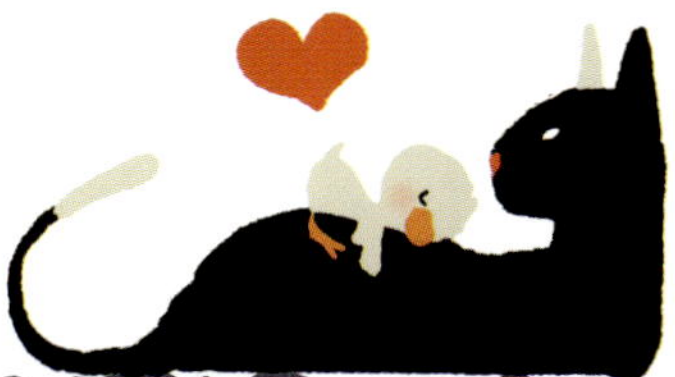

ENDED UP IN THE STRIP.

NOW, HE'S PART OF THE FAMILY.

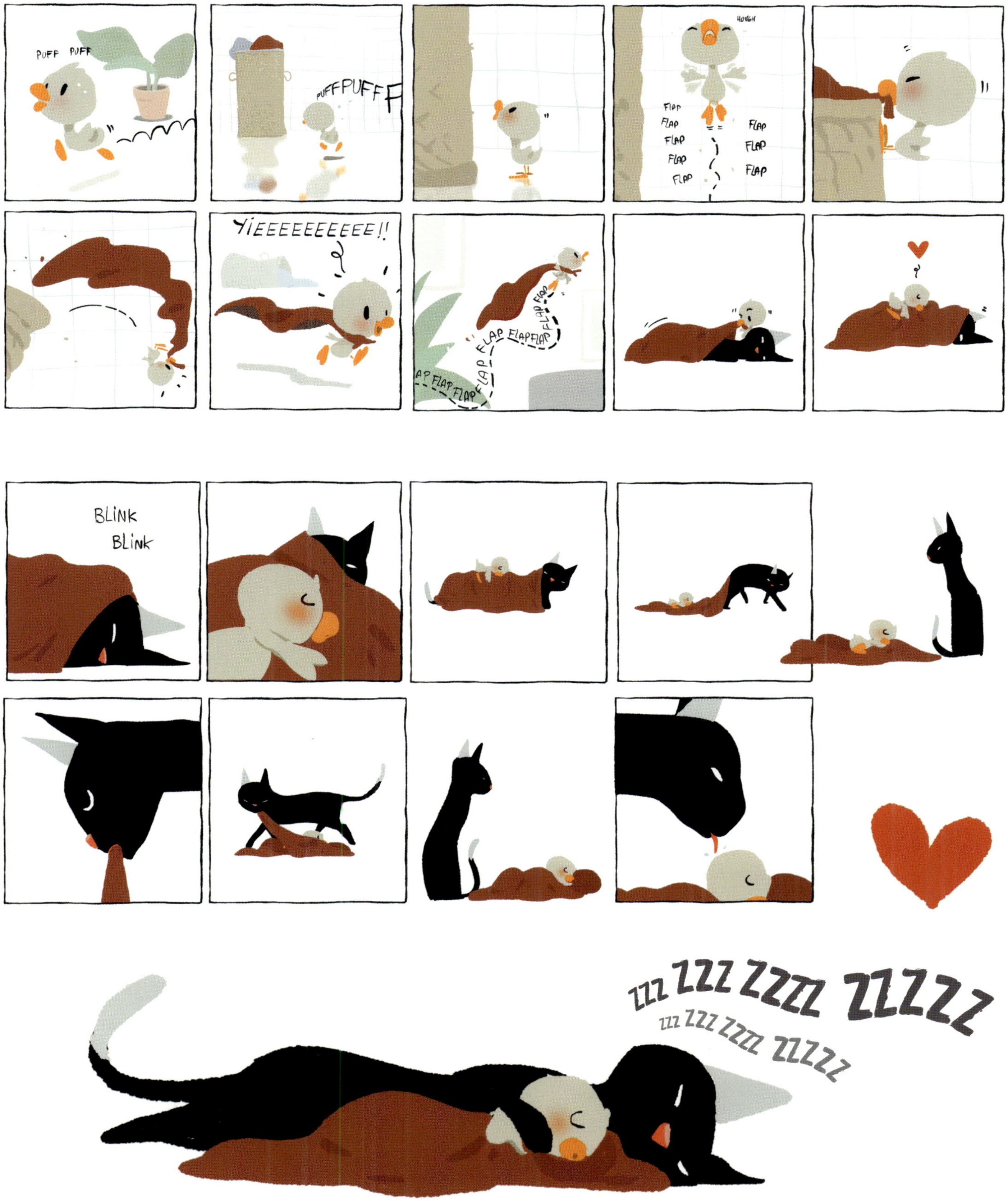
PUFF PUFF
PUFFPUFFF
FLAP
FLAP
FLAP
FLAP
FLAP
FLAP
FLAP
FLAP
YIEEEEEEEEEE!!
FLAP FLAP FLAP FLAPFLAPFLAP FLAP FLAP
BLINK
BLINK
ZZZ ZZZ ZZZZ ZZZZZ
ZZZ ZZZ ZZZZ ZZZZZ

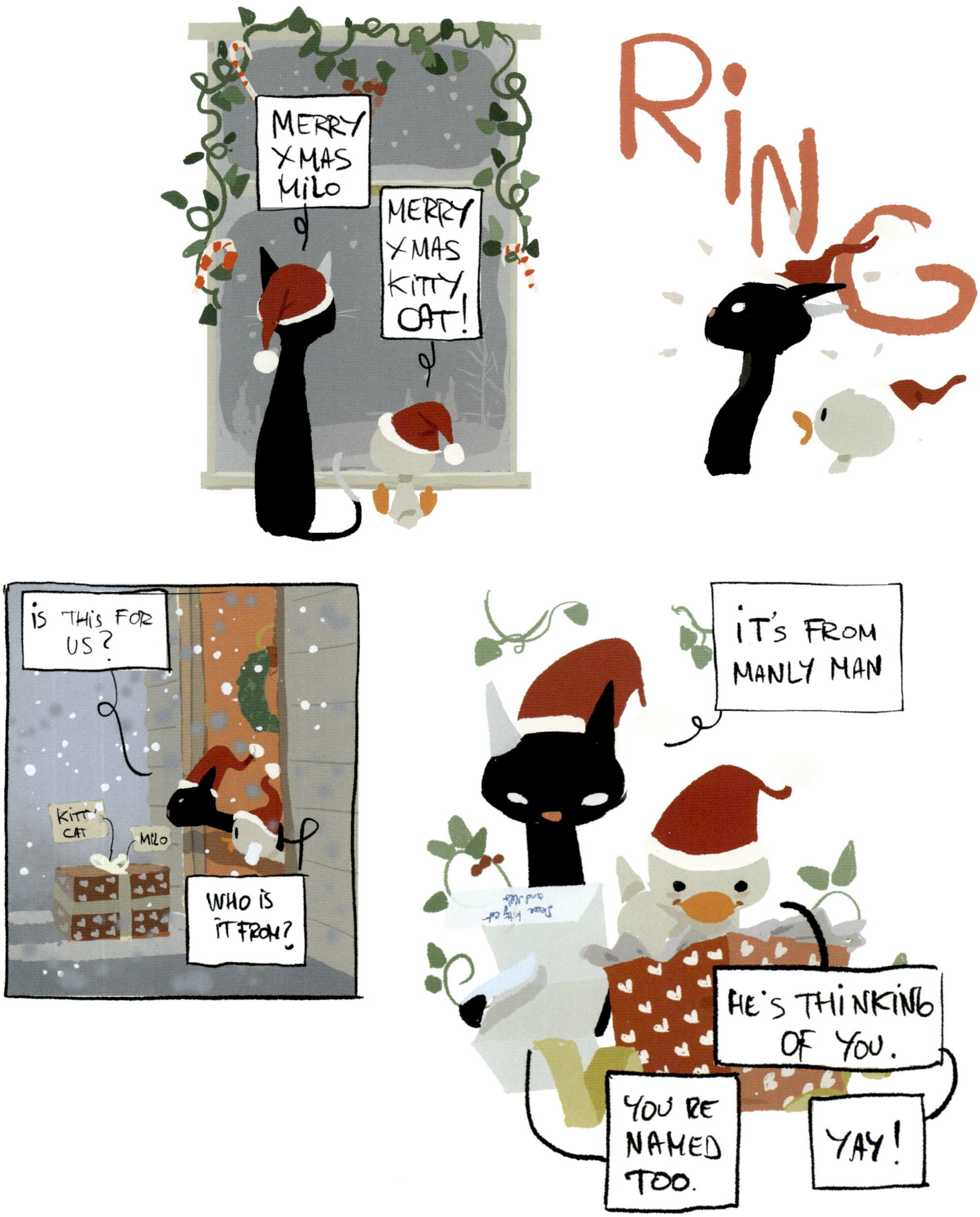
MERRY XMAS MILO
MERRY XMAS KITTY CAT!
RING
IS THIS FOR US?
KITTY CAT
MILO
WHO IS IT FROM?
IT'S FROM MANLY MAN
HE'S THINKING OF YOU.
YOU'RE NAMED TOO.
YAY!

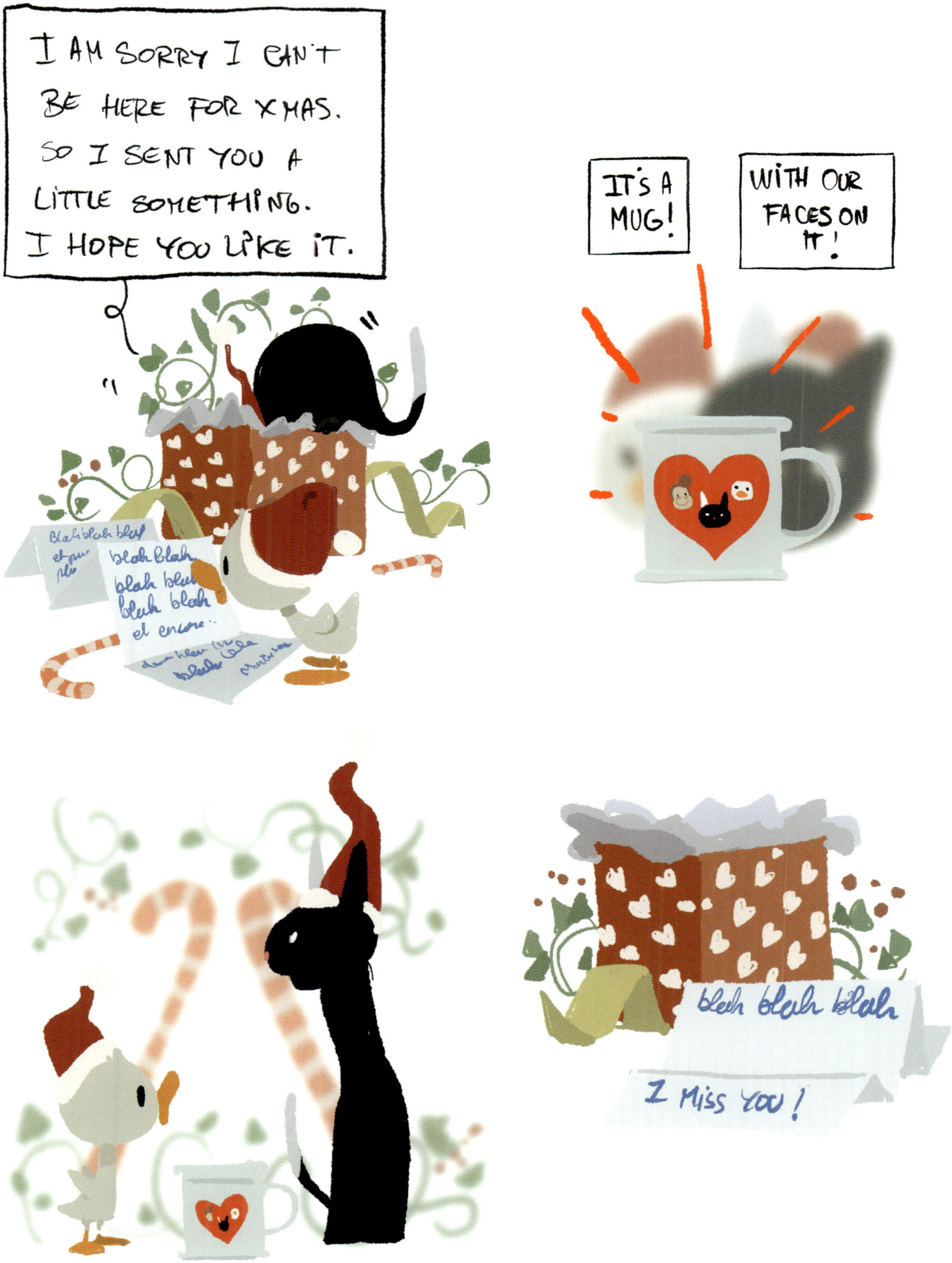
I AM SORRY I CAN'T BE HERE FOR XMAS. SO I SENT YOU A LITTLE SOMETHING. I HOPE YOU LIKE IT.
IT'S A MUG!
WITH OUR FACES ON IT!
blah blah blah
I Miss You!

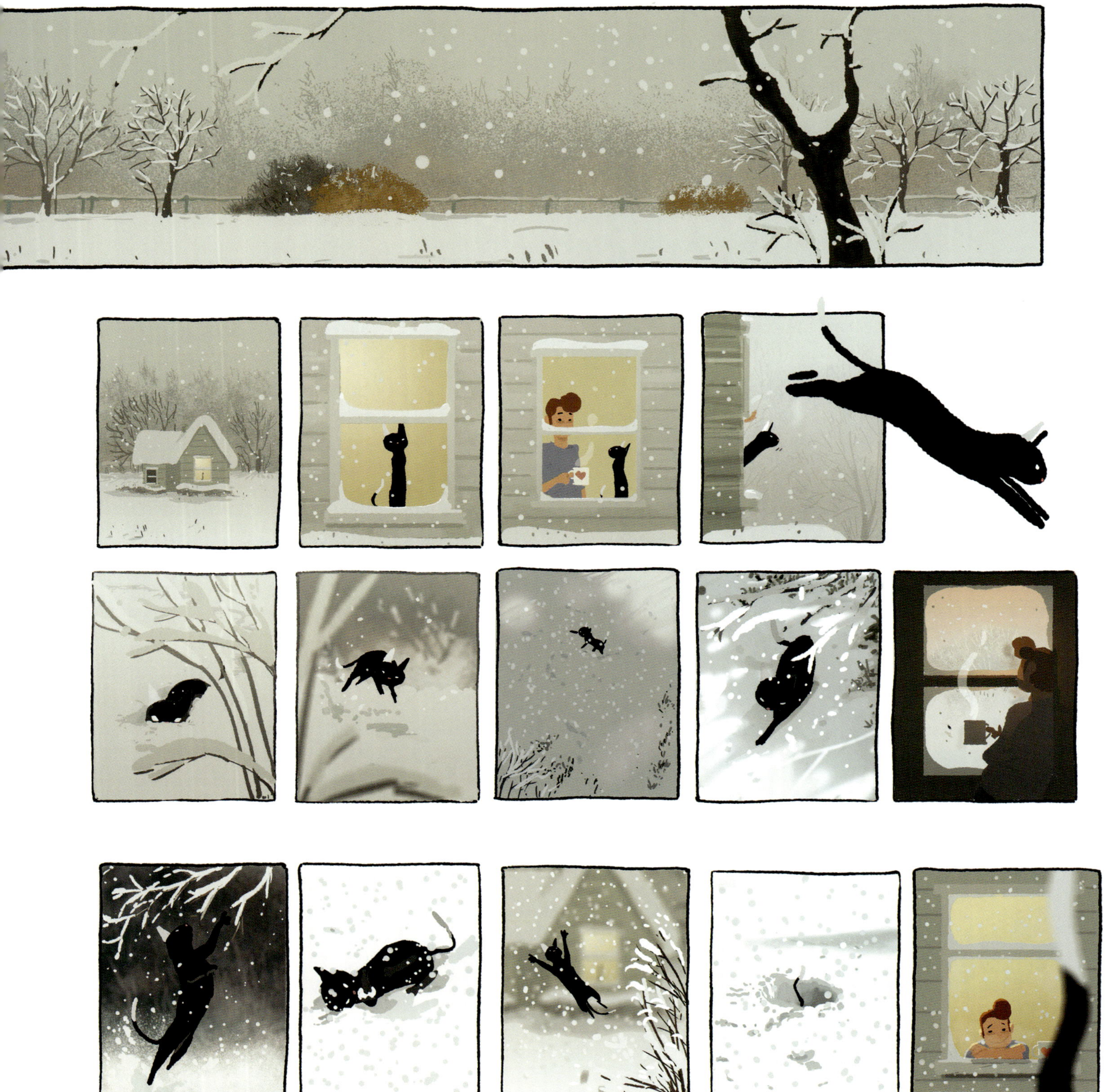

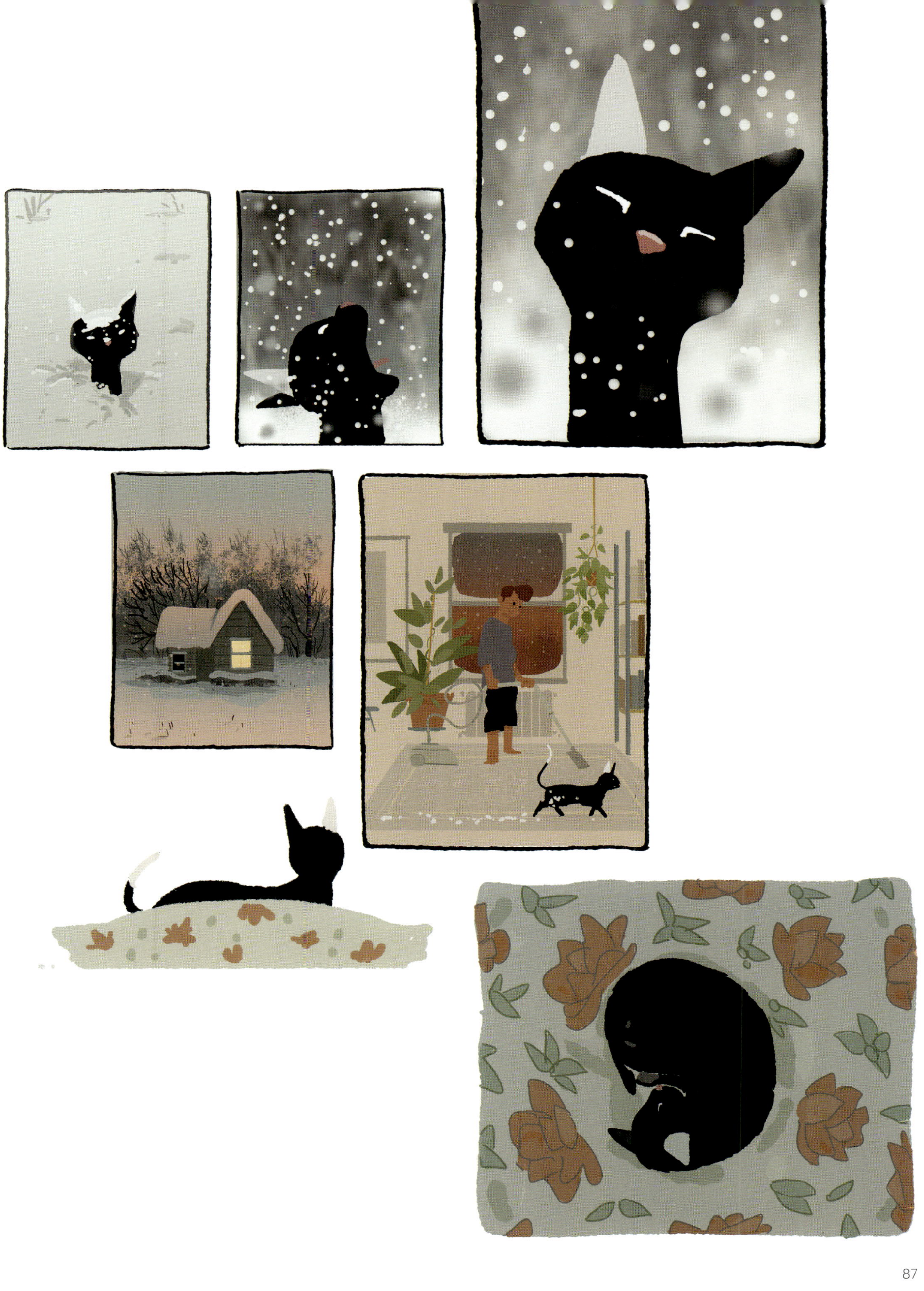

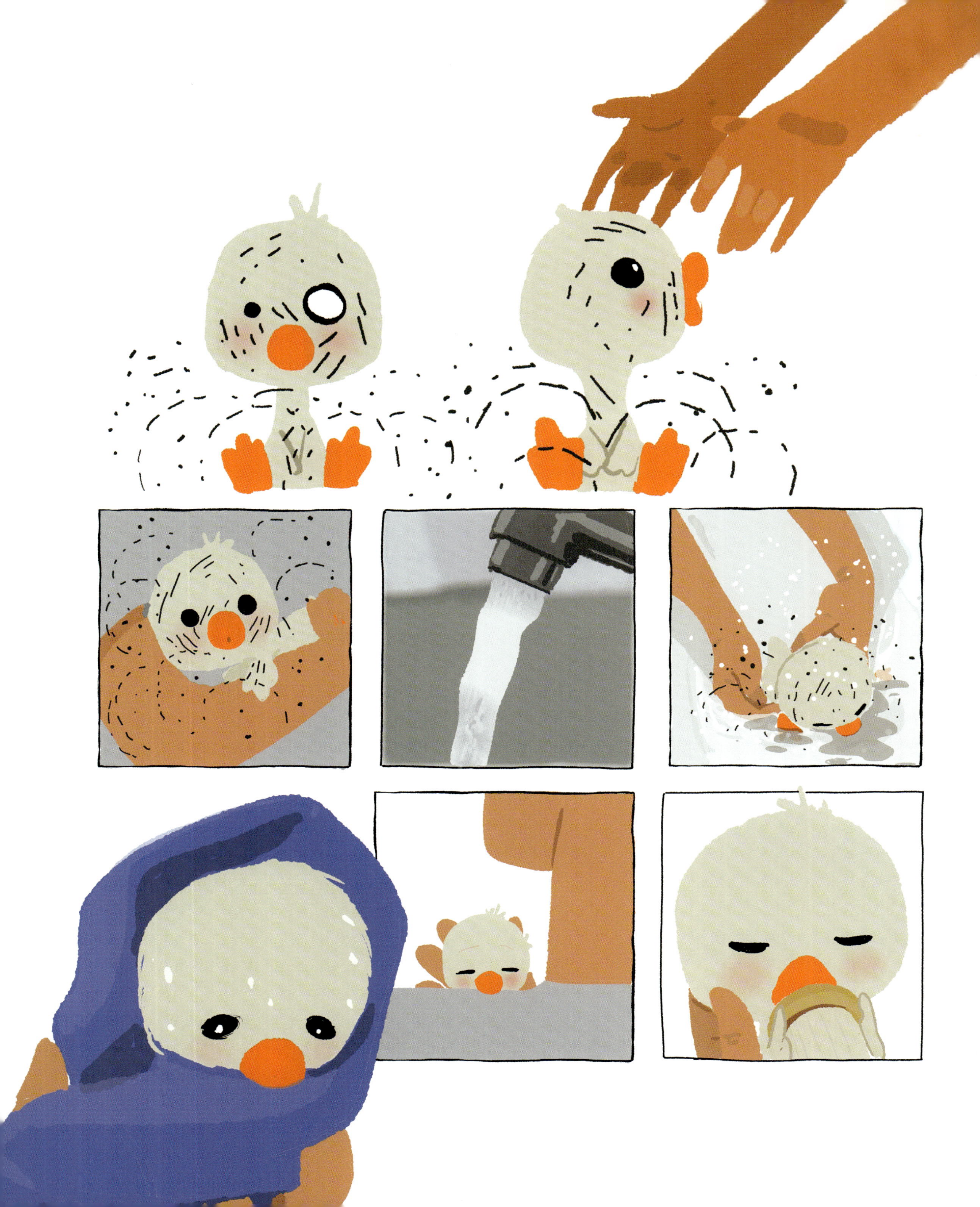

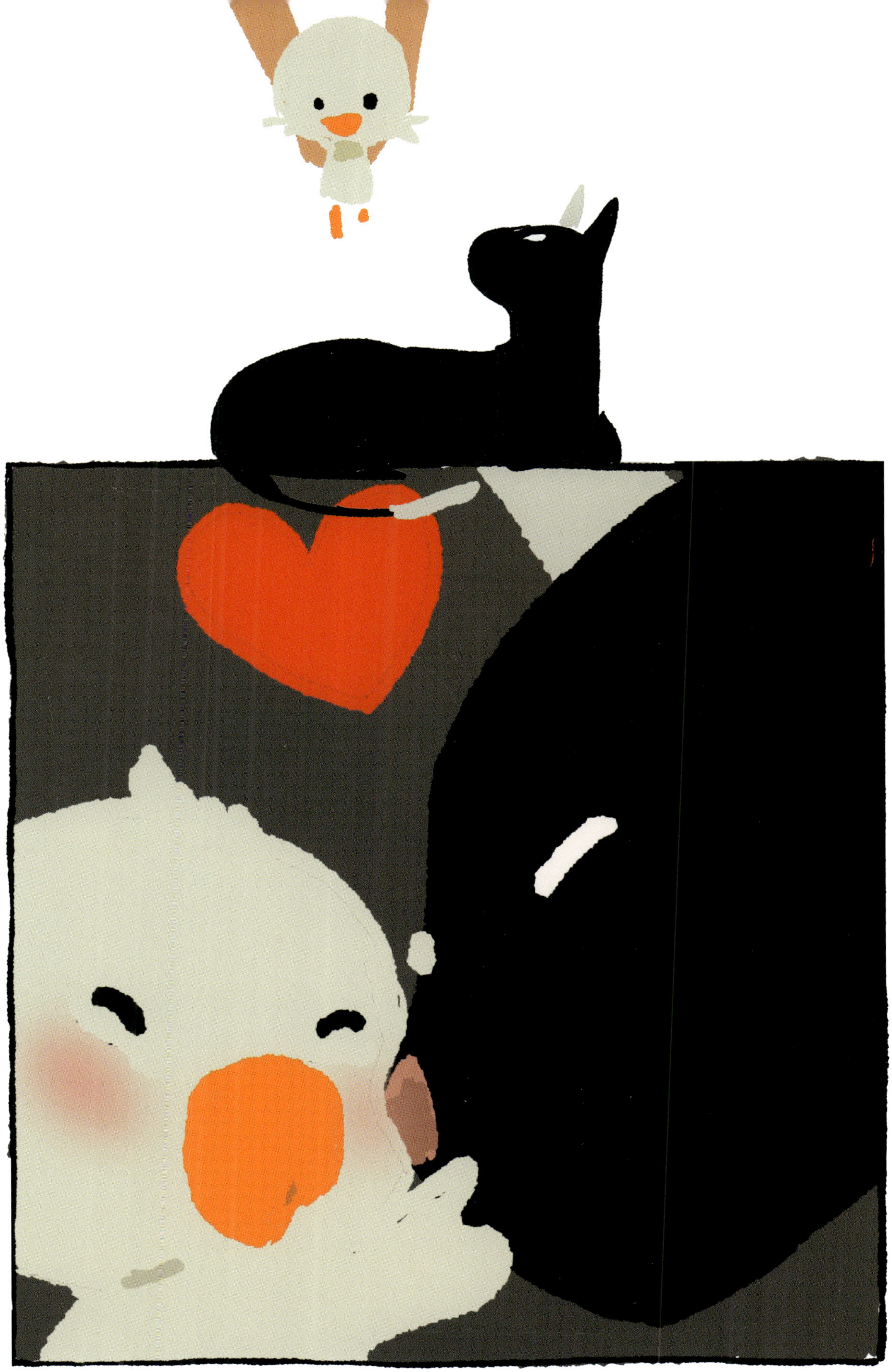

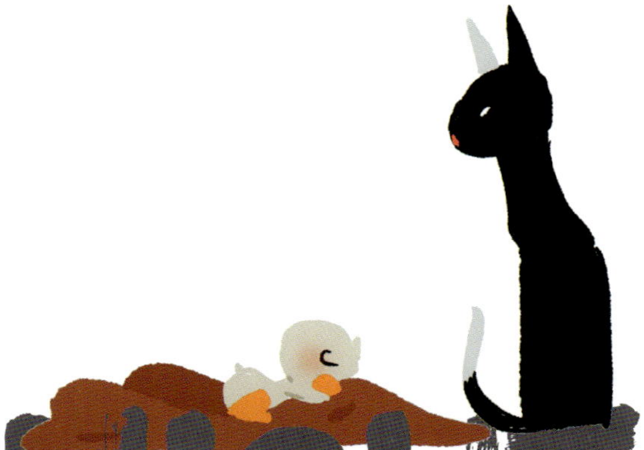

GALLERY: LATE-NIGHT THOUGHTS

THE DOUBTS.
THE BIG QUESTIONS.

WHEN THE PANDEMIC HIT,
OUR LIVES WERE ALTERED IN A BIG WAY.

IN FACT,
ALMOST ALL MY DRAWINGS COULD SIT
UNDER THIS HEADING.

EVEN THE FUN ONES.

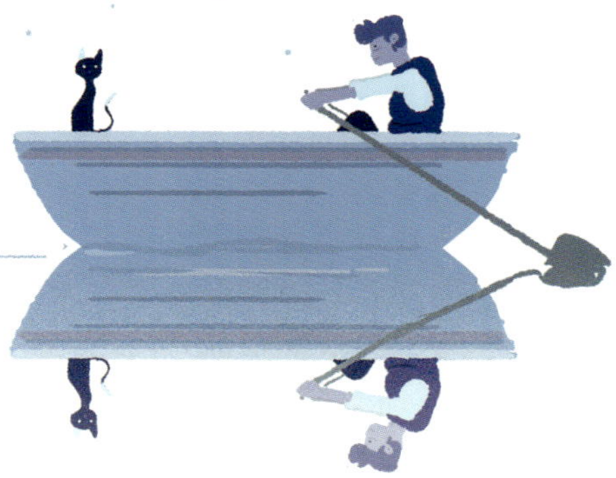

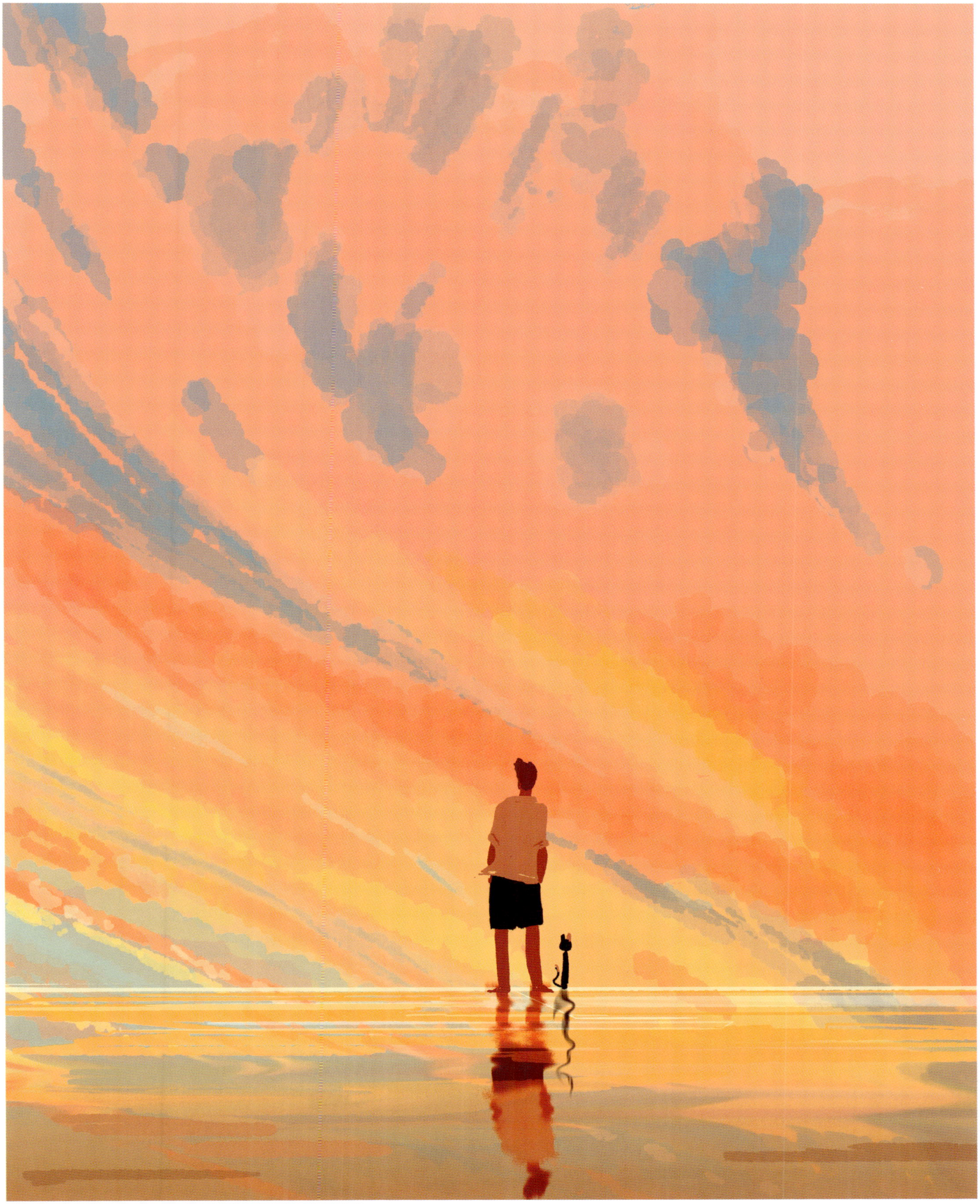

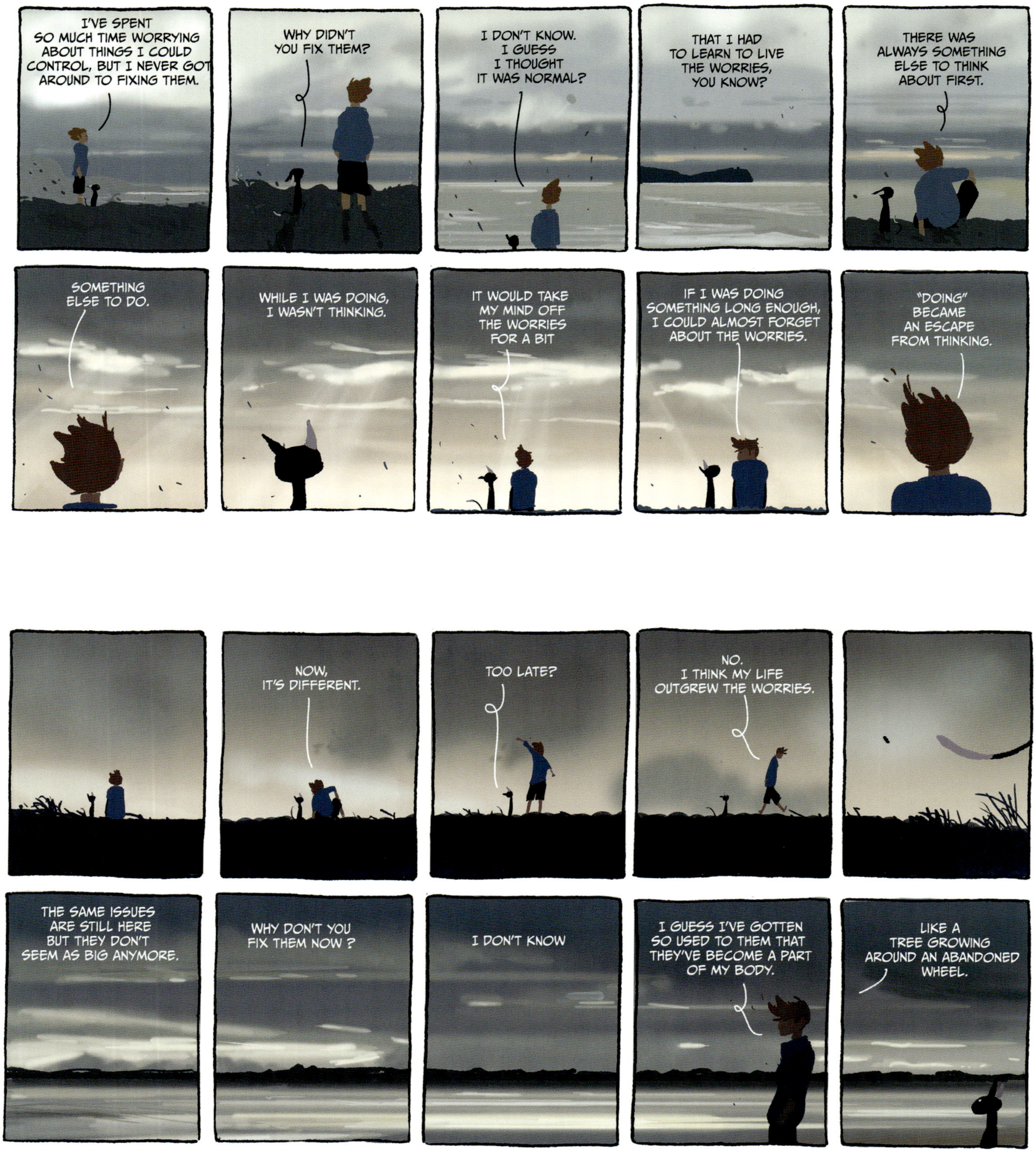

I'VE SPENT SO MUCH TIME WORRYING ABOUT THINGS I COULD CONTROL, BUT I NEVER GOT AROUND TO FIXING THEM.
WHY DIDN'T YOU FIX THEM?
I DON'T KNOW. I GUESS I THOUGHT IT WAS NORMAL?
THAT I HAD TO LEARN TO LIVE THE WORRIES, YOU KNOW?
THERE WAS ALWAYS SOMETHING ELSE TO THINK ABOUT FIRST.
SOMETHING ELSE TO DO.
WHILE I WAS DOING, I WASN'T THINKING.
IT WOULD TAKE MY MIND OFF THE WORRIES FOR A BIT
IF I WAS DOING SOMETHING LONG ENOUGH, I COULD ALMOST FORGET ABOUT THE WORRIES.
"DOING" BECAME AN ESCAPE FROM THINKING.
NOW, IT'S DIFFERENT.
TOO LATE?
NO. I THINK MY LIFE OUTGREW THE WORRIES.
THE SAME ISSUES ARE STILL HERE BUT THEY DON'T SEEM AS BIG ANYMORE.
WHY DON'T YOU FIX THEM NOW ?
I DON'T KNOW
I GUESS I'VE GOTTEN SO USED TO THEM THAT THEY'VE BECOME A PART OF MY BODY.
LIKE A TREE GROWING AROUND AN ABANDONED WHEEL.

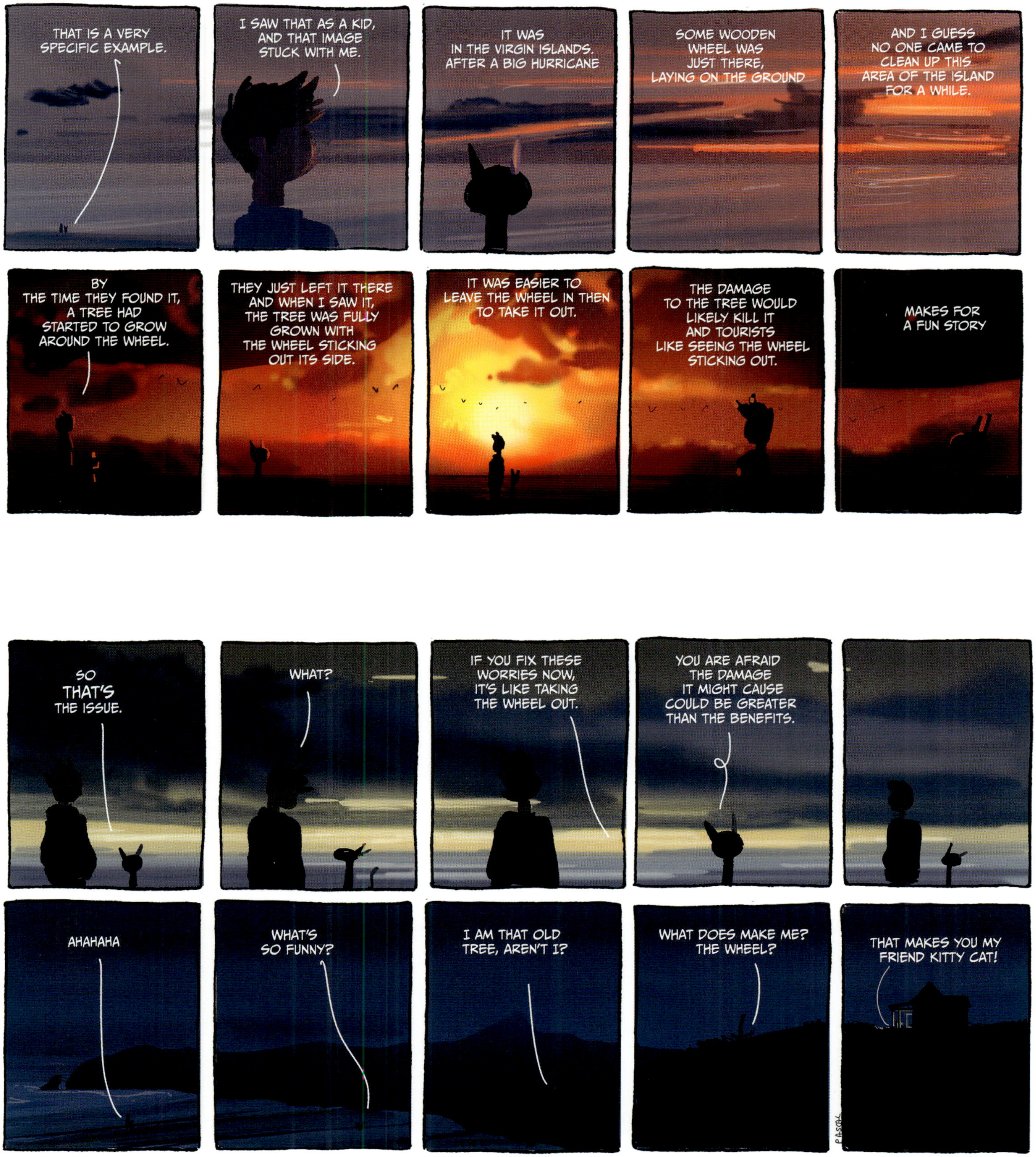
THAT IS A VERY SPECIFIC EXAMPLE.
I SAW THAT AS A KID, AND THAT IMAGE STUCK WITH ME.
IT WAS IN THE VIRGIN ISLANDS. AFTER A BIG HURRICANE
SOME WOODEN WHEEL WAS JUST THERE, LAYING ON THE GROUND
AND I GUESS NO ONE CAME TO CLEAN UP THIS AREA OF THE ISLAND FOR A WHILE.
BY THE TIME THEY FOUND IT, A TREE HAD STARTED TO GROW AROUND THE WHEEL.
THEY JUST LEFT IT THERE AND WHEN I SAW IT, THE TREE WAS FULLY GROWN WITH THE WHEEL STICKING OUT ITS SIDE.
IT WAS EASIER TO LEAVE THE WHEEL IN THEN TO TAKE IT OUT.
THE DAMAGE TO THE TREE WOULD LIKELY KILL IT AND TOURISTS LIKE SEEING THE WHEEL STICKING OUT.
MAKES FOR A FUN STORY
SO THAT'S THE ISSUE.
WHAT?
IF YOU FIX THESE WORRIES NOW, IT'S LIKE TAKING THE WHEEL OUT.
YOU ARE AFRAID THE DAMAGE IT MIGHT CAUSE COULD BE GREATER THAN THE BENEFITS.
AHAHAHA
WHAT'S SO FUNNY?
I AM THAT OLD TREE, AREN'T I?
WHAT DOES MAKE ME? THE WHEEL?
THAT MAKES YOU MY FRIEND KITTY CAT!

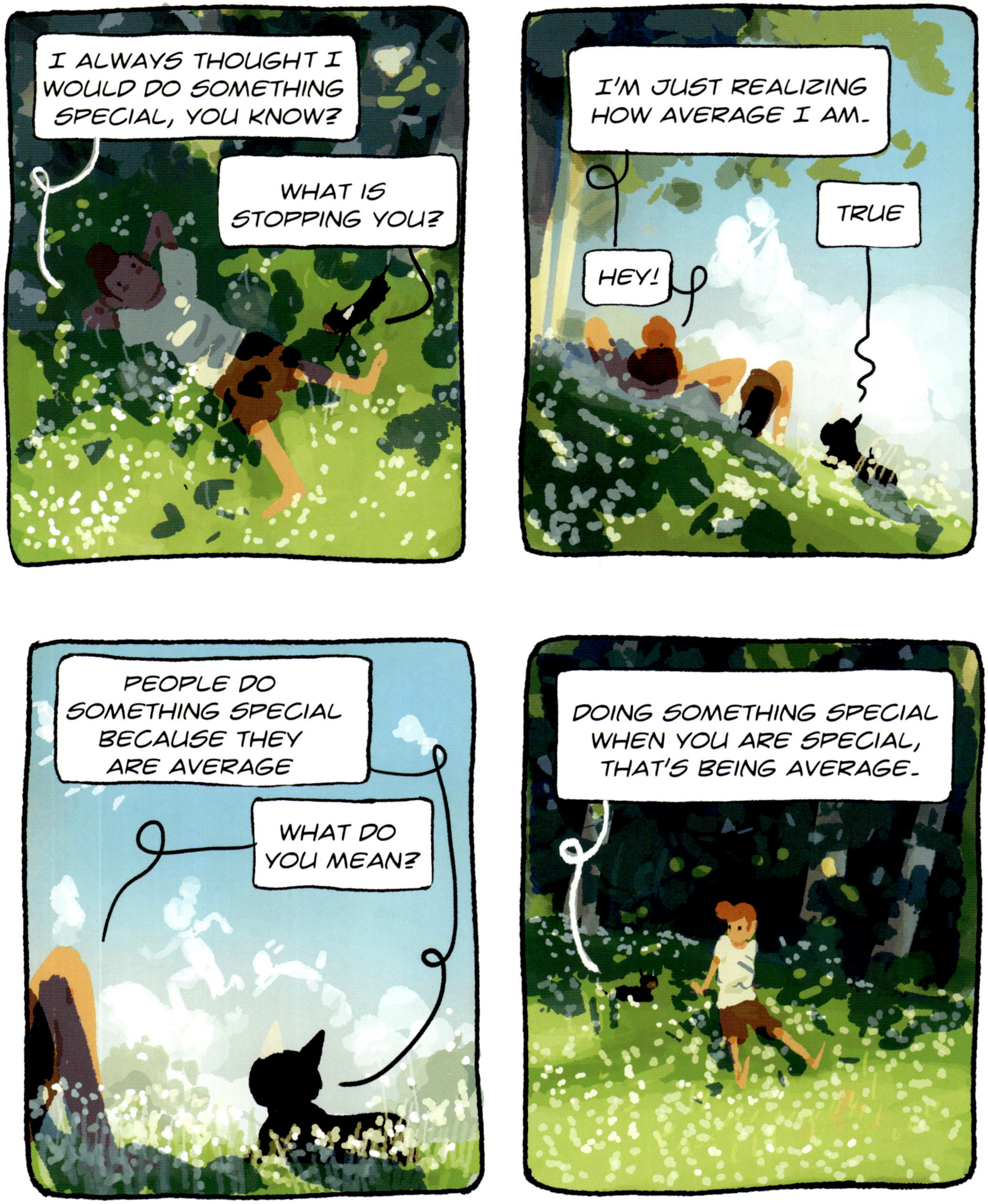
I ALWAYS THOUGHT I WOULD DO SOMETHING SPECIAL, YOU KNOW?
WHAT IS STOPPING YOU?
I'M JUST REALIZING HOW AVERAGE I AM.
HEY!
TRUE
PEOPLE DO SOMETHING SPECIAL BECAUSE THEY ARE AVERAGE
WHAT DO YOU MEAN?
DOING SOMETHING SPECIAL WHEN YOU ARE SPECIAL, THAT'S BEING AVERAGE.

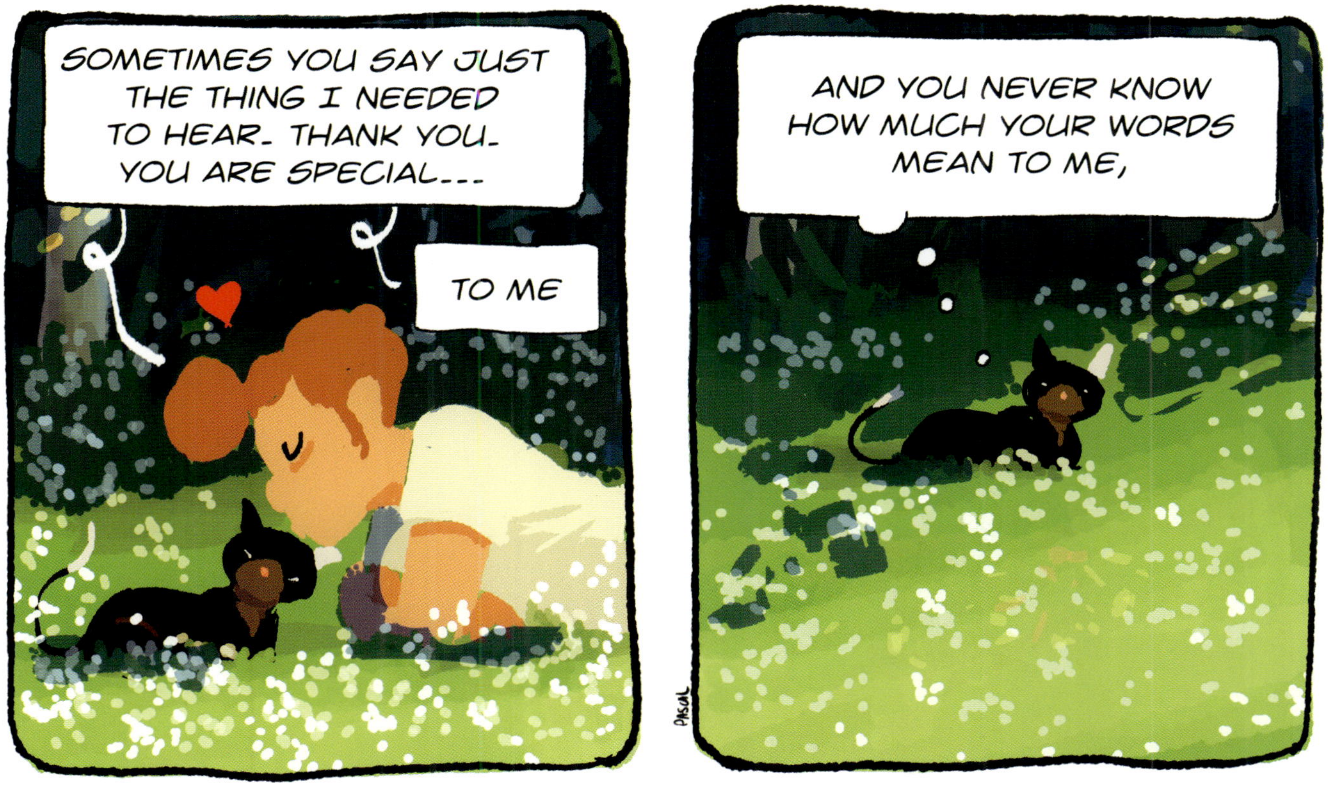
SOMETIMES YOU SAY JUST THE THING I NEEDED TO HEAR. THANK YOU. YOU ARE SPECIAL...
TO ME
PASCAL
AND YOU NEVER KNOW HOW MUCH YOUR WORDS MEAN TO ME,

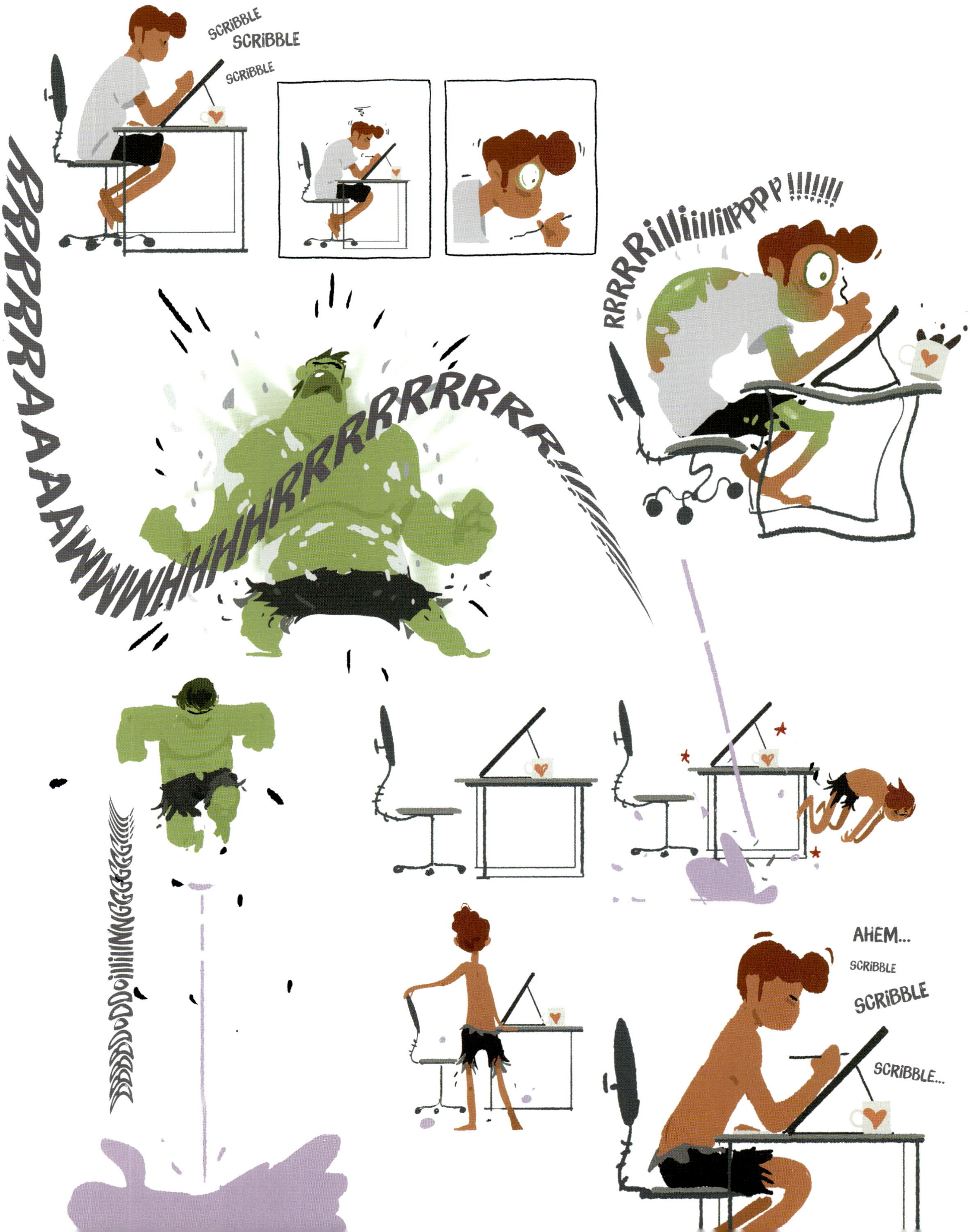
SCRIBBLE
SCRIBBLE
SCRIBBLE
RRRRRiiiiiiiPPPP!!!!!!!
RRRRRAAAAWWWHHHHHHRRRRRRRRRRRRR!!!!
DDDDooiiiiiiNNNGGGGG
AHEM...
SCRIBBLE
SCRIBBLE
SCRIBBLE...

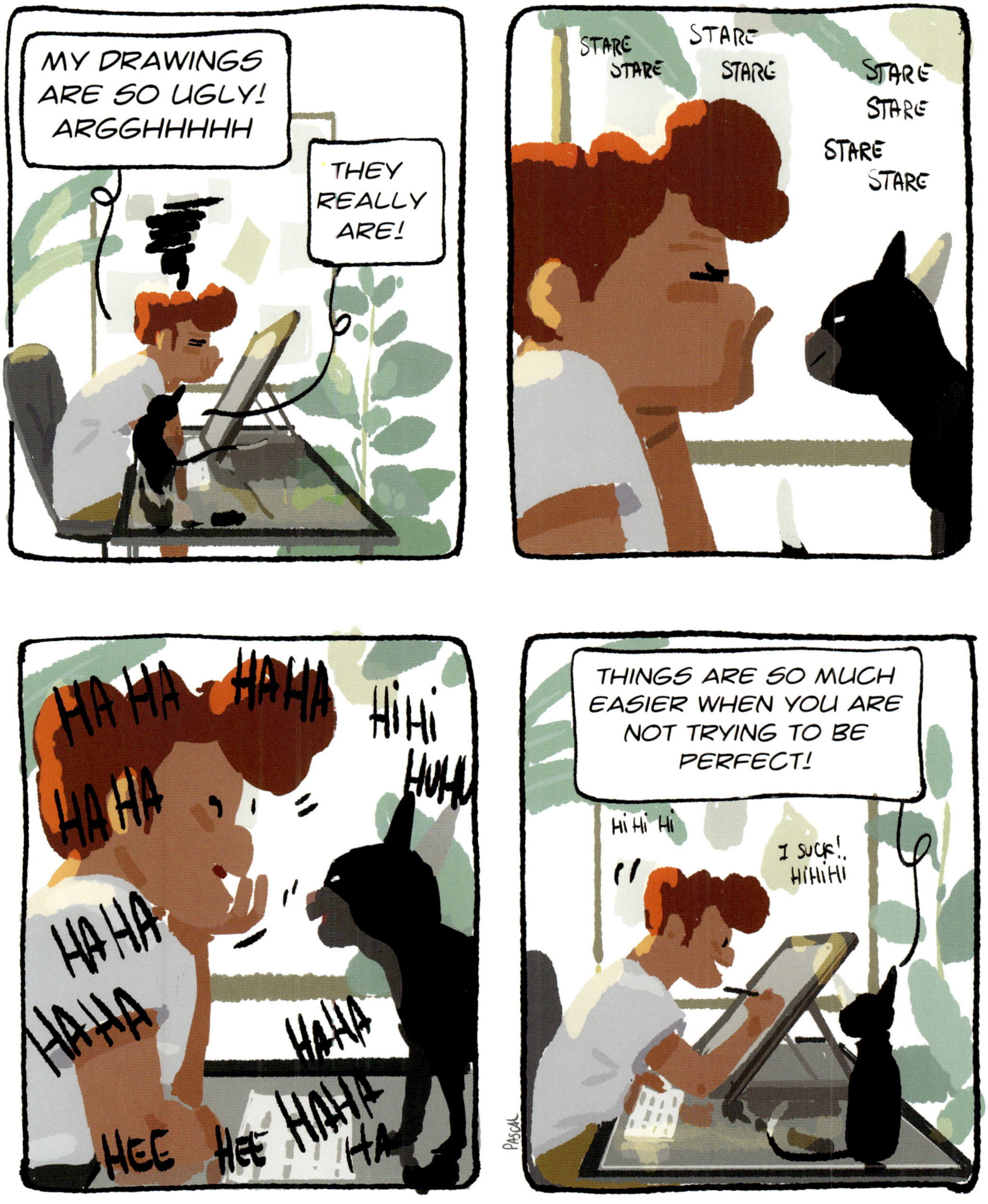
MY DRAWINGS ARE SO UGLY! ARGGHHHHH
THEY REALLY ARE!
STARE STARE STARE STARE STARE STARE STARE STARE
HA HA HAHA HI HI HUHU HA HA HAHA HAHA HAHA HAHA HEE HEE HA
PASCAL
THINGS ARE SO MUCH EASIER WHEN YOU ARE NOT TRYING TO BE PERFECT!
HI HI HI
I SUCK! HIHIHI

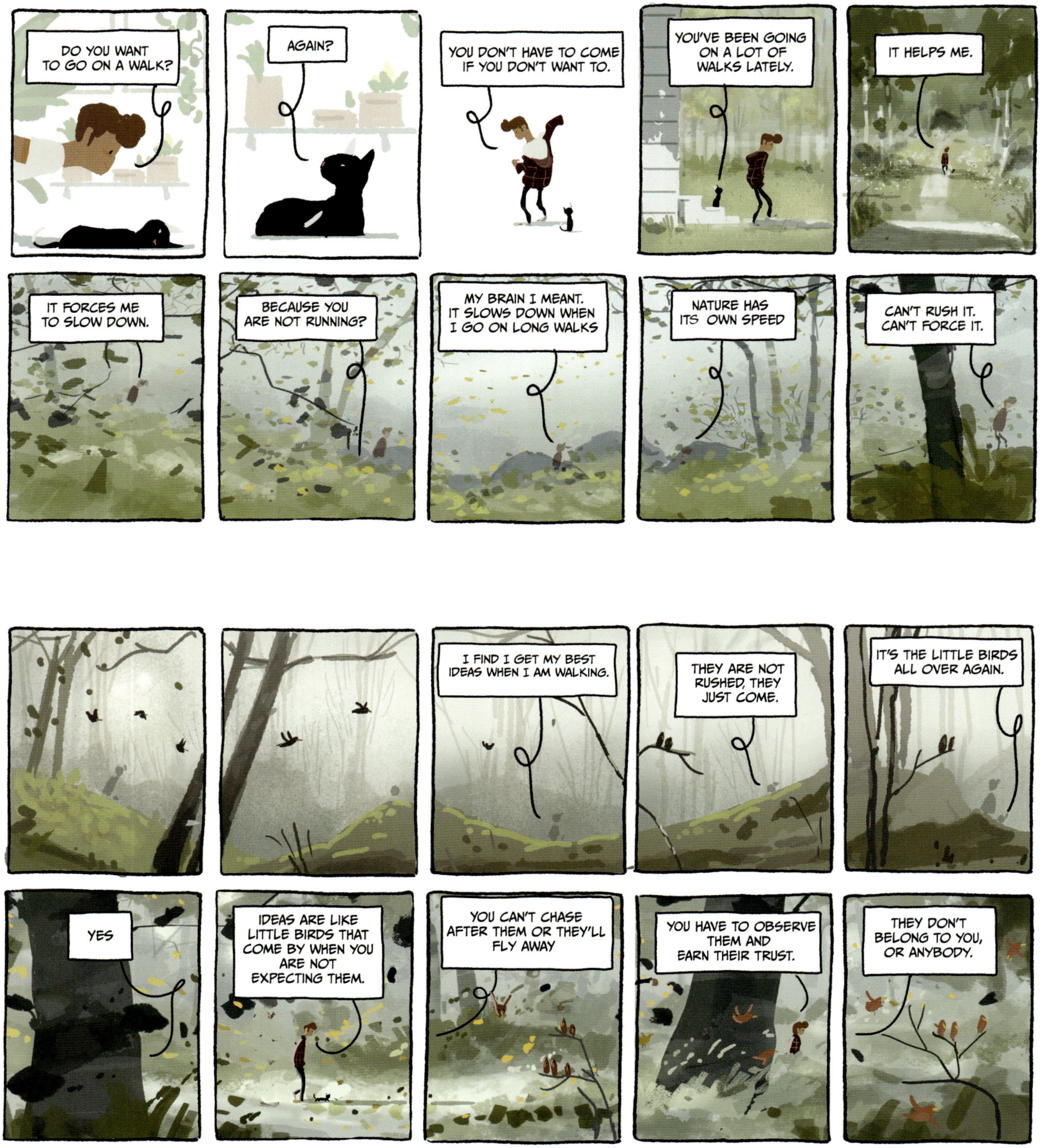
DO YOU WANT TO GO ON A WALK?
AGAIN?
YOU DON'T HAVE TO COME IF YOU DON'T WANT TO.
YOU'VE BEEN GOING ON A LOT OF WALKS LATELY.
IT HELPS ME.
IT FORCES ME TO SLOW DOWN.
BECAUSE YOU ARE NOT RUNNING?
MY BRAIN I MEANT. IT SLOWS DOWN WHEN I GO ON LONG WALKS
NATURE HAS ITS OWN SPEED
CAN'T RUSH IT. CAN'T FORCE IT.
I FIND I GET MY BEST IDEAS WHEN I AM WALKING.
THEY ARE NOT RUSHED, THEY JUST COME.
IT'S THE LITTLE BIRDS ALL OVER AGAIN.
YES
IDEAS ARE LIKE LITTLE BIRDS THAT COME BY WHEN YOU ARE NOT EXPECTING THEM.
YOU CAN'T CHASE AFTER THEM OR THEY'LL FLY AWAY
YOU HAVE TO OBSERVE THEM AND EARN THEIR TRUST.
THEY DON'T BELONG TO YOU, OR ANYBODY.

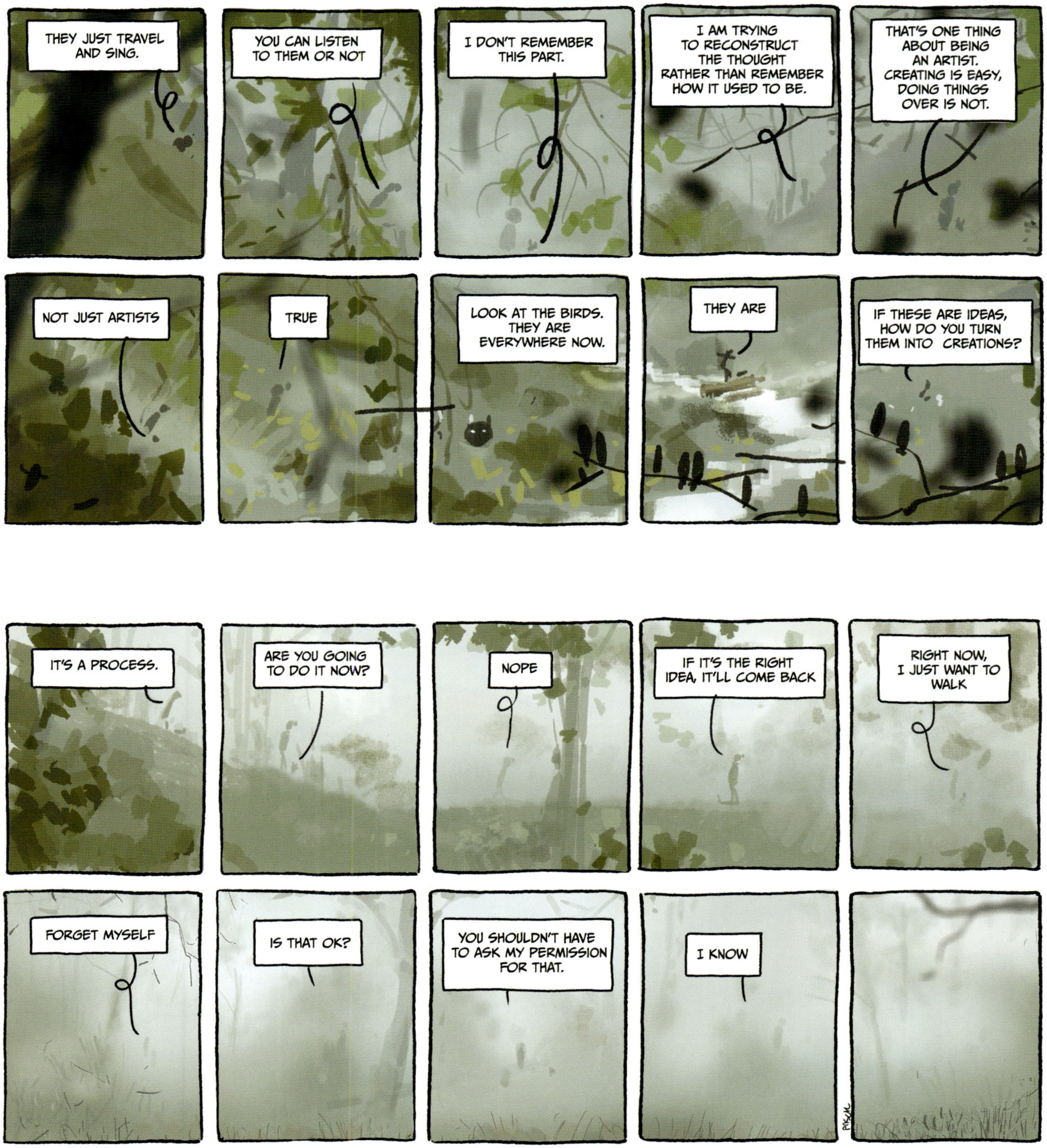
THEY JUST TRAVEL AND SING.
YOU CAN LISTEN TO THEM OR NOT
I DON'T REMEMBER THIS PART.
I AM TRYING TO RECONSTRUCT THE THOUGHT RATHER THAN REMEMBER HOW IT USED TO BE.
THAT'S ONE THING ABOUT BEING AN ARTIST. CREATING IS EASY, DOING THINGS OVER IS NOT.
NOT JUST ARTISTS
TRUE
LOOK AT THE BIRDS. THEY ARE EVERYWHERE NOW.
THEY ARE
IF THESE ARE IDEAS, HOW DO YOU TURN THEM INTO CREATIONS?
IT'S A PROCESS.
ARE YOU GOING TO DO IT NOW?
NOPE
IF IT'S THE RIGHT IDEA, IT'LL COME BACK
RIGHT NOW, I JUST WANT TO WALK
FORGET MYSELF
IS THAT OK?
YOU SHOULDN'T HAVE TO ASK MY PERMISSION FOR THAT.
I KNOW
PASCAL

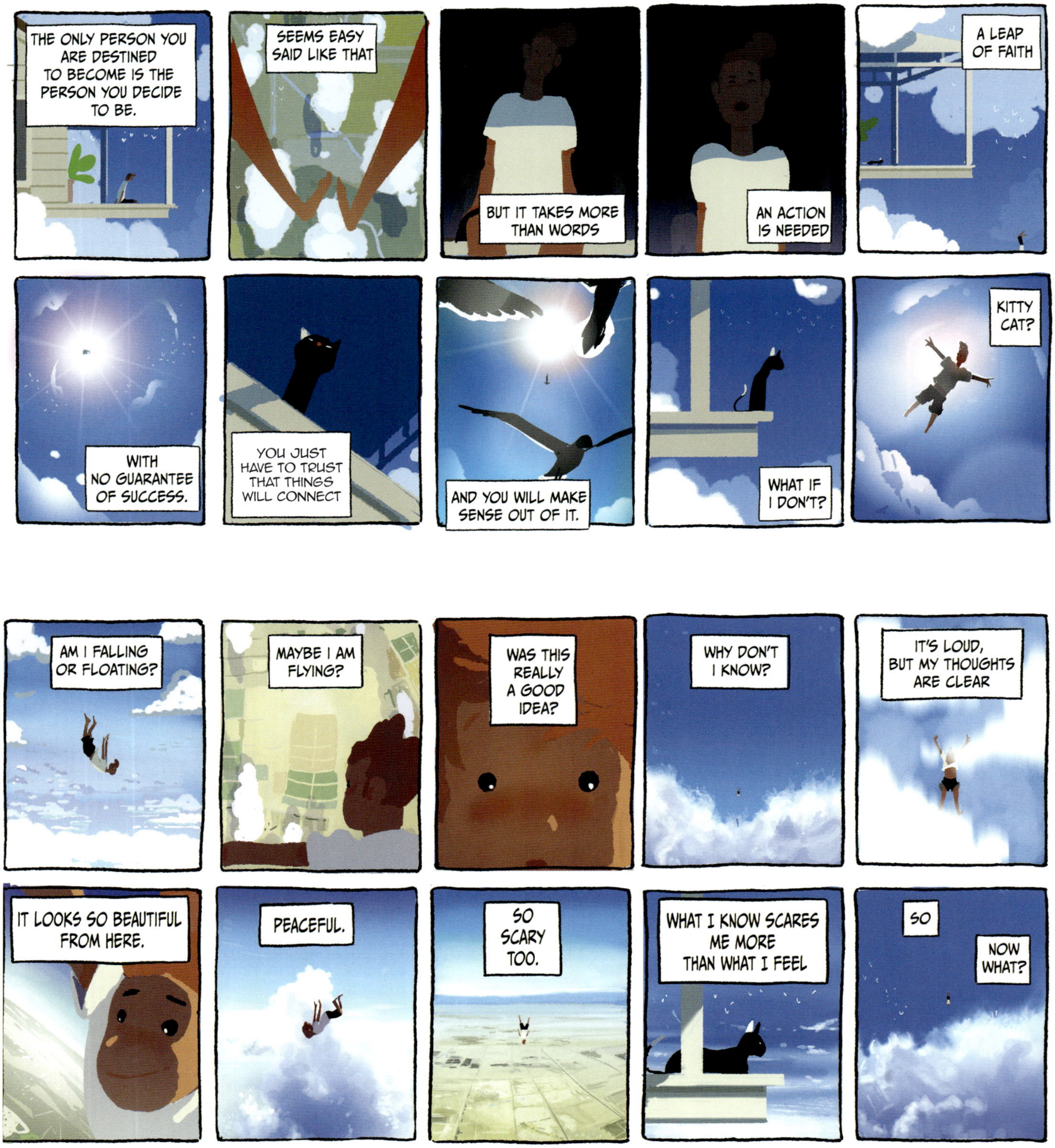
THE ONLY PERSON YOU ARE DESTINED TO BECOME IS THE PERSON YOU DECIDE TO BE.
SEEMS EASY SAID LIKE THAT
BUT IT TAKES MORE THAN WORDS
AN ACTION IS NEEDED
A LEAP OF FAITH
WITH NO GUARANTEE OF SUCCESS.
YOU JUST HAVE TO TRUST THAT THINGS WILL CONNECT
AND YOU WILL MAKE SENSE OUT OF IT.
WHAT IF I DON'T?
KITTY CAT?
AM I FALLING OR FLOATING?
MAYBE I AM FLYING?
WAS THIS REALLY A GOOD IDEA?
WHY DON'T I KNOW?
IT'S LOUD, BUT MY THOUGHTS ARE CLEAR
IT LOOKS SO BEAUTIFUL FROM HERE.
PEACEFUL.
SO SCARY TOO.
WHAT I KNOW SCARES ME MORE THAN WHAT I FEEL
SO
NOW WHAT?

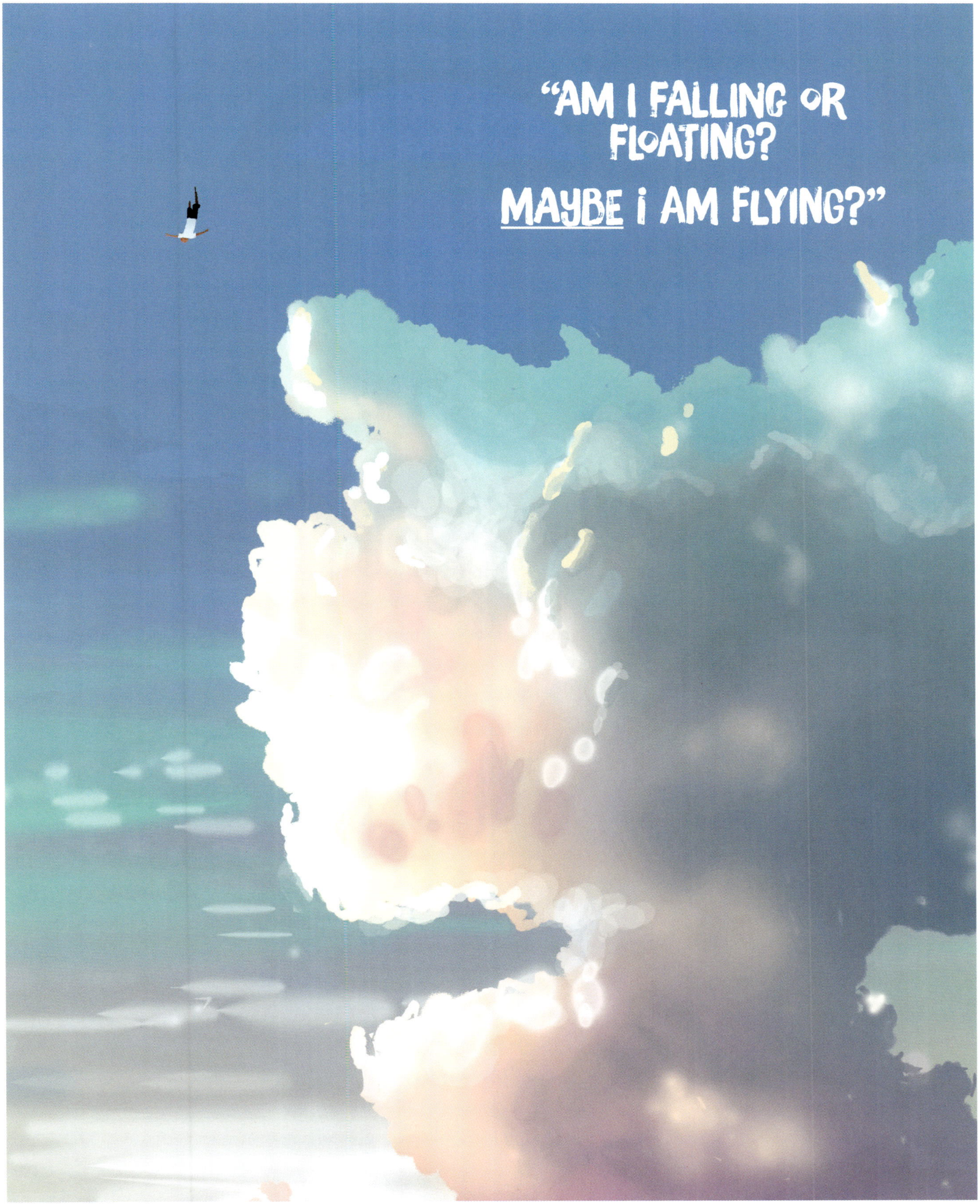
"AM I FALLING OR FLOATING?
MAYBE I AM FLYING?"

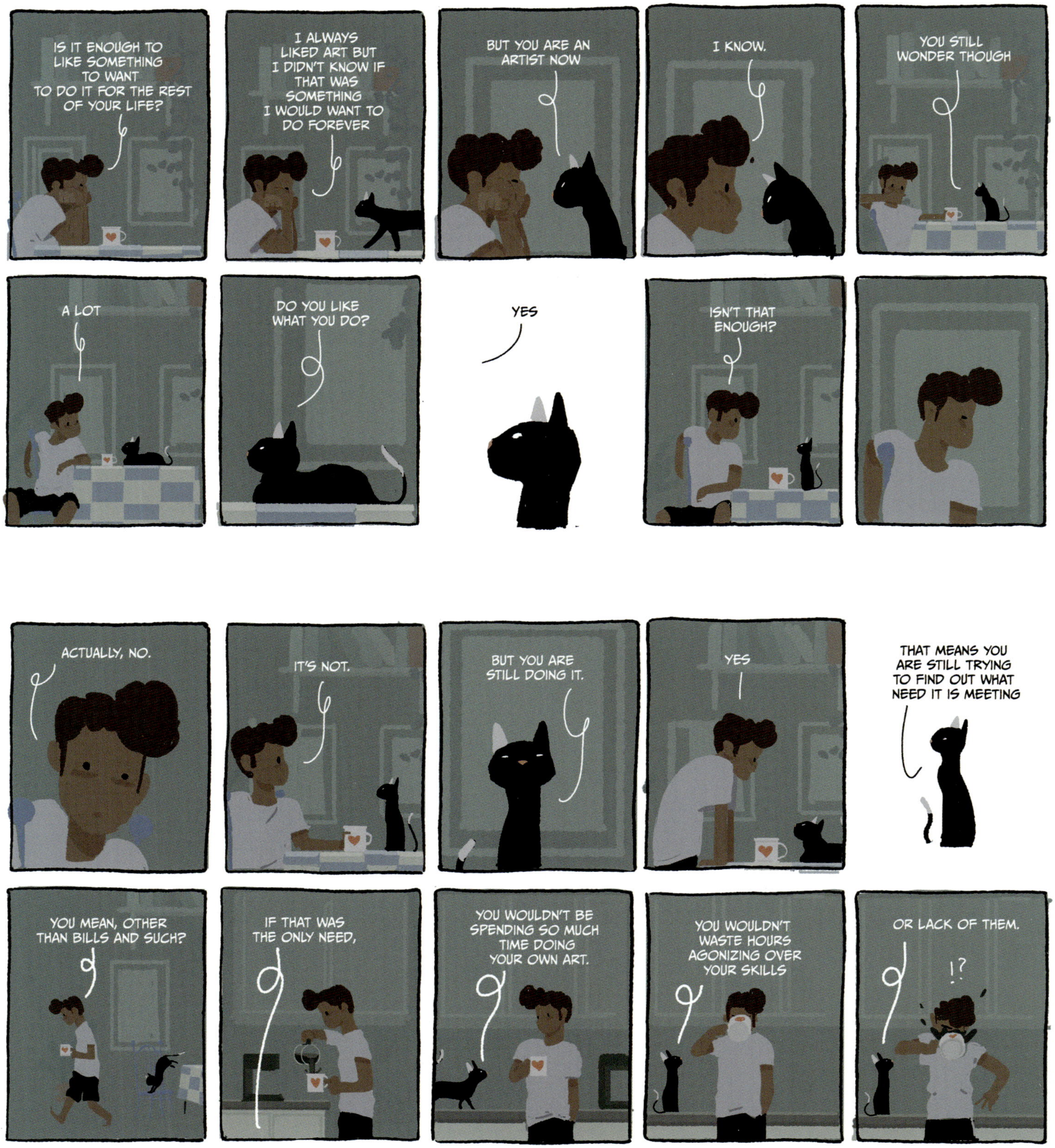
IS IT ENOUGH TO LIKE SOMETHING TO WANT TO DO IT FOR THE REST OF YOUR LIFE?
I ALWAYS LIKED ART BUT I DIDN'T KNOW IF THAT WAS SOMETHING I WOULD WANT TO DO FOREVER
BUT YOU ARE AN ARTIST NOW
I KNOW.
YOU STILL WONDER THOUGH
A LOT
DO YOU LIKE WHAT YOU DO?
YES
ISN'T THAT ENOUGH?
ACTUALLY, NO.
IT'S NOT.
BUT YOU ARE STILL DOING IT.
YES
THAT MEANS YOU ARE STILL TRYING TO FIND OUT WHAT NEED IT IS MEETING
YOU MEAN, OTHER THAN BILLS AND SUCH?
IF THAT WAS THE ONLY NEED,
YOU WOULDN'T BE SPENDING SO MUCH TIME DOING YOUR OWN ART.
YOU WOULDN'T WASTE HOURS AGONIZING OVER YOUR SKILLS
OR LACK OF THEM.
!?

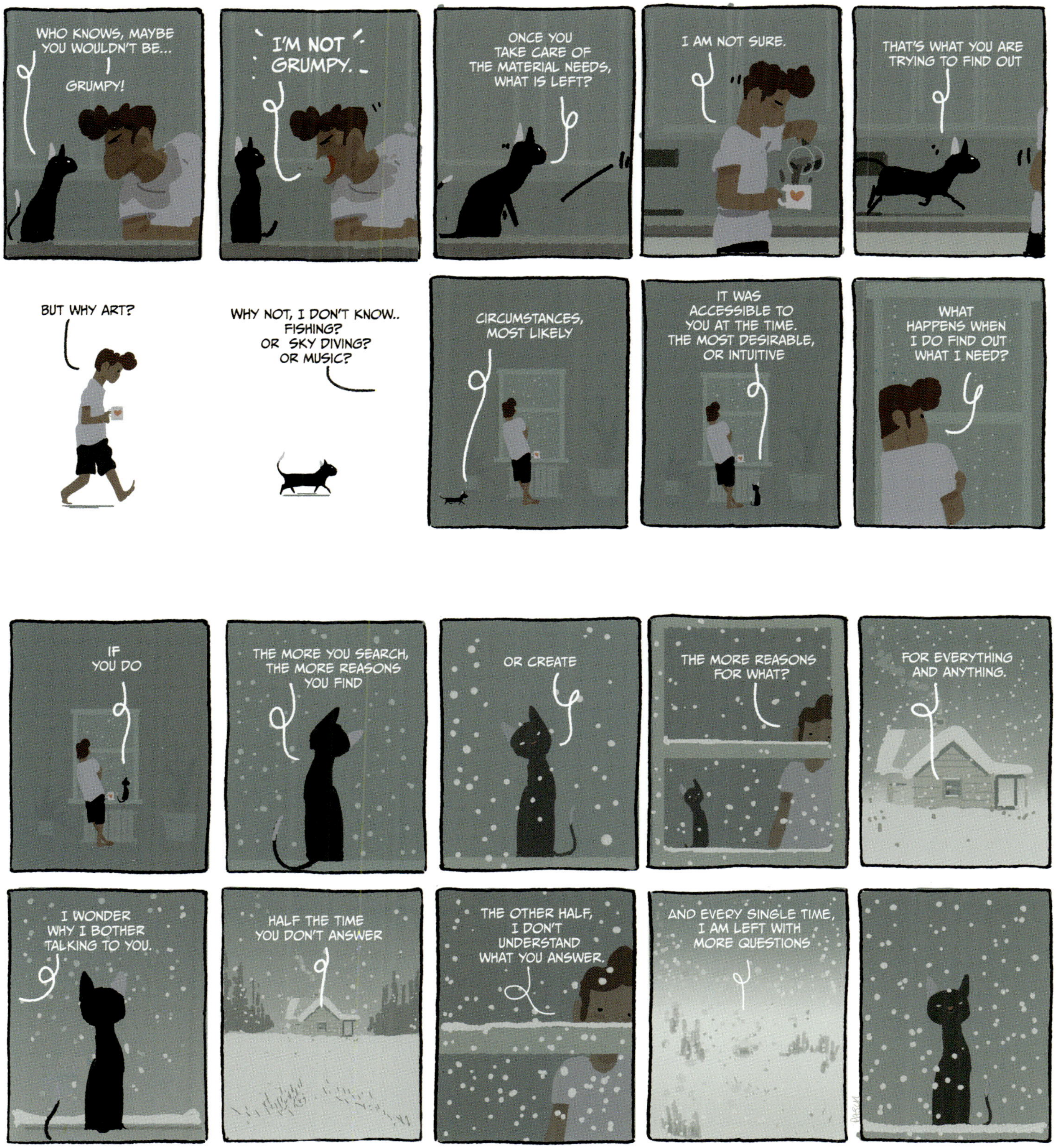
WHO KNOWS, MAYBE YOU WOULDN'T BE...
GRUMPY!
I'M NOT GRUMPY.
ONCE YOU TAKE CARE OF THE MATERIAL NEEDS, WHAT IS LEFT?
I AM NOT SURE.
THAT'S WHAT YOU ARE TRYING TO FIND OUT
BUT WHY ART?
WHY NOT, I DON'T KNOW.. FISHING? OR SKY DIVING? OR MUSIC?
CIRCUMSTANCES, MOST LIKELY
IT WAS ACCESSIBLE TO YOU AT THE TIME. THE MOST DESIRABLE, OR INTUITIVE
WHAT HAPPENS WHEN I DO FIND OUT WHAT I NEED?
IF YOU DO
THE MORE YOU SEARCH, THE MORE REASONS YOU FIND
OR CREATE
THE MORE REASONS FOR WHAT?
FOR EVERYTHING AND ANYTHING.
I WONDER WHY I BOTHER TALKING TO YOU.
HALF THE TIME YOU DON'T ANSWER
THE OTHER HALF, I DON'T UNDERSTAND WHAT YOU ANSWER.
AND EVERY SINGLE TIME, I AM LEFT WITH MORE QUESTIONS

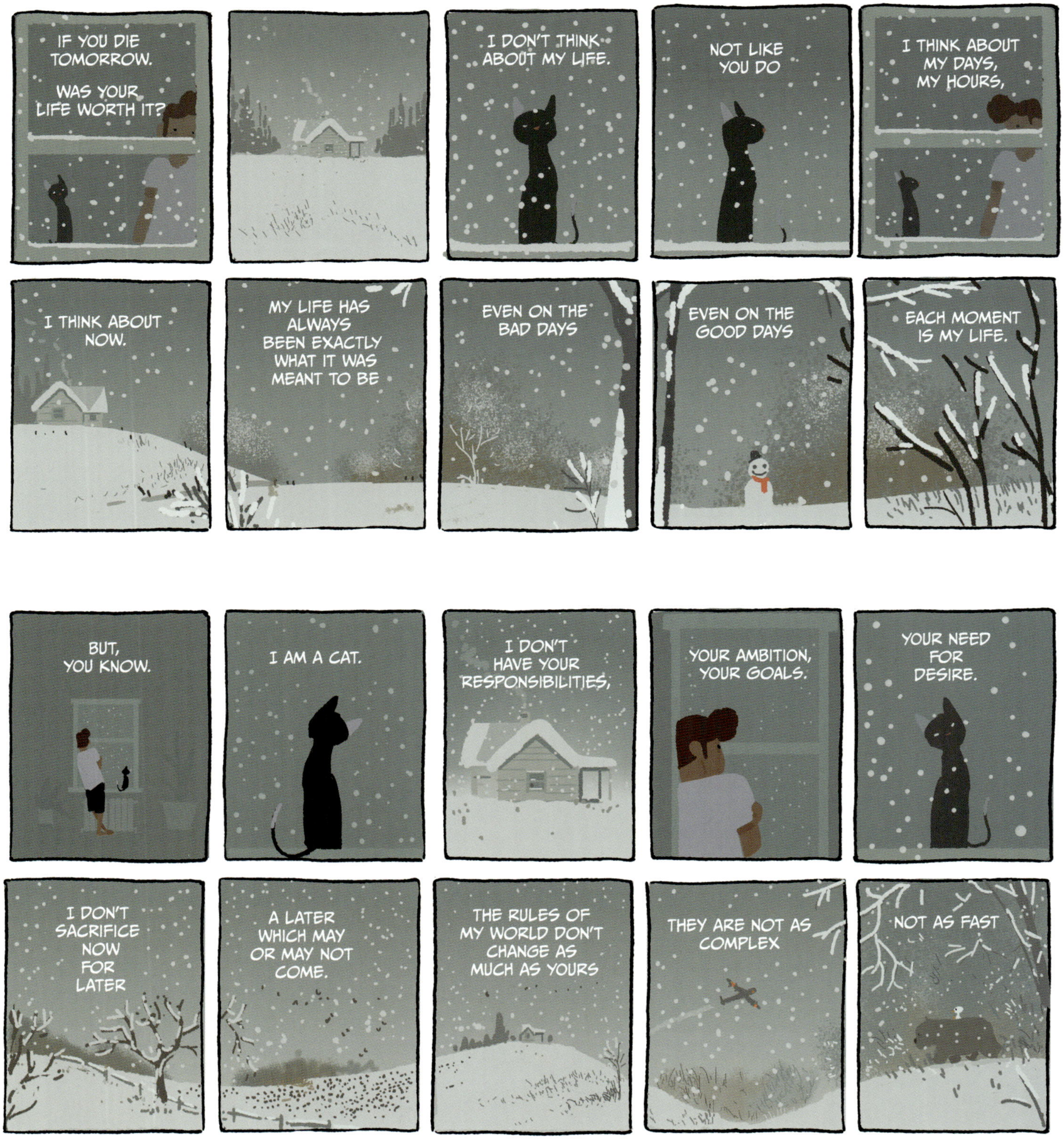
IF YOU DIE TOMORROW.
WAS YOUR LIFE WORTH IT?
I DON'T THINK ABOUT MY LIFE.
NOT LIKE YOU DO
I THINK ABOUT MY DAYS, MY HOURS,
I THINK ABOUT NOW.
MY LIFE HAS ALWAYS BEEN EXACTLY WHAT IT WAS MEANT TO BE
EVEN ON THE BAD DAYS
EVEN ON THE GOOD DAYS
EACH MOMENT IS MY LIFE.
BUT, YOU KNOW.
I AM A CAT.
I DON'T HAVE YOUR RESPONSIBILITIES,
YOUR AMBITION, YOUR GOALS.
YOUR NEED FOR DESIRE.
I DON'T SACRIFICE NOW FOR LATER
A LATER WHICH MAY OR MAY NOT COME.
THE RULES OF MY WORLD DON'T CHANGE AS MUCH AS YOURS
THEY ARE NOT AS COMPLEX
NOT AS FAST

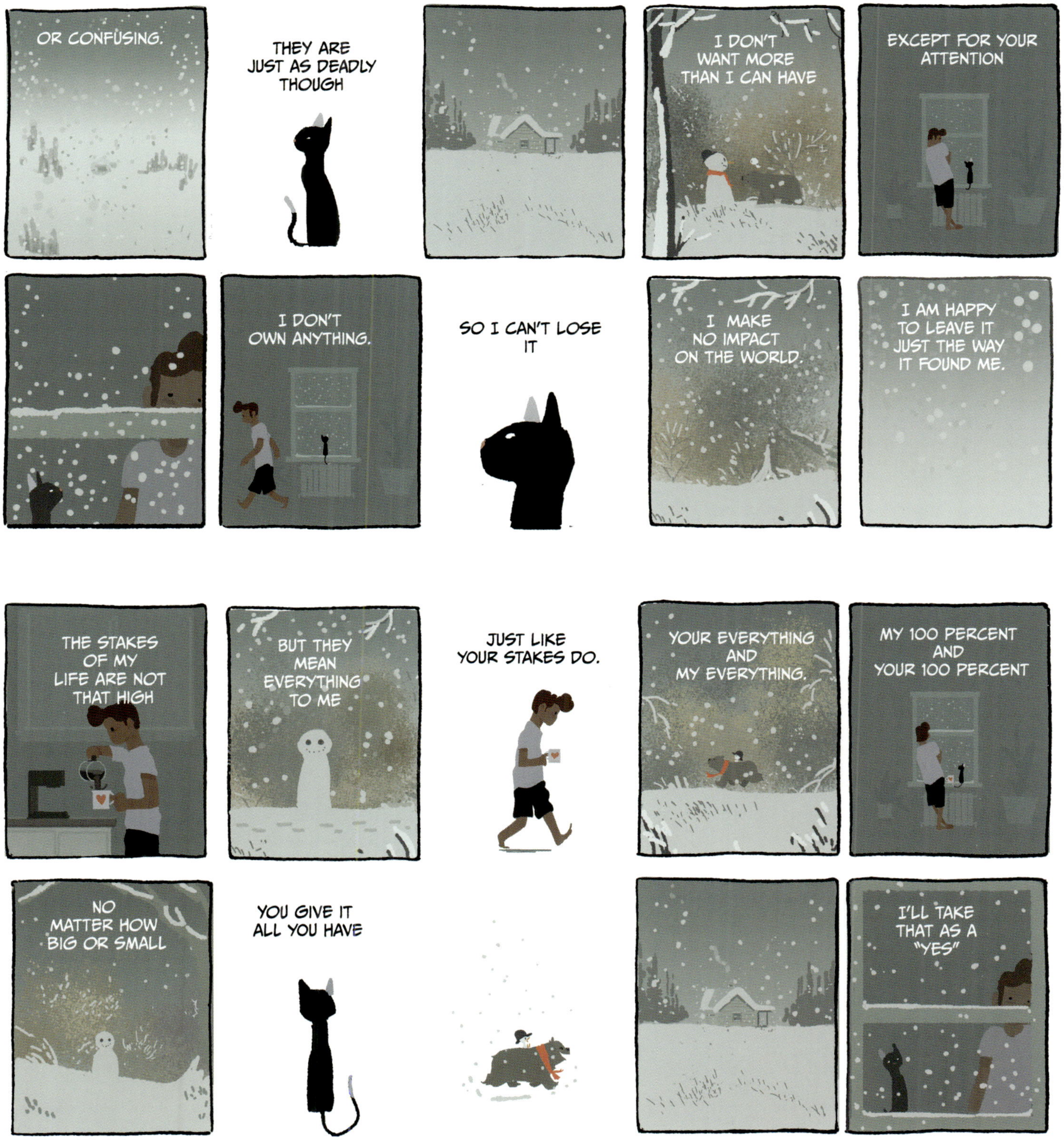
OR CONFUSING.
THEY ARE JUST AS DEADLY THOUGH
I DON'T WANT MORE THAN I CAN HAVE
EXCEPT FOR YOUR ATTENTION
I DON'T OWN ANYTHING.
SO I CAN'T LOSE IT
I MAKE NO IMPACT ON THE WORLD.
I AM HAPPY TO LEAVE IT JUST THE WAY IT FOUND ME.
THE STAKES OF MY LIFE ARE NOT THAT HIGH
BUT THEY MEAN EVERYTHING TO ME
JUST LIKE YOUR STAKES DO.
YOUR EVERYTHING AND MY EVERYTHING.
MY 100 PERCENT AND YOUR 100 PERCENT
NO MATTER HOW BIG OR SMALL
YOU GIVE IT ALL YOU HAVE
I'LL TAKE THAT AS A "YES"

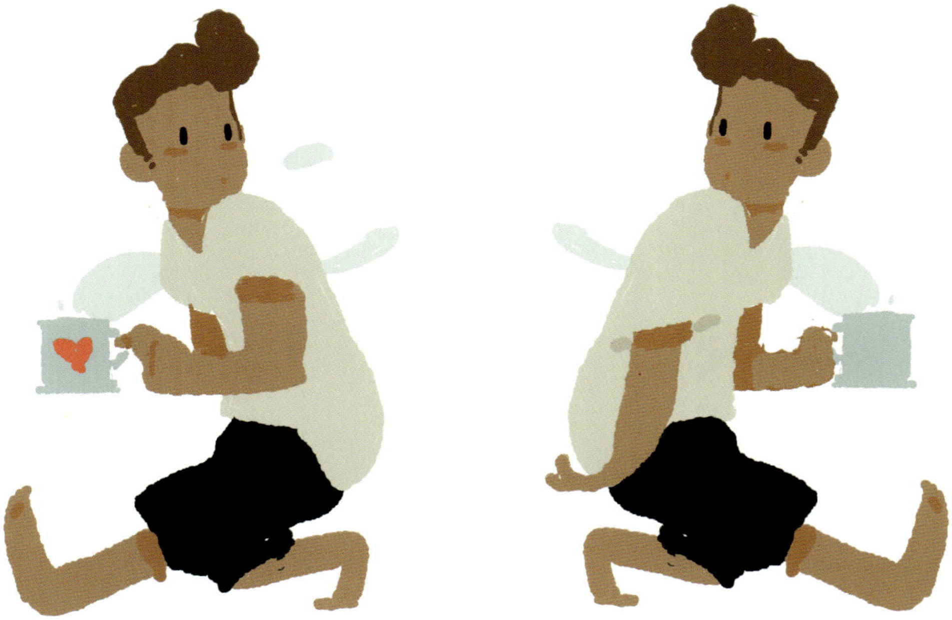

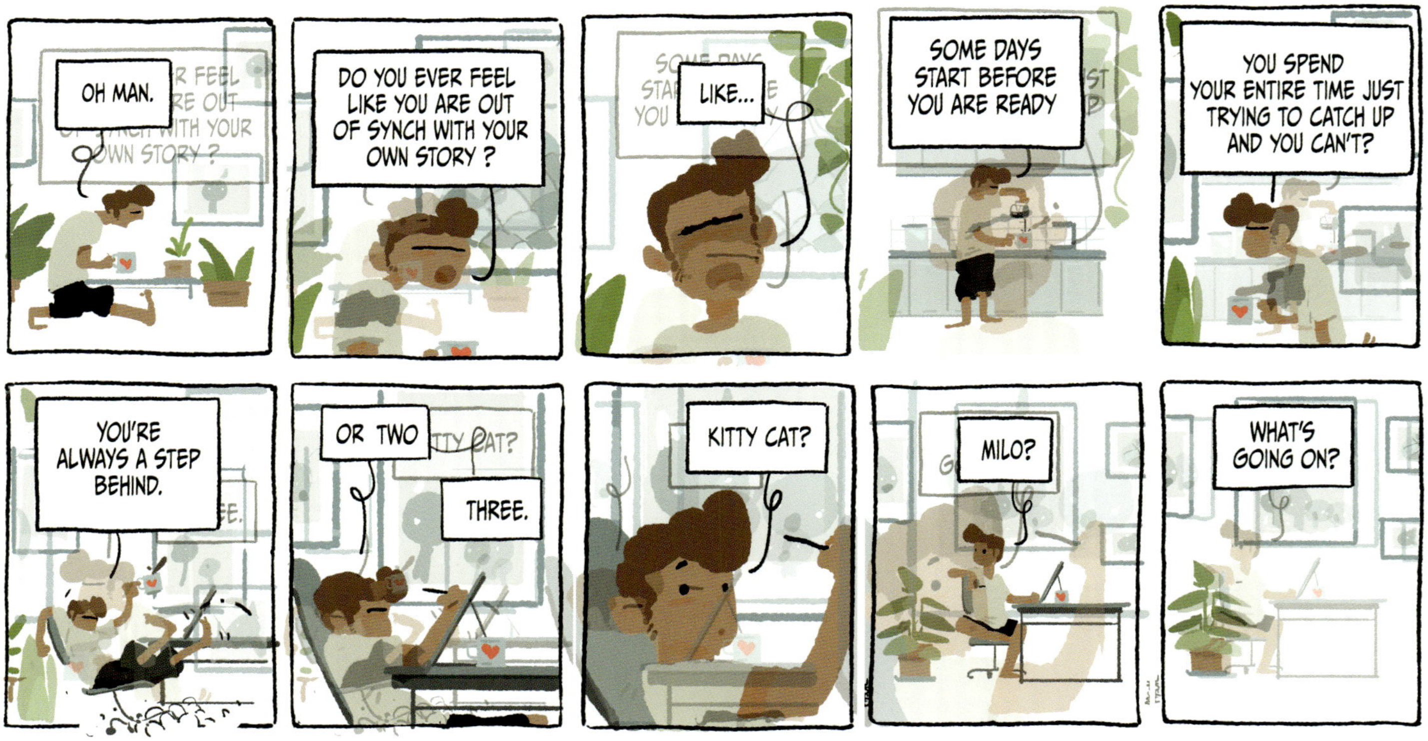
OH MAN.
DO YOU EVER FEEL LIKE YOU ARE OUT OF SYNCH WITH YOUR OWN STORY ?
LIKE...
SOME DAYS START BEFORE YOU ARE READY
YOU SPEND YOUR ENTIRE TIME JUST TRYING TO CATCH UP AND YOU CAN'T?
YOU'RE ALWAYS A STEP BEHIND.
OR TWO
THREE.
KITTY CAT?
MILO?
WHAT'S GOING ON?

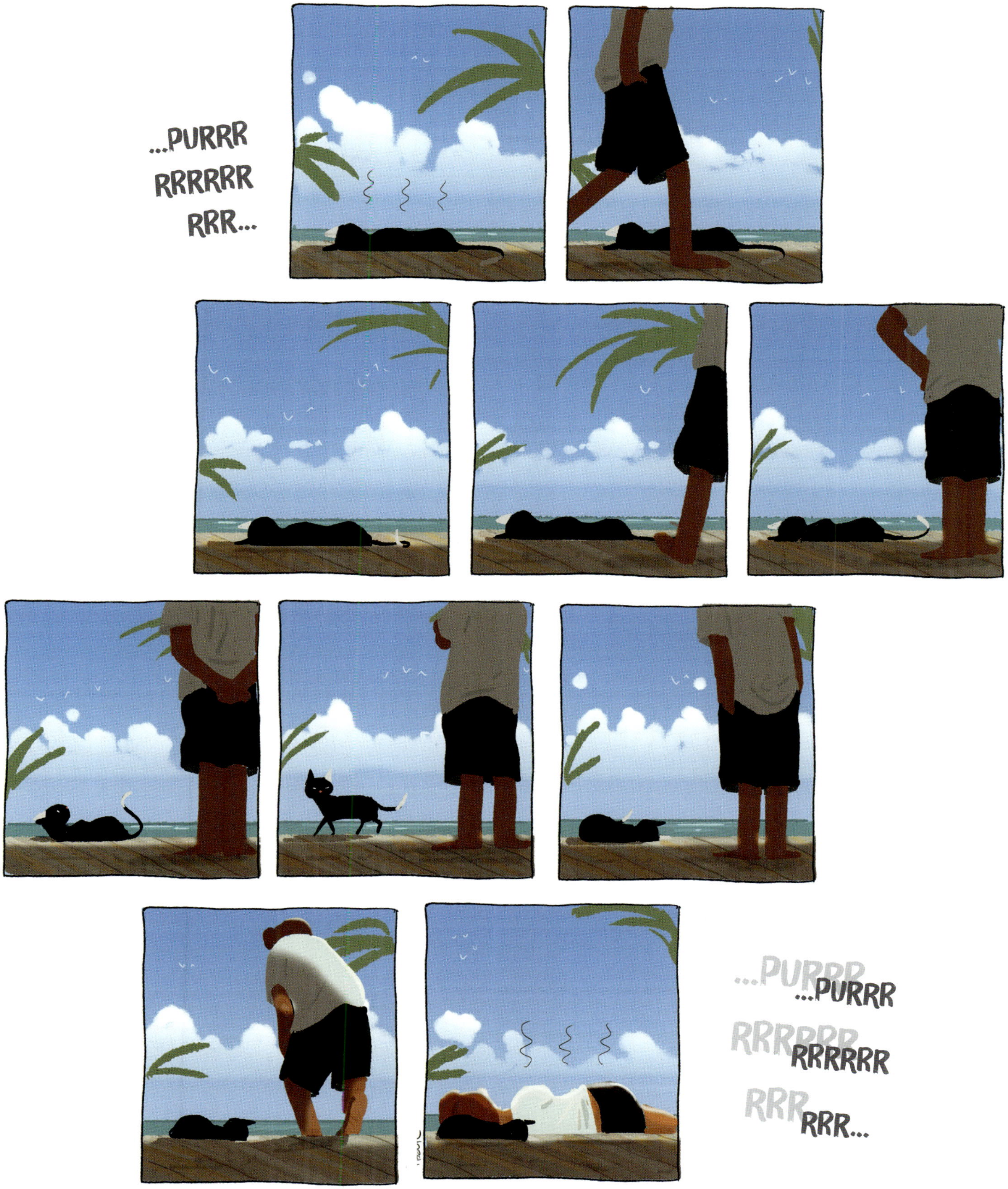
...PURRR
RRRRRR
RRR...
...PURRR
RRRRRR
RRR
...PURRR
RRRRRR
RRR...

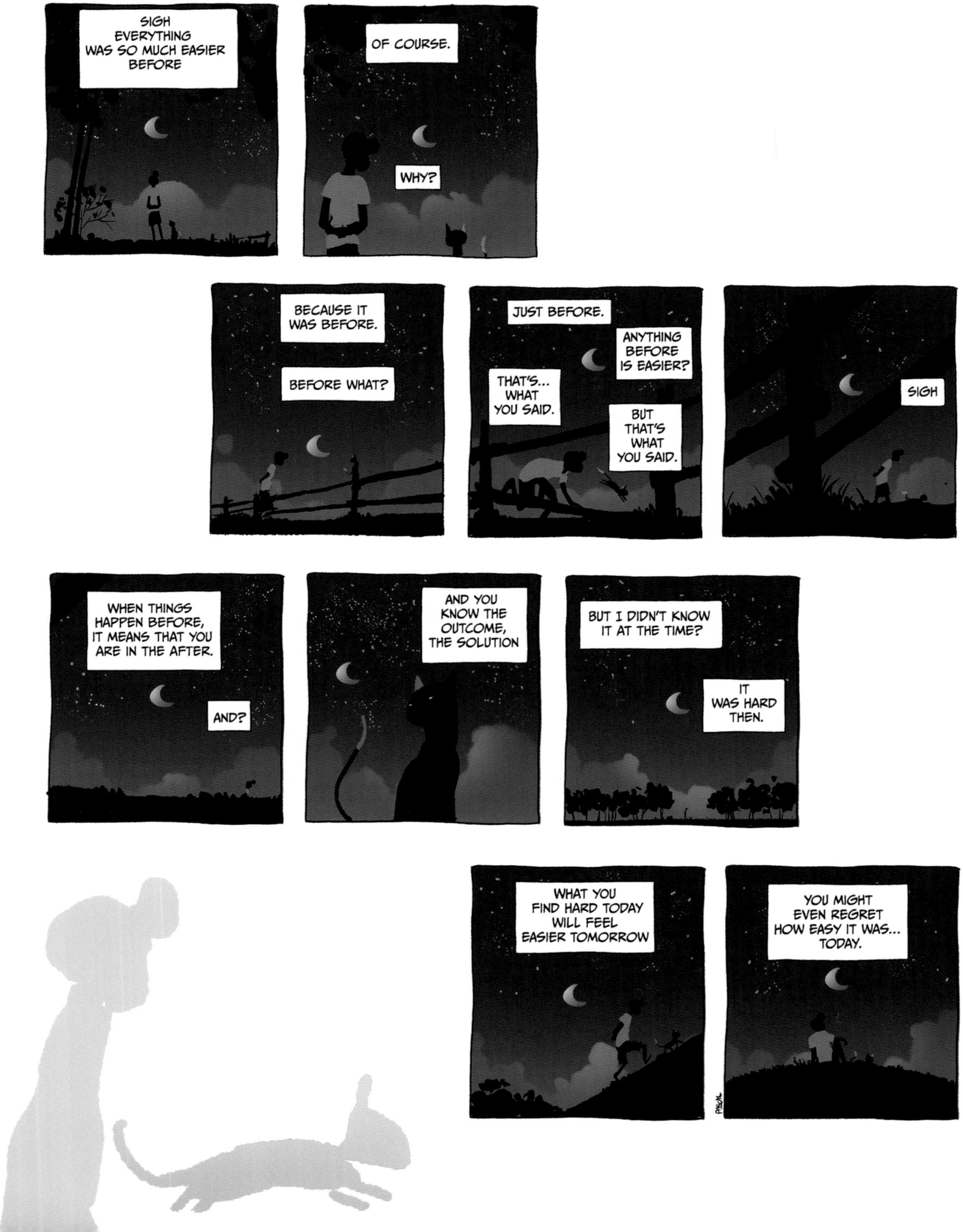
SIGH
EVERYTHING WAS SO MUCH EASIER BEFORE
OF COURSE.
WHY?
BECAUSE IT WAS BEFORE.
BEFORE WHAT?
JUST BEFORE.
ANYTHING BEFORE IS EASIER?
THAT'S... WHAT YOU SAID.
BUT THAT'S WHAT YOU SAID.
SIGH
WHEN THINGS HAPPEN BEFORE, IT MEANS THAT YOU ARE IN THE AFTER.
AND?
AND YOU KNOW THE OUTCOME, THE SOLUTION
BUT I DIDN'T KNOW IT AT THE TIME?
IT WAS HARD THEN.
WHAT YOU FIND HARD TODAY WILL FEEL EASIER TOMORROW
YOU MIGHT EVEN REGRET HOW EASY IT WAS... TODAY.

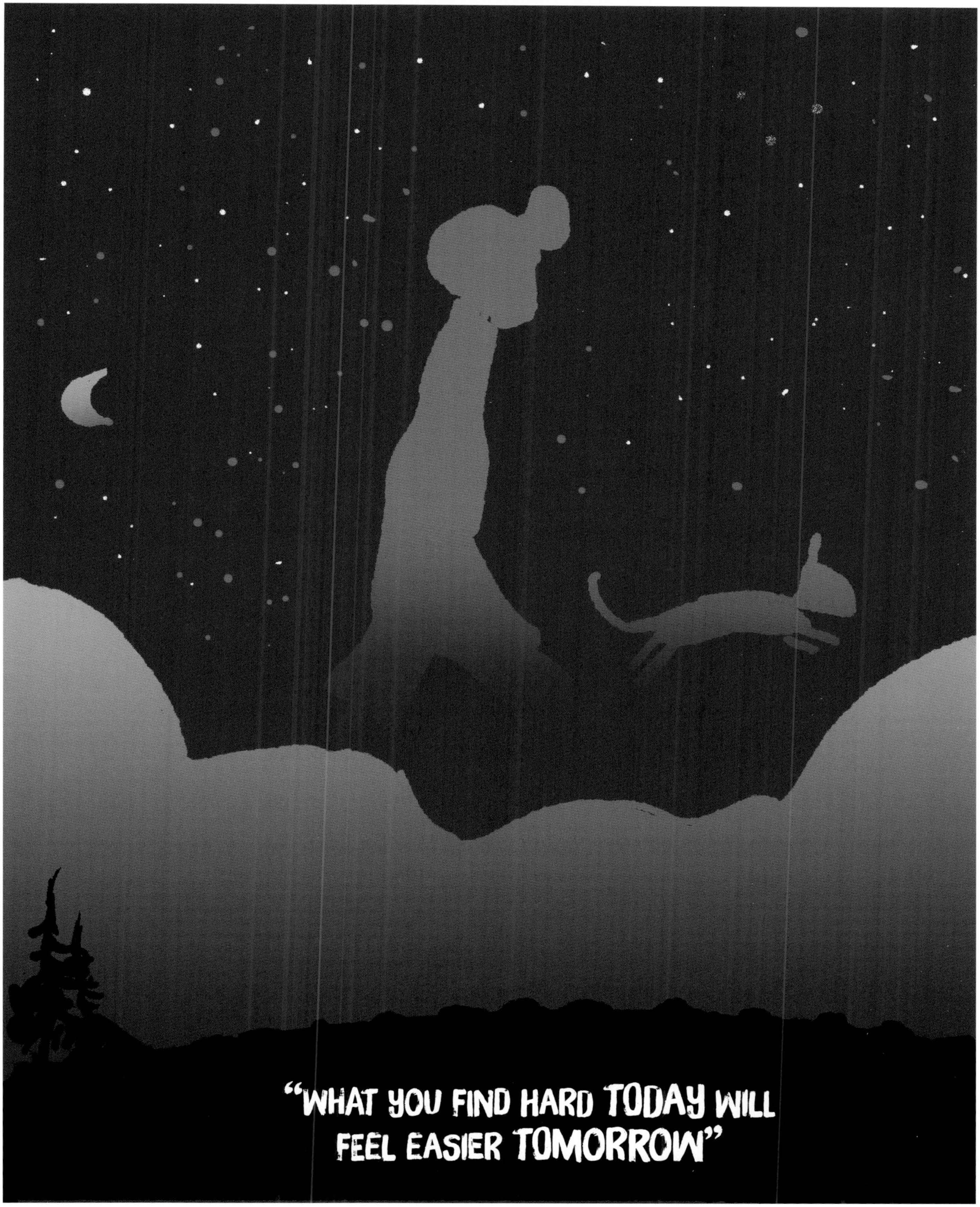
"WHAT YOU FIND HARD TODAY WILL
FEEL EASIER TOMORROW"

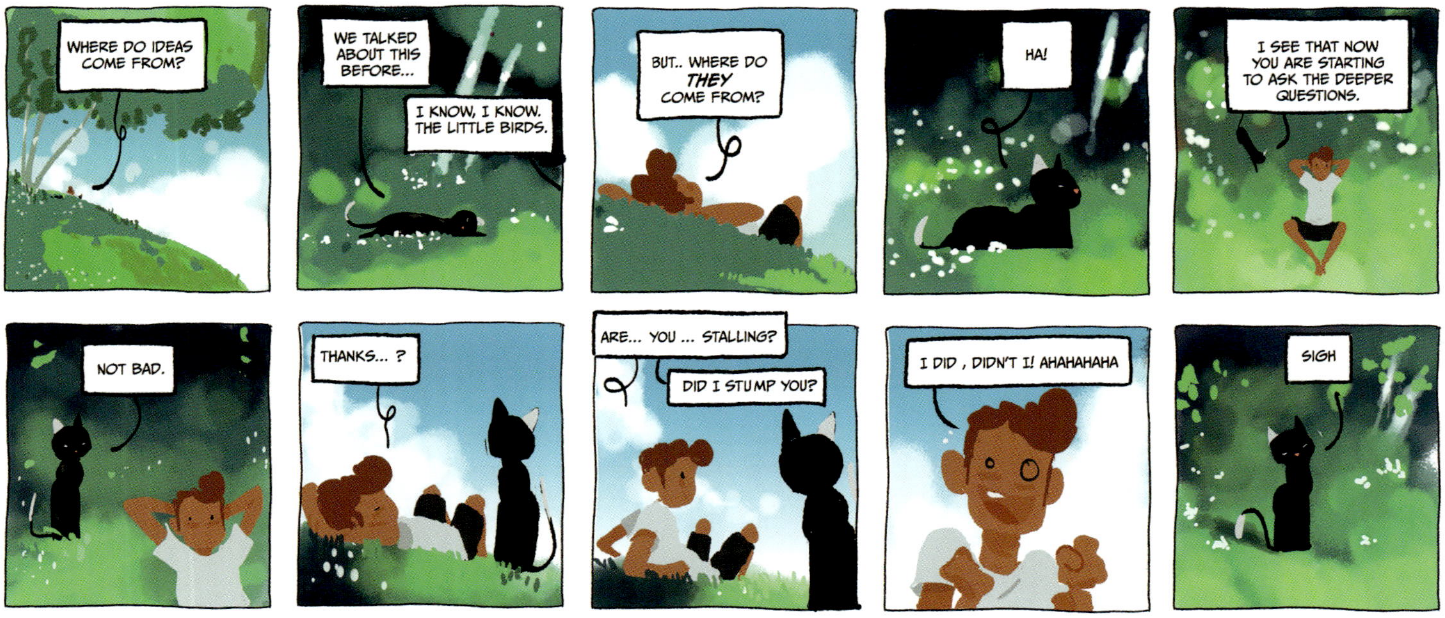
WHERE DO IDEAS COME FROM?
WE TALKED ABOUT THIS BEFORE...
I KNOW, I KNOW. THE LITTLE BIRDS.
BUT.. WHERE DO *THEY* COME FROM?
HA!
I SEE THAT NOW YOU ARE STARTING TO ASK THE DEEPER QUESTIONS.
NOT BAD.
THANKS... ?
ARE... YOU ... STALLING?
DID I STUMP YOU?
I DID , DIDN'T I! AHAHAHAHA
SIGH

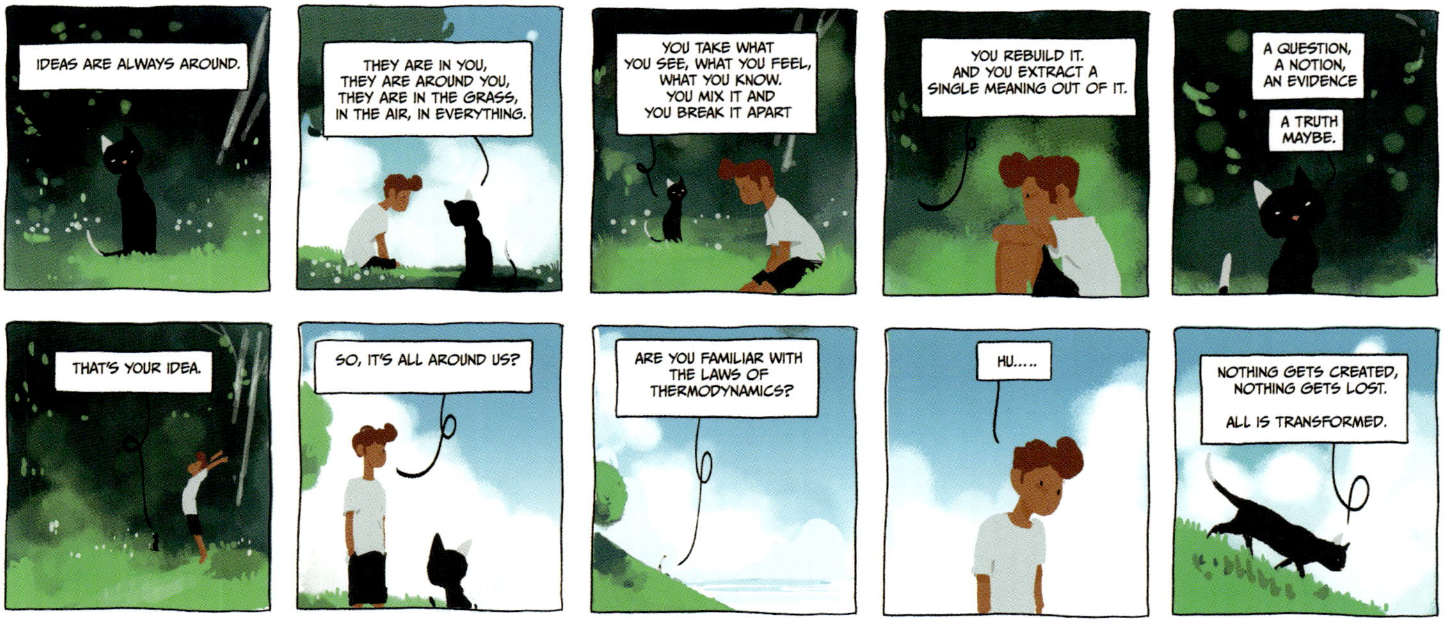
IDEAS ARE ALWAYS AROUND.
THEY ARE IN YOU, THEY ARE AROUND YOU, THEY ARE IN THE GRASS, IN THE AIR, IN EVERYTHING.
YOU TAKE WHAT YOU SEE, WHAT YOU FEEL, WHAT YOU KNOW. YOU MIX IT AND YOU BREAK IT APART
YOU REBUILD IT. AND YOU EXTRACT A SINGLE MEANING OUT OF IT.
A QUESTION, A NOTION, AN EVIDENCE
A TRUTH MAYBE.
THAT'S YOUR IDEA.
SO, IT'S ALL AROUND US?
ARE YOU FAMILIAR WITH THE LAWS OF THERMODYNAMICS?
HU.....
NOTHING GETS CREATED, NOTHING GETS LOST.
ALL IS TRANSFORMED.

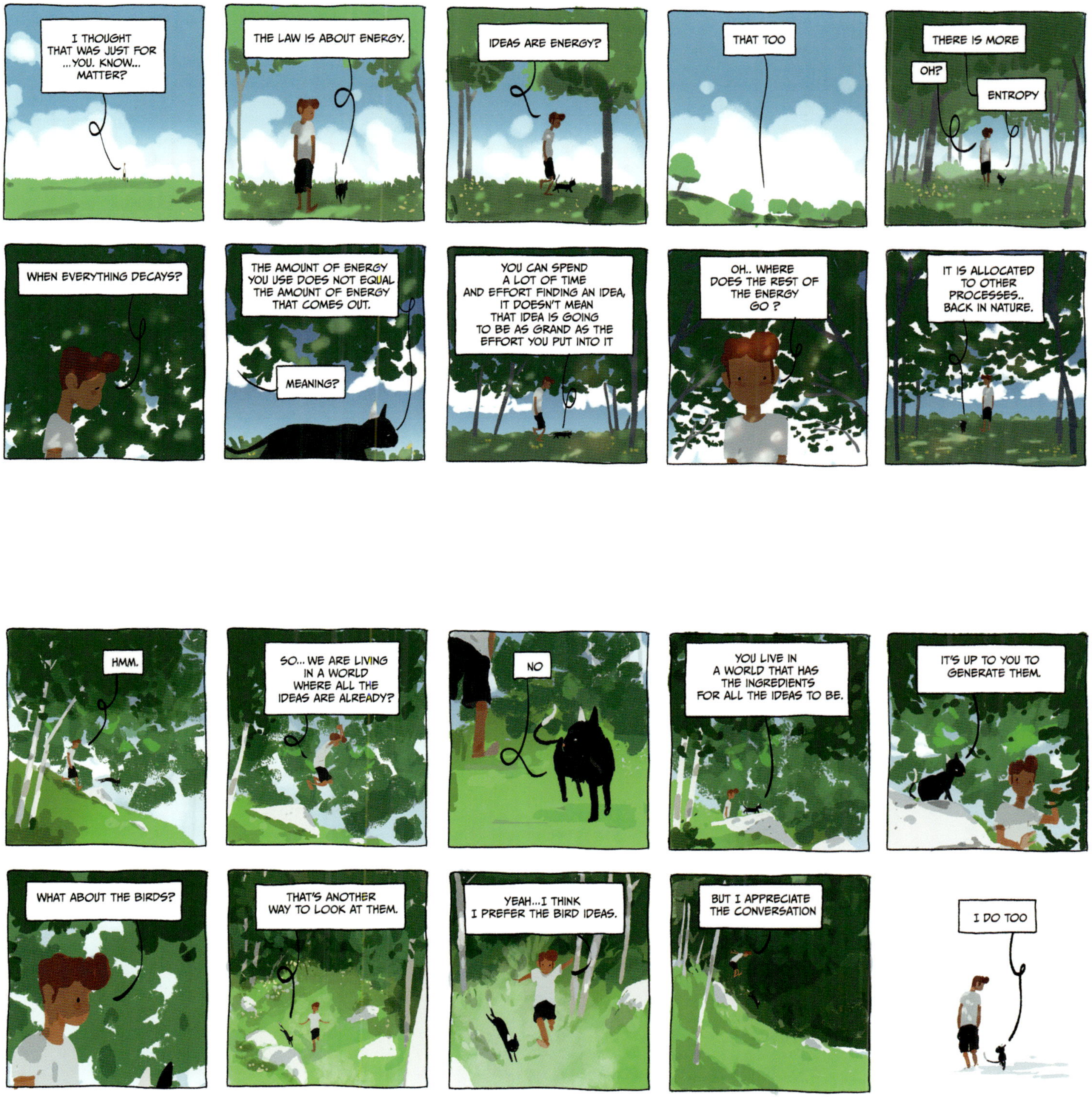
I THOUGHT THAT WAS JUST FOR ...YOU. KNOW... MATTER?
THE LAW IS ABOUT ENERGY.
IDEAS ARE ENERGY?
THAT TOO
THERE IS MORE
OH?
ENTROPY
WHEN EVERYTHING DECAYS?
THE AMOUNT OF ENERGY YOU USE DOES NOT EQUAL THE AMOUNT OF ENERGY THAT COMES OUT.
MEANING?
YOU CAN SPEND A LOT OF TIME AND EFFORT FINDING AN IDEA, IT DOESN'T MEAN THAT IDEA IS GOING TO BE AS GRAND AS THE EFFORT YOU PUT INTO IT
OH.. WHERE DOES THE REST OF THE ENERGY GO ?
IT IS ALLOCATED TO OTHER PROCESSES.. BACK IN NATURE.
HMM.
SO... WE ARE LIVING IN A WORLD WHERE ALL THE IDEAS ARE ALREADY?
NO
YOU LIVE IN A WORLD THAT HAS THE INGREDIENTS FOR ALL THE IDEAS TO BE.
IT'S UP TO YOU TO GENERATE THEM.
WHAT ABOUT THE BIRDS?
THAT'S ANOTHER WAY TO LOOK AT THEM.
YEAH...I THINK I PREFER THE BIRD IDEAS.
BUT I APPRECIATE THE CONVERSATION
I DO TOO

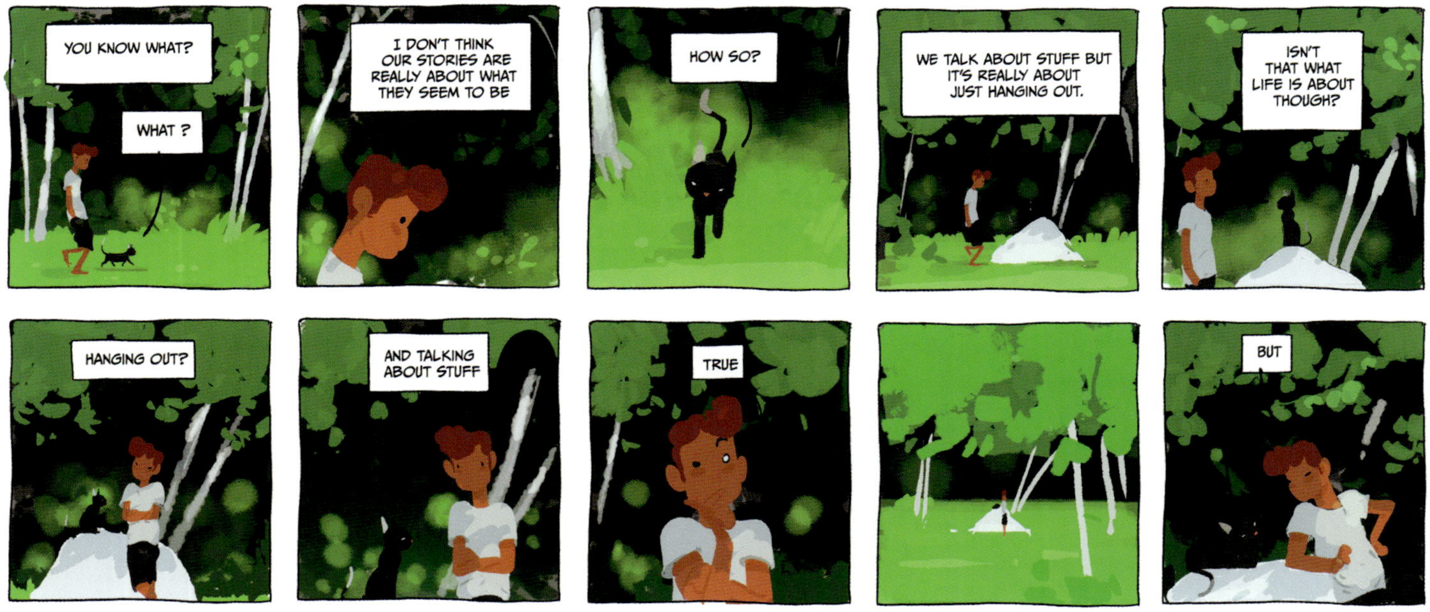
YOU KNOW WHAT?
WHAT ?
I DON'T THINK OUR STORIES ARE REALLY ABOUT WHAT THEY SEEM TO BE
HOW SO?
WE TALK ABOUT STUFF BUT IT'S REALLY ABOUT JUST HANGING OUT.
ISN'T THAT WHAT LIFE IS ABOUT THOUGH?
HANGING OUT?
AND TALKING ABOUT STUFF
TRUE
BUT

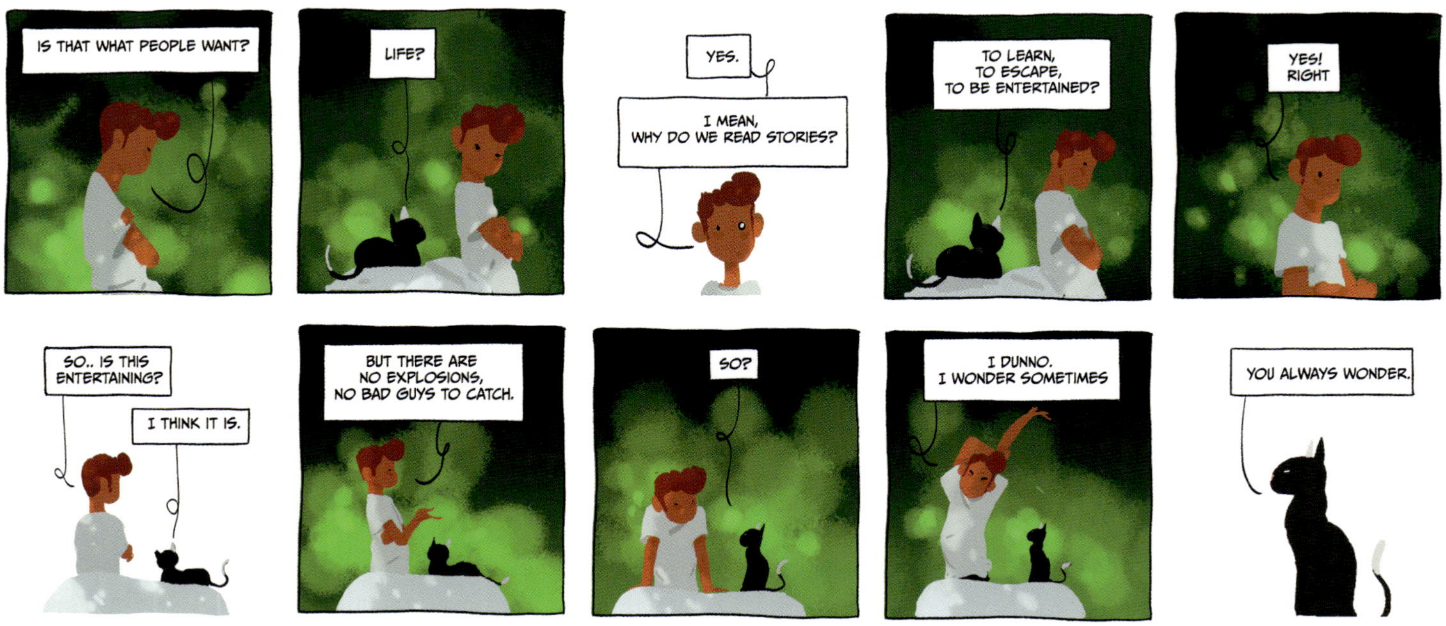
IS THAT WHAT PEOPLE WANT?
LIFE?
YES.
I MEAN, WHY DO WE READ STORIES?
TO LEARN, TO ESCAPE, TO BE ENTERTAINED?
YES! RIGHT
SO.. IS THIS ENTERTAINING?
I THINK IT IS.
BUT THERE ARE NO EXPLOSIONS, NO BAD GUYS TO CATCH.
SO?
I DUNNO. I WONDER SOMETIMES
YOU ALWAYS WONDER.

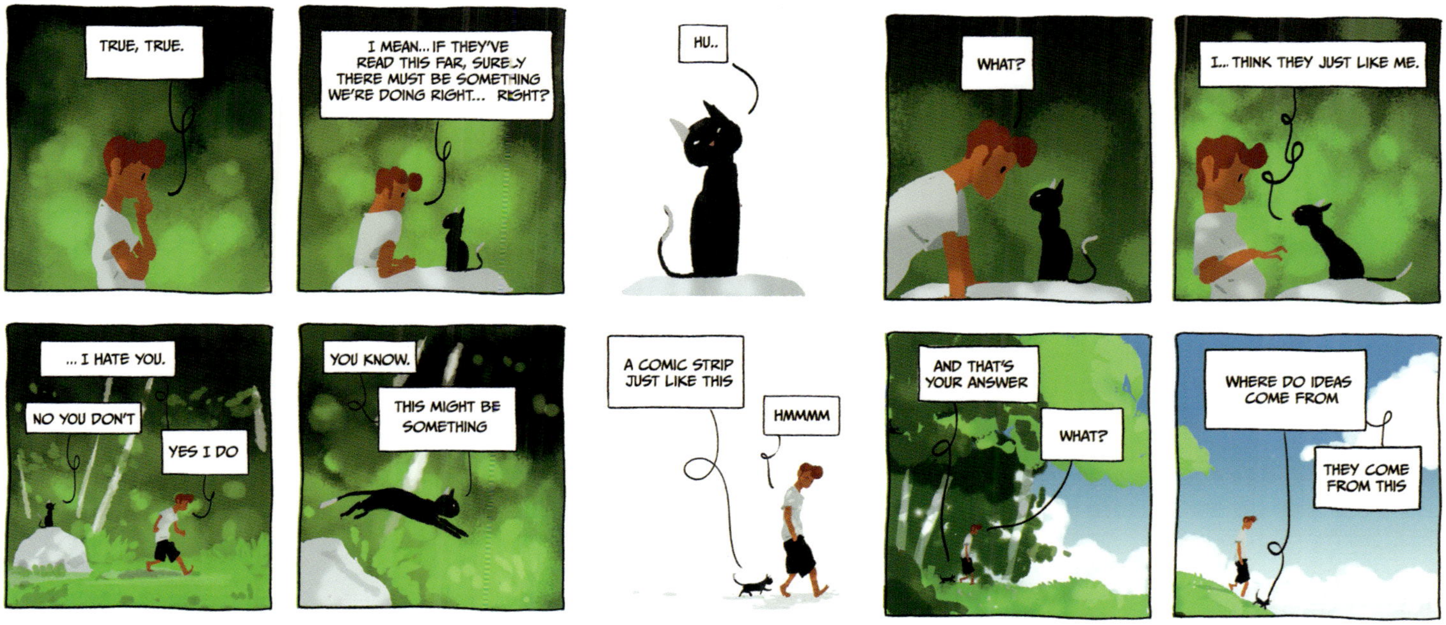
TRUE, TRUE.
I MEAN... IF THEY'VE READ THIS FAR, SURELY THERE MUST BE SOMETHING WE'RE DOING RIGHT... RIGHT?
HU..
WHAT?
I... THINK THEY JUST LIKE ME.
... I HATE YOU.
NO YOU DON'T
YES I DO
YOU KNOW.
THIS MIGHT BE SOMETHING
A COMIC STRIP JUST LIKE THIS
HMMMM
AND THAT'S YOUR ANSWER
WHAT?
WHERE DO IDEAS COME FROM
THEY COME FROM THIS

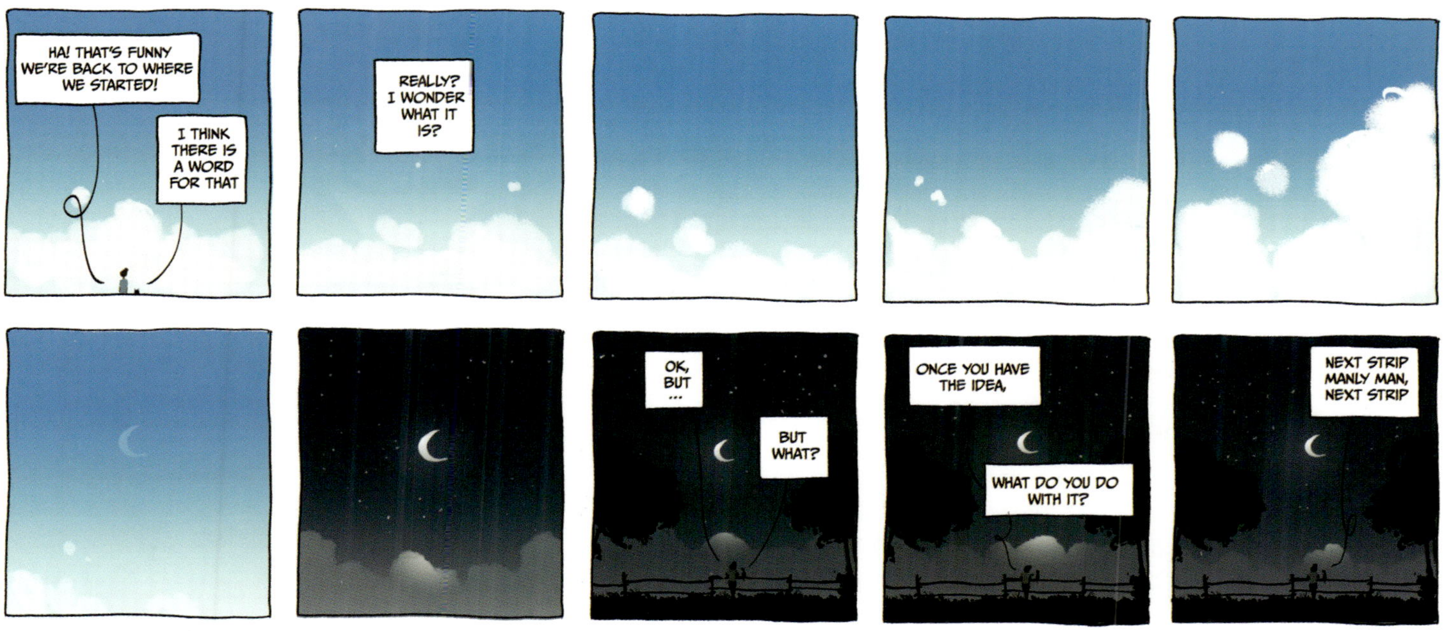
HA! THAT'S FUNNY WE'RE BACK TO WHERE WE STARTED!
I THINK THERE IS A WORD FOR THAT
REALLY? I WONDER WHAT IT IS?
OK, BUT ...
BUT WHAT?
ONCE YOU HAVE THE IDEA,
WHAT DO YOU DO WITH IT?
NEXT STRIP MANLY MAN, NEXT STRIP

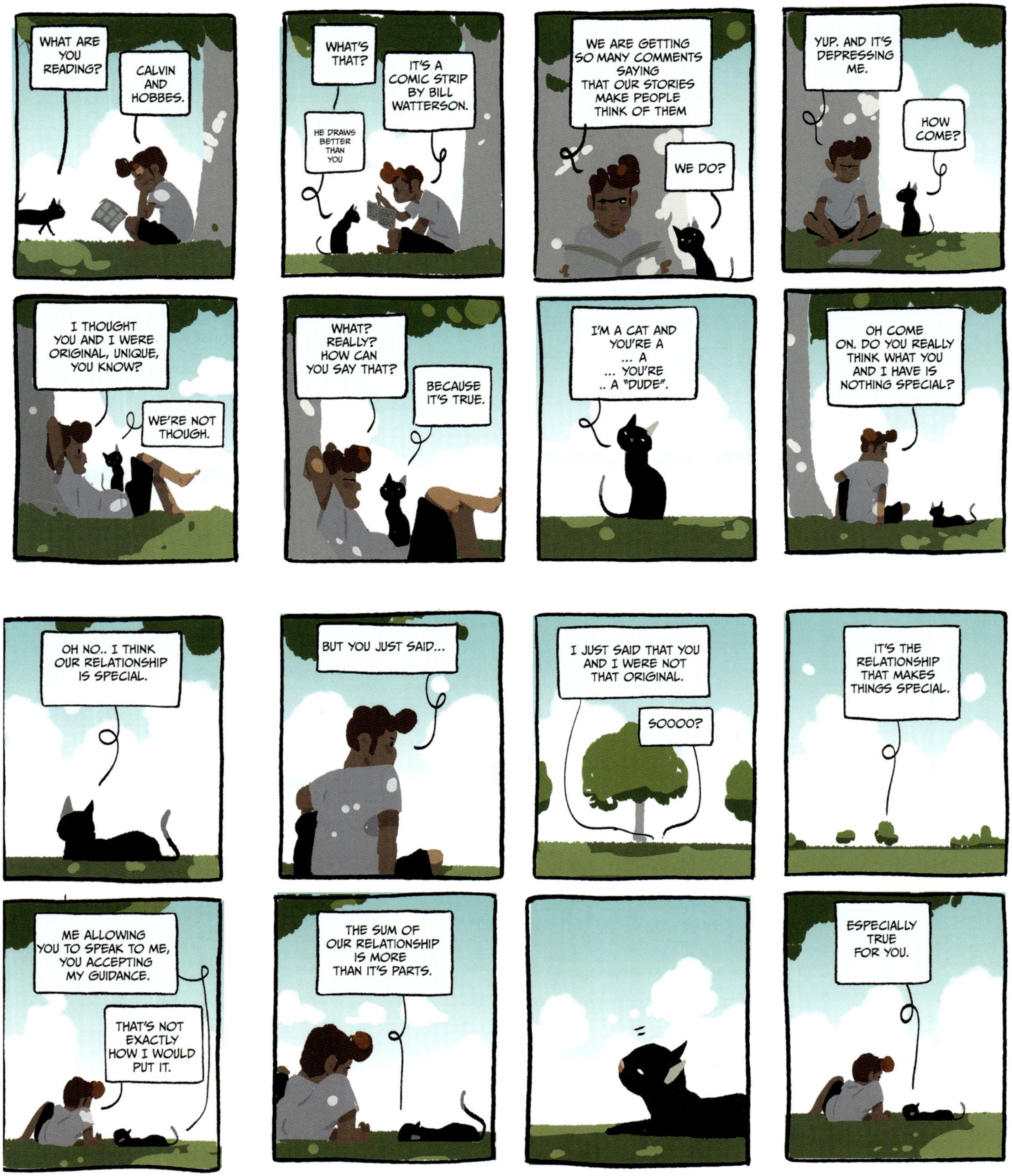
WHAT ARE YOU READING?
CALVIN AND HOBBES.
WHAT'S THAT?
IT'S A COMIC STRIP BY BILL WATTERSON.
HE DRAWS BETTER THAN YOU
WE ARE GETTING SO MANY COMMENTS SAYING THAT OUR STORIES MAKE PEOPLE THINK OF THEM
WE DO?
YUP. AND IT'S DEPRESSING ME.
HOW COME?
I THOUGHT YOU AND I WERE ORIGINAL, UNIQUE, YOU KNOW?
WE'RE NOT THOUGH.
WHAT? REALLY? HOW CAN YOU SAY THAT?
BECAUSE IT'S TRUE.
I'M A CAT AND YOU'RE A ... A ... YOU'RE .. A "DUDE".
OH COME ON. DO YOU REALLY THINK WHAT YOU AND I HAVE IS NOTHING SPECIAL?
OH NO.. I THINK OUR RELATIONSHIP IS SPECIAL.
BUT YOU JUST SAID...
I JUST SAID THAT YOU AND I WERE NOT THAT ORIGINAL.
SOOOO?
IT'S THE RELATIONSHIP THAT MAKES THINGS SPECIAL.
ME ALLOWING YOU TO SPEAK TO ME, YOU ACCEPTING MY GUIDANCE.
THAT'S NOT EXACTLY HOW I WOULD PUT IT.
THE SUM OF OUR RELATIONSHIP IS MORE THAN IT'S PARTS.
ESPECIALLY TRUE FOR YOU.

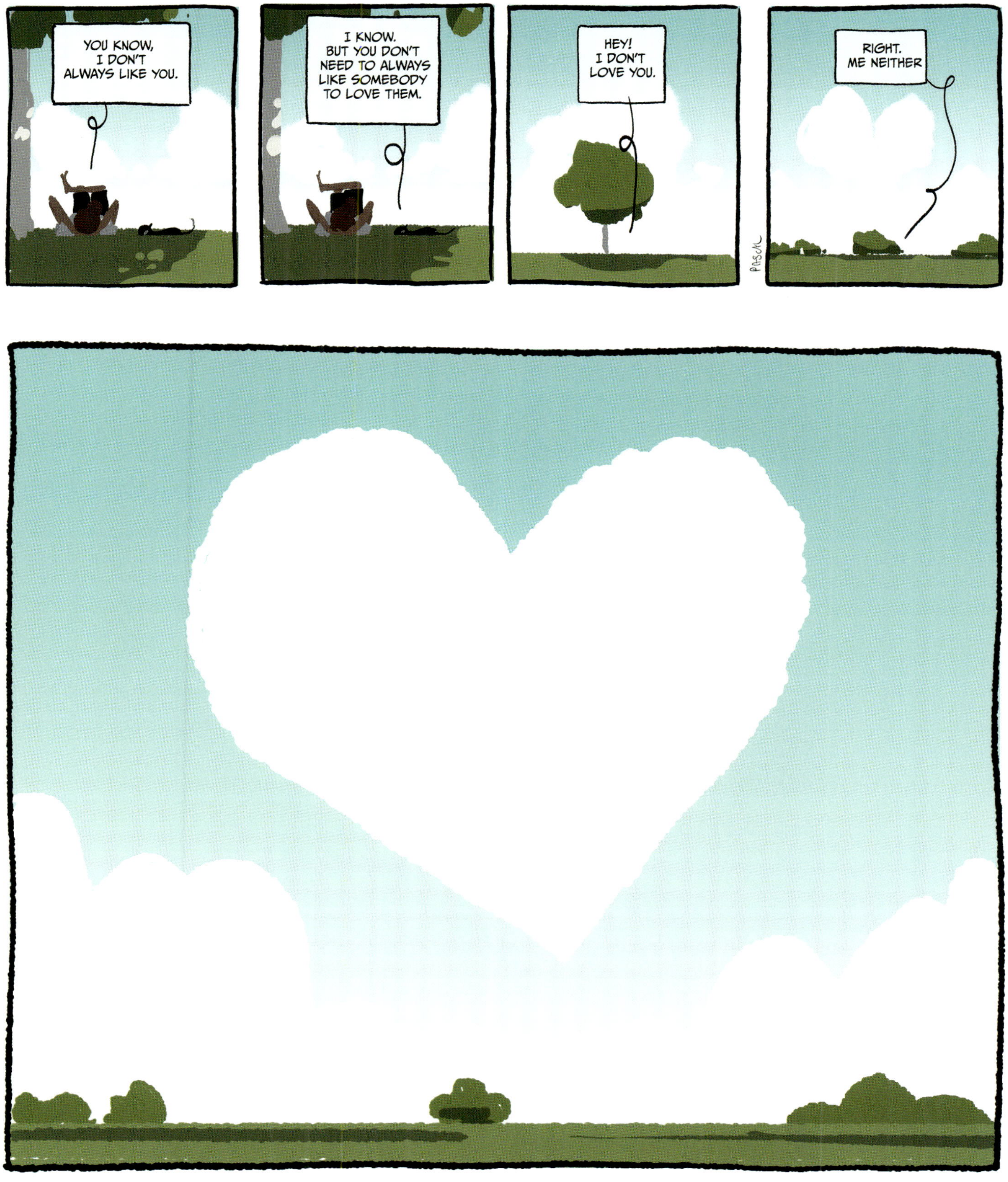
YOU KNOW,
I DON'T
ALWAYS LIKE YOU.
I KNOW.
BUT YOU DON'T
NEED TO ALWAYS
LIKE SOMEBODY
TO LOVE THEM.
HEY!
I DON'T
LOVE YOU.
RIGHT.
ME NEITHER

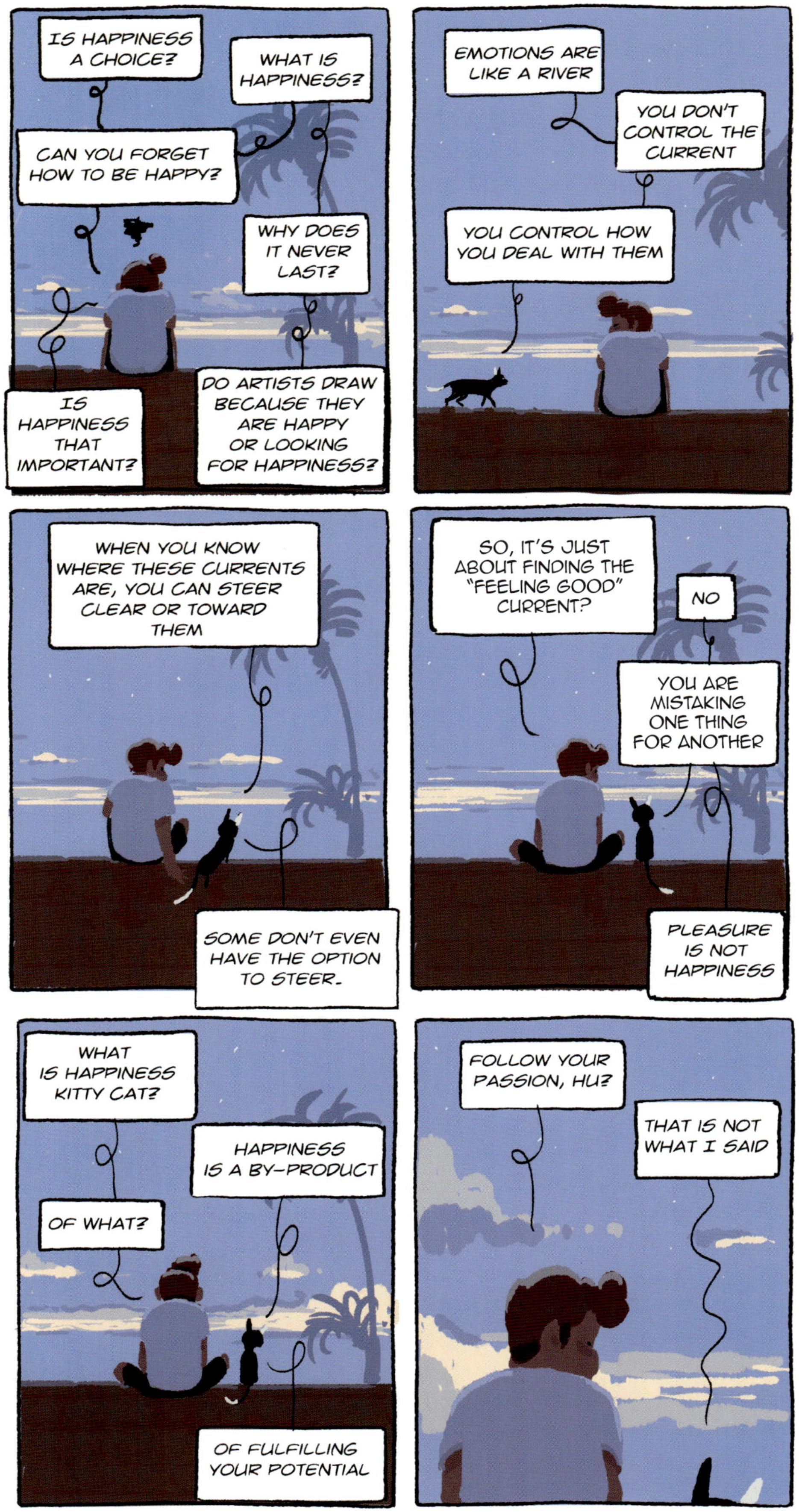
IS HAPPINESS A CHOICE?
WHAT IS HAPPINESS?
CAN YOU FORGET HOW TO BE HAPPY?
WHY DOES IT NEVER LAST?
IS HAPPINESS THAT IMPORTANT?
DO ARTISTS DRAW BECAUSE THEY ARE HAPPY OR LOOKING FOR HAPPINESS?
EMOTIONS ARE LIKE A RIVER
YOU DON'T CONTROL THE CURRENT
YOU CONTROL HOW YOU DEAL WITH THEM
WHEN YOU KNOW WHERE THESE CURRENTS ARE, YOU CAN STEER CLEAR OR TOWARD THEM
SOME DON'T EVEN HAVE THE OPTION TO STEER.
SO, IT'S JUST ABOUT FINDING THE "FEELING GOOD" CURRENT?
NO
YOU ARE MISTAKING ONE THING FOR ANOTHER
PLEASURE IS NOT HAPPINESS
WHAT IS HAPPINESS KITTY CAT?
HAPPINESS IS A BY-PRODUCT
OF WHAT?
OF FULFILLING YOUR POTENTIAL
FOLLOW YOUR PASSION, HU?
THAT IS NOT WHAT I SAID

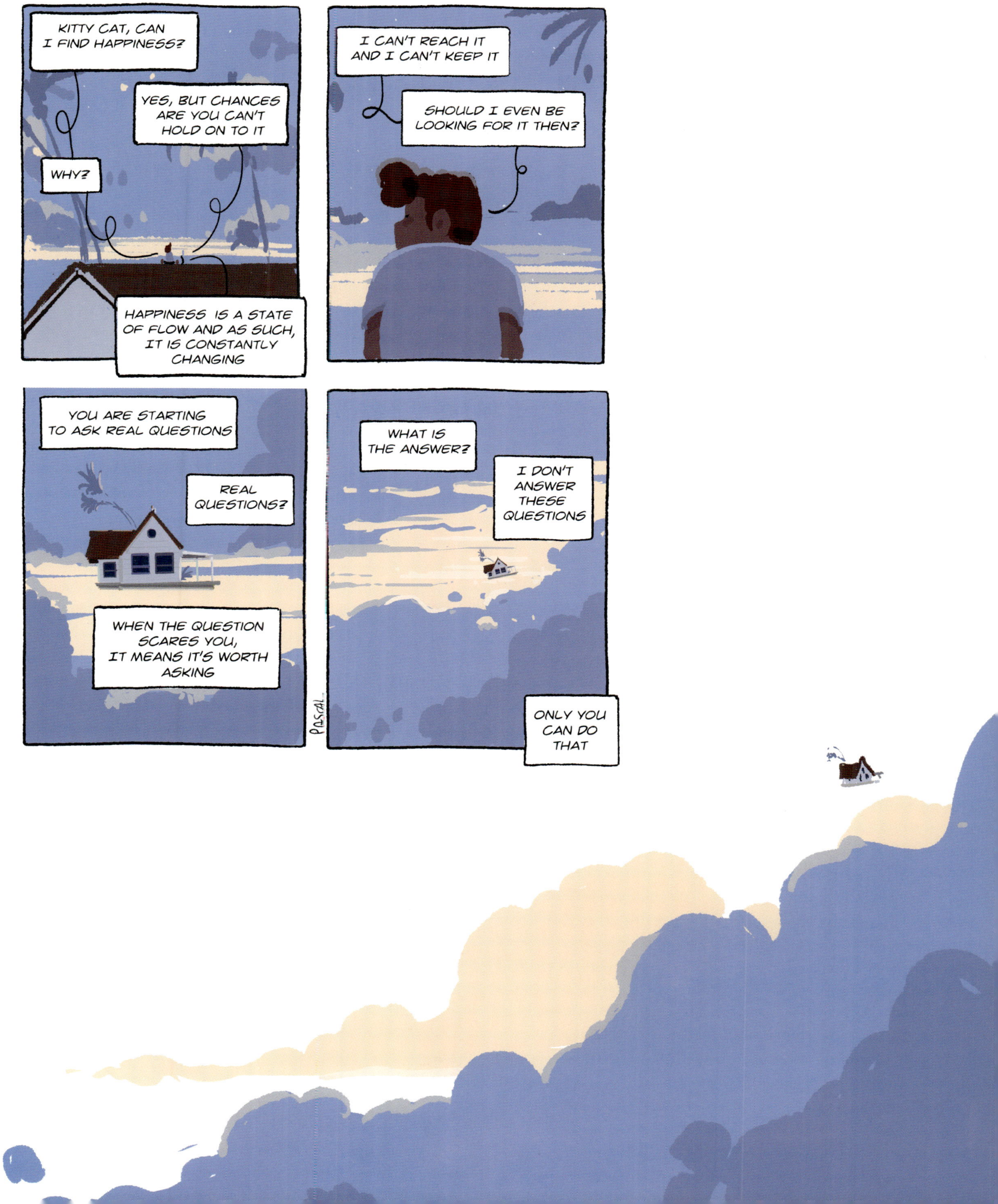
KITTY CAT, CAN I FIND HAPPINESS?
YES, BUT CHANCES ARE YOU CAN'T HOLD ON TO IT
WHY?
HAPPINESS IS A STATE OF FLOW AND AS SUCH, IT IS CONSTANTLY CHANGING
I CAN'T REACH IT AND I CAN'T KEEP IT
SHOULD I EVEN BE LOOKING FOR IT THEN?
YOU ARE STARTING TO ASK REAL QUESTIONS
REAL QUESTIONS?
WHEN THE QUESTION SCARES YOU, IT MEANS IT'S WORTH ASKING
PASCAL
WHAT IS THE ANSWER?
I DON'T ANSWER THESE QUESTIONS
ONLY YOU CAN DO THAT

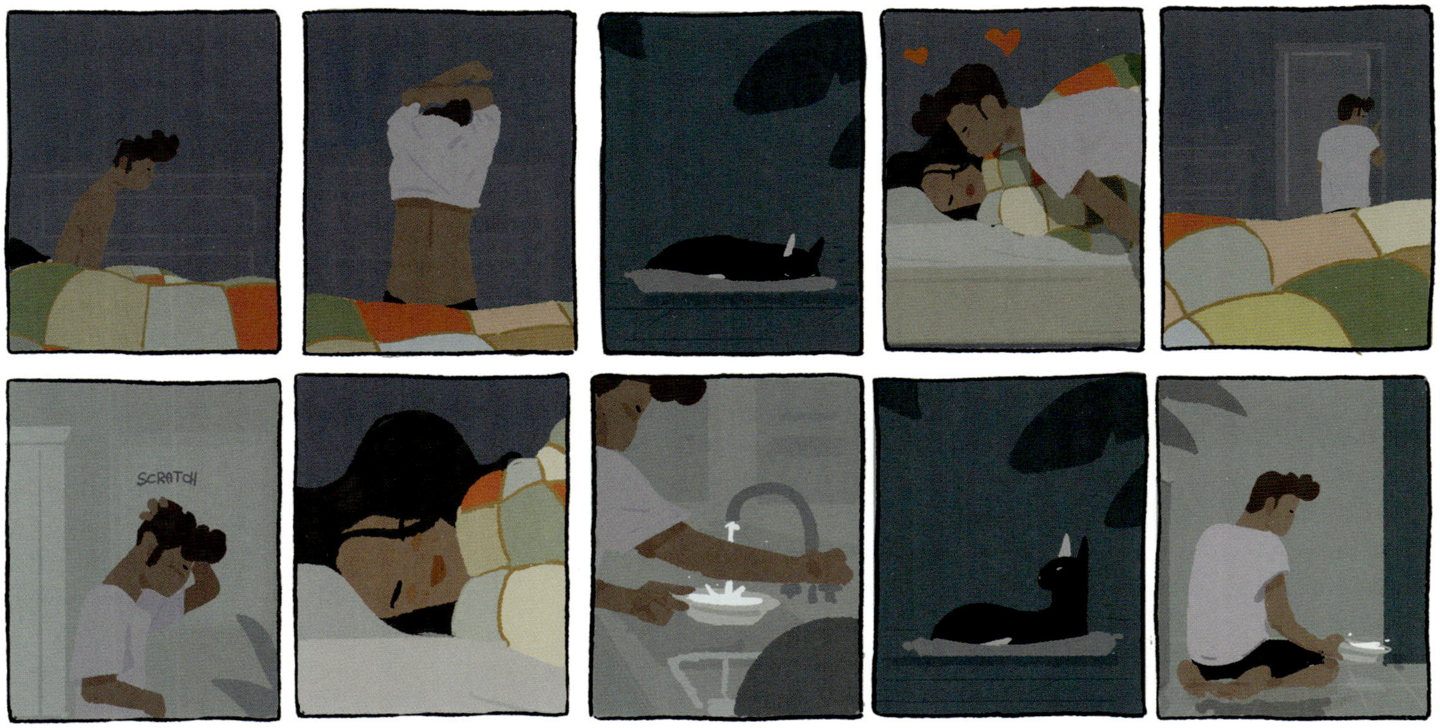
SCRATCH

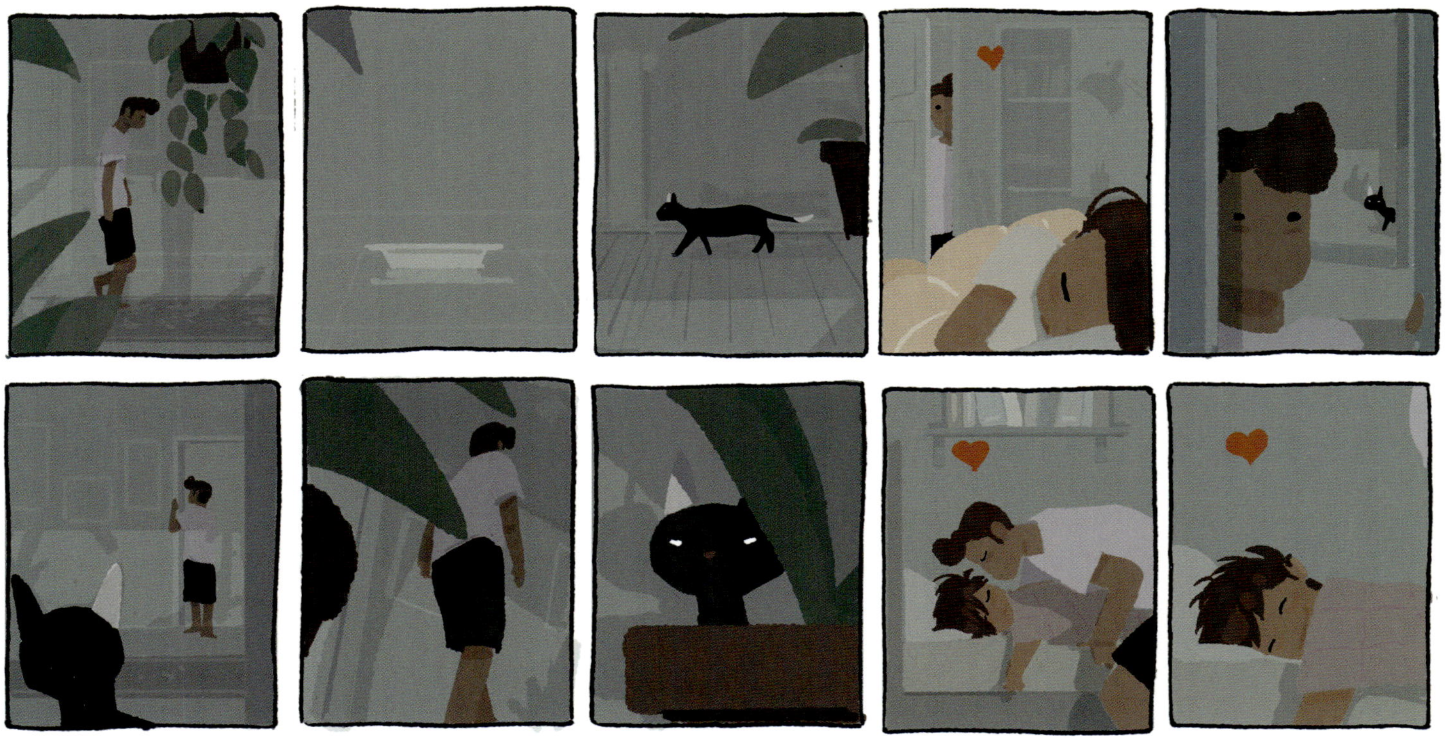

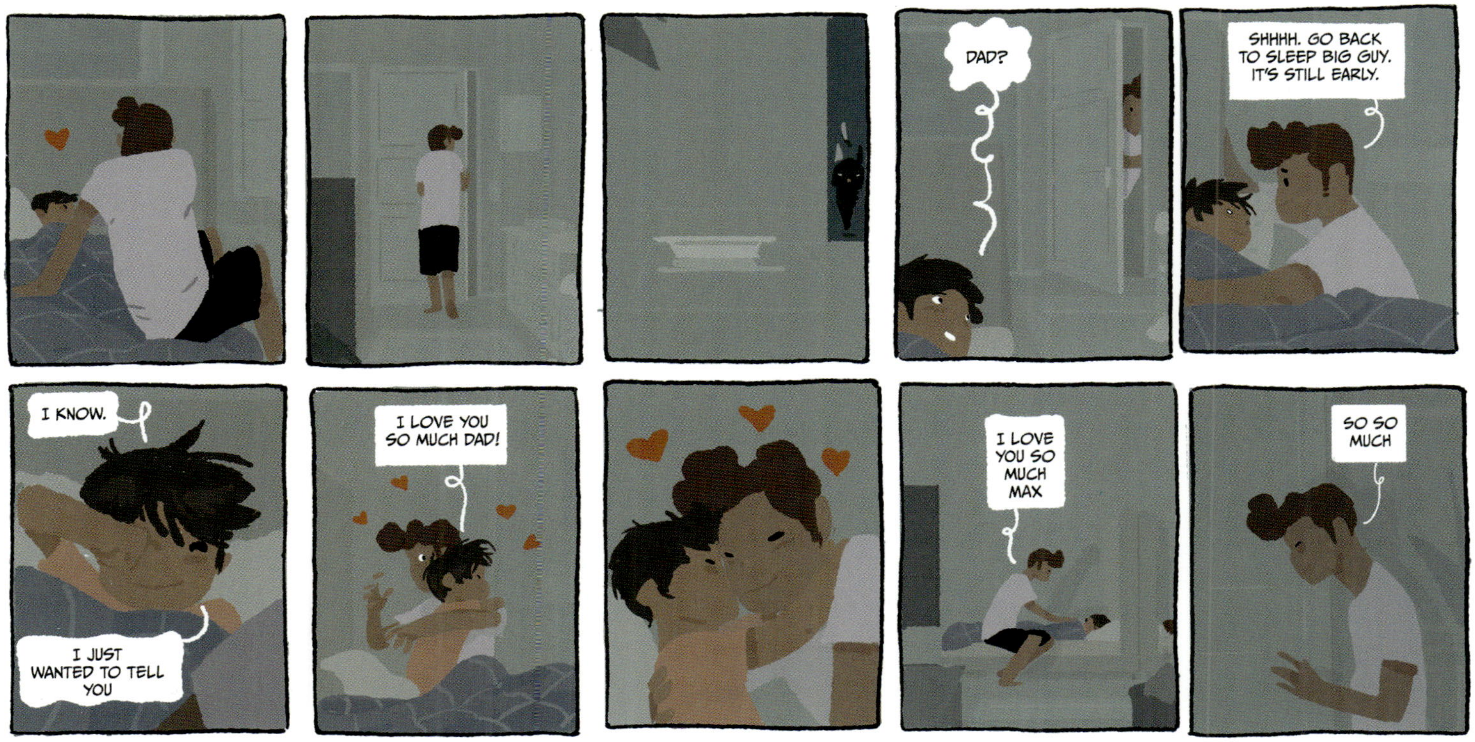
DAD?
SHHHH. GO BACK TO SLEEP BIG GUY. IT'S STILL EARLY.
I KNOW.
I JUST WANTED TO TELL YOU
I LOVE YOU SO MUCH DAD!
I LOVE YOU SO MUCH MAX
SO SO MUCH

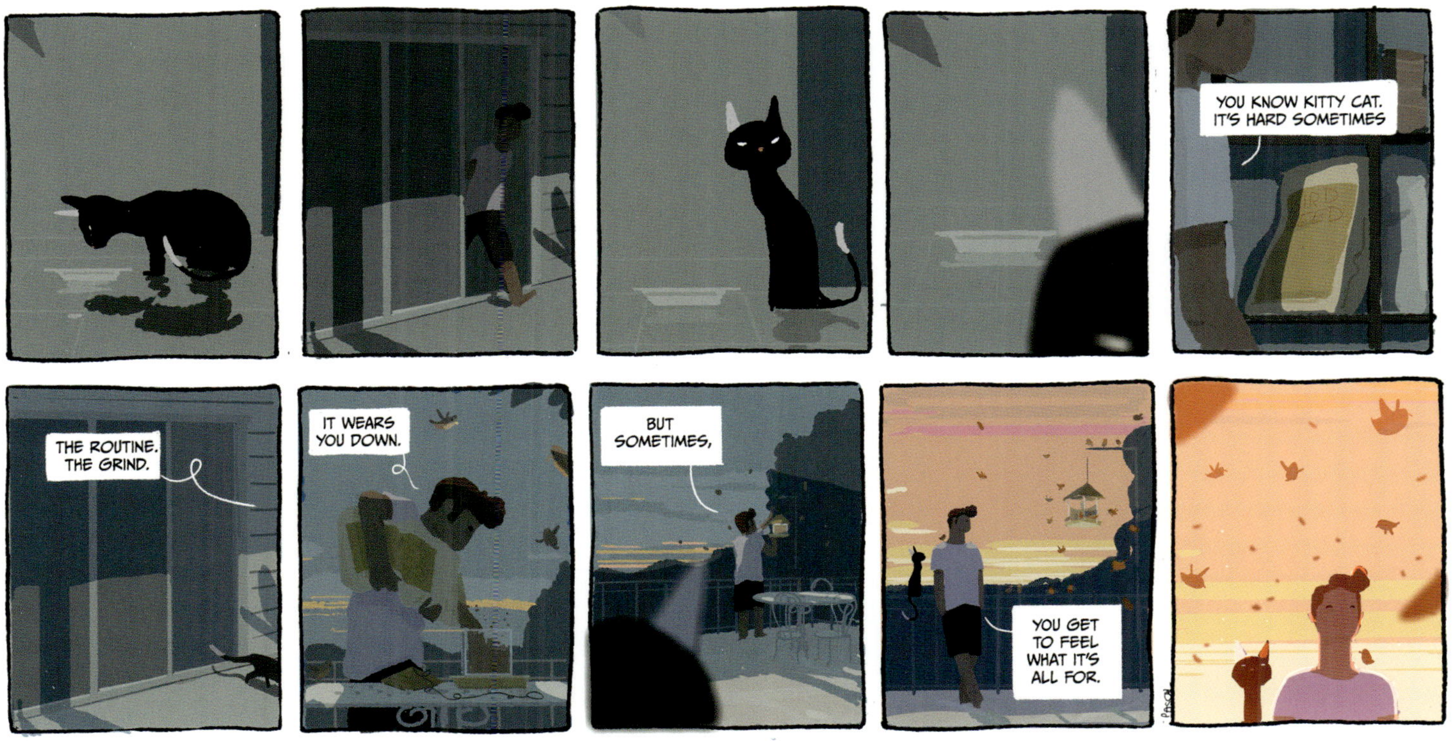
YOU KNOW KITTY CAT. IT'S HARD SOMETIMES
THE ROUTINE. THE GRIND.
IT WEARS YOU DOWN.
BUT SOMETIMES,
YOU GET TO FEEL WHAT IT'S ALL FOR.

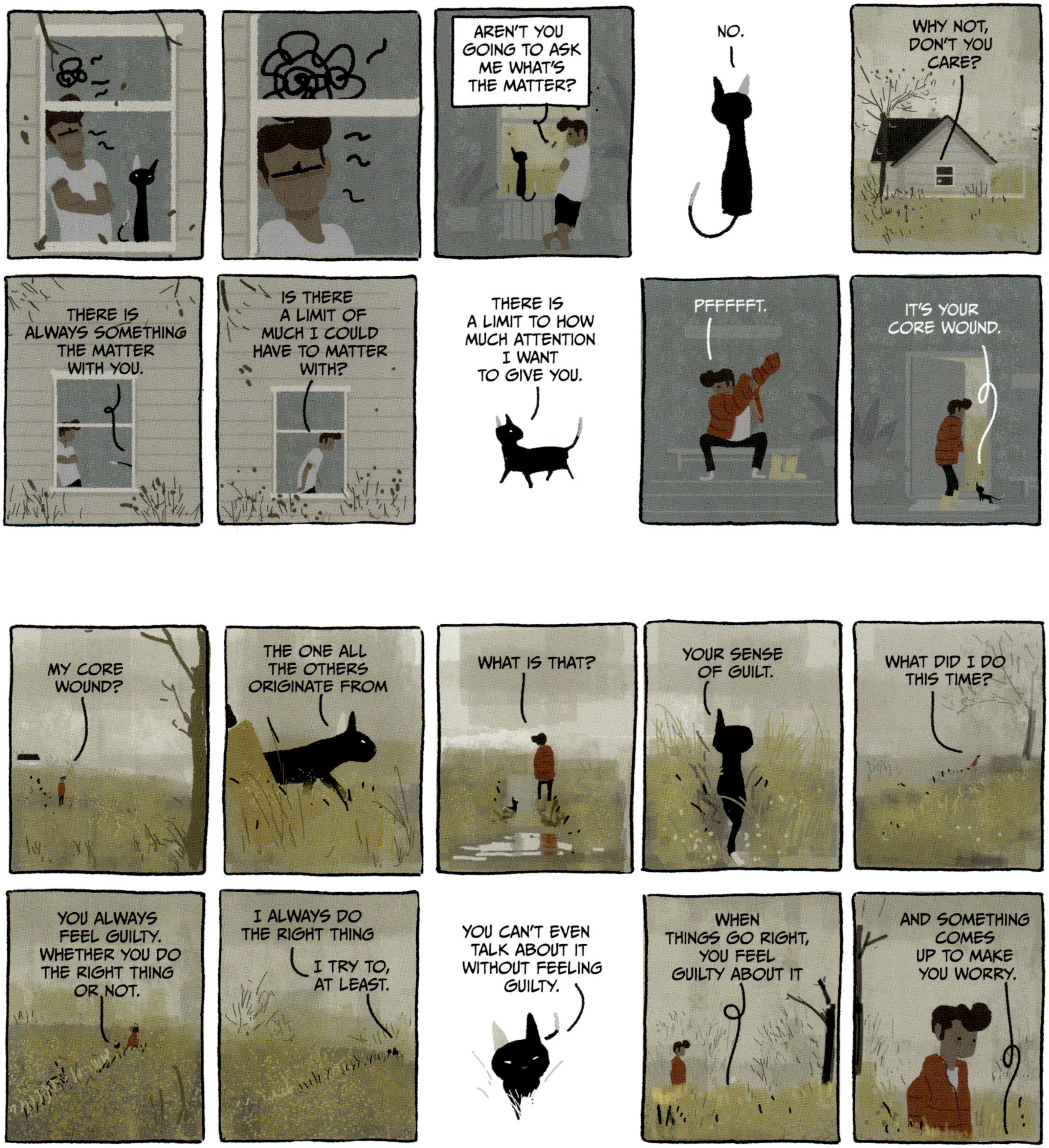
AREN'T YOU GOING TO ASK ME WHAT'S THE MATTER?
NO.
WHY NOT, DON'T YOU CARE?
THERE IS ALWAYS SOMETHING THE MATTER WITH YOU.
IS THERE A LIMIT OF MUCH I COULD HAVE TO MATTER WITH?
THERE IS A LIMIT TO HOW MUCH ATTENTION I WANT TO GIVE YOU.
PFFFFFT.
IT'S YOUR CORE WOUND.
MY CORE WOUND?
THE ONE ALL THE OTHERS ORIGINATE FROM
WHAT IS THAT?
YOUR SENSE OF GUILT.
WHAT DID I DO THIS TIME?
YOU ALWAYS FEEL GUILTY. WHETHER YOU DO THE RIGHT THING OR NOT.
I ALWAYS DO THE RIGHT THING
I TRY TO, AT LEAST.
YOU CAN'T EVEN TALK ABOUT IT WITHOUT FEELING GUILTY.
WHEN THINGS GO RIGHT, YOU FEEL GUILTY ABOUT IT
AND SOMETHING COMES UP TO MAKE YOU WORRY.

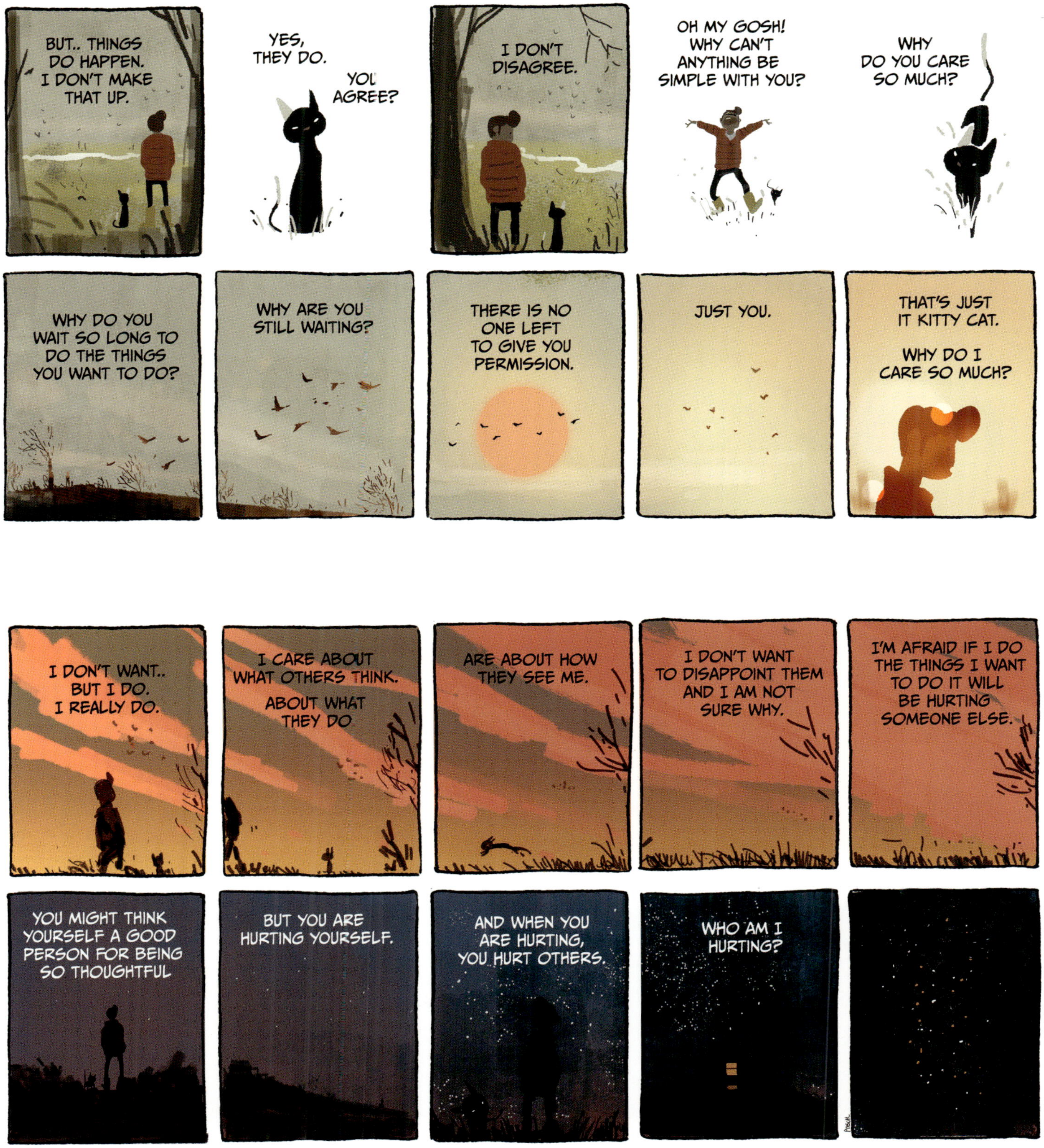

BUT.. THINGS DO HAPPEN. I DON'T MAKE THAT UP.
YES, THEY DO.
YOU AGREE?
I DON'T DISAGREE.
OH MY GOSH! WHY CAN'T ANYTHING BE SIMPLE WITH YOU?
WHY DO YOU CARE SO MUCH?
WHY DO YOU WAIT SO LONG TO DO THE THINGS YOU WANT TO DO?
WHY ARE YOU STILL WAITING?
THERE IS NO ONE LEFT TO GIVE YOU PERMISSION.
JUST YOU.
THAT'S JUST IT KITTY CAT.
WHY DO I CARE SO MUCH?
I DON'T WANT.. BUT I DO. I REALLY DO.
I CARE ABOUT WHAT OTHERS THINK.
ABOUT WHAT THEY DO
ARE ABOUT HOW THEY SEE ME.
I DON'T WANT TO DISAPPOINT THEM AND I AM NOT SURE WHY.
I'M AFRAID IF I DO THE THINGS I WANT TO DO IT WILL BE HURTING SOMEONE ELSE.
YOU MIGHT THINK YOURSELF A GOOD PERSON FOR BEING SO THOUGHTFUL
BUT YOU ARE HURTING YOURSELF.
AND WHEN YOU ARE HURTING, YOU HURT OTHERS.
WHO AM I HURTING?

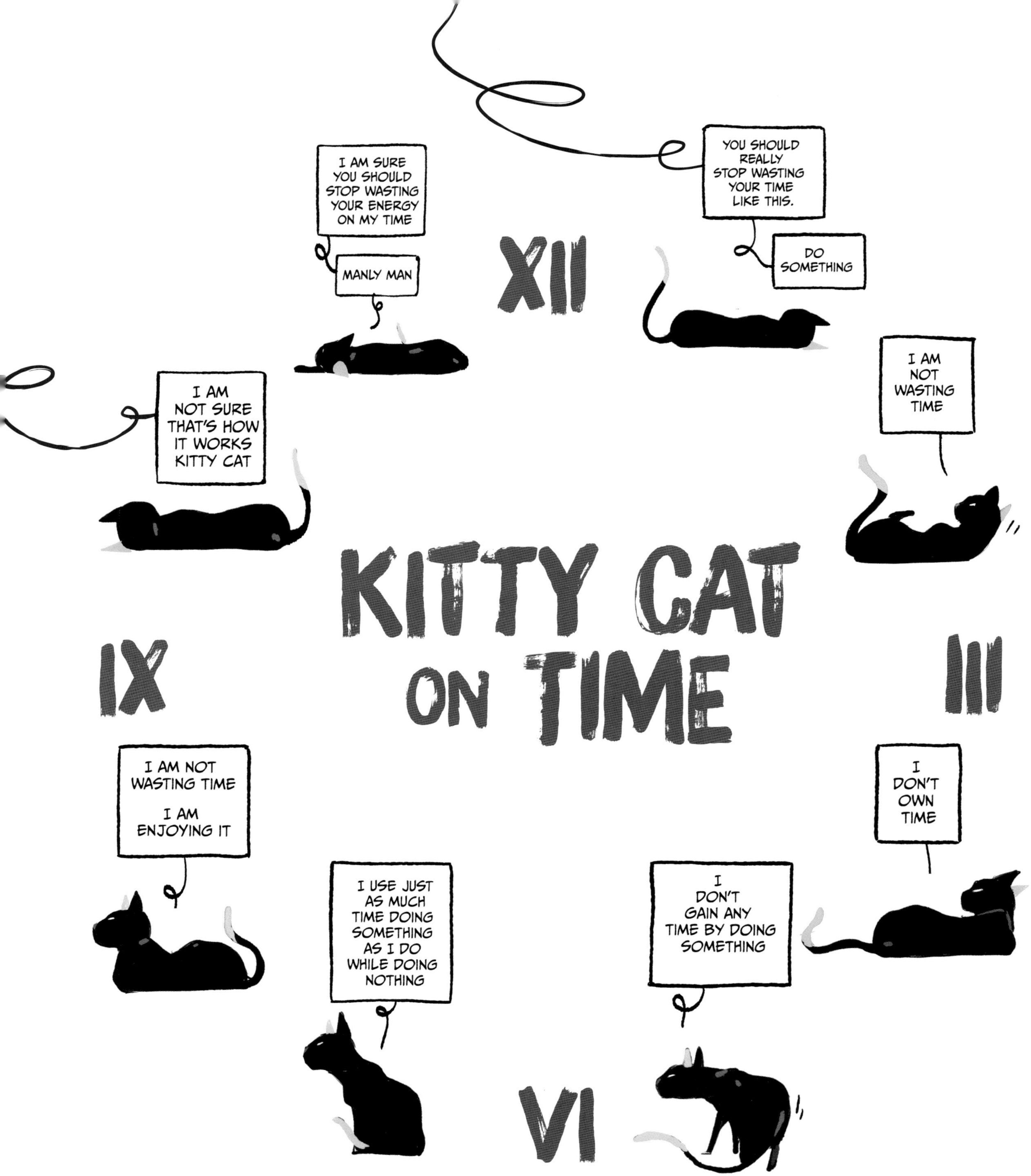
KITTY CAT ON TIME
XII
III
VI
IX
YOU SHOULD REALLY STOP WASTING YOUR TIME LIKE THIS.
DO SOMETHING
I AM NOT WASTING TIME
I DON'T OWN TIME
I DON'T GAIN ANY TIME BY DOING SOMETHING
I USE JUST AS MUCH TIME DOING SOMETHING AS I DO WHILE DOING NOTHING
I AM NOT WASTING TIME
I AM ENJOYING IT
I AM NOT SURE THAT'S HOW IT WORKS KITTY CAT
I AM SURE YOU SHOULD STOP WASTING YOUR ENERGY ON MY TIME
MANLY MAN

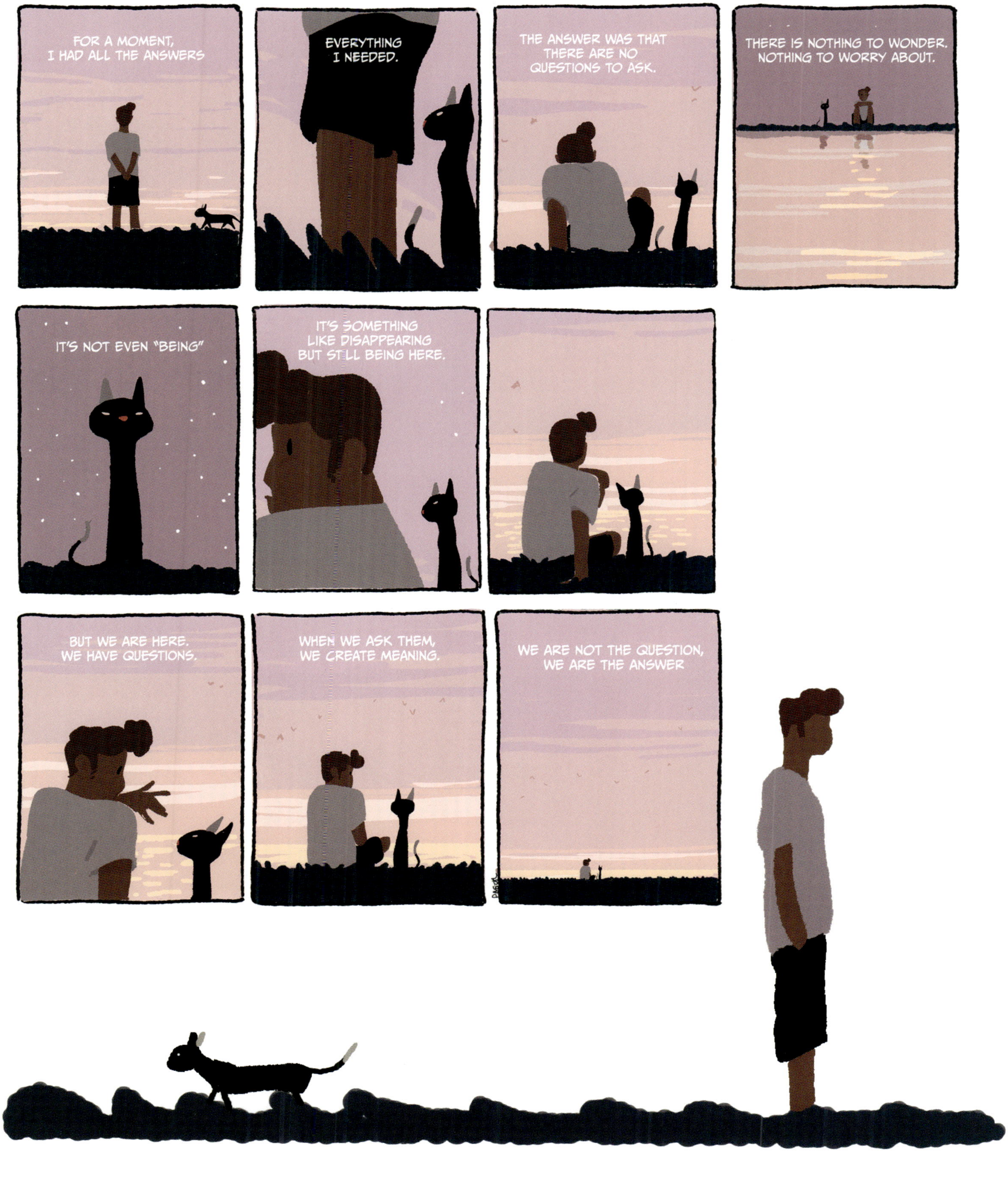
FOR A MOMENT, I HAD ALL THE ANSWERS
EVERYTHING I NEEDED.
THE ANSWER WAS THAT THERE ARE NO QUESTIONS TO ASK.
THERE IS NOTHING TO WONDER. NOTHING TO WORRY ABOUT.
IT'S NOT EVEN "BEING"
IT'S SOMETHING LIKE DISAPPEARING BUT STILL BEING HERE.
BUT WE ARE HERE. WE HAVE QUESTIONS.
WHEN WE ASK THEM, WE CREATE MEANING.
WE ARE NOT THE QUESTION, WE ARE THE ANSWER

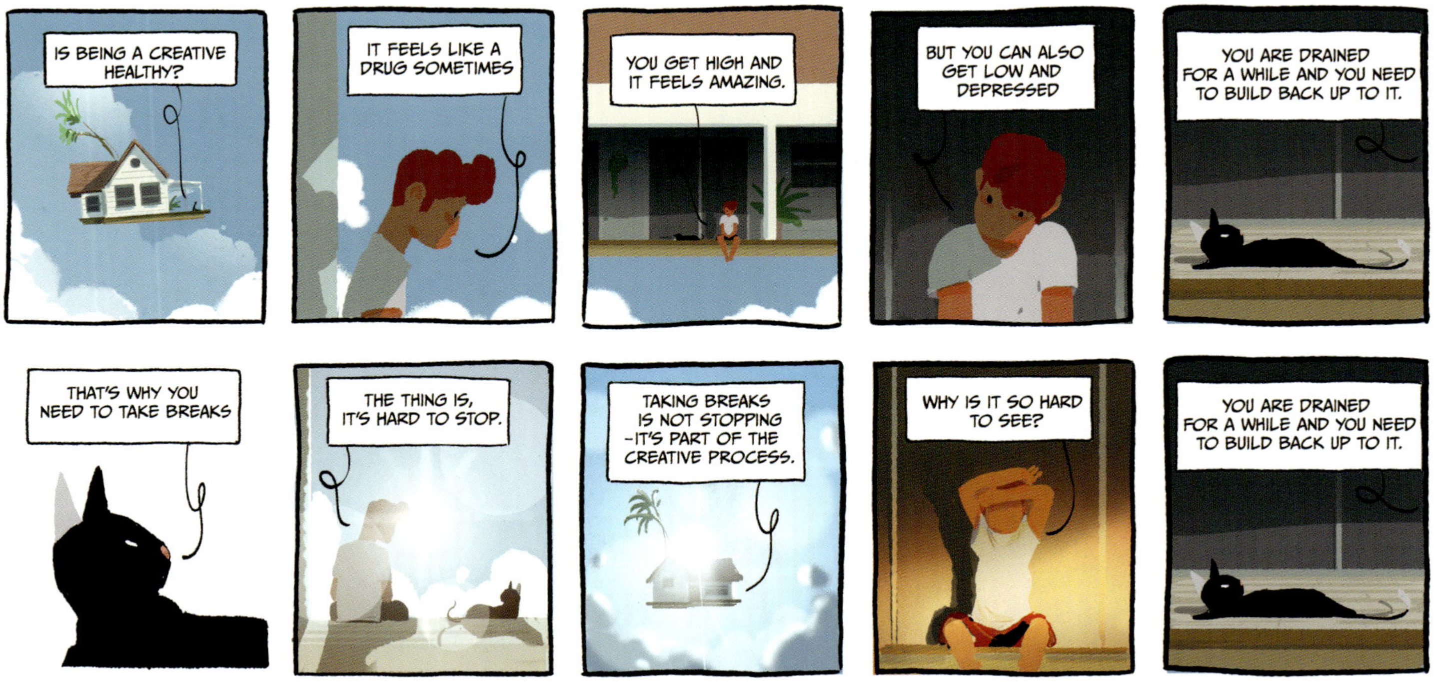
IS BEING A CREATIVE HEALTHY?
IT FEELS LIKE A DRUG SOMETIMES
YOU GET HIGH AND IT FEELS AMAZING.
BUT YOU CAN ALSO GET LOW AND DEPRESSED
YOU ARE DRAINED FOR A WHILE AND YOU NEED TO BUILD BACK UP TO IT.
THAT'S WHY YOU NEED TO TAKE BREAKS
THE THING IS, IT'S HARD TO STOP.
TAKING BREAKS IS NOT STOPPING –IT'S PART OF THE CREATIVE PROCESS.
WHY IS IT SO HARD TO SEE?
YOU ARE DRAINED FOR A WHILE AND YOU NEED TO BUILD BACK UP TO IT.

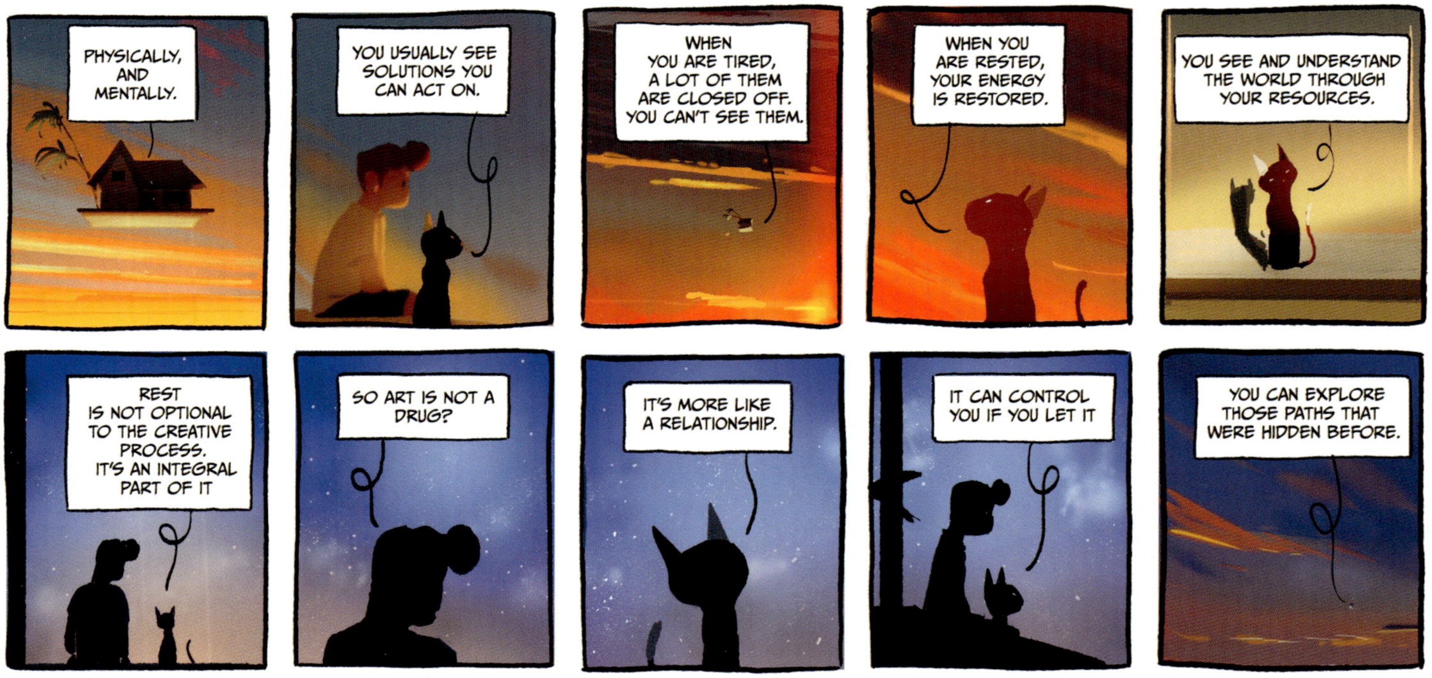
PHYSICALLY, AND MENTALLY.
YOU USUALLY SEE SOLUTIONS YOU CAN ACT ON.
WHEN YOU ARE TIRED, A LOT OF THEM ARE CLOSED OFF. YOU CAN'T SEE THEM.
WHEN YOU ARE RESTED, YOUR ENERGY IS RESTORED.
YOU SEE AND UNDERSTAND THE WORLD THROUGH YOUR RESOURCES.
REST IS NOT OPTIONAL TO THE CREATIVE PROCESS. IT'S AN INTEGRAL PART OF IT
SO ART IS NOT A DRUG?
IT'S MORE LIKE A RELATIONSHIP.
IT CAN CONTROL YOU IF YOU LET IT
YOU CAN EXPLORE THOSE PATHS THAT WERE HIDDEN BEFORE.

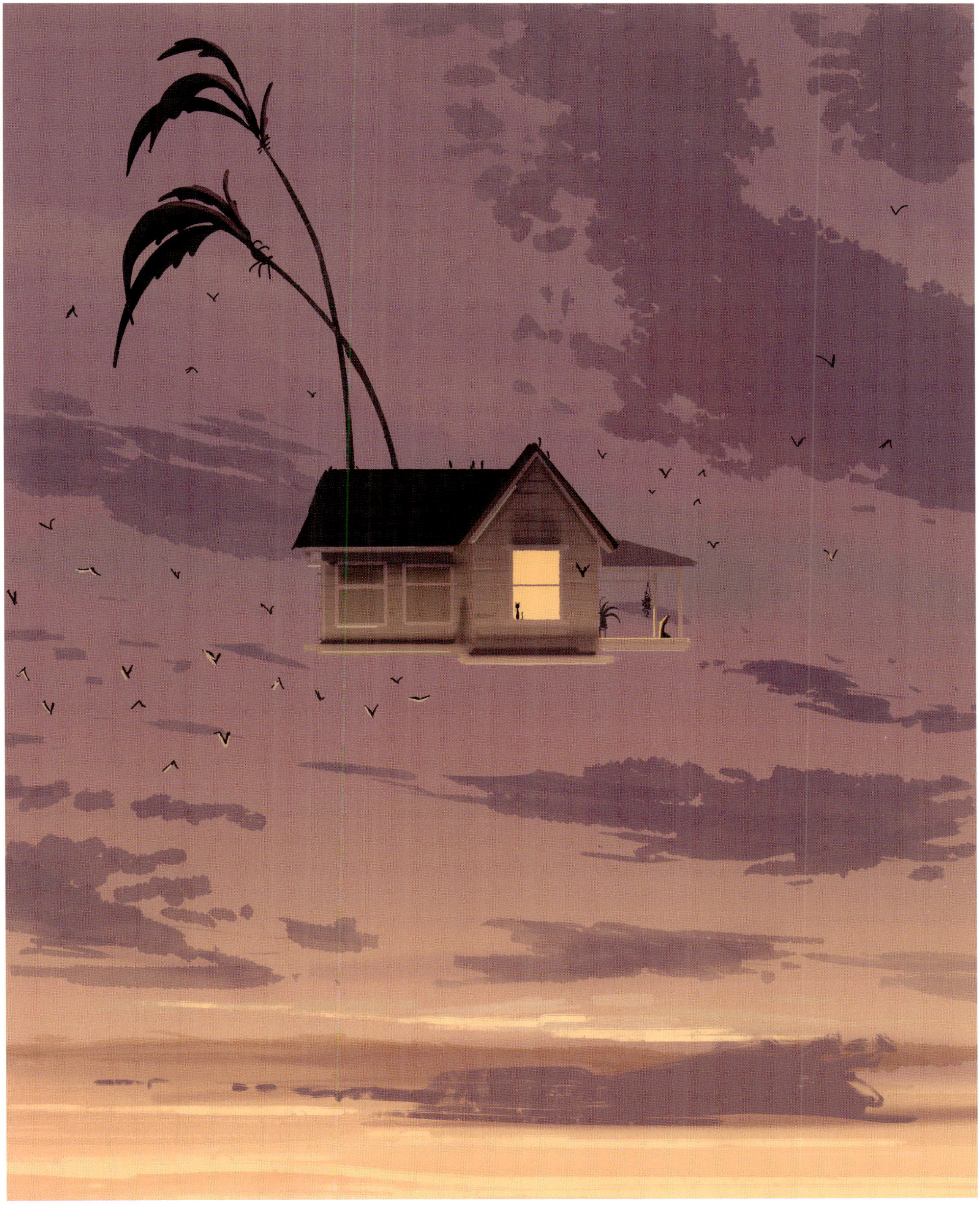

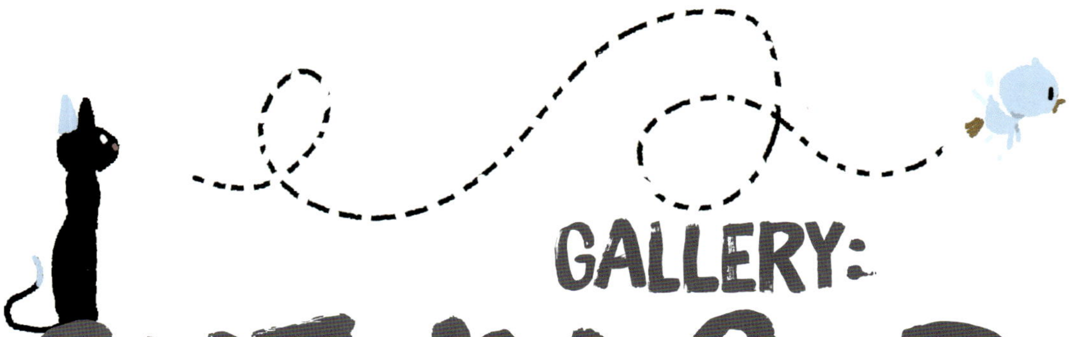

GALLERY:

OUT IN OUR WORLD

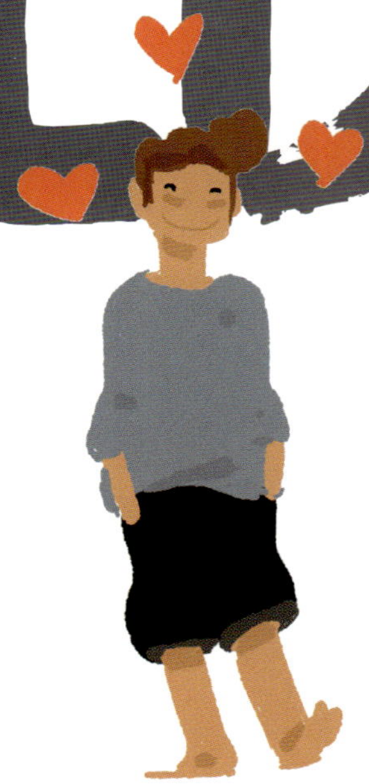

I'M AN INTROVERT.
I WORK WITH
PEOPLE A LOT.
OR AT LEAST, I NEED TO *TALK* TO PEOPLE A LOT.
I DON'T DISLIKE IT AT ALL.
IT JUST TAKES A LOT FROM ME.
LONG WALKS IN THE MOUNTAINS,
OR LONG BIKE RIDES,*

HELP TO CALM MY BRAIN
+ REPLENISH MY ENERGY.

**I WOULD DRAW MORE BIKE RIDES, BUT DRAWING WHEELS IS HARD.*

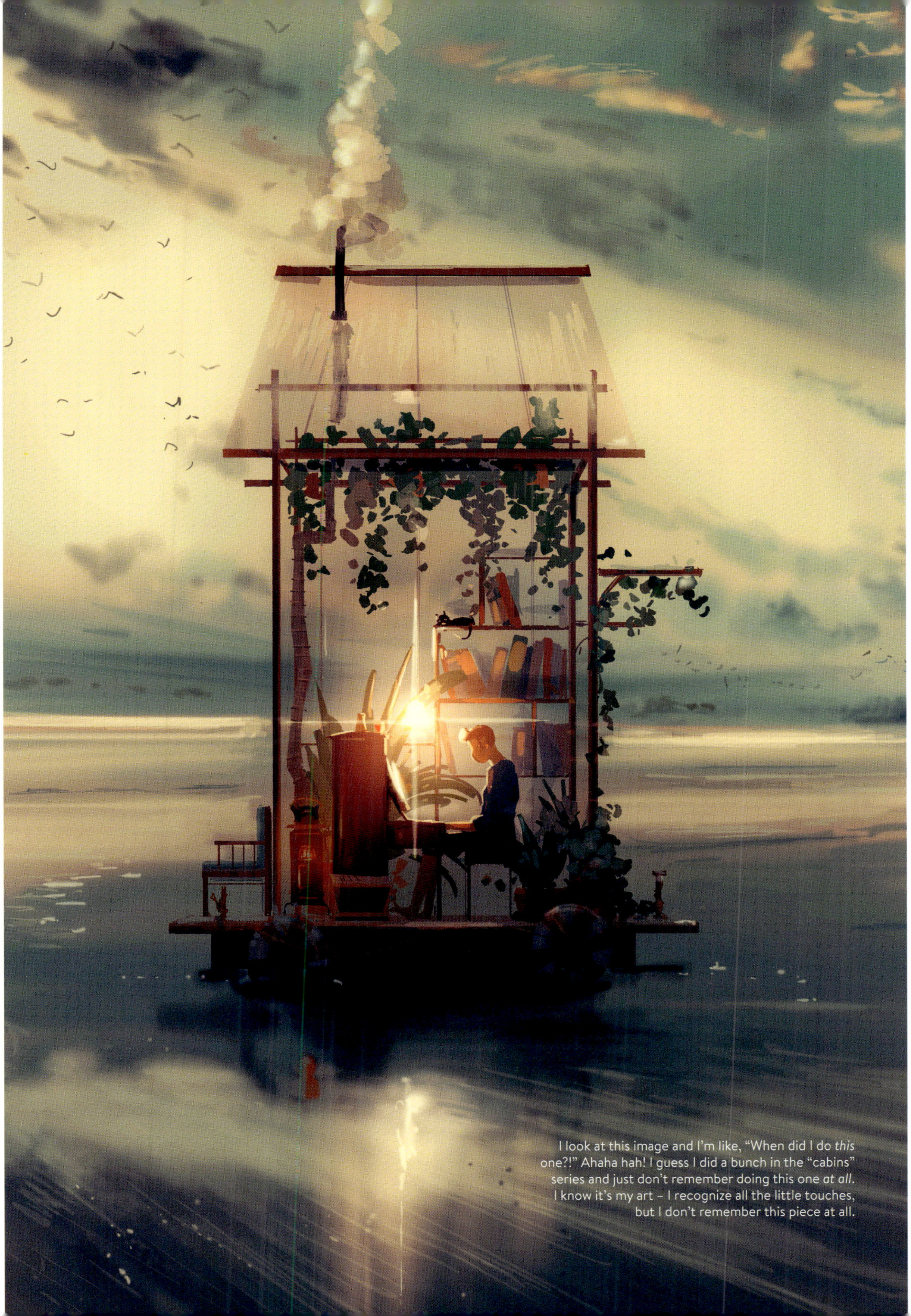

I look at this image and I'm like, "When did I do *this* one?!" Ahaha hah! I guess I did a bunch in the "cabins" series and just don't remember doing this one *at all*. I know it's my art – I recognize all the little touches, but I don't remember this piece at all.

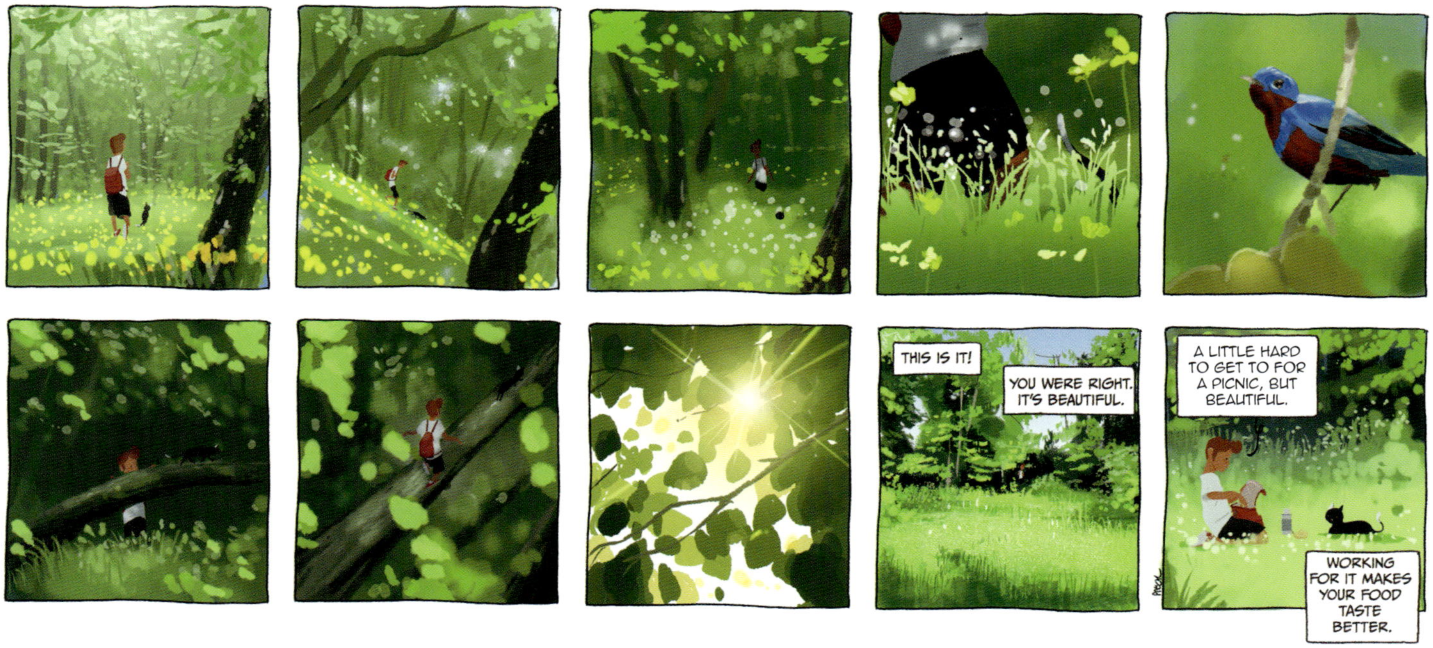
THIS IS IT!
YOU WERE RIGHT. IT'S BEAUTIFUL.
A LITTLE HARD TO GET TO FOR A PICNIC, BUT BEAUTIFUL.
WORKING FOR IT MAKES YOUR FOOD TASTE BETTER.

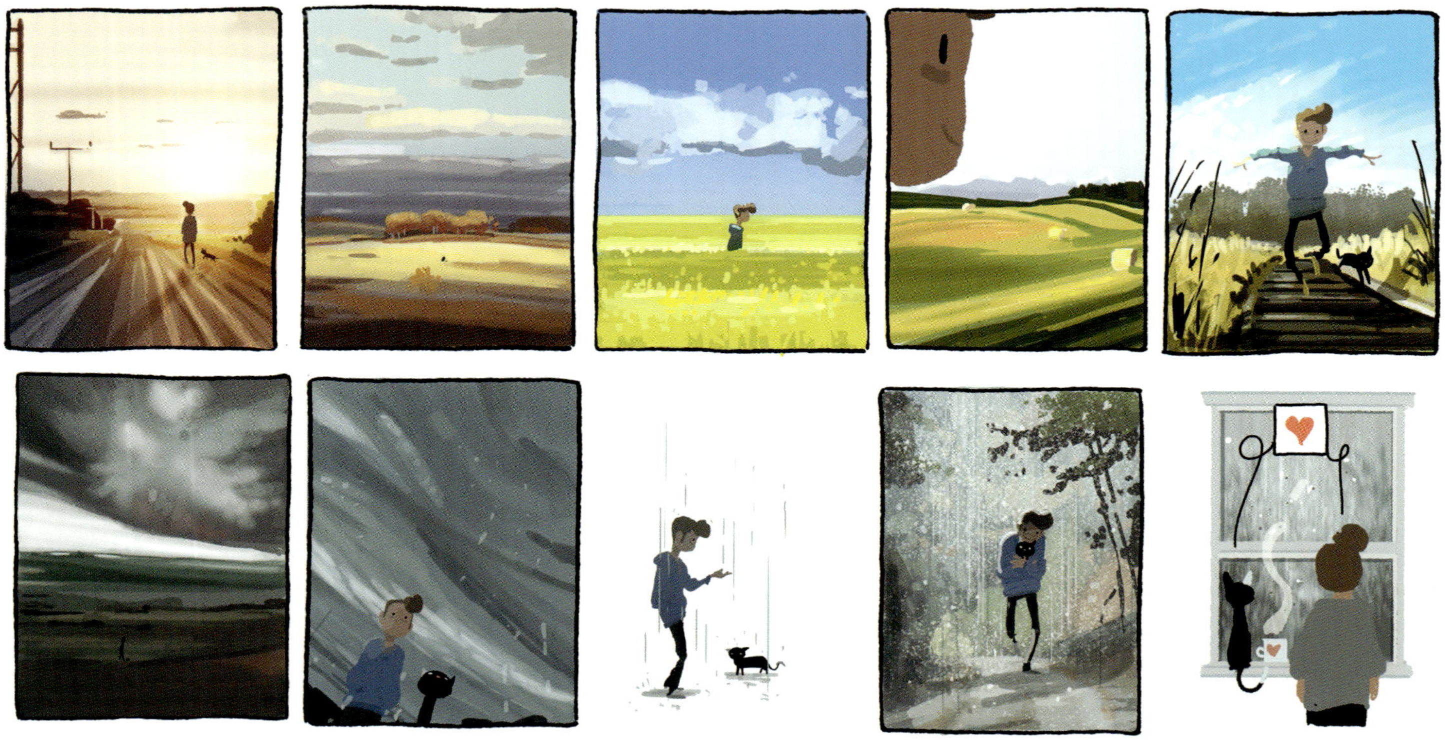

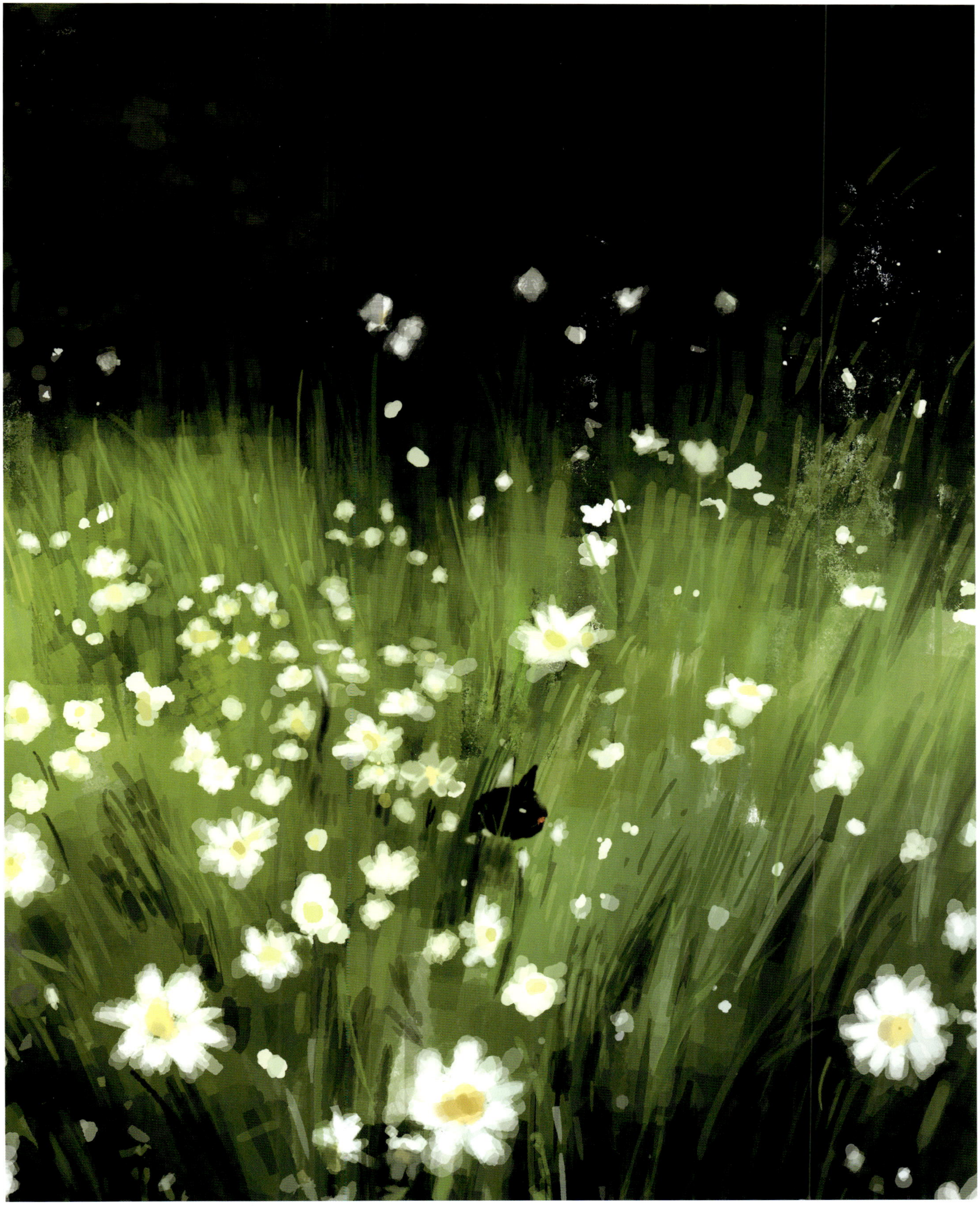

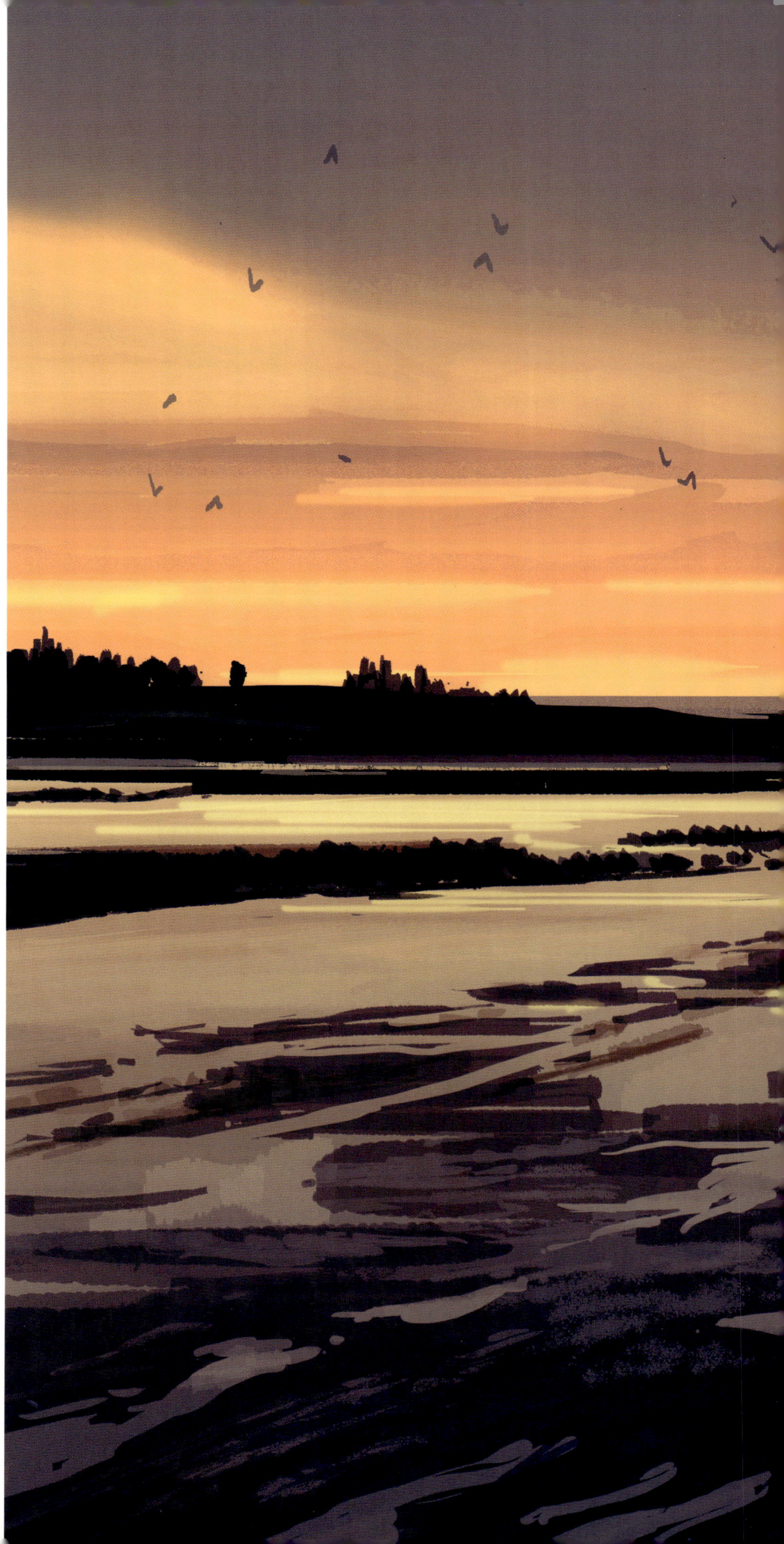

I was *so* disappointed with this. I simply couldn't get physically comfortable while drawing it. I don't know if it happens to other artists, but I have to be mentally *and* physically comfortable to create work that I am happy with. For some reason, I couldn't find the right position for my arm, or my hand, or my back... whatever it was. As a result, I felt the image was so much less than it could have been. But now, a year or so later, I look at it and think it's not so bad!

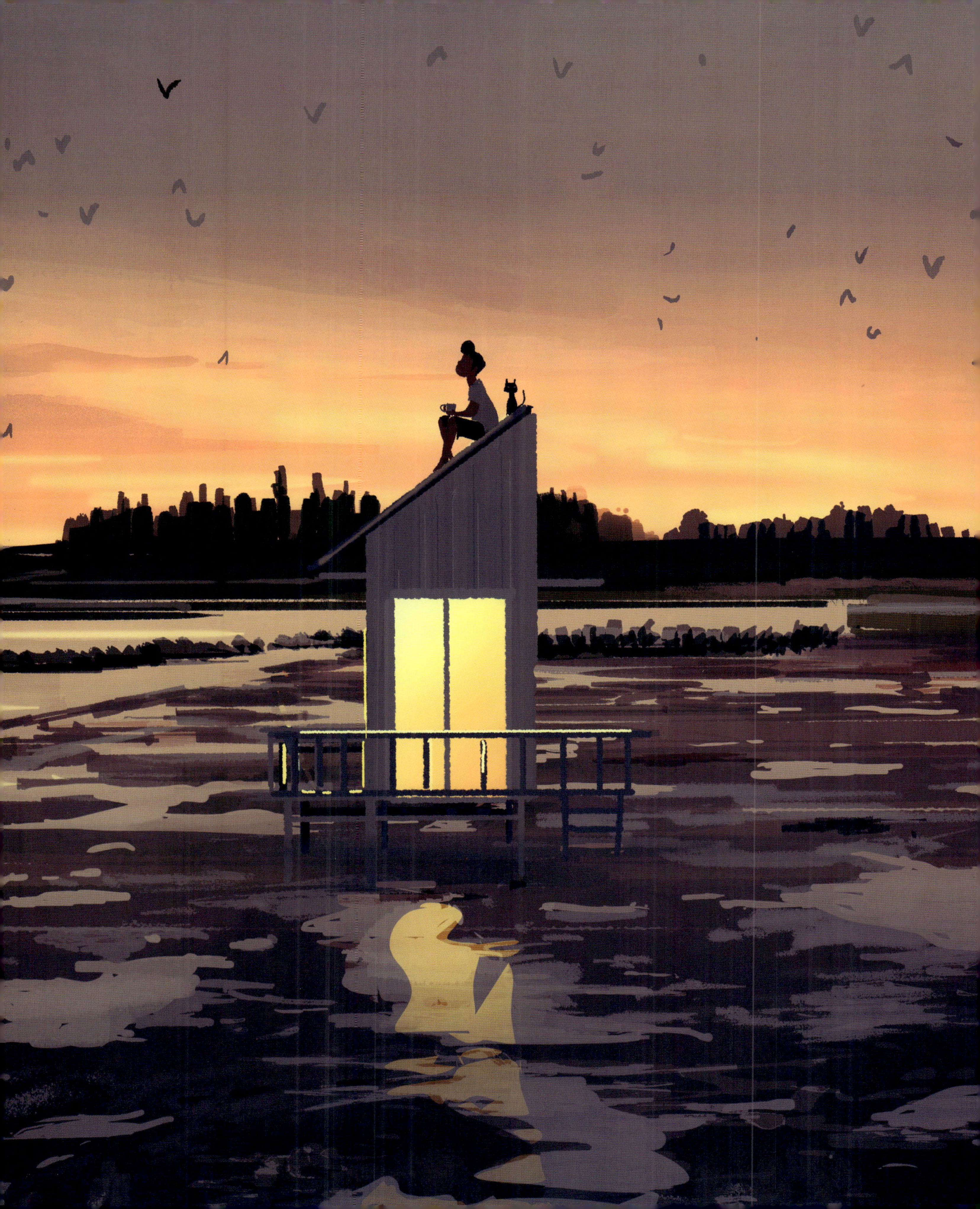

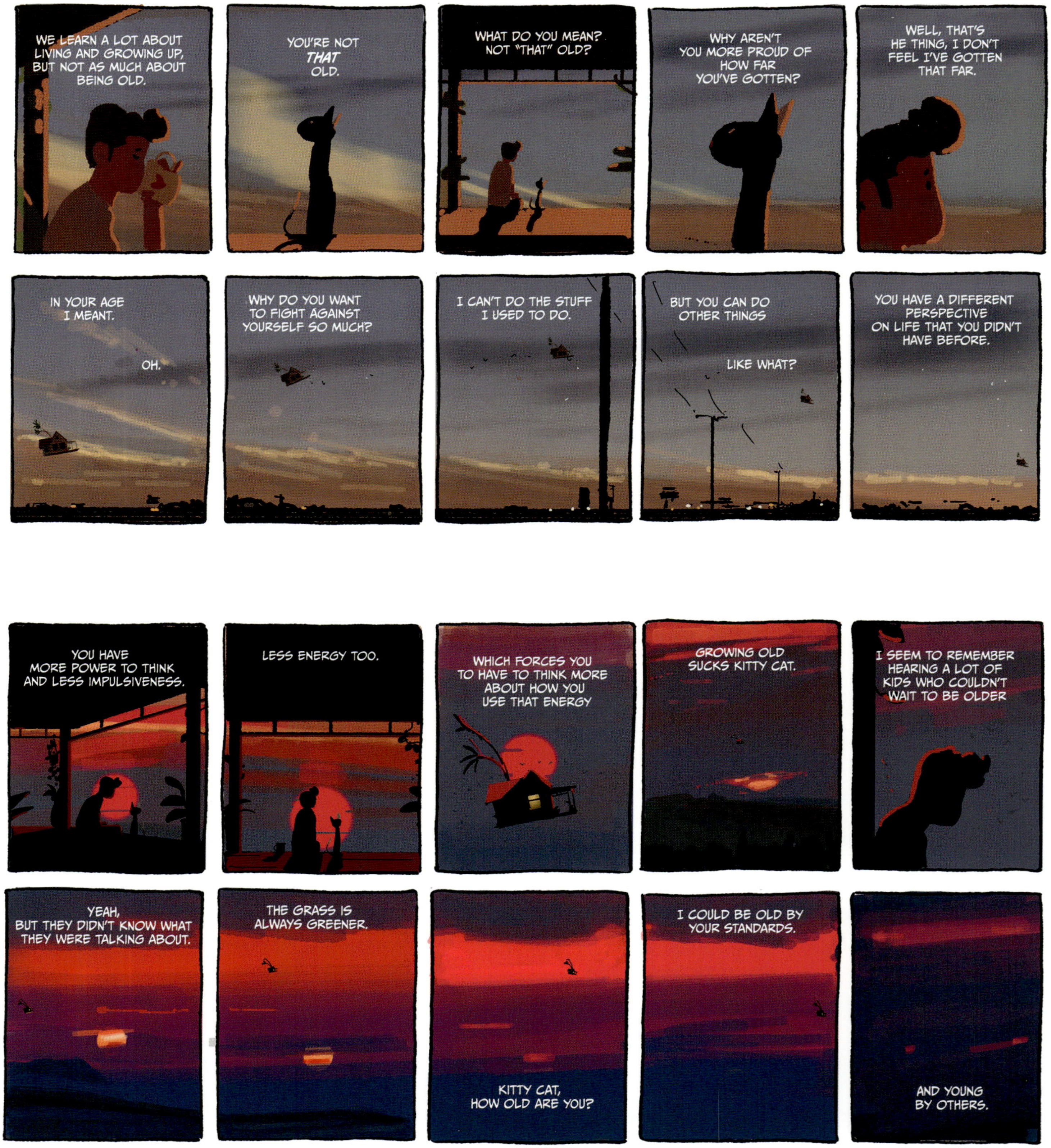
WE LEARN A LOT ABOUT LIVING AND GROWING UP, BUT NOT AS MUCH ABOUT BEING OLD.
YOU'RE NOT *THAT* OLD.
WHAT DO YOU MEAN? NOT "THAT" OLD?
WHY AREN'T YOU MORE PROUD OF HOW FAR YOU'VE GOTTEN?
WELL, THAT'S HE THING, I DON'T FEEL I'VE GOTTEN THAT FAR.
IN YOUR AGE I MEANT.
OH.
WHY DO YOU WANT TO FIGHT AGAINST YOURSELF SO MUCH?
I CAN'T DO THE STUFF I USED TO DO.
BUT YOU CAN DO OTHER THINGS
LIKE WHAT?
YOU HAVE A DIFFERENT PERSPECTIVE ON LIFE THAT YOU DIDN'T HAVE BEFORE.
YOU HAVE MORE POWER TO THINK AND LESS IMPULSIVENESS.
LESS ENERGY TOO.
WHICH FORCES YOU TO HAVE TO THINK MORE ABOUT HOW YOU USE THAT ENERGY
GROWING OLD SUCKS KITTY CAT.
I SEEM TO REMEMBER HEARING A LOT OF KIDS WHO COULDN'T WAIT TO BE OLDER
YEAH, BUT THEY DIDN'T KNOW WHAT THEY WERE TALKING ABOUT.
THE GRASS IS ALWAYS GREENER.
KITTY CAT, HOW OLD ARE YOU?
I COULD BE OLD BY YOUR STANDARDS.
AND YOUNG BY OTHERS.

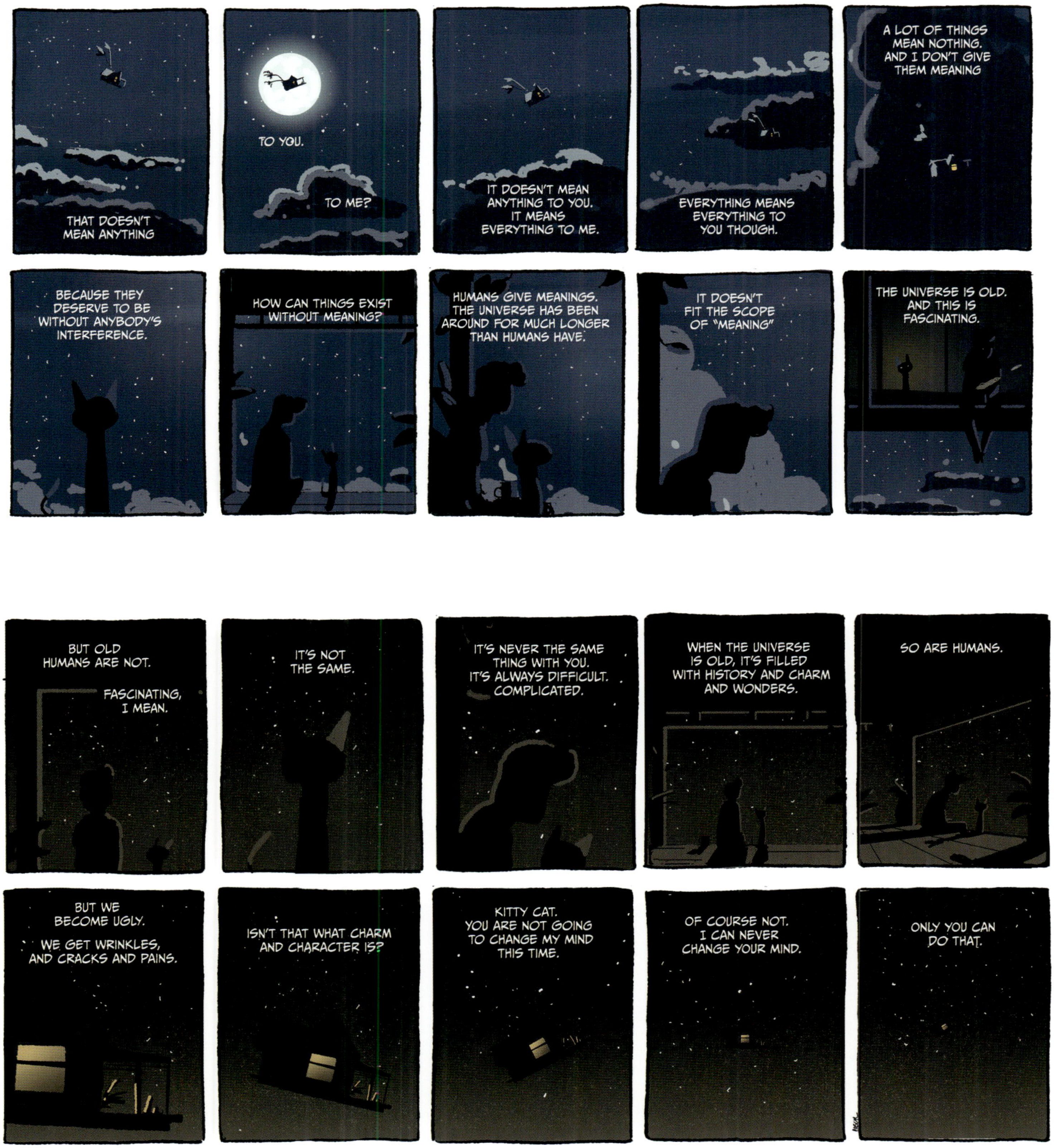
THAT DOESN'T MEAN ANYTHING
TO YOU.
TO ME?
IT DOESN'T MEAN ANYTHING TO YOU. IT MEANS EVERYTHING TO ME.
EVERYTHING MEANS EVERYTHING TO YOU THOUGH.
A LOT OF THINGS MEAN NOTHING. AND I DON'T GIVE THEM MEANING
BECAUSE THEY DESERVE TO BE WITHOUT ANYBODY'S INTERFERENCE.
HOW CAN THINGS EXIST WITHOUT MEANING?
HUMANS GIVE MEANINGS. THE UNIVERSE HAS BEEN AROUND FOR MUCH LONGER THAN HUMANS HAVE.
IT DOESN'T FIT THE SCOPE OF "MEANING"
THE UNIVERSE IS OLD. AND THIS IS FASCINATING.
BUT OLD HUMANS ARE NOT.
FASCINATING, I MEAN.
IT'S NOT THE SAME.
IT'S NEVER THE SAME THING WITH YOU. IT'S ALWAYS DIFFICULT. COMPLICATED.
WHEN THE UNIVERSE IS OLD, IT'S FILLED WITH HISTORY AND CHARM AND WONDERS.
SO ARE HUMANS.
BUT WE BECOME UGLY.
WE GET WRINKLES, AND CRACKS AND PAINS.
ISN'T THAT WHAT CHARM AND CHARACTER IS?
KITTY CAT. YOU ARE NOT GOING TO CHANGE MY MIND THIS TIME.
OF COURSE NOT. I CAN NEVER CHANGE YOUR MIND.
ONLY YOU CAN DO THAT.

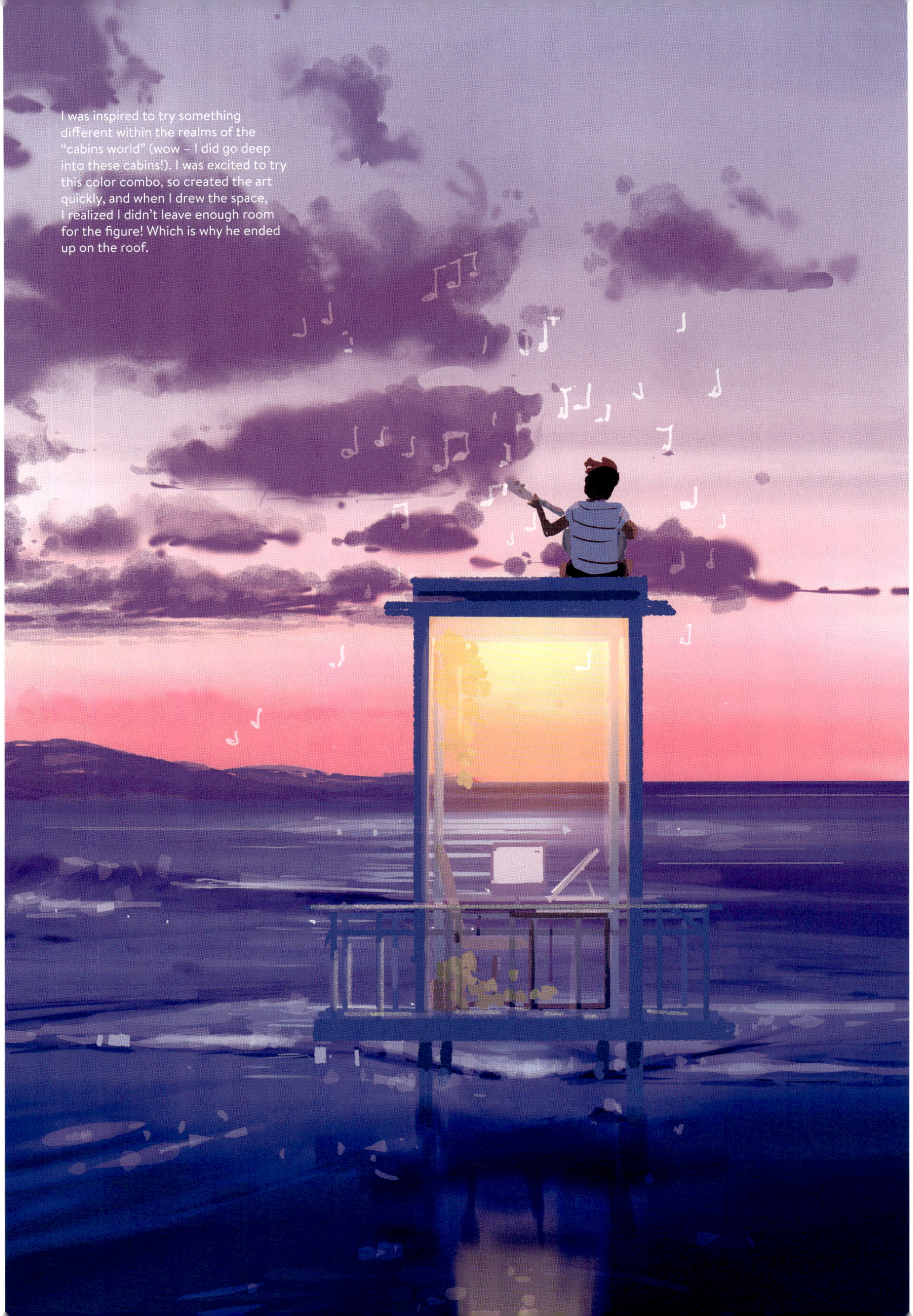

I was inspired to try something different within the realms of the "cabins world" (wow – I did go deep into these cabins!). I was excited to try this color combo, so created the art quickly, and when I drew the space, I realized I didn't leave enough room for the figure! Which is why he ended up on the roof.

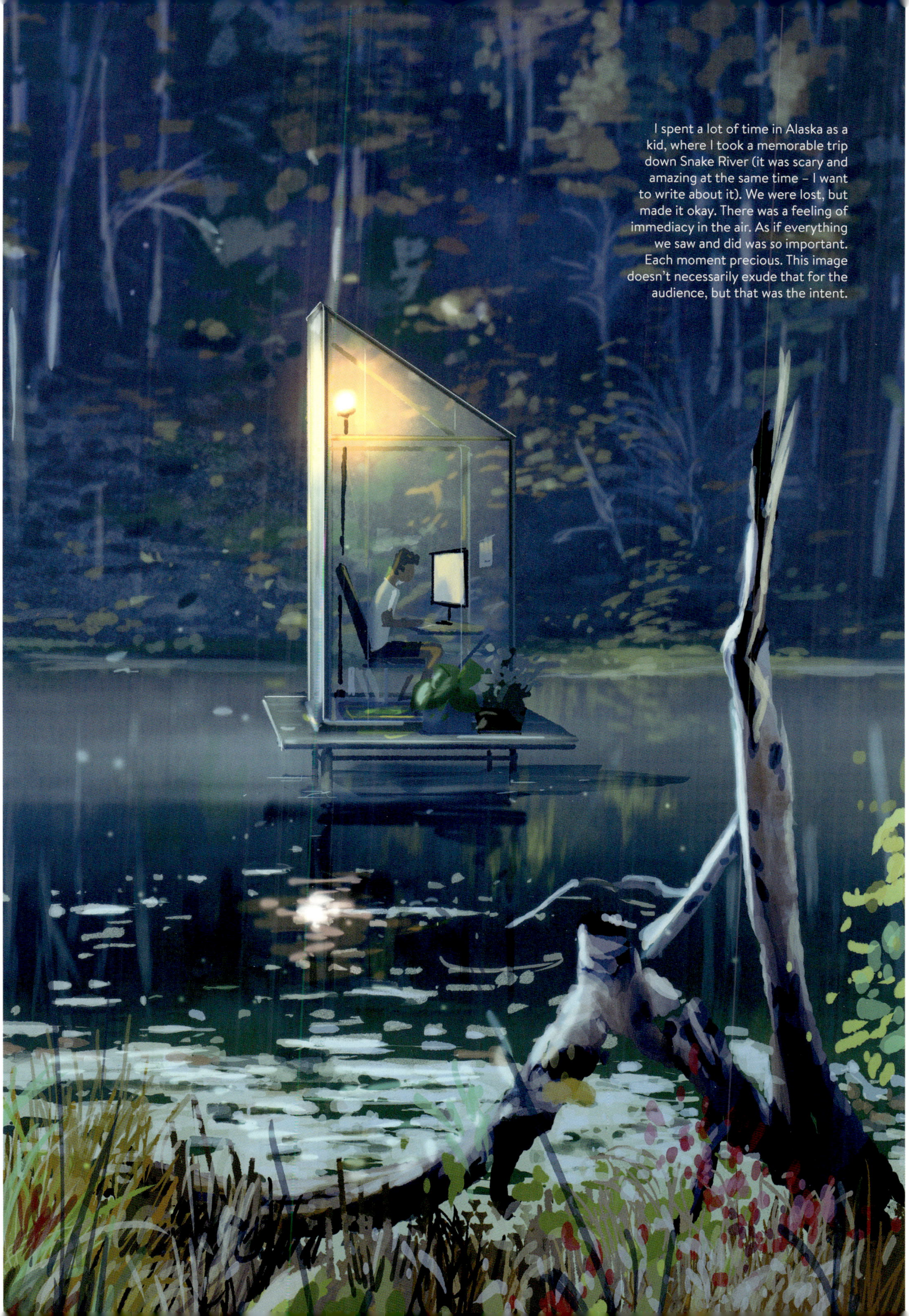

I spent a lot of time in Alaska as a kid, where I took a memorable trip down Snake River (it was scary and amazing at the same time – I want to write about it). We were lost, but made it okay. There was a feeling of immediacy in the air. As if everything we saw and did was so important. Each moment precious. This image doesn't necessarily exude that for the audience, but that was the intent.

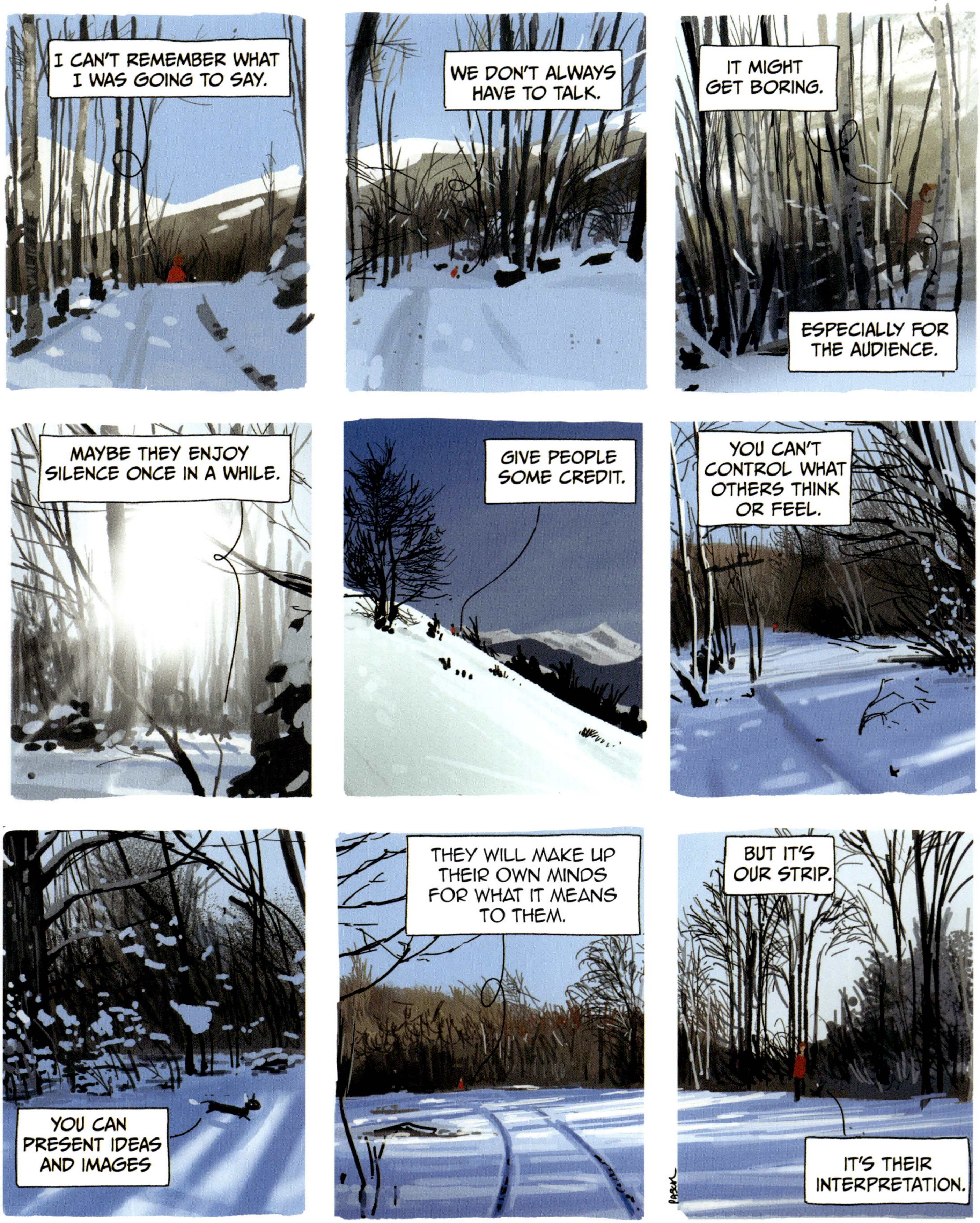
I CAN'T REMEMBER WHAT I WAS GOING TO SAY.
WE DON'T ALWAYS HAVE TO TALK.
IT MIGHT GET BORING.
ESPECIALLY FOR THE AUDIENCE.
MAYBE THEY ENJOY SILENCE ONCE IN A WHILE.
GIVE PEOPLE SOME CREDIT.
YOU CAN'T CONTROL WHAT OTHERS THINK OR FEEL.
YOU CAN PRESENT IDEAS AND IMAGES
THEY WILL MAKE UP THEIR OWN MINDS FOR WHAT IT MEANS TO THEM.
BUT IT'S OUR STRIP.
IT'S THEIR INTERPRETATION.

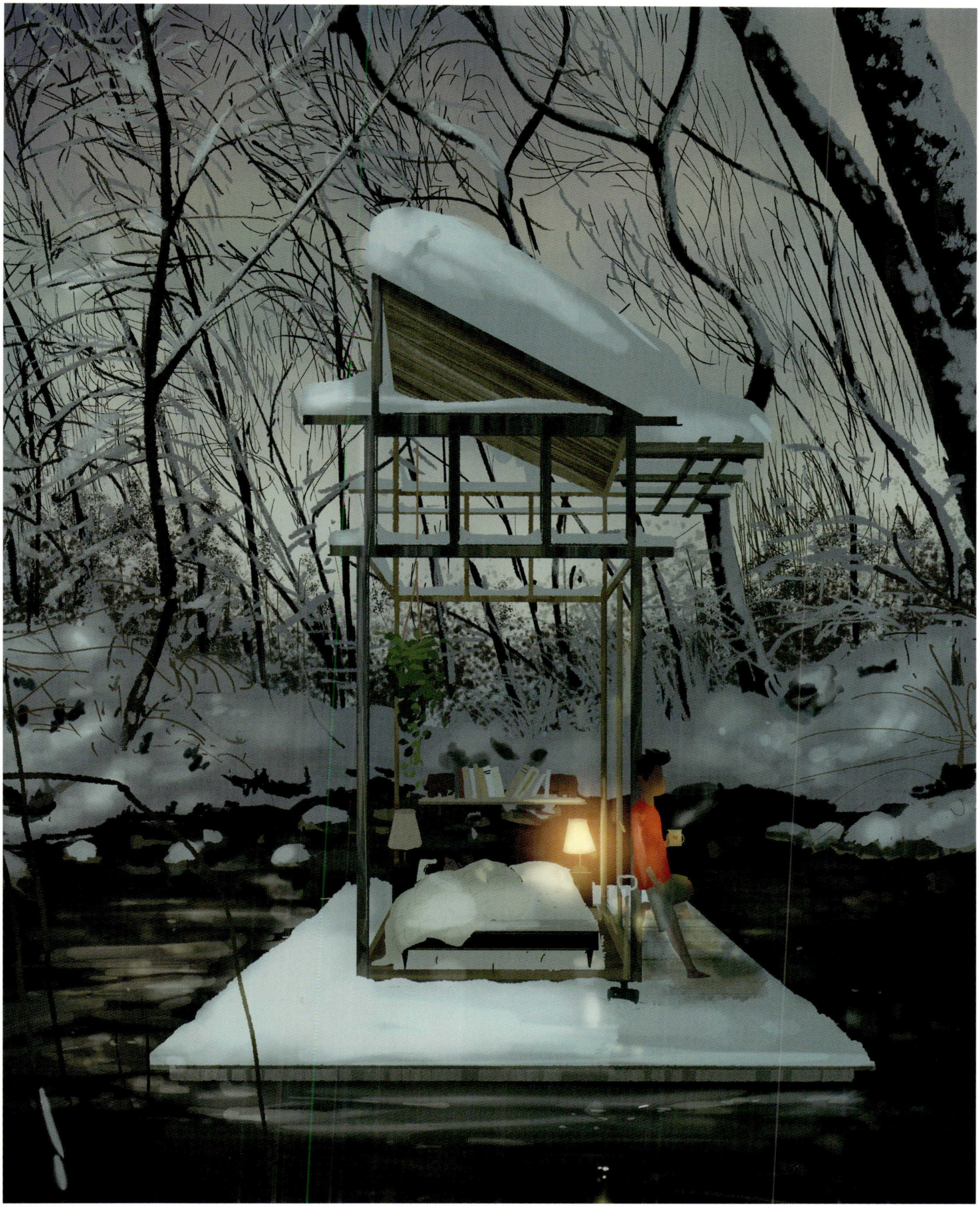

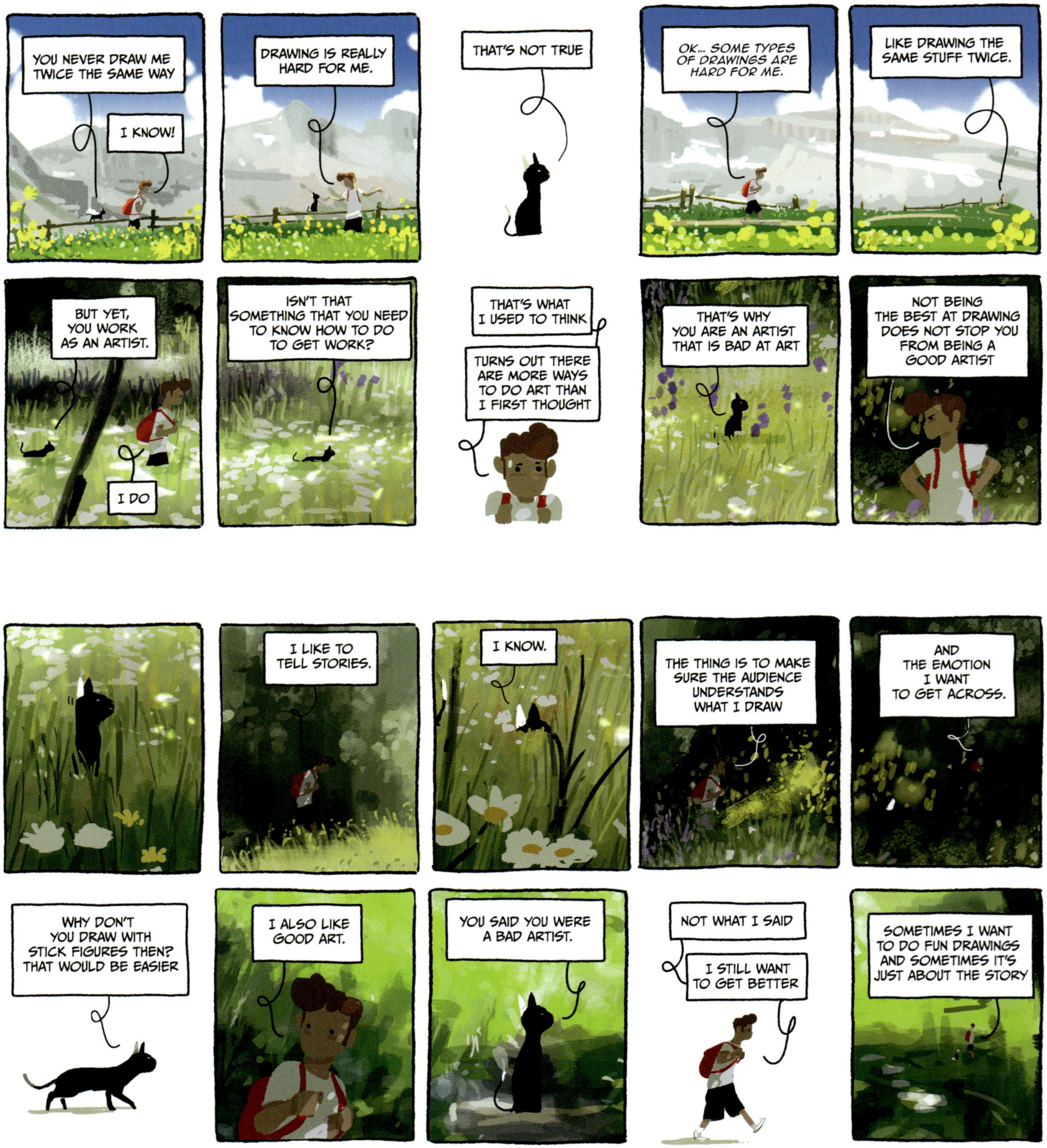
YOU NEVER DRAW ME TWICE THE SAME WAY
I KNOW!
DRAWING IS REALLY HARD FOR ME.
THAT'S NOT TRUE
OK... SOME TYPES OF DRAWINGS ARE HARD FOR ME.
LIKE DRAWING THE SAME STUFF TWICE.
BUT YET, YOU WORK AS AN ARTIST.
I DO
ISN'T THAT SOMETHING THAT YOU NEED TO KNOW HOW TO DO TO GET WORK?
THAT'S WHAT I USED TO THINK
TURNS OUT THERE ARE MORE WAYS TO DO ART THAN I FIRST THOUGHT
THAT'S WHY YOU ARE AN ARTIST THAT IS BAD AT ART
NOT BEING THE BEST AT DRAWING DOES NOT STOP YOU FROM BEING A GOOD ARTIST
I LIKE TO TELL STORIES.
I KNOW.
THE THING IS TO MAKE SURE THE AUDIENCE UNDERSTANDS WHAT I DRAW
AND THE EMOTION I WANT TO GET ACROSS.
WHY DON'T YOU DRAW WITH STICK FIGURES THEN? THAT WOULD BE EASIER
I ALSO LIKE GOOD ART.
YOU SAID YOU WERE A BAD ARTIST.
NOT WHAT I SAID
I STILL WANT TO GET BETTER
SOMETIMES I WANT TO DO FUN DRAWINGS AND SOMETIMES IT'S JUST ABOUT THE STORY

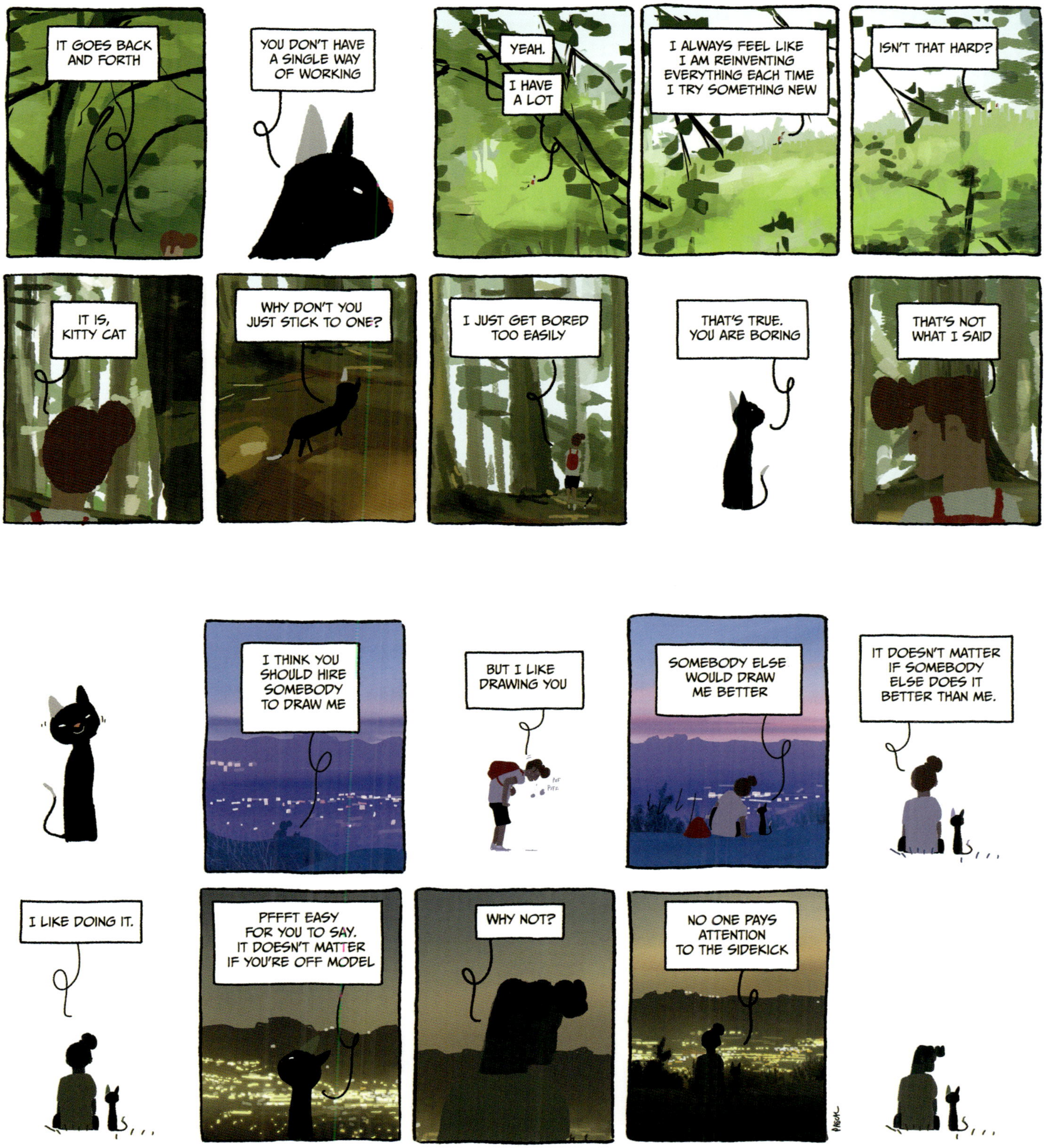
IT GOES BACK AND FORTH
YOU DON'T HAVE A SINGLE WAY OF WORKING
YEAH.
I HAVE A LOT
I ALWAYS FEEL LIKE I AM REINVENTING EVERYTHING EACH TIME I TRY SOMETHING NEW
ISN'T THAT HARD?
IT IS, KITTY CAT
WHY DON'T YOU JUST STICK TO ONE?
I JUST GET BORED TOO EASILY
THAT'S TRUE. YOU ARE BORING
THAT'S NOT WHAT I SAID
I THINK YOU SHOULD HIRE SOMEBODY TO DRAW ME
BUT I LIKE DRAWING YOU
SOMEBODY ELSE WOULD DRAW ME BETTER
IT DOESN'T MATTER IF SOMEBODY ELSE DOES IT BETTER THAN ME.
I LIKE DOING IT.
PFFFT EASY FOR YOU TO SAY. IT DOESN'T MATTER IF YOU'RE OFF MODEL
WHY NOT?
NO ONE PAYS ATTENTION TO THE SIDEKICK

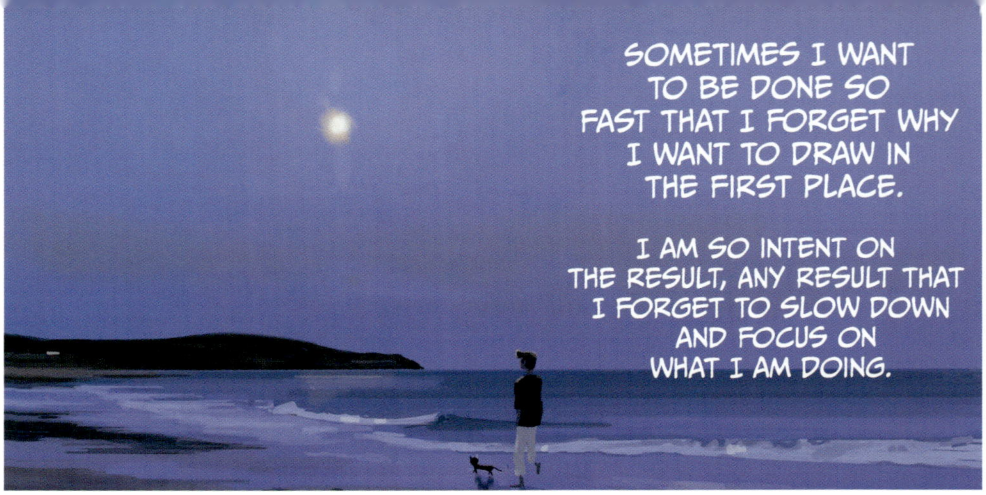
SOMETIMES I WANT TO BE DONE SO FAST THAT I FORGET WHY I WANT TO DRAW IN THE FIRST PLACE.
I AM SO INTENT ON THE RESULT, ANY RESULT THAT I FORGET TO SLOW DOWN AND FOCUS ON WHAT I AM DOING.

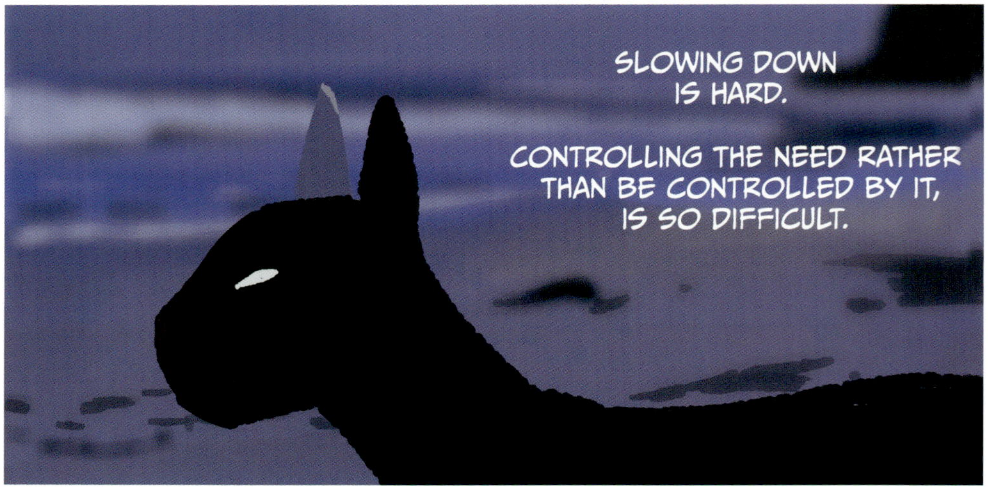
SLOWING DOWN IS HARD.
CONTROLLING THE NEED RATHER THAN BE CONTROLLED BY IT, IS SO DIFFICULT.

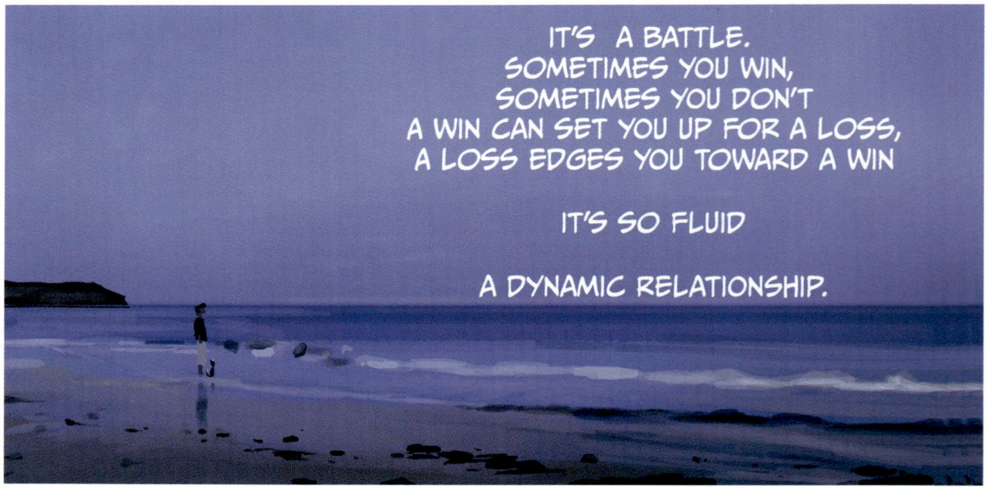
IT'S A BATTLE.
SOMETIMES YOU WIN,
SOMETIMES YOU DON'T
A WIN CAN SET YOU UP FOR A LOSS,
A LOSS EDGES YOU TOWARD A WIN
IT'S SO FLUID
A DYNAMIC RELATIONSHIP.

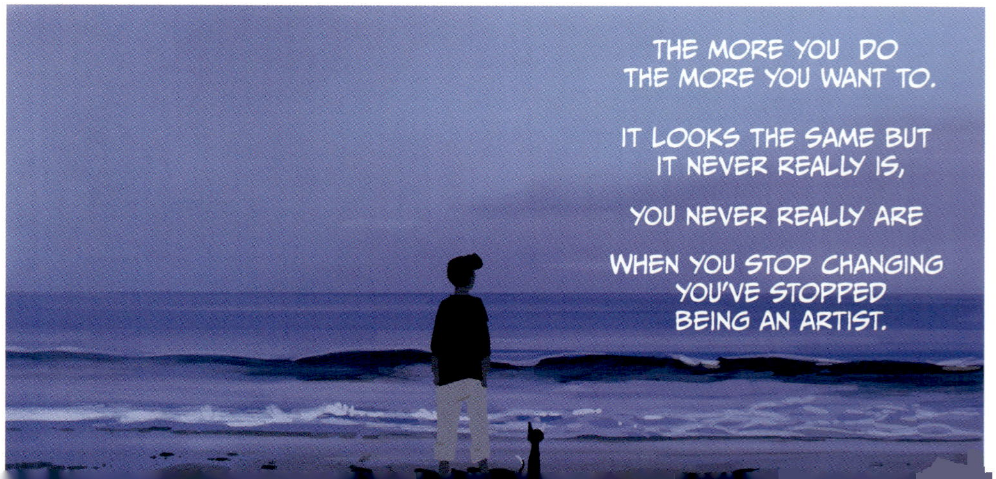
THE MORE YOU DO THE MORE YOU WANT TO.
IT LOOKS THE SAME BUT IT NEVER REALLY IS,
YOU NEVER REALLY ARE
WHEN YOU STOP CHANGING YOU'VE STOPPED BEING AN ARTIST.

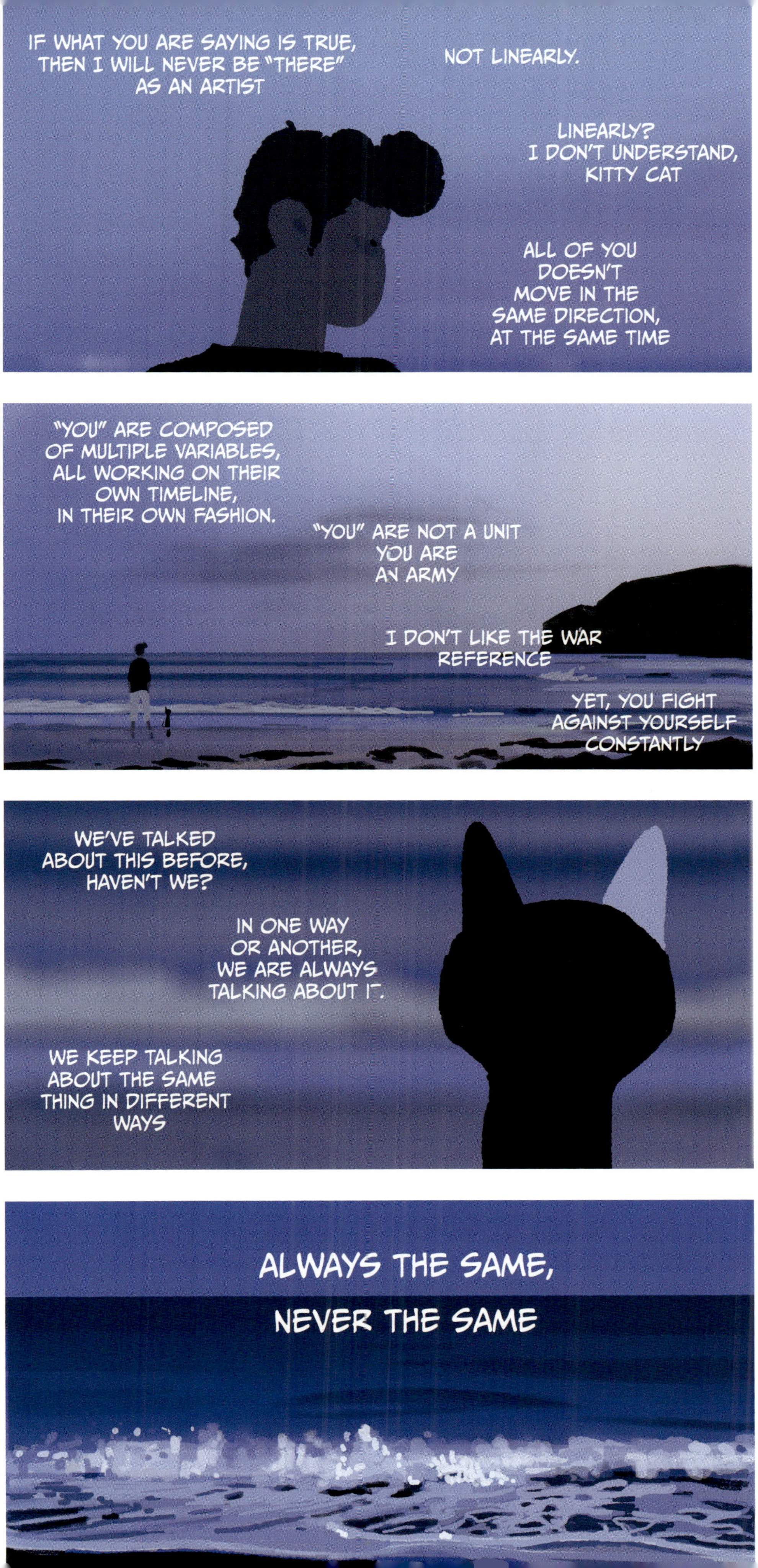
IF WHAT YOU ARE SAYING IS TRUE, THEN I WILL NEVER BE "THERE" AS AN ARTIST
NOT LINEARLY.
LINEARLY? I DON'T UNDERSTAND, KITTY CAT
ALL OF YOU DOESN'T MOVE IN THE SAME DIRECTION, AT THE SAME TIME
"YOU" ARE COMPOSED OF MULTIPLE VARIABLES, ALL WORKING ON THEIR OWN TIMELINE, IN THEIR OWN FASHION.
"YOU" ARE NOT A UNIT YOU ARE AN ARMY
I DON'T LIKE THE WAR REFERENCE
YET, YOU FIGHT AGAINST YOURSELF CONSTANTLY
WE'VE TALKED ABOUT THIS BEFORE, HAVEN'T WE?
IN ONE WAY OR ANOTHER, WE ARE ALWAYS TALKING ABOUT IT.
WE KEEP TALKING ABOUT THE SAME THING IN DIFFERENT WAYS
ALWAYS THE SAME,
NEVER THE SAME

I did this piece after a very long and annoying day at work. I wanted to blow off some creative steam. I can't remember *what* was going off at work, but I remember that feeling. So I took a square brush and started drawing shapes. After about forty minutes, I felt calmer and most of that city was drawn. I liked where it was going and that mood switch made me turn what was originally a dark piece into a romantic moment. That's another reason why I love art so much.

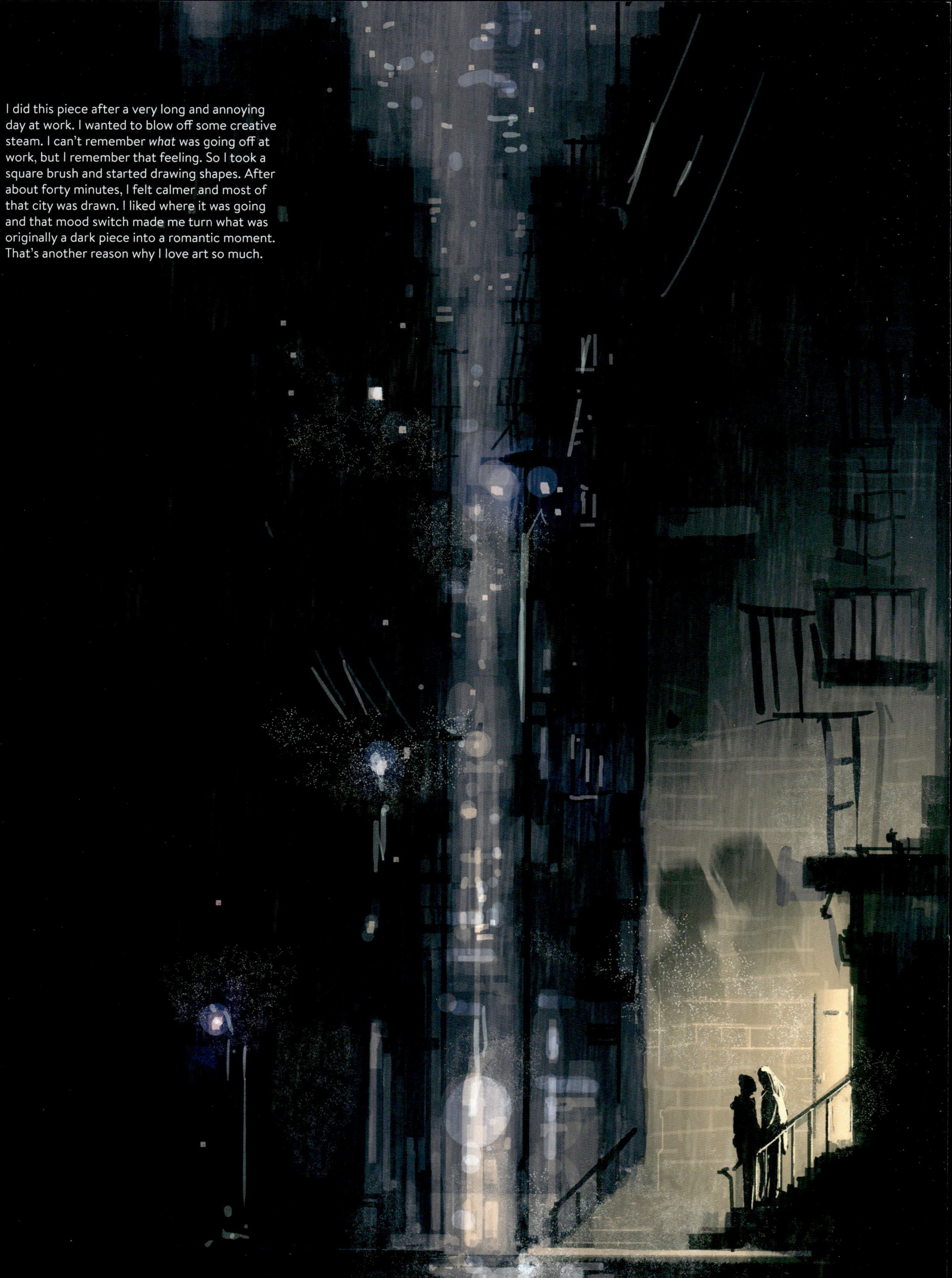

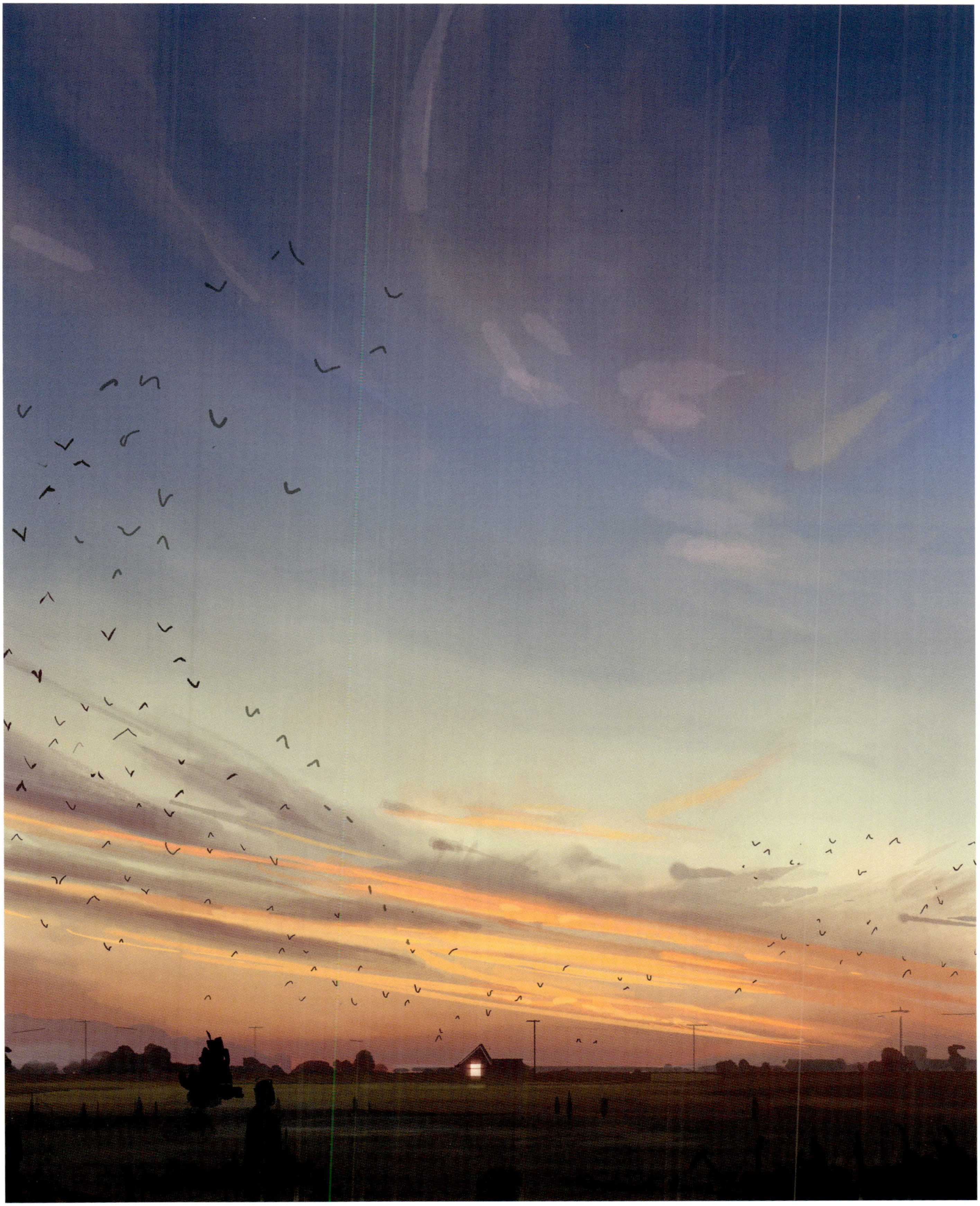

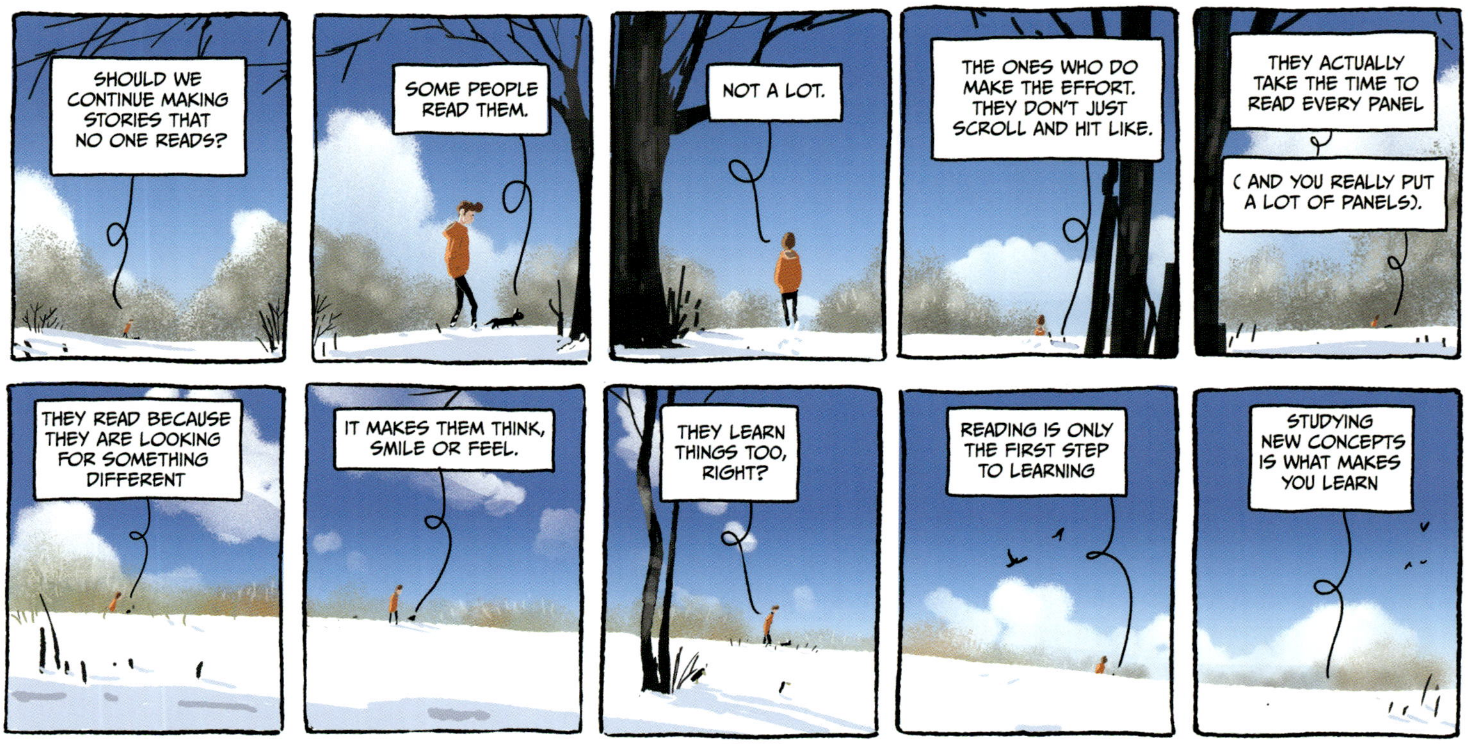
SHOULD WE CONTINUE MAKING STORIES THAT NO ONE READS?
SOME PEOPLE READ THEM.
NOT A LOT.
THE ONES WHO DO MAKE THE EFFORT. THEY DON'T JUST SCROLL AND HIT LIKE.
THEY ACTUALLY TAKE THE TIME TO READ EVERY PANEL
(AND YOU REALLY PUT A LOT OF PANELS).
THEY READ BECAUSE THEY ARE LOOKING FOR SOMETHING DIFFERENT
IT MAKES THEM THINK, SMILE OR FEEL.
THEY LEARN THINGS TOO, RIGHT?
READING IS ONLY THE FIRST STEP TO LEARNING
STUDYING NEW CONCEPTS IS WHAT MAKES YOU LEARN

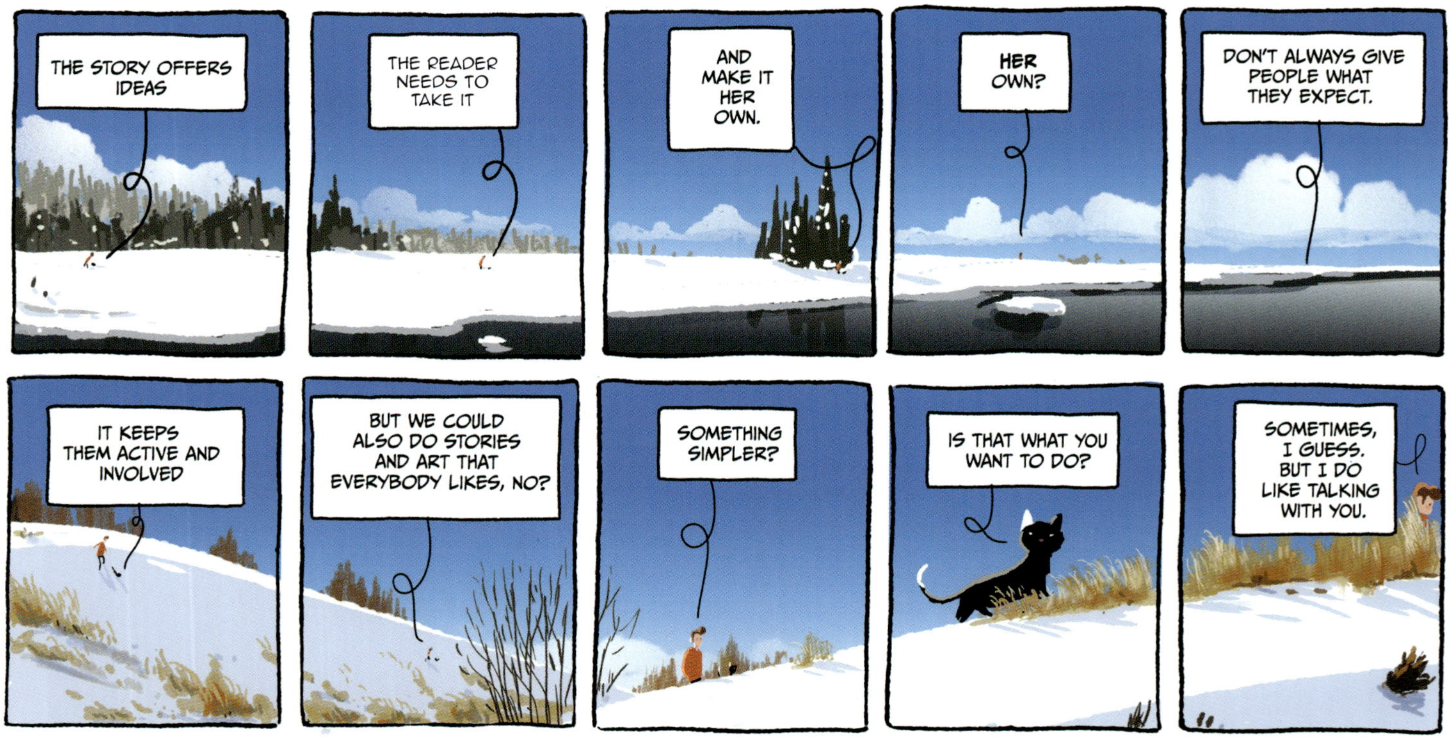
THE STORY OFFERS IDEAS
THE READER NEEDS TO TAKE IT
AND MAKE IT HER OWN.
HER OWN?
DON'T ALWAYS GIVE PEOPLE WHAT THEY EXPECT.
IT KEEPS THEM ACTIVE AND INVOLVED
BUT WE COULD ALSO DO STORIES AND ART THAT EVERYBODY LIKES, NO?
SOMETHING SIMPLER?
IS THAT WHAT YOU WANT TO DO?
SOMETIMES, I GUESS. BUT I DO LIKE TALKING WITH YOU.

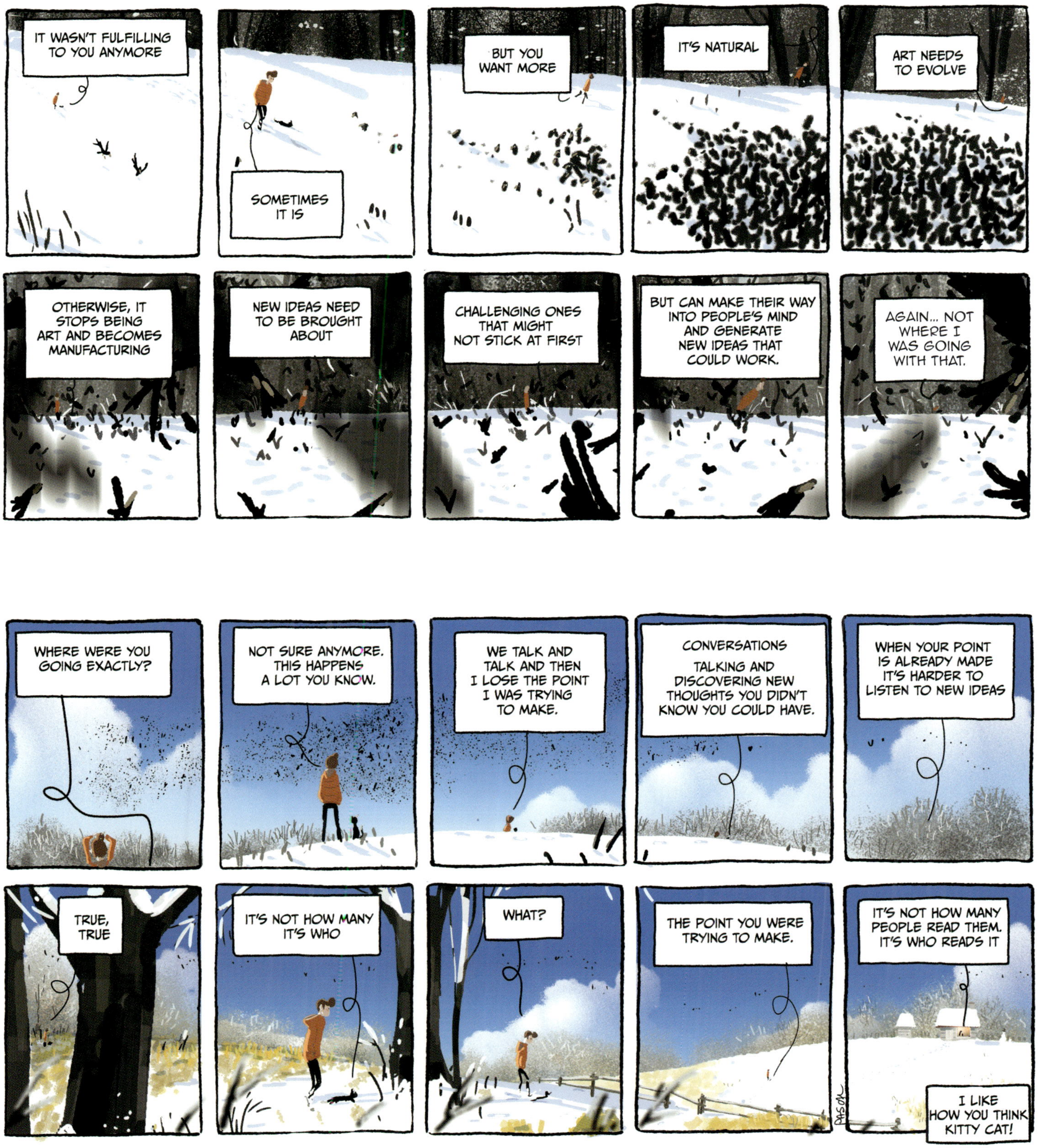
IT WASN'T FULFILLING TO YOU ANYMORE
SOMETIMES IT IS
BUT YOU WANT MORE
IT'S NATURAL
ART NEEDS TO EVOLVE
OTHERWISE, IT STOPS BEING ART AND BECOMES MANUFACTURING
NEW IDEAS NEED TO BE BROUGHT ABOUT
CHALLENGING ONES THAT MIGHT NOT STICK AT FIRST
BUT CAN MAKE THEIR WAY INTO PEOPLE'S MIND AND GENERATE NEW IDEAS THAT COULD WORK.
AGAIN... NOT WHERE I WAS GOING WITH THAT.
WHERE WERE YOU GOING EXACTLY?
NOT SURE ANYMORE. THIS HAPPENS A LOT YOU KNOW.
WE TALK AND TALK AND THEN I LOSE THE POINT I WAS TRYING TO MAKE.
CONVERSATIONS
TALKING AND DISCOVERING NEW THOUGHTS YOU DIDN'T KNOW YOU COULD HAVE.
WHEN YOUR POINT IS ALREADY MADE IT'S HARDER TO LISTEN TO NEW IDEAS
TRUE, TRUE
IT'S NOT HOW MANY IT'S WHO
WHAT?
THE POINT YOU WERE TRYING TO MAKE.
IT'S NOT HOW MANY PEOPLE READ THEM. IT'S WHO READS IT
I LIKE HOW YOU THINK KITTY CAT!
PASCAL

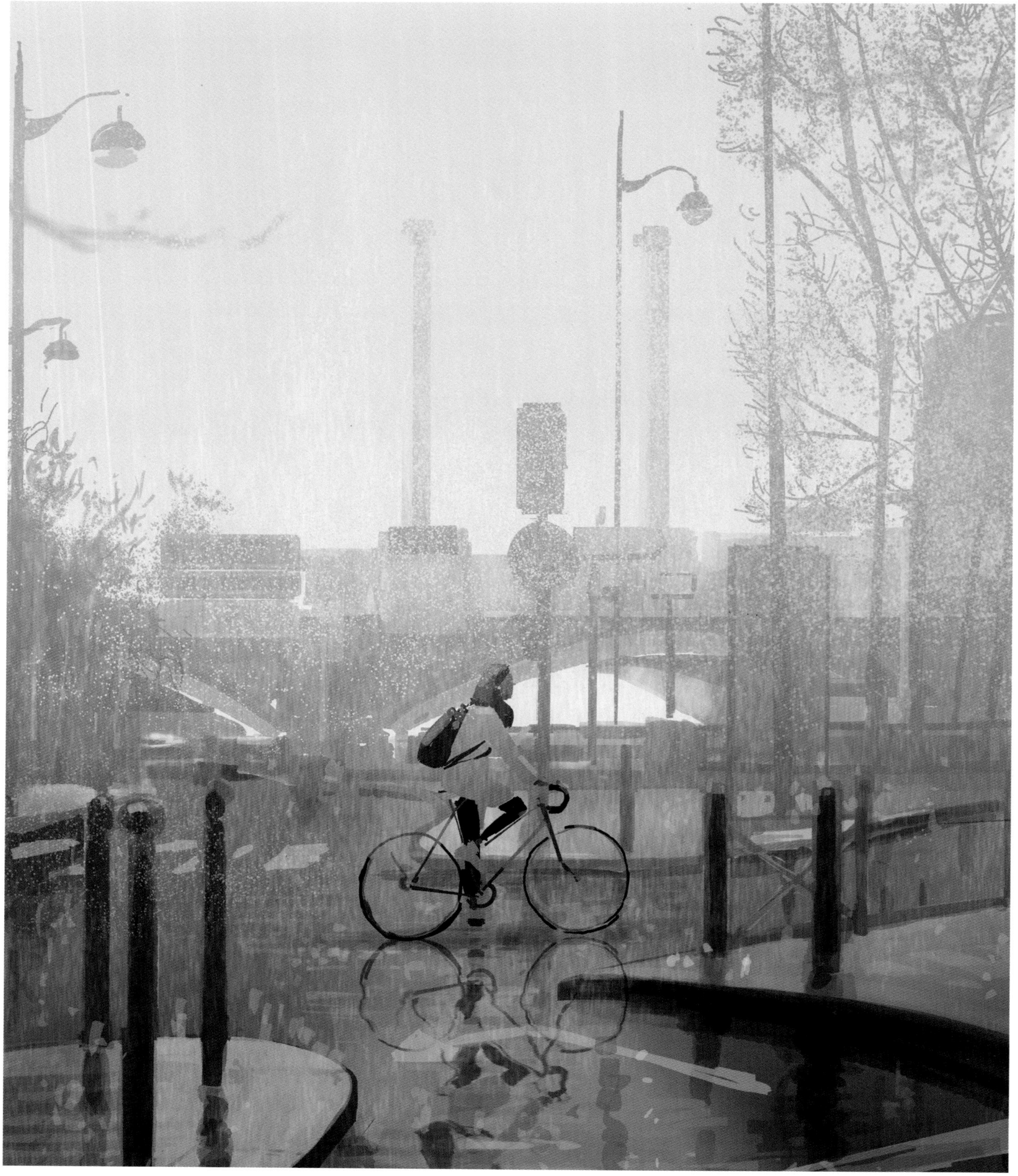

I figured it would be fun to imagine the same scene in different weathers, which led to this series of five (above and on the opposite page). My favorite is this snowy version, but it gets the least attention – sigh. I was happy not so much with the images, but the understanding of what I was doing. Setting and reaching a goal. I see the pieces and think, "Oh! *This* is what it looks like?" I was so focused on capturing the light that the overall image eluded me. Funny.

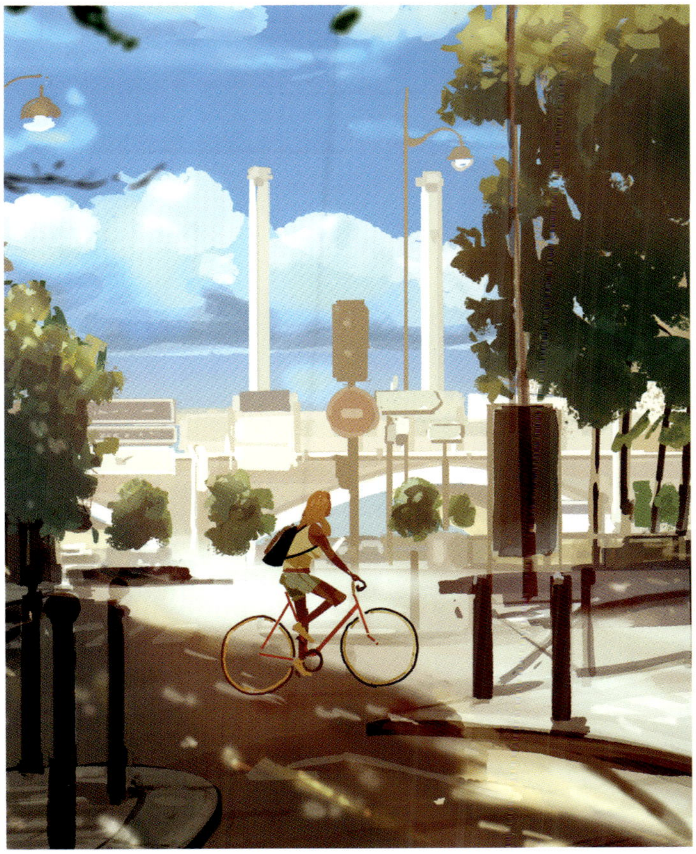

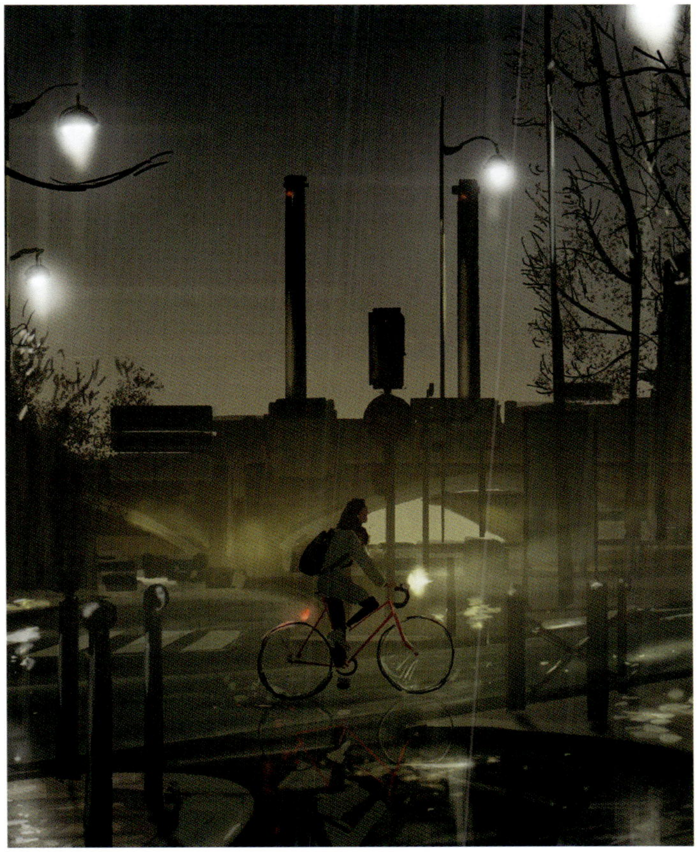

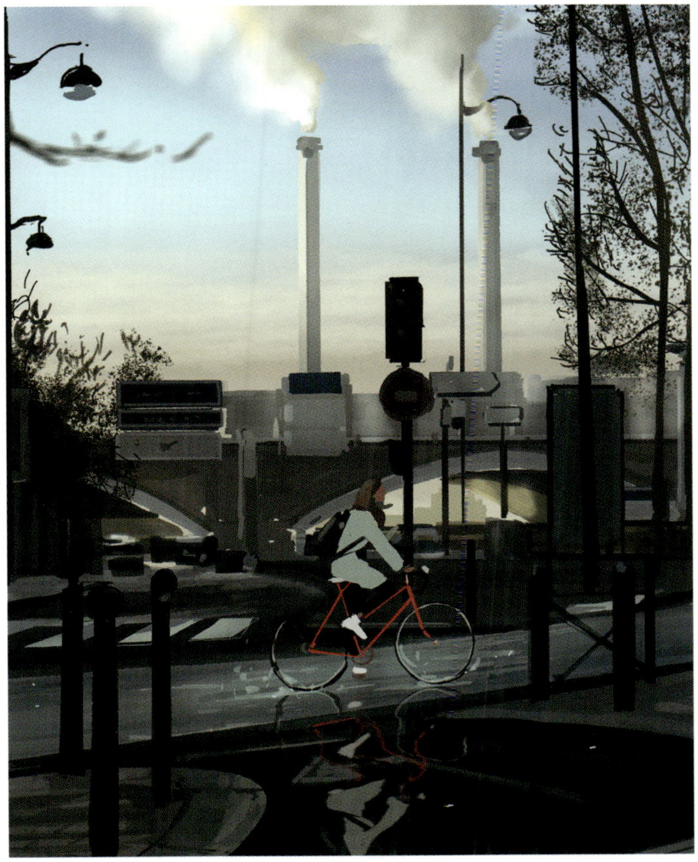

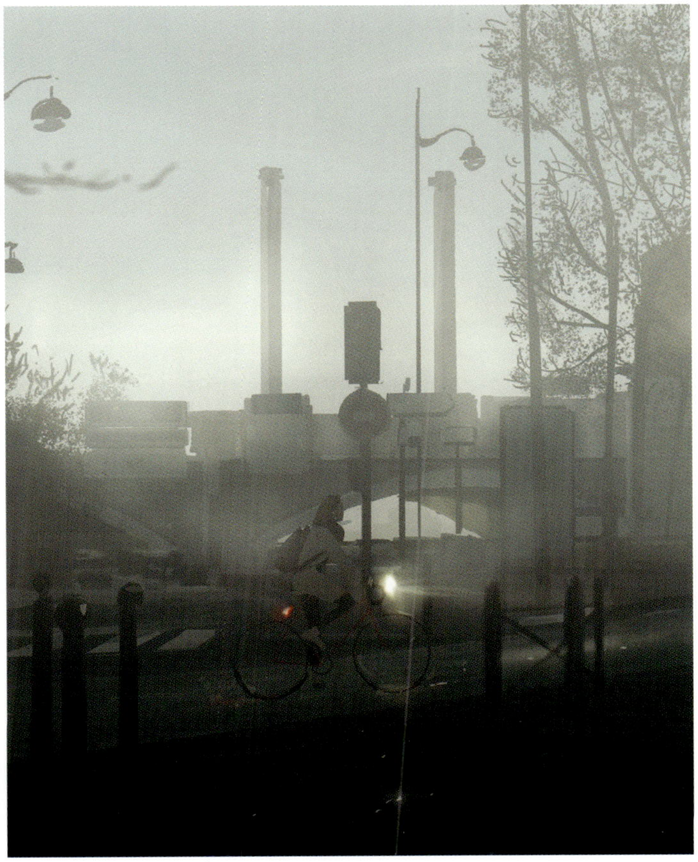

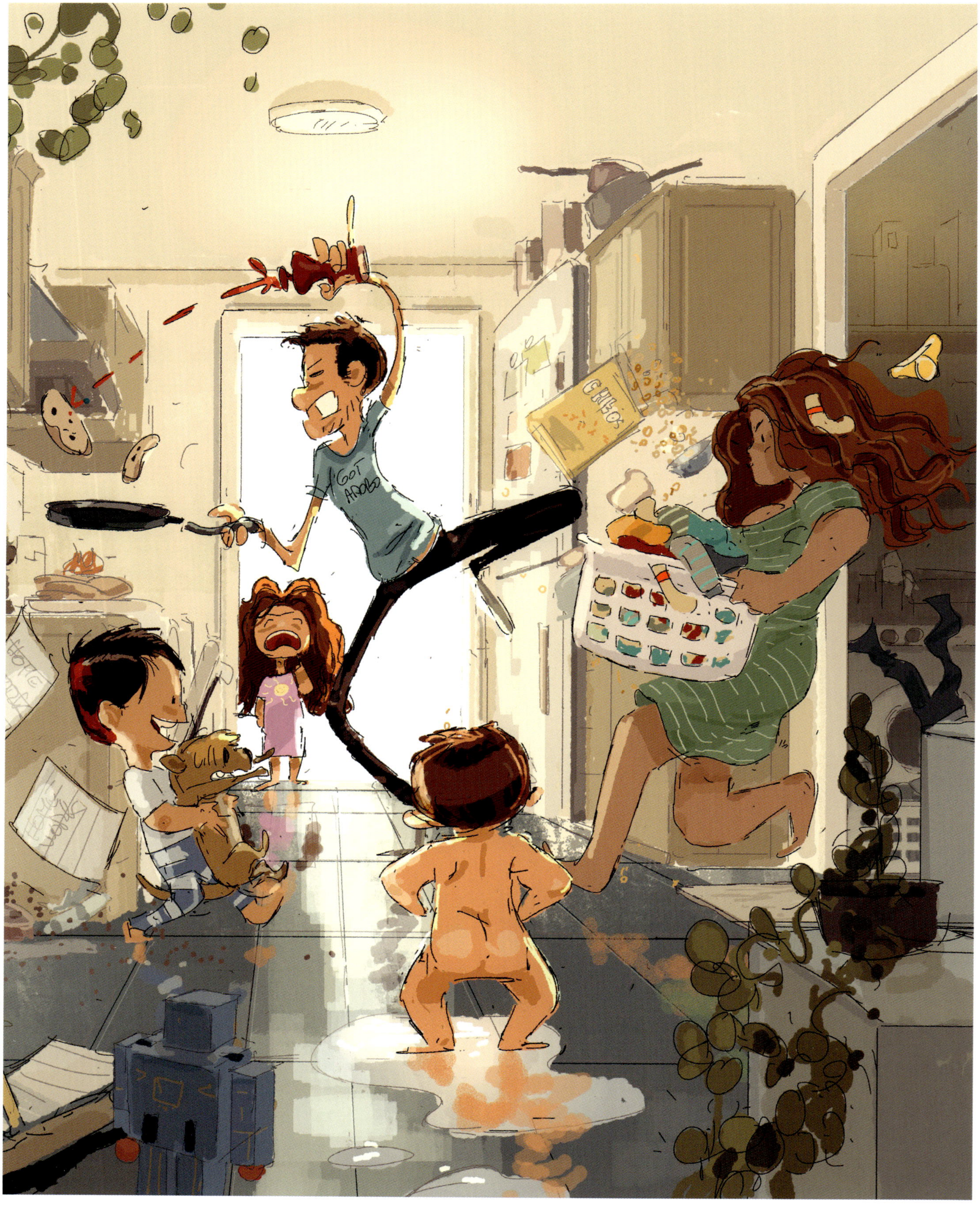
GOT ADOBO

THANK YOU

I REMEMBER DOING A STRIP ONCE,
WONDERING **WHY** PEOPLE WOULD READ STORIES ABOUT
MANLY MAN + KITTY CAT.
THE STORIES ARE NOT **FUNNY**.
THEN SOMEONE TOLD ME THAT **NOT EVERYTHING** IN LIFE IS **ABOUT FUN**.
IT'S MOSTLY ABOUT **MEANINGFULNESS**.
IT MEANS THE WORLD TO ME THAT YOU HAVE READ THIS BOOK
(OR AT LEAST THIS PAGE).

THANK YOU VERY MUCH.

I wanted to keep the best for the end:
Thank you Lily, Max, and Colin.
I love you three so much.

Thank you Manly Man and Kitty Cat. I know it's weird to thank you, but you've helped me a lot.

Thank you Katrina. For everything you do on a daily basis. I love you.

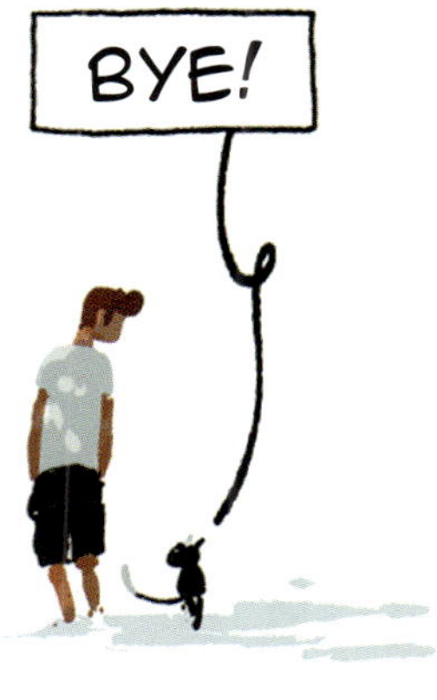

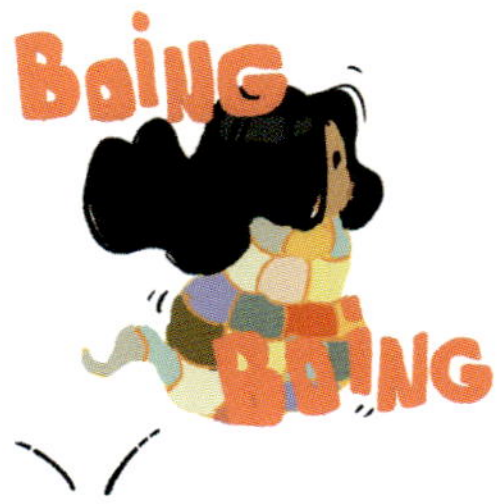

ABOUT 3DTOTAL PUBLISHING

3dtotal Publishing is a trailblazing, creative publisher specializing in inspirational and educational resources for artists.

Our titles feature top industry professionals from around the globe who share their experience in skillfully written step-by-step tutorials and fascinating, detailed guides. Illustrated throughout with stunning artwork, these best-selling publications offer creative insight, expert advice, and essential motivation. Fans of digital art will enjoy our comprehensive volumes covering Adobe Photoshop, Procreate, and Blender, as well as our superb titles based around character design, including *Fundamentals of Character Design* and *Creating Characters for the Entertainment Industry*. The dedicated, high-quality blend of instruction and inspiration also extends to traditional art. Titles covering a range of techniques, genres, and abilities allow your creativity to flourish while building essential skills.

Well-established within the industry, we now offer over 100 titles and counting, many of which have been translated into multiple languages around the world. With something for every artist, we are proud to say that our books offer the 3dtotal package:

LEARN • CREATE • SHARE

Visit us at 3dtotalpublishing.com
3dtotal Publishing is part of 3dtotal.com, a leading website for CG artists founded by Tom Greenway in 1999.